D0205991

AMERICA'S OLDER POPULATION

AMERICA'S OLDER POPULATION

Paul E. Zopf, Jr.

Dana Professor of Sociology
Guilford College

Cap and Gown Press, Inc.
Houston

LIBRARY
WITHDRAWN
COLLEGE
EMMITSBURG, MARYLAND

Copyright © 1986 by Cap and Gown Press, Inc.

All rights reserved. No part of this book may be reproduced or
transmitted in any form whatsoever or by any means, electronic
or mechanical, including photocopying, recording, or by any
information storage and/or retrieval system,
without written permission from the Publisher.

Cap and Gown Press, Inc.
Box 58825
Houston, Texas 77258 - U.S.A.

Library of Congress Catalog Card Number 84-71505

Library of Congress Cataloging in Publication Data

Zopf, Jr., Paul E.
    America's older population.

    Bibliography
    Includes indexes.
    1. Aged—United States—Social conditions. 2. Aged—
United States—Statistics. I. Title.
HQ1064.U5Z67 1986   305.2'6'0973   84-71505
ISBN 0-88105-055-5
ISBN 0-88105-056-3 (paper)

Printed in the United States of America

Dedicated to

Eric and Mary

CONTENTS

viii

List of Figures

List of Tables

Preface

America's Older Population examines the characteristics of older people and the ways in which those characteristics are interwoven, using data for 1980 and later years. The book is concerned, too, with the combined effects of fertility, mortality, and migration in aging America's population and shaping its major features. The study is also comparative, contrasting America's elderly population with those in other societies. Within the United States it compares men and women, blacks and whites, Hispanics and non-Hispanics, and rural and urban people. Moreover, the work assesses the social, economic, political, and other results of the process of aging in America's population, basically along two lines: (1) the impact that the elderly and their characteristics have on society, and (2) the consequences that those characteristics have for the elderly themselves.

The book also has a pervasive humanistic component, for it deals with the welfare and rights of older people and their relationships with younger ones. The roles that the elderly have played historically in American society are also accounted for, traced by using the trends to which the older population has been subject.

Overall, the book emphasizes social demography, which brings together the data and methods of the demographer, the analyses of the sociologist, and the insights and concerns of the humanist. Therefore, I hope the work will be useful as a text or collateral reading for teachers who approach the subject from any of those perspectives, and that it will serve as a reference work for other professionals in gerontology.

America's Older Population also examines the stereotypes about elderly people and submits those assumptions to as factual an examination as possible. Thus, the book confronts the belief that most elderly are abandoned by their adult offspring, that large proportions live in nursing homes, that most older persons are poor, senile, and sexless, and other commonly held misconceptions about those aged 65 and older.

Finally, most chapters of the book offer projections, meant to be a contribution to rational social planning for the numbers and proportions of older people who will be part of American society well into the next century, and for the needs they and the working population will have.

Twentieth century trends and their potential changes allow one to infer much that will apply in the twenty-first century, despite the risks inherent in making projections. I hope those conclusions will prove useful and reasonably accurate.

The topics in *America's Older Population* are as follows: (1) number and distribution of older people; (2) age composition; (3) sex composition; (4) marriage and family status; (5) educational status; (6) work characteristics; (7) retirement; (8) income and poverty status; (9) mortality levels, differentials, and trends; (10) internal migration; and (11) some implications of America's aging population.

I am deeply indebted to the many people who have contributed so significantly to knowledge and insight in the fields represented in this work. Their numbers are so large that I can only acknowledge them collectively here, while I cite them individually in my references. Their work has been invaluable, as have the data collected and published by the U.S. Bureau of the Census, the National Center for Health Statistics, the United Nations, and other agencies. Without those very significant materials I could not have prepared a study such as this. I hope those persons and agences will accept my gratitude for their major contributions to demography and gerontology, and that they will forgive any misinterpretations of their work that mine may contain.

My colleagues at Guilford College, as always, deserve special thanks for moral support in my research endeavors, and I am indebted to the college itself for a study leave that provided the time to do this research and for several grants that helped underwrite its costs. In particular, I appreciate the encouragement of Vernie Davis, Cyrus Johnson, William Rogers, Sam Schuman, and other friends at this institution. I am also deeply indebted to my students, who helped me develop and refine many of the ideas that are in this volume.

There is no way I can express my full appreciation to Evelyn Zopf for her patience as I dash off to meet deadlines, come home late because of my research projects, and rely repeatedly on her for help. But she has my heartfelt devotion nonetheless. So does Eric Zopf, whose own career is now unfolding and who is also supportive of my work.

PAUL E. ZOPF, JR.

Chapter 1

Number and Distribution
Of Older People

Introduction

America's older population is larger than at any time in history, and so is its proportional representation in the total population. This is one of the fundamental facts shaping American society and its economic system, tax structure, and human relationships, and it calls for substantial social innovation to accommodate the aging of its population. Moreover, stereotypes and misconceptions abound about the roles that elderly people play in the social drama, the strains they endure, and how they mesh with the rest of us. Most serious is the tendency to lump all elderly together as sick, poor, senile, sexless, and generally unproductive, while we also sometimes venerate their wisdom and experience. Either attitude, however, places the whole group on the fringes of the society and denies the very integration that makes social life useful, for as Simon de Beauvoir argues, "either by their virtue or by their degradation they stand outside humanity."[1]

Perhaps these attitudes are less significant where the proportion of older people in a population is relatively small; certainly they are minimal or absent in traditional societies that integrate the elderly fully into social life. But America's older population is large numerically and proportionately and promises to become more so; we are not a traditional society and we do tend to isolate and stereotype our older people, partly because Americans see death as an enemy to be eluded and don't want the presence of their elderly to remind them of their own mortality. In turn, that mindset helps to create a youth-oriented culture and to convert the elderly into a minority group whose ranks eventually will include all those younger people who manage to avoid dying prematurely. Given present

1

age-specific death rates and life expectancy, about 77 of each 100 babies born today will reach age 65, so the chances are good that any one of us will enter what has become one of America's largest minorities. Therefore, considering the demographic realities and the perceptions about "old age," we need to take both an objective and a compassionate look at the size of the enlarging group of older persons, the reasons for its growth, the composition of that population, its migratory patterns and death rates, the probable size of the elderly group in the next century, and some of the consequences of an aging population. All of this adds up to a demographic profile that includes insights from formal demography, sociology, psychology, economics, health research, and other fields that help enlighten the realities of America's aging population in the 1980s and 1990s.

Master Trends

Demographers are concerned with th ee related aspects of aging in the United States:

(1) The absolute numbers of older persons in the population, the extent to which those numbers are increasing, and the demographic characteristics of the older group; (2) the proportion of people who are defined as elderly, which reflects the aging of the population; and (3) the longevity of individuals, which shows up as declining death rates and increases in the expectation of life at specific ages. Therefore, while these aspects are closely linked, it is important to remember that the number of older people, the aging of a whole population, and the aging of individuals are not the same thing.[2] Moreover, while the aging of a whole population is largely a socially determined process, the aging of individuals is primarily a physiological one.[3]

Given these strategic variations, the demographic circumstances of America's elderly are being shaped by several major trends that contribute to the continuing growth of this older group, their larger proportional representation in the total population, their greater average life expectancy, and their changing demographic relationships with the rest of the population. In these master trends appear some of the basic processes that produce America's aging and the complex relationships between those processes, along with some of the more significant socioeconomic implications.[4]

1. Continuing a long trend, life expectancy at birth has increased markedly since 1940 — about 9 years for males and 12 years for females. Consequently, male babies born today can expect to live an average of 71 years, female babies approximately 78 years. Everyone does die of something, of course, but the much larger number of people who now live longer gives the country a rapidly growing elderly population, while the average person who reaches 65 has many additional years of life remain-

ing. The man who attains that age can expect an average of 14 additional years, the woman an average of 18 more years.[5]

2. The nation's birth rate, which was high during the baby boom after World War II, began to fall significantly in 1960, and by 1976 it was lower than ever before. Though the rate has climbed a little since then, it is still so low that the infant and child population is a comparatively small share of the total. Consequently, older groups, especially people 65 and over, are becoming a larger percentage of the nation's total. This shows clearly that fluctuations in the birth rate are ordinarily more important than any other factor in determining the percentage of people aged 65 and over, or of those in any other age range.

3. The huge baby boom of 1945-1960 will show up as an unusually large elderly population in the years after 2010, and 40 years later people 65 and over will be about 22 per cent of the entire population, as compared with just over 11 per cent in 1980. By 2050 the nation will have at least 67 million older citizens, or more than two and half times the number living in 1980.[6]

4. The survivors of the great waves of foreign immigration, which reached most of its highest peaks between 1905 and 1914, are a relatively old population, with fully a third of them 65 or more. Only a fraction of their original ranks have been replenished by younger legal immigrants, however, because of restrictive legislation, so the elderly foreign-born group also contributes somewhat to the aging of the population. But given the average age of foreign-born people — now over 52 years compared with 30 years for the total population — that group will become continually smaller, and the major cause of aging will be the balance between birth and death rates. That process is already far along, for the impact of the aging immigrant population was greater two or three decades ago than it is now.

5. Despite greater life expectancy, people tend to retire from their jobs younger than they did earlier, even though the mandatory retirement age was raised in 1978 from 65 to 70. Earlier retirement means additional years of reliance on Social Security and various private pension plans, some of which are already seriously strained by the growing retired population, built-in cost-of-living increases, and inflation rates in the whole economy.

6. As the postwar baby-boom population ages, the proportion of active workers will decrease dramatically while that of older people rises, and the ratio of workers to retirees will decline steadily for some time. Therefore, while 1980 saw about five people aged 20-64 for each person over 65, 2050 will see less than three in the younger age group for each one in the older category. So the cost of retirement, a large share of which is borne by the employed population, will increase and the proportion of people available to carry it will shrink. At the same time, however, the overall support burden will be lightened by a small number of children per

worker, so there will be significant compensations for increases in the elderly support burden, though part of it will continue to shift from private to public funds.

These are some of the basic trends involved in the steady increase in the percentage of people who are aged 65 and older. The trends will promote substantial social change, new stresses for the older and younger populations, and more demands for a decent old age for all citizens, including those who are now young. Moreover, the aging process and the expanding elderly population will have a powerful impact on all sorts of social services, especially medical care, and on America's family systems, concepts of marriage, and ability to care for retired people, particularly the oldest ones.

Factors That Affect the Age Profile

The master trends show that the only thing which can alter a nation's age profile is the balance between rates of fertility, mortality, and migration — the three components of all population change. If birth and death rates remained constant and there were no net gains or losses by migration in particular age groups, a country's age profile eventually would consist of unchanging proportions of children, the elderly, and younger adults.[7] But those three demographic processes rarely stay the same over long periods, and most populations have abnormally large percentages of people in some ages that reflect increases in fertility at one time, relatively small percentages in other ages that mirror low rates of reproduction at other times, and variations from heavy net gains or losses by migration in given years.

Changes in death rates at various times also affect the age profile, but unless they are concentrated heavily among one group, they exert far less impact on the age profile than do fertility rates. Even the general decline in death rates that enlarged the *number* of older people has not raised their *proportion* in the United States recently, because the improvements in mortality have been greater at the lower end of the age scale than at the upper end, and have actually served to increase the percentage of children, not the elderly.[8] That pattern could change, but at present the aging of America's population results primarily from long-term fluctuations in the birth rate and lower proportions of children now than in the past, because that drop makes older people a much larger share.

Given these relationships among the population processes, current growth in the number of America's elderly people reflects high birth rates 65 and more years ago and the decreasing death rates since then, while growth in their proportion reflects both the earlier high birth rates and the lower ones that prevail now.[9] Moreover, the fluctuations in the numbers of older people that will occur until the year 2050 or so can be projected with reasonable accuracy, for they will result largely from past birth rates that obviously cannot change, though the projection rationale does assume no drastic increases in the death rate because of epidemics, wars, or other massive causes, nor major decreases because of new life-saving events. The percentages of older people are less easy to project, however, for a new baby-boom could expand the child population and thus decrease the proportional importance of the elderly. In addition, a spectacular decrease in mortality is possible because we will learn to control cancer, heart disease, or other major killers of older people, and it could reduce their death rates markedly and raise both their numbers and proportions.[10] But although such advances could raise life expectancy several years and experiments in cell biology and other areas could even increase the biological limits of the human life span — now estimated at about 100 years by some — they would simply shift the older population upward in the age scale. The death rates of the elderly would still be relatively high as compared with other age groups, and membership in their age category would still be comparatively short, though it might be useful to raise the generally accepted threshold of "old age" from 65 to 75 or even 85 years.

Immigration has its impact, too, though it affects the age profile less now than formerly. When the volume of immigration is heavy and consists mostly of young adults, it contributes to a relatively large number of elderly people about 45 or 50 years later; that fact accounts for a considerable amount of the growth in America's elderly population until about 1960. But when immigration falls off sharply, as it did in the United States after 1914, though with a few important increases in the early 1920s, its later impact on the aging of the population is far less.

In fact, the relative youthfulness of the present large illegal immigration to the United States, coupled with that of the smaller group of legal entrants, will tend to slow the demographic aging of the whole population, though the actual impact is difficult to measure. But even if we know relatively little about the size and demographic composition of the illegal group, it is clear that most of the new immigrant populations do consist heavily of young adults and children, and they will keep the percentage of older people from increasing even faster than it is already, at least for a time. Considering the patterns of the twentieth century, however, the largest impact of immigration on the aging of the population has probably passed, and future changes in age composition will depend even more heavily on fertility than they have many times in the past.

Organization of the Book

Give these basic conditions, the purpose of this book is to explore the demographic realities of the older population and some of the meanings of those realities for the entire society and for the elderly themselves.

The remainder of this chapter considers the past, present, and projected size and proportion of the aging group and the way in which they are distributed geographically throughout the country. Included are variations by metropolitan and nonmetropolitan residence and some of the redistribution now underway because of variations from place to place in net migration and fertility.

Chapter 2 looks at the age breakdown of the overall elderly group, and at the changing ratio of older people to younger adults and what that means for support burdens. There the study explores the demographic relationships between the declining percentages of children and the increasing proportions of elderly people as components of the total dependency burden that producing adults must carry.

Chapter 3 turns attention to the balance between men and women and what it means for older people who have lost their mates and for their ability to deal with solitude, diminished income, and other unhappy realities that affect many. That chapter also focuses on the male-female differences in death rates and longevity that distort the sex balance and create a superabundance of women in the older ages.

Chapter 4 deals with the marital status and family characteristics of the older population, particularly the effects of widowhood and its aftermath. The loss of a mate is predominantly a problem of women because of sex differences in life expectancy, and calls for a careful look at the impact of widowhood on them.

Chapter 5 assesses the educational standing of older people and the reasons why it averages below that of younger people. Included, too, are the patterns of re-education among some of the many older people who remain viable and optimistic.

Chapter 6 considers the work characteristics of older people, including the extent to which they continue in the labor force, the occupations they hold, the industries that employ them, and their problems with unemployment.

Chapter 7 concerns retirement, including the composition of the retired population, why people retire and how they adjust, and changes in the nature of retirement. The study examines the trend toward early retirement and how inflation, recessions, and high unemployment rates affect that trend.

Chapter 8 is an account of income distribution and poverty status, and deals with the degree of income equitability that exists between elderly people and other groups. Important also are income differences by race and sex, the principal sources of income for the elderly, and the features of the older segment that falls below the official poverty line.

Chapter 9 explores the mortality levels and differentials among older people and the principal causes of death that finally end their lives. That chapter examines life expectancy and mortality differences by race and sex, the long-term reduction in the death rates of older people, and changes in the importance of various causes.

Chapter 10 concerns the relatively small share of America's older people who migrate after they reach age 65, especially those who move from place to place within the United States in search of retirement opportunities. Included are the movements to Florida, Arizona, California, and other Sunbelt states, and the way in which migration selects for certain characteristics. The reasons for elderly migration and its basic trends are also explored.

Chapter 11, which concludes the book, is an account of some social consequences of America's aging population, both for the elderly and the larger society. Some aspects are the role ambiguity, isolation, minority group status, and other problems faced by some elderly, and the adjustment, productivity, and good health enjoyed by many others. Included, too, are the prospects to intervene in the aging process, thereby increasing both life expectancy and life span itself.

Why 65 and Over?

Even though biological aging takes place at very different rates for individuals, this book uses 65 and over as the ages defining the older population. It is an arbitrary choice that should not imply uniformity in people's social and economic performance, for the category does include people well past age 65 who are not old physiologically and others who have just turned age 65 but who are very old biologically. Moreover, 65 marks the popularly accepted threshold of the older ages simply because it was arbitrarily selected as the forced retirement age in Germany's social welfare system that was created in 1889 by Chancellor Otto von Bismarck.[11] Bismarck actually set retirement at 70, but it was dropped to 65 in 1916,[12] partly because the German government assumed few people would live past that age to collect benefits from a program that was created in the first place to offset the appeals of socialism.

The U.S. Census Bureau also defines the elderly as those aged 65 and older and reports its data on that basis, and if those valuable data are to be useful, there is little choice but to accept its classification. In addition, the Social Security Administration uses 65 as the point for beginning to pay full benefits, and many other agencies employ that age in their operations. Therefore, it is simply practical for this study to use 65 as the threshold for becoming "elderly," even though the mandatory retirement age is now 70 and the average retirement age at this writing is actually lower than 65.

The most accurate measure would really be *functional age,* which reflects the person's ability to work, engage in intellectual activity, and be self-maintaining.[13] But there is little agreement on how to assess functional age, and because it varies from person to person the index is difficult to use as a standard or to represent statistically. Furthermore, in large groups of people, such as the nation, "the aging process, functional age, and physiological age follow chronological age closely,"[14] though there are wide individual variations within those large populations. In this search for an ideal index, however, it is most important to avoid any implication that the elderly are all alike and all share poverty or affluence, good health or illness, social disengagement or integration, or any other features that encourage stereotyping and thus obscure the group's great diversity. The older contingent is nearly as heterogeneous as many others in American society, except that all of its members are at least age 65.

The analyses in the following chapters refer mainly to people aged 65-84, because they are the vast majority of the elderly group. In 1980, for example, they made up 91 per cent of the whole category 65 and over, though the proportion 85 and over is increasing rapidly. In addition, there are serious distortions in the data beyond age 84, basically for two reasons: (1) The numbers in some categories beyond that age are so small that a few individuals more or less can change the statistical pattern significantly; and (2) because it is prestigious to be a centenarian and one receives attention as a curiosity if not a respected elder, there are substantial distortions in age-reporting among people approaching the century mark; some are not even sure of their correct age. Therefore, the data for people aged 85 and older need to be used cautiously, though some things about that group can be reported separately, especially the large sex imbalance.

Numbers and Proportions of Elderly People

Numbers

In 1980 there were 25.5 million people aged 65 and older in the United States. They were a larger number than ever before and they are continuing to increase. That group is more than eight time as large as the one in 1900, because birth rates were high when today's elderly generation was born, death rates have fallen off dramatically during their lifetimes, and the survivors of the large immigrant populations of the early twentieth century are now quite old.[15] Thus, the large numbers of older people are the collective result of the aging process among increasing millions of individuals. This is not the same thing, however, as the "aging" of the nation's whole population, which occurs when elderly people grow not just in numbers, but as a percentage of the total.

Proportions

In 1980 the nation's older people were 11.3 per cent of the whole population, which is a higher proportion than ever in the past and which is certain to increase markedly over the next several decades, probably to level out only after the middle of the next century. There will also be a brief leveling and perhaps even a slight proportional decline just after the turn of the century, however, when the small baby crops of the 1930s are elderly.

The major statistical relationships between various age groups appear in the 1980 portion of Figure 1-1, which is an age-sex pyramid that portrays the percentages of males and females by five-year age ranges. In that diagram the present relative abundance of older people is easily apparent, as is the comparative scarcity of children. All of this contrasts sharply with the situation in 1870, when older people were a far smaller share of the total population, young people a much larger part. Moreover, the aging of the whole population, represented by more than a century of dramatic change in the proportions of people at various age levels, has created new implications for the nation's ability to absorb older people into satisfying roles, including occupations, and for family structure, the political process, investment policies, and other basic social matters that tend to differ from one age group to another.[16]

Despite the high percentage of elderly people in America's present population, however, they do not come close to being a world record. In fact, the United States ranks only twentieth in the proportions of those aged 65 and older; the other 19 countries are all European and have had extremely low birth and death rates for a considerable time. (See Table 1-1.) Most are in Western Europe, though several other Eastern European countries would join those already on the list if the partial success of recent pro-natalist policies had not increased their percentages of children and caused their proportions of older people to fall, at least temporarily.[17]

These aging populations in the developed countries contrast sharply with the much younger ones in most developing nations, where relatively high birth rates and declining death rates, especially among infants, elevate the percentages of children and depress those of elderly people. In Mexico, for example, the elderly are less than 3.5 per cent of the population, as they are in Indonesia, Brazil, and most other developing nations with recent population explosions and life expectancies well below those of the industrialized countries. Thus, by world standards the United States has a very high percentage of older people, though a fairly low one by European standards.

Growth Trends in America's Older Population

Even though fluctuations in fertility, mortality, and migration have made the population of the United States younger at certain times and older at others, the long-term trend has been toward a larger number and higher proportion of elderly people. That is true of most industrialized nations, where the percentages of children have fallen and those of elderly inhabitants have risen substantially in recent decades. Furthermore, as America's proportion of children has shrunk, the percentages of people in many of the age groups between 20 and 64 have grown, but not as rapidly as the share of the elderly. As a result of these patterns, the median age in the United States went from less than 17 years in 1820, to 23 years in 1900, to 30 years in 1980. The average age was even a bit higher in 1940 and 1950 than in 1980, for it reflected the very low birth rates of the 1930s and

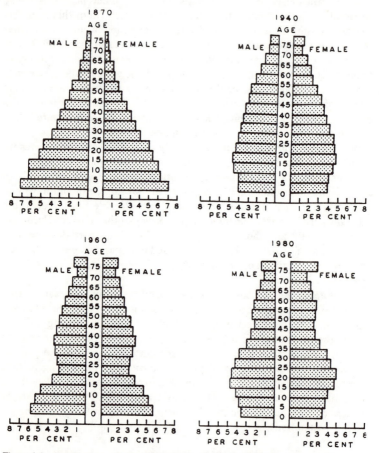

Figure 1-1. Age-Sex Pyramids for the United States: 1870, 1940, 1960, and 1980
Sources: U.S.Census Office, *Ninth Census of the United States, Vital Statistics of the United States* (1872), table 22; U.S.Bureau of the Census, *U.S. Census of Population: 1960, Characteristics of the Population, U.S. Summary* (1964), table 47; *1980 Census of Population, Supplementary Reports*, PC80-S1-1, *Age, Sex, Race, and Spanish Origin of the Population by Regions, Divisions, and States: 1980* (1981), table 1.

early 1940s and the aging immigrant population. Then in 1960 and 1970 the median age was down some because of the high post-World War II fertility levels, though the reductions proved to be temporary. These changes also reflect the rapid growth in the numbers of older people from 1900 to 1952 or so, followed by somewhat slower increases in their ranks. Despite the fluctuations, however, the long-term aging of the population resumed after 1970, and the 11.3 per cent of America's population who were aged 65 and older in 1980 contrasted markedly with the 3 per cent in 1870.

Table 1-1. Elderly Population of Countries Having
1 Million or More Inhabitants and
Higher Percentages of Elderly Than
the United States

Country	Year	Total Population (000)	Population 65+ Number (000)	Population 65+ Per Cent
Sweden	1980	8,310	1,354	16.3
East Germany	1980	16,737	2,661	15.9
Austria	1980	7,505	1,162	15.5
West Germany	1980	61,566	9,550	15.5
England & Wales	1980	49,244	7,424	15.1
Norway	1980	4,086	603	14.8
Denmark	1980	5,123	739	14.4
Belgium	1979	9,855	1,410	14.3
France	1980	53,583	7,535	14.1
Scotland	1980	5,153	724	14.1
Switzerland	1980	6,314	872	13.8
Italy	1980	57,070	7,676	13.5
Hungary	1980	10,711	1,438	13.4
Greece	1979	9,449	1,233	13.0
Czechoslovakia	1978	15,137	1,892	12.5
Finland	1980	4,780	572	12.0
Bulgaria	1980	8,861	1,051	11.9
Netherlands	1980	14,091	1,616	11.5
Northern Ireland	1978	1,539	175	11.4
UNITED STATES	1980	226,505	25,544	11.3

Sources: United Nations, Demographic Yearbook,
1979, table 7; 1980, table 7; 1981, table 7.

The proportion of older people actually grew rather slowly between 1870 and 1930, but then their rate of increase picked up considerably for several reasons. (See Table 1-2.) (1) Many older people were products of a large fertility increase after the Civil War, and by 1935 much of their sizable age cohort had reached age 65. (2) Decreases in the birth rates between 1900 and 1935 made children and young adults proportionately less abundant in the population and elderly people more so. (3) By the last quarter of the twentieth century the millions of immigrants who had arrived early in the 1900s had aged past 65, and because they were not fully replaced by young immigrants, the average age of the foreign-born population was significantly higher than that of the native-born group. (4) The increases in life expectancy that occurred after 1930 allowed more infants to survive and more people of other ages to live longer.

Table 1-2. People 65 and Over in the American Population, 1870-1980

Year	Total Population (000)	Population 65+	
		Number (000)	Per Cent
1870	38,558	1,154	3.0
1880	50,156	1,723	3.4
1890	62,622	2,417	3.9
1900	76,212	3,084	4.0
1910	92,229	3,954	4.3
1920	106,022	4,940	4.7
1930	123,203	6,645	5.4
1940	132,165	9,036	6.8
1950	151,326	12,295	8.1
1960	179,323	16,560	9.2
1970	203,212	20,066	9.9
1980	226,505	25,544	11.3

Sources: U.S. Bureau of the Census, Sixteenth Census of the United States: 1940, Characteristics of the Population, U.S. Summary (1943), table 8; U.S. Census of Population: 1970, General Population Characteristics, U.S. Summary (1972), table 53; 1980 Census of Population, Supplementary Reports, PC80-S1-1, Age, Sex, Race, and Spanish Origin of the Population by Regions, Divisions, and States: 1980 (1981), table 1.

These four conditions that favored aging of the population were augmented by significant fertility reductions after 1960. Therefore, between 1870 and 1980 the number of people 65 and over grew 2,114 per cent, while the total population increased only 487 per cent. The group of children under 15 was 239 per cent larger in 1980 than in 1870, and the group aged 15-64 was 572 per cent greater. All of these changes contributed to the gradual aging of the American population. In fact, just in the twentieth century the elderly population has increased more than three and a half times as fast as the population of all ages. Figure 1-1 shows how this process has appeared on the age-sex pyramid at particular times.

State-to-State Increases

Elderly people are most numerous, of course, in the states with the largest total populations. Therefore, in 1980 California had the largest number, followed in order by New York, Florida, Pennsylvania, Texas, Illinois, and Ohio. In fact, those seven states accounted for 11.6 million elderly people, or 45 per cent of the nation's total.

The number of people aged 65 and older increased in each of the 50 states and the District of Columbia between 1970 and 1980 and, therefore, in each of the regions and divisions, but the rates of increase varied widely, with some far below the national average of 27 per cent, others substantially above. (See Table 1-3 and Figure 1-2.) The proportions grew only slightly in the District of Columbia and modestly in New York, Iowa, Nebraska, South Dakota, and Massachusetts. At the same time, the percentages of elderly people increased tremendously in Nevada, Arizona, Hawaii, and Florida, though the 1980 populations were relatively small in all except Florida, and even modest numerical increases produced high rates of growth in some states. Other states that experienced at least 40 per cent increases in the elderly population are Alaska, New Mexico, South Carolina, North Carolina, Utah, and Georgia. The largest numerical increases occurred in Florida, California, and Texas. California registered a proportional increase of only 34 per cent and Texas one of 38 per cent, however, because their total populations and influxes of younger people are so large that even the addition of huge numbers of older people produces fairly modest proportional increases overall.

In every state except Wyoming, the elderly population grew faster than the total population. In most states of the Northeast and North Central regions, the older group increased several times more rapidly than the total, and it even grew substantially where the total populations declined — Rhode Island and New York. In the Southern and Western States, whose overall growth rates were unusually high, the older population also grew more rapidly than the total, even expanding modestly in the nation's capital despite an overall population decrease of 16 per cent. Rates of increase among older Americans in the states of the South and West were often two or three times higher than the rates for total populations, though Wyoming's elderly increased at only about half the state's overall rate.

Some Projections

The nation's elderly population is certain to become substantially larger than it is now, because the people who will enter this category in the next

Table 1-3. Percentage Change in the Elderly and Total Populations of Each Region and Division, 1970-1980

Region and Division	Population 65+, 1980 (000)	Per Cent Change, 1970-80	
		65+	All Ages
United States	25,544	27.3	11.4
Northeast	6,072	16.8	0.2
New England	1,520	19.7	4.2
Middle Atlantic	4,551	15.8	-1.1
North Central	6,691	16.8	4.0
East North Central	4,492	17.9	3.5
West North Central	2,199	14.8	5.2
South	8,484	40.4	20.0
South Atlantic	4,363	48.6	20.4
East South Central	1,657	30.5	14.5
West South Central	2,463	34.2	22.9
West	4,298	38.8	23.9
Mountain	1,060	52.5	37.1
Pacific	3,237	34.8	19.8

Sources: U.S. Bureau of the Census, U.S. Census of Population: 1970, General Population Characteristics, U.S. Summary (1972), tables 57 and 72; 1980 Census of Population, Supplementary Reports, PC80-S1-1, Age, Sex, Race, and Spanish Origin of the Population by Regions, Divisions, and States: 1980 (1981), table 2; Statistical Abstract of the United States: 1981 (1981), table 9.

15

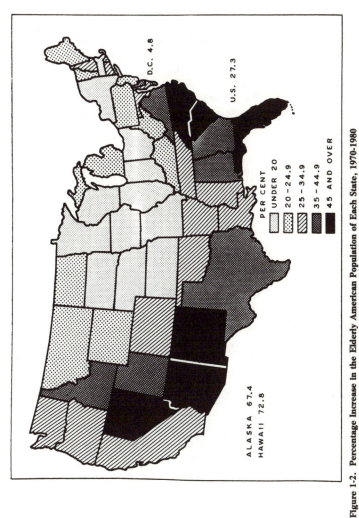

Figure 1-2. Percentage Increase in the Elderly American Population of Each State, 1970-1980

Sources: U.S.Bureau of the Census, *U.S. Census of Population: 1970, General Population Characteristics, U.S. Summary* (1972), table 62; *U.S. Census of Population, Supplementary Reports,* PC80-S1-1, *Age, Sex, Race, and Spanish Origin of the Population by Regions, Divisions, and States: 1980* (1981), table 2.

several decades are already alive and subject to age-specific death rates
that have been predictable so far. The rate of growth, however, will vary
substantially over time, and the numbers and proportions of elderly people will even fall now and then because of fluctuating birth rates in past
years.

Table 1-4 shows the probable patterns, based on Series II projections of
the population made by the U.S. Bureau of the Census. It should be made
clear, however, that those data depend on several assumptions about
rates of fertility, mortality, and net immigration, any of which could be
altered by unpredictable events, such as a new baby boom that would
increase the infant population significantly, or some major disaster or
health improvements that would alter the death rate drastically. In particular, Series II projections assume a level of fertility intermediate between
the highest (Series I) and the lowest (Series III) that seem possible in light

Table 1-4. Projected Numbers and Percentages of
People 65 and Over, 1980-2050

Year	Total Population (000)	Population 65+	
		Number (000)	Per Cent
1980[a]	226,505	25,544	11.3
1985	238,648	28,673	12.0
1990	249,731	31,799	12.7
1995	259,631	34,006	13.1
2000	267,990	35,036	13.1
2025	301,022	58,636	19.5
2050	308,856	67,060	21.7

Sources: U.S. Bureau of the Census, 1980 Census of
Population, Supplementary Reports, PC80-S1-1, Age,
Sex, Race, and Spanish Origin of the Population by
Regions, Divisions, and States: 1980 (1981), table
1; "Projections of the Population of the United
States: 1982 to 2050" (advance report), Current
Population Reports, P-25, no. 922 (1982), table 2.

[a]Census data.

Projections based on Series II assumptions.

of the American demographic experience and the social, cultural, and economic factors that influence population processes. Moreover, all of the projections assume that future mortality levels will decline but that the balance between immigration and emigration could add from 250,000 to 750,000 people each year. Series II projections assume annual net immigration of 450,000, although that figure does omit the large undocumented immigration to the United States, much of it from Latin America.[18] In addition, legal immigration is sometimes higher than 450,000 (in 1981 it was 597,000), although between 1970 and 1980 it did average 450,000 annually.

If Series II assumptions do prove reasonably accurate, the combination of fertility, mortality, and migration will raise the nation's elderly population by about 3 million per year until 1995, when that group will represent about 13 per cent of the total population. Then the proportion of older inhabitants will stop growing and their numbers could even drop some, because the low birth rates before World War II will appear around the turn of the century as comparatively stable numbers of people aged 65 and older. But when the products of the postwar baby boom move into the older ages, the numbers and percentages will increase once again. By 2030 the large elderly group, which in its younger years has already caused great expansions in school systems that are now having to reduce operations and which has placed heavy burdens on the job market, will have one last major impact on society as it reaches the ages 65 and beyond.[19] Eventually, if fertility and mortality rates do not change much, the proportions of children, younger adults, and older people will approach a stable equilibrium. Such a population would not have severe indentations or large bulges anywhere in the age profile, and the aging of the population would stop. While all of this is going on, Series II projections imply that the proportion of children under age 15 will drop to 21 per cent of the total population by 2000 and to 17 per cent by 2050.

Projections are risky, however, and there is still the possibility of a significant fertility increase in the 1980s or 1990s that would raise the percentages of children in the nation's population and thereby reduce the share of older people. Some demographers predict just such a baby boom, ironically because of the relatively small cohort who will be in their most fertile years. Richard Easterlin, for instance, suggests that when the small baby crops of the period after 1965 reach their most fertile stage about two and a half decades later, those people will experience fewer economic pressures than some earlier cohorts, because their small numbers will put them in demand in the job market. Their incomes will be relatively high as a result and will allow them to get material things and also raise somewhat larger families than their parents,[20] other influences being equal. If so, the percentage of children will rise and that of the elderly will be lower than expected. In the same vein, Easterlin interprets the low birth rates of the late 1960s and the 1970s as a reaction to the relative deprivation felt by the large age cohort that achieved its peak reproductive potential during that period. They reduced their fertility levels, he argues, because of the employment squeeze, inflation, and other economic constraints generated in part by the relatively large size of their age group. Therefore, as fertility and the proportion of children dropped in response to these conditions, the percentage of older people was able to rise sharply. If any new increase in fertility comes, it will change the age profile by broadening the base of the age-sex pyramid and slowing proportional growth at the apex, at least temporarily. Even if fertility levels were to rise, however, the proportion of older people would still increase between 2010 and 2020, when the huge baby boom of the late 1940s and the 1950s becomes 65 and over. Therefore, while the aging of the population could slow in that decade, the massive new baby boom that would be required to reverse it seems highly unlikely.[21]

We shall have to see what happens, although the constraints imposed on fertility by inflation, unemployment, energy shortages, changes in women's roles and opportunities, and other realities are all variables in the equation, and they will probably cause relatively small cohorts to give birth to other relatively small cohorts in the foreseeable future. If fertility and mortality then come into equilibrium and neither changes appreciably over a long period, the proportions of people in the major age groups will stabilize and the percentage of elderly people will stop growing; the progressive aging of America's population will then be over, at least for a time. It is worth noting also, however, that even at low rates of reproduction, large cohorts produce other large cohorts who will later reach the older years.

Geographic Distribution

The distribution of elderly people in the United States is far from even, with the largest percentages to be found in New England and the Middle Atlantic division, the Great Plains area, and a few sections of the South. The older group is underrepresented in several other parts of the South, various industrialized districts of the North Central region, and almost all of the Mountain and Pacific divisions. The parts of the country with high percentages of elderly often have low birth rates, which help increase the proportional importance of older age groups. Some places, especially in the Sunbelt, have received relatively large migrations of the elderly. Still other ''aging'' sections are quite rural and have lost large proportions of young adults by net migration, which not only reduces their proportional significance, but also that of the children they bear. Conversely, the places with comparatively few older people either have high birth rates or large migratory influxes of people under age 65, though fertility and migration frequently act in concert.

Patterns by States

As in the case of the regions and divisions, the 50 states vary widely in their proportions of people aged 65 and older, ranging from a 1980 high of 17.3 per cent in Florida to only 2.9 per cent in Alaska. (See Figure 1-3.) As is well known, Florida receives a large retired population by migration, though younger adults are also part of the massive flow and help keep the elderly group from being an even larger percentage than it is. The movement to Alaska, on the other hand, consists chiefly of young adults, often with children, and very few older people are part of that migration. A large share of Alaska's population growth has also been quite recent, so those people have not yet had a chance to become 65. Furthermore, some people in that state's population who do reach the older ages migrate to warmer places, sometimes those from which they came. The other chief cause of Alaska's youthful age profile is its relatively high fertility level, for in 1980 its birth rate was exceeded only by those of Utah and the District of Columbia.

In addition to Florida, the elderly group is 13 per cent or more in Arkansas, Rhode Island, Iowa, South Dakota, and Nebraska, and is between 12 and 13 per cent in Pennsylvania, Kansas, Massachusetts, Maine, Oklahoma, New York, North Dakota, West Virginia, and Wisconsin. Several of these states, such as the ones in the Northeast, have comparatively low birth rates that account for their relatively large shares of elderly people, whereas other states, such as those in the Midwest, have high birth rates but also comparatively large rural populations with fairly sizable numbers of older people. In fact, in 1980 the influences of farm and nonfarm residence at the national level were such that older people made up 12.3 per cent of the farm population but only 10.9 per cent of the nonfarm group.[22] Furthermore, the farm population is the nation's only major residence segment in which the number of elderly men exceeds that of elderly women, though by a far smaller margin than in the past.

The states with unusually low percentages of older people, besides Alaska and Utah, are Hawaii, Wyoming, Nevada, Colorado, and New Mexico, each of which had less than 9 per cent elderly in 1980. All have birth rates above the national average. In addition, such states as Michigan, Maryland, Virginia, South Carolina, Georgia, Louisiana, Texas, and Idaho have between 9 and 10 per cent older people. The last five have birth rates well above the national average, but they and the others also have unusually large groups of working-age people, because they are either highly industrialized or suburbanized and do not draw or retain abnormally large elderly groups.

These cases all underscore the fact that the causes of high or low proportions of older people are extremely complex. If one considers only the migration component, for example, a particular state may have had a

20

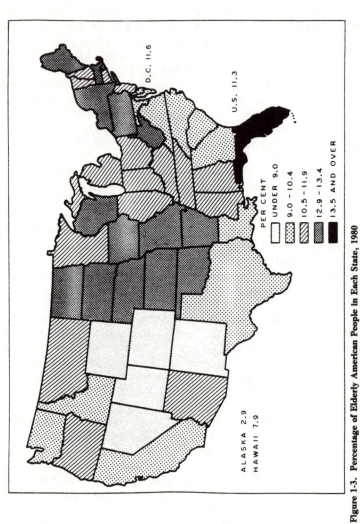

PER CENT

- UNDER 9.0
- 9.0 – 10.4
- 10.5 – 11.9
- 12.9 – 13.4
- 13.5 AND OVER

D.C. 11.6

U.S. 11.3

ALASKA 2.9

HAWAII 7.9

Figure 1-3. Percentage of Elderly American People in Each State, 1980

Source: U.S.Bureau of the Census, *1980 Census of Population, Supplementary Reports,* PC80-S1-1, *Age, Sex, Race, and Spanish Origin of the Population by Regions, Divisions, and States: 1980* (1981), table 2.

great economic boom 40 or 50 years ago that attracted many young adults who have aged but stayed put. Another may have a high proportion of elderly because large numbers of immigrants settled there in the early twentieth century. In some states, such as Alaska, the population migrating in now is quite young and also relatively fertile, and those realities help keep down the percentages of older people. In California, whose total and elderly populations are the nation's largest, the age composition of in-migrants has been so mixed that, while the number of older people increased 34 per cent between 1970 and 1980, their proportion only rose from 9 to 10.2 per cent. These are a few of the ways migration affects the state-to-state differences in the share of older people. The influences of birth and death rates are equally complex and usually even more significant than migration.

Metropolitan-Nonmetropolitan Patterns

In many instances, the degree to which an area is rural or urban shapes the ways that birth, death, and migration affect its age structure. Therefore, we need to consider how the proportions of older people differ between the metropolitan and nonmetropolitan areas of the nation.

Metropolitan elderly. The bulk of the nation's people of all ages, including the elderly, live in metropolitan areas, but older people are still underrepresented there because of their relative scarcity in some of the sections just outside the central cities. On the other hand, older people are fairly heavily represented within those large central cities, especially those with 1 million or more inhabitants. (See Table 1-5.) Middle-aged people are more apt to avoid those places, and in that sense, the elderly are more like young adults, who are disproportionately represented in large urban centers, though usually for different reasons. At the same time, the elderly account for a relatively small share of the people residing outside the central cities of metropolitan counties. Therefore, a comparatively large percentage of the elderly is highly urbanized, living amidst the advantages and disadvantages of the nation's great cities, even though that tendency is not as strong as it was in the past. Some were born in the places where they reside, others are first-generation immigrants, and still others have moved to the cities from other parts of the nation; many of them were part of the huge rural-to-urban migration that shifted more than 55 million people off the farms between 1933 and 1970.[23]

Certain parts of the central cities often contain dense concentrations of the elderly, sometimes because their incomes are too low to allow them to migrate elsewhere, or because they choose to remain in familiar neighborhoods among friends, particularly those of the same ethnic background and age.[24] Many of those elderly are simply left behind as younger family members flee poor educational and occupational opportunities, deterioriating housing, high crime rates, and other conditions that the elderly who remain must endure. The older people then may form "gerontological enclaves,"[25] and because they tend to succumb more readily to the role of "victim" in such places, the loss of younger people also represents a decreasing level of protection for many elderly. As a result of these residential dynamics, the relatively high overall proportions of older people in many large central cities often reflect specific concentrations here and there within those centers, sometimes troubled by problems that intensify as the elderly concentrate more heavily and younger people become even scarcer.[26] These enclaves often degenerate into "gray ghettos" in some sections of nearly all central cities, usually the aging and deteriorating parts of the urban core.[27]

Suburban elderly. The older people who inhabit the suburgs have been a comparatively small group historically, but more elderly now live there than in the central cities. Therefore, suburban groups are aging along with the rest of the population, and the percentages of people 65 and over are growing there just as they are in the cities and the countryside.

Table 1-5. Proportional Representation of Persons in Various Residence Classes, by Selected Age Groups, 1980

Residence Class	Age Group				
	25-34	35-44	45-54	55-64	65+
All Classes	16.4	11.3	10.1	9.6	11.3
Metropolitan	16.9	11.5	10.2	9.5	10.7
In Central Cities	17.3	10.3	9.6	9.6	11.9
Outside Central Cities	16.6	12.3	10.6	9.4	9.9
Nonmetropolitan	14.9	10.7	9.7	9.8	13.0
Farm	10.0	11.8	13.2	13.3	12.3

Sources: U.S. Bureau of the Census, State and Metropolitan Area Data Book, 1982 (1982), p. 357; "Farm Population of the United States: 1980," Current Population Reports, P-27, no. 54 (1981), table 2.

In some cases, gerontological clusters are appearing in the suburbs, too, though some of them are related to the location of nursing homes, retirement condominiums, and other developments that are not really part of "natural" neighborhoods. In other instances, suburban populations are aging because relatively high percentages of younger people are migrating out to opportunities elsewhere, especially in times of high unemployment. The aging process is also hastened by the high cost of homes and mortgage money, which tends to keep many young couples from moving into the types of suburban housing that their parents were once able to afford more easily and where they still live. Moreover, the average age of a suburban population tends to rise as the suburb itself ages, creating substantial proportions of people 65 and over in many older suburban communities.

Small-town and farm elderly. Another large group of elderly people can be found in the more rural nonmetropolitan parts of the nation. They are heavily represented in the counties with no urban places and in all other types of nonmetropolitan territory, including farms. They have a special affinity, however, for the villages and hamlets with 1,000-2,500 inhabitants, and only a slightly lesser attraction to towns and small cities having between 2,500 and 25,000 inhabitants. Some of those small-town people have simply remained in the places they were born, while others have left nearby farms and moved into these centers, perhaps after a farm has been sold or transferred to an adult son or daughter. Still other elderly residents of the towns have migrated longer distances to find better climatic and other conditions, often leaving large cities as they move. Very few of the elderly people in these nonmetropolitan areas are an aging immigrant group, however, for the small towns attracted far less than their fair share of foreign-born people, while the cities drew relatively large proportions.

The nation's most rural elderly people as a group tend to be especially disadvantaged and to have more than their share of poverty, poor health, deteriorated housing, and psychosocial isolation.[28] This is so partly because the rural areas lost services and income during the huge twentieth-century migration to cities, and partly because subsequent increases in rural incomes and services have not kept pace with the significant regrowth that has occurred in nonmetropolitan places since 1970. Therefore, on the average the most isolated rural people of all ages have fewer advantages than other groups, and older people have the least advantages of the rural segment. Consequently, the rural elderly have lower average incomes than their urban counterparts and are more apt to suffer from chronic illnesses and disabilities, partly because poor public transportation in rural areas keeps many from visiting the health-care facilities that do exist.

The rural elderly also have lower average levels of education than the urban and suburban elderly, are more likely to occupy substandard housing, and are less apt to have joined pension funds and other plans that provide retirement income; even Social Security coverage has been poorer historically for rural than for urban workers. However, elderly rural workers who are self-employed, principally in farming and small-town businesses, may have more discretion in choosing when or even whether to retire than do people employed by someone else, though financial realities influence most of those decisions.[29] As expected, these problems all tend to be more serious for elderly women than for elderly men in the rural areas, and those women probably have fewer alternatives available to them than virtually any other segment of the population.[30]

Race and sex patterns. The patterns of rural-urban distribution by race are similar to the ones just described for the total elderly population. That is, both black and white elderly people, along with those of Spanish origin, are heavily represented in large central cities but are relatively scarce in the metropolitan sections just outside those cities. They are especially abundant in the nonmetropolitan counties, particularly the ones with sizable towns and small cities. The only exception is the relative scarcity of elderly Spanish-origin people in nonmetropolitan counties with places of 25,000 or more inhabitants. Furthermore, only in the rural-farm residence category do elderly men outnumber older women regardless of race or ethnic origin. The sex imbalance is greatest in central cities, where there are only 63 men aged 65 and over for each 100 women in those ages. But even in the nonmetropolitan counties collectively, where the sex imbalance is less, there are only 78 men for every 100 women. In the farm population, however, the ratio is still 112.[31]

The geographic patterns emphasize the heterogeneity of the elderly population and show that some residence groups in the United States are aging somewhat faster than others. Nonetheless, the birth rate has fallen so significantly in virtually all parts of the nation, that the aging of the population is one of its universal demographic phenomena. Therefore, while the average age is a bit higher in the central cities and the more rural nonmetropolitan places than in the suburbs and is substantially higher in the farm population than any other aggregate, most of the differences are narrowing. Consequently, the graying of America's population pervades all of the major residence categories.

Redistribution

As a result of the variable growth patterns from one section to another, the nation's major regions and divisions have added older people at very different rates. In turn, those variations are redistributing the older group more evenly throughout most of the nation, though not necessarily by physical movement. Thus, the Northeast, which has long had higher proportions of older people than the national average, has been witnessing below-normal growth in their numbers, which is bringing the share of older people in that region closer to the national figure. The North Central region, which also has had more than its fair share of elderly during most of the present century, now has approximately the national average because of comparatively slow growth between 1970 and 1980. On the other hand, the South and the West, which historically have had less than their shares of older people, are adding them rapidly. The South is now at the national average, while the West is coming closer to it. Many of the individual states in those regions, however, are still far below the national figure, partly because their birth rates are comparatively high, and partly because of influxes of young adults.

While the elderly population is becoming somewhat more evenly distributed among the major regions, it is also concentrating more heavily in a handful of states in the South and West, largely because of net in-migration. At the same time, the states whose populations show exceptionally low rates of growth among the elderly generally have lost many of them by net out-migration. Migration affects redistribution in other ways, too, however, for many states with extremely high percentages of older people are losing young adults by net migration, while those aged 65 and older stay behind and their proportion remains high.[32] This is going on in parts of the Midwestern farm belt, such as Iowa, where the number of elderly is growing rather slowly (11% between 1970 and 1980), while they also remain a comparatively high proportion of the total (13% in 1980) because of the exodus of younger adults, some of them accompanied by children. Much the same is true in Kansas, Nebraska, South Dakota, and other states with percentages of older people well above the national average, but whose numbers of elderly are growing at rates far below the national norm.

Despite their various movements from place to place, older people don't shift around nearly as much as young adults, for while as many as 25 per cent of the people aged 20-24 change residence in a given year, it is rare for more than 6 per cent of the elderly to do so. Moreover, the moves that most older people do make tend to be of relatively short distance, despite the well-known treks to Florida, California, and other Sunbelt areas. And if they are going to move any considerable distance, older people generally do so in their early or mid-60s, often as part of the adjustment that accompanies retirement. Those past age 75, on the other hand, are much less likely to leave their present homes for faraway sections of the nation, though some may move short distances, perhaps to live near their children or to enter retirement or nursing homes. Others, especially recent

LIBRARY OF MOUNT ST. MARY'S COLLEGE

widows, return to the local area they may have left a few years earlier.

These dynamics raise the proportions of elderly people slowly in some places and rapidly in others, though it is noteworthy that since 1900 the elderly contingent has grown at least twice as fast as the total population in every state, including Alaska and Hawaii. Clearly, it is possible for the proportion of older people to rise significantly in a state even if practically no increase occurs by net migration of the elderly themselves. Therefore, the changes in the states underscore the intricate interplay of fertility, mortality, and migration which affects numbers, proportions, and growth rates of the elderly population, both directly and indirectly, and which redistributes them throughout the nation's population.

Summary

The United States has never had a larger number of people aged 65 and older than it does now, nor has that group ever been a greater percentage of the total population. Furthermore, the average individual can expect to live longer than his/her counterpart in any previous generation. These basic facts have major implications for many aspects of American life and for the elderly themselves as individuals and as a group.

The three population processes — fertility, mortality, and migration — are variously involved in these basic changes. The *absolute number* of older people is large now because of the high fertility rates when they were born, the reductions in the death rate during their lifetimes, and the huge immigrations of the early twentieth century. The relatively high and climbing *percentage* of elderly people, which "ages" the nation's population, is primarily the result of recent low birth rates that decrease the proportions of children and young adults in the population, though the aging of the immigrant population has also played a part in the process. Death rates, however, have been dropping faster for infants and children than for the elderly, so this actually helps depress the percentage of the latter. Finally, the greater longevity of individuals does depend on long-term reductions in the death rates of all age groups and consequent increases in life expectancy.

Both the numbers and proportions of the elderly will continue to grow until well into the next century, because the group from which they will come is already alive and subject to fairly predictable death rates. Then, numbers and percentages will level out or even drop for a time, only to rise again, provided the nation experiences no major wars or epidemics, unexpected life-saving miracles, baby booms, mass immigrations or emigrations, or other events that would drastically alter the statistical relationship between the age categories.

The elderly population is not distributed evenly throughout the nation, despite a trend in that direction, but shows high concentrations in New England and the Middle Atlantic states, the Great Plains, and a few sections of the South, most notably Florida. Older people are somewhat underrepresented in metropolitan areas as a whole, though they are overrepresented in certain parts of central cities and in the towns and on the farms of nonmetropolitan counties. They have increased in the suburbs, and their percentages are rising there. Moreover, the proportion of older people is growing virtually everywhere, and their rate of increase between 1970 and 1980 was greater than that of the total population in 49 of the 50 states; Wyoming was the only exception. These changes suggest the pervasive nature of the aging that now typifies America's population and raise strategic questions about its economic and political implications, the needs for medical and retirement provisions, and the form and dynamics of the nation's future social system.

NOTES

1. Simon de Beauvoir, *The Coming of Age*. New York: Putnam's Sons, 1972, p. 4.

2. For a discussion of these aspects, see Matilda White Riley and Anne Foner, *Aging and Society*, v. 1, *An Inventory of Research Findings*. New York: Russell Sage Foundation, 1968, pp. 15-35.

3. Joseph J. Spengler, *Population and America's Future*. San Francisco: Freeman, 1975, p. 90.

4. Some of the trends are adapted from Joseph A. Califano, Jr., "The Aging of America: Questions for the Four-Generation Society," *Annals of American Academy of Political and Social Science* 438 (1978): 97-98.

5. Data are from the U.S. Bureau of the Census, *Statistical Abstract of the United States: 1982-83*. Washington, DC: U.S. Government Printing Office, 1982, table 107.

6. U.S. Bureau of the Census, "Projections of the Population of the United States: 1982 to 2050," *Current Population Reports*, P-25, no. 922 (1982): 13; *1980 Census of Population, Supplementary Reports*, PC80-S1-1, *Age, Sex, Race, and Spanish Origin of the Population by Regions, Divisions, and States: 1980* (1981), table 1.

7. Charles B. Nam and Susan O. Gustavus, *Population: The Dynamics of Demographic Change*. Boston: Houston Mifflin, 1976, p. 190.

8. Henry S. Shryock and Jacob S. Siegel, *The Methods and Materials of Demography*, v. 1. Washington, DC: U.S. Government Printing Office, 1973, p. 248. Cf. U.S. Bureau of the Census, "Demographic Aspects of Aging and the Older Population in the United States," *Current Population Reports*, P-23, no. 59 (1978), pp. 10-11.

9. U.S. Bureau of the Census, "Demographic Aspects of Aging...," *ibid.*, p. 4.

28

10. See Ansley J. Coale, "The Effects of Changes in Mortality and Fertility on Age Composition," *Milbank Memorial Fund Quarterly,* 34 (1956): 79-114.

11. J. John Palen, *Social Problems.* New York: McGraw-Hill, 1979, p. 388.

12. Harrison Givens, Jr., "An Evaluation of Mandatory Retirement," *Annals, op. cit.,* p. 52.

13. Beth J. Soldo, "America's Elderly in the 1980s," *Population Bulletin,* 35 (1980): 5.

14. U.S. Bureau of the Census, "Demographic Aspects of Aging...," *op. cit.,* p. 1.

15. Riley and Foner, *op. cit.,* p. 16.

16. *Ibid.,* p. 21.

17. For a discussion, see Henry P. David, "Eastern Europe: Pronatalist Policies and Private Behavior," *Population Bulletin,* 36 (1982).

18. For a discussion of the projection method, see U.S. Bureau of the Census, "Projections of the Population...," *op. cit.,* pp. 2-3.

19. Leon F. Bouvier, "America's Baby Boom Generation: The Fateful Bulge," *Population Bulletin* 35 (1980): 30.

20. Richard A. Easterlin, "What Will 1984 Be Like? Socioeconomic Implications of Recent Twists in Age Structure," *Demography* 15 (1978): 397-421. Cf. Ronald D. Lee, "Demographic Forecasting and the Easterlin Hypothesis," *Population and Development Review* 2 (1976): 459-468. See the discussion of Easterlin's work by Glenn Collins, "The Good News About 1984," *Psychology Today* 12 (1979): 34-48.

21. Soldo, *op. cit.,* p. 10.

22. For the data, see U.S. Bureau of the Census, "Farm Population of the United States: 1980," *Current Population Reports,* P-27, no. 54 (1981), table 2.

23. For an account of the rural-to-urban migration, see T. Lynn Smith and Paul E. Zopf, Jr., *Demography: Principles and Methods,* 2nd ed. Port Washington, NY: Alfred, 1976, pp. 498-513.

24. Jacob S. Siegel, "On the Demography of Aging," *Demography* 17 (1980): 353. Cf. Donald O. Cowgill, "Residential Segregation by Age in American Metropolitan Areas," *Journal of Gerontology* 33 (1978): 446-453.

25. Siegel, *op. cit.,* p. 353.

26. On this matter, see Stephen M. Golant, ed., *Location and Environment of the Elderly Population.* New York: Wiley, 1979.

27. Soldo, *op. cit.,* p. 13.

28. National Council on the Aging, "Special Concerns II," *Perspective on Aging,* v. 9 (1980), p. 20.

29. For a study of this matter, see Norah Keating and Judith Marshall, "The Process of Retirement: The Rural Self-Employed," *The Gerontologist* 20 (1980): 437-443.

30. National Council on the Aging, *op. cit.,* p. 24.

31. U.S. Bureau of the Census, "Farm Population of the United States," *op. cit.,* table 2.

32. U.S. Bureau of the Census, "Some Demographic Aspects of Aging in the United States," *Current Population Reports,* P-23, no. 43 (1973): 9.

Chapter 2

Age Composition of the
Older Population

America's elderly are far from a homogeneous group, for the aging process is based on such a wide range of environmental causes and individualized physiology and heredity, that persons go through it at very different rates.[1] In addition, at any given moment a person's aging represents a unique accumulation of experiences that also affect his/her remaining life expectancy. Therefore, while 65 is the accepted threshold of the older ages because American society causes several things to happen to most people then, the group that has crossed the threshold is tremendously varied, with quite different individual prospects for good health and additional years of life. Even the elderly themselves often do not fully appreciate the heterogeneity of their own age category. This was reflected in the 1974 survey by the National Council on the Aging which found that most tend to overestimate the seriousness of problems faced by their group and believe their own individual maladies to be more common than they actually are, while the ones with relatively few problems tend to believe they are rather rare exceptions.[2] Therefore, the great majority of elderly "who said they faced very serious problems imputed that same experience to most of the other elderly."[3] The end result is often a misleading assumption of homogeneity within and about the older population concerning not only health and finances but many other aspects as well.

Given these perceptions and the stereotypes widely held by younger people, it is important to emphasize the substantial variations that exist within the group aged 65 and older, and that the problems associated with the aging of a population depend as much on the composition of the elderly group as they do on its size.[4] One reflection of the variability is

29

the way the elderly population is distributed among its several age categories from 65-69 to 85 and older and the features that tend to accompany each of the narrower age groupings. No matter what the patterns or indexes used to explore them, however, the key to a view of the people 65 and over is heterogeneity in terms of employment, income, sexual activity, and other factors, though homogeneity does increase gradually as the elderly age.[5] Moreover, there tends to be considerable continuity among older people in the sense that levels of happiness, activity, life satisfaction, and other features neither improve nor deteriorate dramatically relative to those of other cohort members with whom individuals have reached the older years.[6]

Distribution of Ages

Within the elderly population the great majority are concentrated relatively close to age 65, whereas those aged 85 and older are a small minority, though they are increasing as a proportion. (See Table 2-1.) Thus, the present percentages represent less concentration at the lower end of the 65-and-over scale than in the past. In 1900, for example, 71 per cent of the elderly were between 65 and 74 and only 4 per cent were 85 and older. The recent tendency for people to be more heavily represented in the oldest ages is not yet due primarily to any significant increases in the human life span, which is regarded by some as a biological attribute of the species and only now on the verge of significant extension. Changing age distribution has resulted instead from the larger proportions of people who survive to the older ages of that life span.[7] In addition, the higher percentages of very elderly people who appear at certain times are due to high fertility levels when their cohort was born, as was the case with the group born just after the Civil War. The survivors of that cohort were in their late 70s and 80s in the decade after World War II, when the proportion of people aged 75 and older rose to about a third of the entire elderly group. Finally, the aging of people who immigrated in the early 1900s also contributed to the size of the group 75 and over, for by 1980 an abnormally large share of those foreign-born people still surviving were in the oldest categories, though migration is usually less important than fertility and mortality in shaping a nation's age profile.[8]

Differences by Sex and Race

Females have a greater survival potential than males at all ages, from the newborn to centenarians, for the death rates of females are substantially lower than those of males across the entire age spectrum. Therefore, men in the older ages are more likely than women to cluster near 65, whereas the women are distributed more evenly among the age ranges. In 1980, for instance, only 34 per cent of the nation's older men but 42 per cent of the women were aged 75 and older. (See Table 2-1.)

In general, elderly black people concentrate more heavily in the ages near 65 than do white people, and they are less represented in most of the older years. At fault is the higher death rate that has prevailed among blacks throughout America's history and which is still in evidence, though less dramatically than it was. Nevertheless, if a black person is able to survive the relatively high death rates until age 75 or 80, his/her survival potential actually is somewhat better than that of a white person. Thus, while the death rates of white males are lower than those of black males at all ages until 75, the reverse is true beyond that age. This "crossover"

Table 2-1. Percentages of Older People in Specific Age Groups, by Sex, Race, and Spanish Origin, 1980

Race and Sex	Per Cent				
	65-69	70-74	75-79	80-84	85+
All Races	34.4	26.5	18.9	11.4	8.8
Male	37.9	27.7	17.9	9.9	6.6
Female	32.0	25.9	19.3	12.6	10.2
White	34.0	26.6	18.8	11.7	8.9
Male	37.8	27.7	17.9	10.0	6.7
Female	31.6	25.8	19.4	12.8	10.4
Black	37.2	27.0	18.6	9.6	7.6
Male	39.1	27.7	18.1	8.9	6.3
Female	35.9	26.5	19.0	10.1	8.5
Spanish Origin[a]	37.3	27.3	19.2	9.3	6.9
Male	37.9	27.8	19.3	9.0	6.1
Female	36.7	26.9	19.2	9.7	7.5

Source: U.S. Bureau of the Census, 1980 Census of Population, Supplementary Reports, PC80-S1-1, Age, Sex, Race, and Spanish Origin of the Population by Regions, Divisions, and States: 1980 (1981), table 1.

[a]May be of any race.

also occurs for women, but at a somewhat older age than for men. As a result of the reversal, the white man who reaches age 85 has an average of 5.3 years remaining, the black man an average of 7.8 years; the figures for women are 6.7 years and 9.9 years, respectively.

Despite the crossover effect in the oldest ages, however, the higher birth rates of black people and their higher death rates at most ages cause only 8 per cent of all American blacks to be aged 65 and older, contrasted with about 12 per cent of all whites. Those proportions are shaped, too, by the fact that immigrants are a far smaller share of the black than of the white population, while those black immigrants who do enter the country now tend to be significantly younger on the average than the white immigrants.

When age and sex are accounted for together, white women are far more likely than any other group to show up in the 75-and-over category, whereas black men are the most poorly represented in those ages. But none of the racial discrepancies is as great as in the past, for the death rates of black people have been falling faster than those of whites and the distributions of the races within the older age ranges are slowly growing more alike. At the same time, death rates have fallen faster for women than for men in both racial groups, so the distribution of the sexes throughout the elderly ages is less similar than in the past. Those dynamics all contribute to the substantial majorities of older women, both black and white.

The Role of Mortality

The preceding comments suggest that differential death rates by race and sex powerfully affect how the various age groups appear in the 65-and-over category, though other significant factors are also involved. The influence of mortality can be examined by looking briefly at differences in the proportion of people who survive to particular ages and at the average number of years of life remaining to those who do make it to age 65, 75, and the older years. The appropriate data appear in Table 2-2 on the percentages of survivors and Table 2-3 on life expectancy. Both sets of data use the racial categories "white" and "other races," who have been at least 90 per cent black in all years.

Proportion of survivors. In 1980 about 77 per cent of all races collectively could expect to survive from birth to age 65, compared with only 41 per cent at the turn of the century, when the first national life tables were compiled. This remarkable improvement has been most impressive among women, for about 85 per cent of the whites and 75 per cent of the blacks can now expect to reach age 65. Naturally, beyond that age the comparatively high death rates for all race and sex groups reduce the percentages who reach the older years, but the current figures all represent substantial improvements over 1900-1902, especially for black women, who fared much worse relative to white women than they do now.

The situation has been and still is less favorable for men, and the rate of improvement in their survival potential has been slower than that among women. Thus, in 1980 about 72 per cent of the white men and only 58 per cent of the blacks could plan to see age 65. Moreover, just 17 per cent of the white men and 14 per cent of the blacks could anticipate reaching age 85 — proportions which are less than half those for women in each race. In 1900-1902, however, the sexes were more nearly alike in their probability to attain the older ages, while the races were less alike than they are now. This change shows that the nation's older population is becoming increasingly female in the sense that a growing share of the whole group aged 65 and older consists of women. At the turn of the century they made up 50

Table 2-2. Percentages of Persons Surviving to Specified Ages, by Race and Sex, 1901 and 1980

Race and Sex	Per Cent Surviving to					
	Age 65		Age 75		Age 85	
	1901[a]	1980	1901[a]	1980	1901[a]	1980
White						
Male	39.2	72.3	21.4	47.5	5.2	18.3
Female	43.8	84.7	25.4	68.5	7.1	38.4
Other Races						
Male	19.0	58.0	8.9	35.5	2.0	13.9
Female	22.0	75.0	11.1	55.7	3.6	29.6

Sources: National Center for Health Statistics, Vital Statistics of the United States: 1978, vol. 2, sec. 5, Life Tables (1980), table 5-4; "Advance Report of Final Mortality Statistics, 1980," Monthly Vital Statistics Report, vol. 32, no. 4 (1983), table 2.

[a]Average of data for 1900-1902 in the death-registration states.

34

per cent of the total, while in 1980 they were 60 per cent. Particularly
striking is the fact that improvements in life expectancy for black men lag
far behind those for black women. On the other hand, the proportions of
black and white men who survive to age 65 are now more nearly alike than
they were in 1900-1902, as are those of black and white women. So while
the races have converged in this respect, the sexes have diverged.

Table 2-3. Average Number of Years of Life
Remaining at Specified Ages, by Race
and Sex, 1901 and 1980

Race and Sex	Remaining Life Expectancy at					
	Age 65		Age 75		Age 85	
	1901[a]	1980	1901[a]	1980	1901[a]	1980
White						
Male	11.5	14.2	6.8	8.8	3.8	5.0
Female	12.2	18.5	7.3	11.5	4.1	6.3
Other Races						
Male	10.4	13.5	6.6	8.9	4.0	5.3
Female	11.4	17.3	7.9	11.4	5.1	7.0

Sources: National Center for Health Statistics,
Vital Statistics of the United States: 1978, vol.
2, sec. 5, Life Tables (1980), table 5-4; "Advance
Report of Final Mortality Statistics, 1980,"
Monthly Vital Statistics Report, vol. 32, no. 4
(1983), table 2.

Remaining life expectancy. Americans aged 65 and older can expect an
average of 16.4 additional years of life, though individuals range widely
around that norm. This compares with an average of 11.9 years in
1900-1902. But while the changes during the century did add about 4.5
years of life expectancy for the elderly, it is a fairly small increase, given
the huge improvements in health and nutrition that have lowered general
death rates and infant mortality levels so drastically. Therefore, the relatively small magnitude of the change suggests that reductions in the death
rates of older age groups have not been as great as those of younger
ages.[9] In turn, it shows that the death rates of older people continue to
be high relative to those of other age groups and that their time in the
65-and-over category is really quite brief, though more people do survive

over a longer portion of the age span than ever before.[10] Once again, females have a marked advantage over males, for the average life expectancy of elderly women in both major races has improved considerably more than that of elderly men.

Some Trends and Projections

Age composition within the elderly group keeps changing because of variations in fertility, mortality, and net migration, but a few long-term trends have remained relatively constant. In particular, the whole group has grown less concentrated near 65 and an increasing share is in the oldest ages. (See Figure 2-1.) But the major increases in the proportion 75 and over came after 1940, for in each decade prior to that year only about 29 or 30 per cent fell into that age group. Conversely, seven-tenths or so of all elderly appeared in the ages under 75. The familiar factors involved in

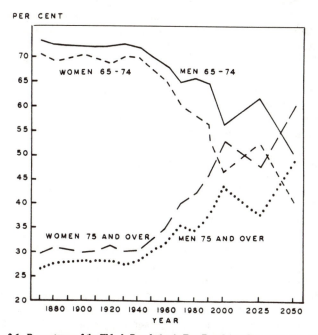

Figure 2-1. Percentages of the Elderly Population in Two Broad Age Groups, by Sex, 1870-2050
Sources: U.S.Bureau of the Census, *Sixteenth Census of the United States: 1940, Characteristics of the Population, U.S. Summary* (1943), table 8; *U.S. Census of Population: 1970, General Population Characteristics, U.S. Summary* (1972), table 53; *1980 Census of Population, Supplementary Reports*, PC80-S1-1, *Age, Sex, Race, and Spanish Origin of the Population by Regions, Divisions, and States: 1980* (1981), table 1; "Projections of the Population of the United States: 1982 to 2050" (advance report), *Current Population Reports*, P-25, no. 922 (1982), table 2.

preserving the lopsided distribution were relatively high rates of death that allowed comparatively few people to reach the oldest ages, high birth rates that enlarged the lower end of various cohorts 65 years later, and an immigrant population that was still relatively youthful early in the century.

By 1950, however, the proportion 65-74 had begun to decline significantly and those 75 and older had started to rise, thereby accelerating a trend which had slow beginnings much earlier and which seems likely to persist into the twenty-first century. In fact, given the age groups of people already alive and their probable death rates, it is likely that by 2050 people 75 and over will be considerably more than half the entire elderly population. This represents a remarkable change since 1940, when people in the 65-74 age bracket outnumbered those 75 and over by more than two to one, and is still another reflection of the aging of America's population.

The group aged 85 and older has grown especially rapidly while the elderly population as a whole has been increasing in numbers and proportions. Between 1950 and 1980, for example, people aged 85 and older increased from about 600,000 to 2.2 million, or 288 per cent. At the same time, the number aged 65-74 increased 85 per cent and those aged 75-84 expanded 136 per cent. As a consequence, people aged 85 and older went from 4.7 per cent of the total elderly population in 1950 to 8.8 per cent in 1980. Given these rates, they promise to number at least 16 million by 2050, or more than seven times the figure in 1980, and to be about 24 per cent of all elderly.

Figure 2-1 also indicates that women have long been more heavily represented than men in the oldest age group and that they will continue to be so; even in 1870 about 30 per cent of the elderly women but only 27 per cent of the men were 75 and over. Moreover, given the differential death rates by sex, the gap will widen, and by 2050 it is likely that 60 per cent of America's elderly women but only 49 per cent of the men will be aged 75 and older.

We can expect some temporary reversals in the overall trends, however, which correspond to earlier variations in fertility. For example, in 2000 the percentages of both sexes aged 74-75 will drop significantly, for that comparatively small group will consist of the survivors of the small baby crops born in the 1920s and 1930s. The decline will enhance the statistical importance of people 75 and over and their percentages will grow. By 2025, though, the large baby boom of 1945-1960 will have reached the elderly ages and the percentage of people 65-74 will rise dramatically as that of older ones falls. In the two decades to follow the trends will again reverse, as the much lower birth rates after 1960 show up in the form of smaller percentages of people aged 65-74 and consequent increases of those 75 and over.

These dynamics all have significant implications for the kinds of facilities American society must provide in the next half century or so. We will need to focus rather heavily on medical care, nursing homes, and other services for extremely old people and on their social and emotional needs. On the whole, that group begins to develop quite a different health profile than people who have just become 65, because many of the older ones suffer the ravages of illness and disability that most of the younger ones can still avoid for a decade or so. Therefore, it is not enough to plan for an expanding group 65 and over, which is certainly on its way. The nation has to account for the proportions who will be over 75 and 85 and for the things that happen to those older people. For example, while 41 per cent of the women aged 65-74 are already widowed, 69 per cent of those 75 and over have lost their mates, and the proportion reflects a great

Table 2-4. Percentages of the Elderly Population in Two Broad Age Groups, by Race and Sex, Selected Years

Age and Year	All Races		White		Other Races	
	Male	Female	Male	Female	Male	Female
65-74						
1910	71.8	69.7	71.9	70.0	71.2	65.9
1940	71.9	69.6	71.5	69.3	76.2	72.7
1980	65.6	57.9	65.4	57.4	66.7	62.4
2000[a]	56.5	46.6	56.2	45.8	59.5	52.7
75+						
1910	28.2	30.3	28.1	30.0	28.8	34.1
1940	28.1	30.4	28.5	30.7	23.8	27.3
1980	34.4	42.1	34.6	42.6	33.3	37.6
2000[a]	43.5	53.4	43.8	54.2	40.5	47.3

Sources: U.S. Bureau of the Census, U.S. Census of Population: 1970, General Population Character-istics, U.S. Summary (1972), table 53; 1980 Census of Population, Supplementary Reports, PC80-S1-1, Age, Sex, Race, and Spanish Origin of the Population by Regions, Divisions, and States: 1980 (1981), table 1; "Projections of the Population of the United States: 1982 to 2050" (advance report), Current Population Reports, P-25, no. 922 (1982), table 2.

[a]Projections based on Series II assumptions.

number of personal tragedies in the oldest years.

Also, the death rates for males and females aged 75-84 are more than double those for people aged 65-74, and while the higher levels do result in part from many sudden, relatively painless deaths, they also reflect a large number of people who suffer prolonged illnesses marked by physical and emotional pain and deterioration. Therefore, the growing abundance of people in the oldest ages calls for a heavy focus on hospice facilities, home care for invalids, and warmth and understanding for those whose lives are ebbing slowly and who are easy to pity, resent, or neglect. These and other realities suggest the great differences a society confronts when it has either an abundance of older people near age 65 or a heavy concentration in the upper 70s and beyond.[11]

The proportion of people in the 75-and-over group is increasing among both blacks and whites. (See Table 2-4.) Early in the twentieth century the percentages aged 75 and older in both races tended to be only half or less those of people aged 65-74 — a situation that persisted until 1940. That was the census year when the large number of people born just after the Civil War were aged 65-74, and while both races tended to concentrate in that category, it was more true of blacks than whites. Since 1940, however, the proportions of elderly people who are 75 and older have been increasing in both racial groups, while the percentages of those 65-74 have been dropping. Moreover, the extremely old, especially women, will continue to become a larger share of both racial groups and will stand in marked contrast with the proportions in 1910, when both blacks and whites clustered close to 65 and very old people of either race were quite scarce.

If Series II projections prove accurate, the changes will probably leave the nation with at least 17 million people aged 75 and older in 2000 and 37 million by 2050. Moreover, nearly two-thirds of the latter group will consist of women, most of them widows. In the ages 85 and older, increases will be especially rapid and the number of women in those ages will be nearly the same as that in the group aged 75-84. The oldest women will outnumber men by about 2.5 to one. But the very existence of these large groups of the old-old reflects improvements in health and longevity and a prolonged ability to be useful in American society. At the same time, however, increasing percentages of the elderly have been leaving responsible roles in jobs and the economy in general, whether voluntarily or involuntarily, and many more are apt to be perceived as the wards of a welfare state that expects its oldest citizens to withdraw from full productivity. Therefore, while the older population has higher levels of education and better average health than ever before, the society makes it more difficult for them to perform constructively, while it also grows more resentful about the cost of their support. Aggravated by the pressures of high unemployment rates among the baby-boom generation now become adult, the failure to make fully productive use of the elderly is a problem for the nation and for many elderly themselves, especially those 65-74.[12] It is this combination of circumstances that deprives some older Americans of purpose and meaning, and the one that stems not from changes in fertility, mortality, and migration, but from restrictive social attitudes. We have added several years to the lives of many more Americans but tend to make those years less useful; in the process we have converted numerous contributing people into dependents. Therefore, the analysis now turns to some aspects of that dependency.

Dependency Ratios

An evaluation of the average burden of support for elderly people, carried essentially by younger adults, logically accompanies the assessment of age distributions and their underlying population processes. In a broader sense, demographers are also concerned with the child-support burden, for many questions about population pressures involve the proportions of people available to look after those whose age and its social correlates keep them from caring fully for themselves and who make up the dependent population. The latter group consists of people aged 0-19 and those 65 and older,[13] and while this study focuses on the elderly, it must also account for the youth support burden as part of the total responsibility that falls on people aged 20-64. In that connection, it is important to emphasize that in all industrialized countries the child support burden has dropped very significantly as that for the elderly has risen, thus producing a net decrease in the total dependency burden.

One principal index of support burdens is the *dependency ratio,* calculated as follows:

$$\text{Dependency ratio} = \frac{\text{Population aged 0-19 and 65 and over}}{\text{Population aged 20-64}} \times 100$$

It is expressed as the number of dependents for each 100 producers. People aged 15-19 could also be considered part of the producing population, especially in any study of the developing countries where many enter the labor force at those younger ages, but in the United States so many people aged 15-19 are still in school that the majority are not self-supporting. In addition, some people under 65 are not producers and many older ones are; indeed, one of the judgments in this book is that more older people should be allowed to produce more fully if they wish and are able. Whether or not a particular person is really dependent is affected by health, financial standing, occupational involvement, the cultural definitions that surround age, and other factors.[14] But a demographic study can only deal with categories of people, not individuals, and the decision was made earlier to use 65 as the threshold of the older ages. In fact, occupational involvement does drop substantially by that age and drastically afterwards. In 1980, for example, about 91 per cent of the men aged 45-54, 72 per cent of those aged 55-64, and only 19 per cent of the ones 65 and older were in the labor force; for women the decline was from 60 per cent, to 41 per cent, to 8 per cent.[15] Nor is official inclusion in the labor force the only way for older people to be productive. Nonetheless, while there is much variation in what dependency means socially and individually, the Census Bureau reports the majority of its age data for five-year ranges, and it seems most useful to classify Americans aged 0-19 and 65 and over as dependents and those aged 20-64 as producers.

Use of the dependency ratio could also imply that the support burden is distributed evenly among people aged 20-64, which is not so in any society. Nor does the index allow for the levels of living at which the support burden is carried in various populations.[16] Thus, while the dependency ratio does describe the statistical relationship between the older population and younger adults over time and in different places, its variations should not be taken to reflect differences in levels of living. Moreover, when the ratio can be refined to relate the elderly who actually do not work to the group aged 20-64 who do, it is more accurate than when it is based only on age categories,[17] though the data rarely permit such refinements by sex, race, and other characteristics.[18]

Some International Comparisons

In 1980 there were about 76 Americans aged 0-19 and 65 and over for each 100 aged 20-64, which is a relatively low figure compared with many earlier periods and with the bulk of the world's countries now. (See Table 2-5.) The dependency ratio for the elderly (20) accounted for a quarter of the overall support burden, the youth ratio (56) for the other three-quarters, and while the former is continuing to grow and the latter to shrink, the two together do not represent a particularly heavy burden of support. In fact, relatively few of the world's countries have smaller youth dependency ratios, though not many have larger elderly ratios either.

The youth dependency ratios are low and the elderly ones high in the urban-industrial countries, because fertility and mortality rates have been quite low for some time and the populations in those places are aging ones in the sense that people 65 and over range between 11 and 16 per cent of the total in most cases. About 20 countries have higher elderly dependency ratios than the United States, and all are European. As shown by the 10 representative ones in Table 2-5, almost all are highly industrialized, though other factors are also at work in such nations as Bulgaria and Hungary, where the percentages of workers engaged in agriculture are still relatively high, while elderly dependency ratios are also about 20. In fact, the aging of those populations demonstrates that effective fertility control can exist where levels of industrial development are substantially below those in the more urbanized nations. Despite the large elderly populations and comparatively small youthful segments in the representa-

Table 2-5. Selected Countries With Low and High Dependency Ratios, 1980

Country	Dependency Ratio			Number 20-64 for each One 65+
	Elderly	Youth	Total	
Sweden	28.5	46.2	74.7	3.5
East Germany	28.4	50.4	78.8	3.5
Austria	28.0	52.6	80.6	3.6
England & Wales	27.0	52.0	79.0	3.7
West Germany	26.8	46.1	72.9	3.7
Norway	26.6	53.9	80.5	3.8
Scotland	25.4	55.3	80.7	3.9
Denmark	25.3	50.1	75.4	4.0
France	25.3	54.7	80.0	4.0
UNITED STATES	19.9	56.4	76.3	5.0
Nicaragua	8.0	154.3	162.3	12.6
Ecuador	7.9	138.7	146.6	12.6
Bolivia	7.6	123.1	130.7	13.2
Thailand	7.5	118.0	125.5	13.3
Brazil	7.4	113.3	120.7	13.5
India	7.4	109.3	116.7	13.5
Guatemala	6.8	130.2	137.0	14.7
Zaire	6.1	138.7	144.8	16.3
Sudan	5.9	111.3	117.2	16.9
Gambia	4.7	113.0	117.7	21.2

Sources: United Nations, Demographic Yearbook, 1980, table 7; 1981, table 7; U.S. Bureau of the Census, 1980 Census of Population, Supplementary Reports, PC80-S1-1, Age, Sex, Race, and Spanish Origin of the Population by Regions, Divisions, and States: 1980 (1981), table 1.

tive developed countries, however, people under age 20 still outnumber those aged 65 and older in every case, though the two groups are much nearer the same size than they are in all of the developing nations with recent or present high birth rates. Paradoxically, therefore, the industrialized countries best able to support large numbers of children have the smallest proportions of them, whereas the heaviest youth support burdens occur in the developing countries least equipped to carry them. At the same time, while the developed countries have the largest percentages of older people, most also use mechanisms that either force or encourage the elderly to be less than fully productive or even fully integrated into their societies.[*19*]

Though the least developed nations have the lowest elderly dependency ratios, those for youth are so high that the two combine to produce high overall support burdens.[*20*] Those societies are concentrated largely in Africa, parts of Asia, and all but the temperate sections of Latin America. In fact, the 10 representative countries with extremely high rates shown in Table 2-5 have such youthful age profiles that the elderly group is only 4 per cent or less of the total population in each case. In some of them the birth rate has dropped in very recent years; in others it has risen a bit; and in the rest it has remained fairly static at a high level. But in all of the countries the basic cause of the huge child burdens and the small elderly ones is the high level of fertility coupled with recent precipitous declines in mortality, especially among infants. The populations in those places have become more youthful in the past few decades as they incurred their population explosions, and child care is a tremendously larger concern than is support for the small percentage of elderly, many of whom must keep working and fill economically useful roles anyway. In the future, however, the number of elderly people is likely to increase faster than that of children in most parts of the world, so the elderly segment will gradually become a larger part of the dependent population, children a somewhat smaller part.[*21*] Nevertheless, the latter will still account for the great bulk of the world's dependency situation, particularly in the developing countries.[*22*]

Some other countries not listed in Table 2-5 have moderate overall support burdens, but the relative importance of young and elderly people varies widely among them. One group consists of developing countries with relatively high youth ratios but low ones for the elderly; most have experienced drastic reductions in mortality and about half also have declining birth rates. These changes in the vital processes are comparatively new, however, and the percentages of children are still fairly high, those of older people relatively low. The countries in another group with moderate burdens have fairly low youth ratios but rather high elderly indexes; they include Canada, Australia, New Zealand, some temperate parts of South America, and a few European nations. There the birth and death rates have been low enough long enough for the elderly to become increasingly large parts of the total populations, though they are still below the proportions in the United States and most of Europe. Those countries are unlikely to experience reductions in infant and youth mortality comparable to earlier decreases, and if fertility rates hold at a relatively low level, the proportions of producers and older people will rise and the elderly support burdens will grow.[23]

Ratio of workers to older people. Given the dependency ratios for the elderly in the United States, there are now about five people aged 20-64 for each person aged 65 and older. That figure closely resembles those in the other urban-industrial nations, whereas the developing countries have relatively large numbers of workers for each older person. (See Table 2-5.) But when the ratio of workers to each child is added, the great strains in the developing countries become obvious. For example, while there are 13 producers for each 10 dependents in the United States, there are only 6 in Nicaragua. Thus, the vast child population, not the growing elderly group, imposes the large majority of the support burden in most countries, as it did earlier in the United States. The present huge group of children in the developing nations also imperils levels of living and the world ecosystem far more than do dependent elderly people, for today's child population will draw from the earth's resources for many decades, and even at relatively low birth rates they will still produce huge numbers of children of their own. Eventually, the large child populations will also become large elderly populations and will still impose heavy support burdens on the producing population and strains on the ecosystem. Thus, past high birth rates make their effects felt for the better part of a century, even if a society has managed to achieve low ones recently.

Racial and Ethnic Differences in the United States

The total dependency ratio in the white population is low compared with that among blacks and is much below those of other races and Spanish-origin people. (See Table 2-6.) The components of those various ratios also differ widely, because whites have a comparatively light support burden for youth and a relatively heavy one for the elderly, while blacks bear a heavier burden for children and a lighter one for the elderly. As birth and death rates become more alike for the two races, however, the component ratios also grow more similar. The group of "other races" and the people of Spanish origin have especially high youth dependency ratios and low ones for the elderly. As a result of these variations, the number of workers for each elderly person is lowest among whites and rises successively for blacks, Spanish-origin people, and other races. But the population of white children is now so small relative to the group of producing adults, that even when those aged 0-19 are compared with the group of white elderly, there are more workers for each dependent person among whites than among blacks, other races, and the Spanish-origin population.

The youth dependency ratio would be even higher for Spanish-origin people and their elderly dependency figure would be lower if it were not for the Cuban contingent, because their proportion of children is far smaller than those of people with Mexican, Puerto Rican, or Central and South American backgrounds. Thus, while the Spanish-origin group as a whole has a relatively high support burden for youth and a comparatively low one for the elderly, the reverse is true for Cubans, many of whom came to the United States in 1960 or so and who are now an aging population.[24]

Even though these patterns underscore the greater weight of child care and the lesser burden of older people that tend to be borne by blacks and Spanish-origin people, the statistical situation should not imply that the actual support burdens of blacks are all carried exclusively by blacks, any more than those of whites are carried entirely by their race. American society is far more complex than that, with many mechanisms that both disperse and concentrate income irrespective of average dependency ratios by race.

Nonetheless, the statistical differences do have fundamental implications for social and economic conditions, particularly when they are coupled with the fact that median per capita family income is still significantly higher for whites than for blacks and Spanish-origin people. That is particularly true among elderly people, which means the average older black or Spanish-background person has a greater financial struggle to be self-supporting than does the older white, though family ties and other sources of assistance do alter the situation in many individual cases. But on balance and because of the combination of age patterns and income-distribution mechanisms, the average black wage earner carries a much heavier total support burden than does his/her white counterpart, and still does so at a substantially lower level of income. The fact that elderly dependency ratios are lower for blacks than for whites doesn't change that basic condition, because the relative scarcity of older blacks is more than offset by the numbers of children. Therefore, the data on dependency ratios also underscore the differences in fertility and mortality that still persist between racial and ethnic groups, even though the rates have become more alike for blacks and whites.

Some Changes and Projections

The various changes in age composition in the United States, produced

Table 2-6. Dependency Ratios in the United States, by Race and Spanish Origin, 1980

Race	Dependency Ratio			Number 20-64 for each One 65+	Number 20-64 for each Dependent[a]
	Elderly	Youth	Total		
All races	19.9	56.4	76.3	5.0	1.31
White	21.2	52.7	73.9	4.7	1.35
Black	15.1	76.6	91.7	6.6	1.09
Other Races	8.1	82.5	90.6	12.4	1.20
Spanish Origin[b]	9.3	82.5	91.8	10.8	1.09

Source: U.S. Bureau of the Census, 1980 Census of Population, Supplementary Reports, PC80-S1-1, Age, Sex, Race, and Spanish Origin of the Population by Regions, Divisions, and States: 1980 (1981), table 1.

[a]Dependents are those aged 0-19 and 65+.

[b]May be of any race.

by fluctuations in the three population processes, have decreased the overall dependency ratio very significantly, though not without some temporary increases reflected in the censuses of 1950, 1960, and 1970. (See Table 2-7.) Moreover, the youth ratio has fallen continually, except for those three times, while the elderly ratio has risen in each succeeding decade. In fact, the youth burden has been cut nearly in half since 1870, while the elderly support burden has more than tripled, though the net result in 1980 was a total dependency ratio little more than two-thirds that in 1870. This has happened because fertility declined in the long run and reduced the proportional significance of the child population, mortality decreased significantly and raised life expectancy for all age groups, and immigration introduced progressively fewer young adults. These factors changed the age profile so much that the upward surge in the birth rate after World War II was neither great enough nor sustained enough to offset fully the far longer period when both vital rates fell rapidly and immigration dropped off drastically. Consequently, there have been only a few temporary reversals in the trend toward a higher median age and a lower overall support burden, and no halt at all in the movement toward a higher elderly dependency ratio.

It seems likely that the elderly dependency ratio will continue to increase gradually until 2000 or so, when the relatively small birth cohorts of the Depression will be in the older years. At the same time, barring any new baby boom the youth dependency ratio should continue to fall steadily, until it is only half that in 1880. Therefore, the overall dependency ratio will also fall between now and 2000. By 2025, however, the elderly dependency ratio will leap upward as the postwar baby boom inhabits the older ages, the youth ratio will continue to fall gradually, but the total ratio will rise because of the large group aged 65 and older. Those trends will continue until at least 2050, when the youth and elderly dependency ratios won't be far apart. But the total ratio will still be lower than the one in 1970, even though the relative importance of its components will have changed dramatically.

Table 2-7 also shows the steady decline in the ratio of workers to elderly people and indicates that the figure in 1980 was less than a third that in 1870. But the great decline in the proportion of children actually increased the ratio of workers to all dependents. As Americans enter the twenty-first century, the number of workers for each older person will continue to decline, which will certainly increase the average cost per worker for Social Security taxes, Medicare and other health payments for older people, and similar services. But the reductions in child-care responsibilities will compensate partly for increases in those for the elderly, so we can expect more of a realignment in expenditures than vast increases for both dependent parts of the population combined. In addition, there is more opportunity for the elderly than for young children to be self-supporting,

47

Table 2-7. Dependency Ratios in the United States,
           1870-2050

Year	Dependency Ratio			Number 20-24 for each One 65+	Number 20-64 for each One 0-19 and 65+
	Elderly	Youth	Total		
1870	6.3	105.0	111.3	15.8	0.90
1880	7.1	99.2	106.3	14.1	0.94
1890	7.7	92.2	99.9	12.9	1.00
1900	7.9	86.3	94.2	12.7	1.06
1910	8.0	78.2	86.2	12.5	1.16
1920	8.6	74.7	83.3	11.7	1.20
1930	9.7	69.6	79.3	10.3	1.26
1940	11.7	58.6	70.3	8.6	1.42
1950	14.0	58.7	72.7	7.1	1.38
1960	17.7	73.6	91.3	5.7	1.10
1970	18.9	72.5	91.4	5.3	1.09
1980	19.9	56.4	76.3	5.0	1.31
1990	21.7	48.9	70.6	4.6	1.42
2000	22.2	47.3	69.5	4.5	1.44
2025	34.8	43.7	78.5	2.9	1.28
2050	39.5	42.5	82.0	2.5	1.22

Sources: U.S. Bureau of the Census, Sixteenth Census of the United States: 1940, Characteristics of the Population, U.S. Summary (1943), table 8; U.S. Census of Population: 1970, General Population Characteristics, U.S. Summary (1972), table 53; 1980 Census of Population, Supplementary Reports, PC80-S1-1, Age, Sex, Race, and Spanish Origin of the Population by Regions, Divisions and States: 1980 (1981), table 1; "Projections of the Population of the United States: 1982 to 2050" (advance report), Current Population Reports, P-25, no. 922 (1982), table 2.

Projections based on Series II assumptions.

and while all infants do have to rely on someone else for survival, many elderly do not. The group of self-sufficient older people certainly can be enlarged by more imaginative social and economic arrangements that provide better access to jobs and other opportunities, especially as the small birth cohorts of the 1970s and subsequent years finally shrink the proportion of younger workers and put skilled older ones in greater demand. If the cost of living can be kept reasonable, the tradeoff of a heavier elderly support burden for a much lighter youth burden should be manageable for the working population, though not without problems and even potential intergenerational conflict.

Naturally, the numbers and proportions of people aged 20-64 also affect the size of the dependency ratio, for they are the base group to which the two dependent ones are related statistically. Therefore, changes in that category are just as strategic as fluctuations among younger and older people. The absolute numbers of people in the group 20-64 have grown sevenfold since 1870 and the group increased from 47 per cent of the total population in that year to 57 per cent in 1980. The increases that took place at more specific times during that period generally represent the movement of progressively larger birth cohorts into the 20-64 category, while periodic decreases, especially in 1960 and 1970, reflect new growth spurts in the child population. The numbers aged 20-64 promise to continue increasing until about 2020, to decline temporarily, and then to increase slowly once again. By 2050 those people will number about 170 million and will be about 56 per cent of the total population.

The total dependency ratio has fallen at various times in the past because a given child population was proportionately smaller than several which preceded it, and because those earlier large cohorts entered the group of producers. Therefore, if the birth rate remains reasonably stable at a low level, the large cohorts that eventually will age into the 65-and-over category will raise the elderly dependency ratio for a time and then will die. If fertility and mortality both remain comparatively stable, the three large age groups will come into equilibrium with each other, the dependency ratio will neither rise nor fall markedly, and the nation will be able to count on fairly stable support burdens, at least demographically. That outcome is not guaranteed, of course, given the historical capriciousness of the birth rate and potential increases in the average life span; nor does it imply anything about the financial ability of people to carry even a demographically stable support burden. But the size and age composition of future populations may be more predictable than many in the past, which should make certain social and economic planning easier. It will still be a long time, however, before families and the society can expect the elderly support burden to stop fluctuating, and during most of the next half century it will still grow substantially and the locus of financing will shift more from private to public funds.[25]

49

Aged-Child Ratios

One infrequently used but sensitive index of aging in a population is the *aged-child ratio,* which accounts simultaneously for the numbers of people and changes at both ends of the age scale.[26] In using this index and to be sure it refers to children, the data are based on the numbers of those aged 0-14 rather than 0-19, and on those aged 65 and older. The index is computed as follows:

$$\text{Aged-child ratio} = \frac{\text{Number of persons 65 and over}}{\text{Number of persons 0-14}} \times 100$$

In societies with large proportions of children, such as India, Thailand, and other so-called developing countries, the aged-child ratios are commonly under 10 older people for each 100 children, whereas in the developed nations with relatively large shares of older people, the index is often 50 or higher. (See Table 2-8, which uses the same countries as Table 2-5.) Indeed, increases in the aged-child ratio are actually an index of aging in a population.[27] For example, India, with a total population nearly three times that of the United States, has more than five times as many children but 3 million fewer elderly. As a result, the aged-child ratio in India is less than 9, while that in the United States is 50. Nonetheless, even though the American child population is much smaller relative to that of older people than it was in the past, the United States still has far from the world's highest aged-child index, for it is surpassed by nine countries listed in Table 2-8 and several others. They are all European, but include some in both the East and the West.

The aged-child ratios in most of the developing countries, on the other hand, are close to the one in the United States in 1870, when the index was only 8 and children were 39 per cent of the total population, elderly people a mere 3 per cent. Thus, the developing countries in Table 2-8, as well as many others not listed, have such huge proportions of children and so few elderly people that their aged-child ratios are commonly only a small fraction of those in the industrialized nations. In India, for example, about 41 per cent of the population consists of children, whereas the elderly are only 3 per cent. In contrast, children are 18 per cent of West Germany's population, older people 16 per cent. The two countries have aged-child indexes of 9 and 85, respectively.

Within the United States the aged-child ratio is highest for the white population, less than half as great for blacks, and even lower for the Spanish-origin contingent. (See Table 2-9.) These data reflect the signifi-

Table 2-8.   Selected Countries With Low and High
             Aged-Child Ratios, 1980

Country	Number 0-14 (000)	Number 65+ (000)	Aged-Child Ratio[a]
West Germany	11,187	9,550	85.4
Sweden	1,628	1,354	83.2
East Germany	3,290	2,661	80.8
Austria	1,540	1,162	75.5
England & Wales	10,289	7,424	72.2
Denmark	1,068	739	69.2
Norway	908	603	66.4
Scotland	1,125	724	64.4
France	11,997	7,535	62.8
UNITED STATES	51,282	25,544	49.8
India	262,656	22,762	8.7
Brazil	49,973	4,140	8.3
Thailand	19,378	1,575	8.1
Bolivia	2,412	184	7.6
Ecuador	3,810	269	7.1
Guatemala	3,201	208	6.5
Nicaragua	1,310	83	6.3
Sudan	8,383	510	6.1
Zaire	12,189	661	5.4
Gambia	252	13	5.2

Sources: United Nations, Demographic Yearbook,
1980, table 7; 1981, table 7; U.S. Bureau of the
Census, 1980 Census of Population, Supplementary
Reports, PC80-S1-1, Age, Sex, Race, and Spanish
Origin of the Population by Regions, Divisions,
and States: 1980 (1981), table 1.

[a]Number aged 65+ per 100 aged 0-14.

cantly lower proportions of children and higher percentages of elderly people in the white group than in the other two. Moreover, the aged-child ratios in all groups increased very substantially during the twentieth century, and they will probably leap forward in the next century as the population ages rapidly. In fact, by 2025 there will probably be more elderly people than children in the white population, though the numbers in the two age groups will also become more nearly alike among blacks. If Series II projections made by the Census Bureau hold up, in 2050 children should be about 17 per cent of the total population, elderly people around 22 per cent. But the two groups together will be only a little less than they were in 1870 (42%), when children outnumbered elderly people 13 to one.

Table 2-9. Changes in Aged-Child Ratios in the United States, by Race, 1900-2050

Year	Number Aged 65+ per 100 Aged 0-14		
	All Races	White	Other Races
1900	11.8	12.5	7.6
1910	13.4	14.1	8.2
1920	14.6	15.4	9.2
1930	18.4	19.5	9.6
1940	27.3	29.0	15.6
1950	30.2	32.0	17.7
1960	29.7	31.9	16.3
1970	34.7	37.4	19.5
1980	49.8	57.2	23.3
1990	58.2	65.2	29.4
2000	62.7	70.4	32.9
2025	106.2	118.7	65.5
2050	124.5	134.6	94.3

Sources: U.S. Bureau of the Census, U.S. Census of Population: 1970, General Population Characteristics, U.S. Summary (1972), table 53; 1980 Census of Population, Supplementary Reports, PC80-S1-1, Age, Sex, Race, and Spanish Origin of the Population by Regions, Divisions, and States: 1980 (1981), table 1; "Projections of the Population of the United States: 1982 to 2050" (advance report), Current Population Reports, P-25, no. 922, table 2.

Projections based on Series II assumptions.

In fact, in 2050 the proportion of the two groups together will be virtually identical to the one in 1900, though the relative shares of children and the elderly will have changed radically.

The aged-child ratios have also changed greatly for whites and blacks in the twentieth century, more than quadrupling between 1900 and 1980 among whites and more than tripling among blacks. But the figure for blacks remained consistently behind that for whites and increased more slowly, basically because of the higher birth rates and larger proportions of children in the black population, along with the higher death rates of black people at most ages and the lower percentage of survivors to age 65. As a result, the black aged-child ratio was 61 per cent of the white ratio in 1900, but only 41 per cent in 1980. But given the rapid rate at which black fertility is now falling and its tendency to approach that of whites even more closely, the black ratio will probably rise considerably faster than the white figure, especially after 2000. To the extent the index represents growing similarity between the races in fertility rates and proportions of elderly people, it also reflects improvements in the socioeconomic conditions that earlier kept the black child population relatively large, the black elderly one comparatively small. In turn, the racial convergence in at least some of these conditions mirrors the impressive growth of the black middle class and its norms, despite the persistence of serious problems for those black people who live in poverty and the ghettos.

Summary

The nation's elderly population contains very different percentages of people in the several age ranges which make up the 65-and-older group, because of variable levels of health and other factors that raise the death rate as people age increasingly beyond 65, and because of the past fluctuations in fertility. Even now most elderly are concentrated fairly close to age 65, though the proportion of those 75 and older is expanding the most rapidly. Consequently, the elderly population is dispersed somewhat more evenly throughout all of the ages, and the young-old are becoming a smaller share of the 65-and-over age group, the old-old a greater share. That is so because larger proportions of people now have more years of life expectancy remaining than did their parents, and because the survivors of large birth cohorts and the last remnants of large immigrations have moved into the oldest ages. Women are more heavily represented than men in those ages and whites are proportionately more abundant than blacks, though with notable exceptions in a few of the oldest years, essentially because of previous fertility patterns and differential death rates by race and sex. These differences among various groups can be measured by the percentages in a birth cohort who survive to the various older years and by the average life expectancy that remains to people who have already reached particular ages.

The dependency ratio also enables a look at how the numbers of elderly people and children relate to the numbers of those aged 20-64 available to support the two dependent groups, though categorical designations of "dependent" and "producer" do ignore many individual variations. In the United States the ratio of children to producers has fallen markedly as the birth rate has dropped, and it will amount certainly continue to decline well into the twenty-first century. At the same time, the elderly support burden has risen significantly and will continue on that course. These changes together, however, have produced an overall dependency ratio which has dropped a great deal since 1870, which will fall even more until about 2010, and which will then rise a bit above the 1980 level. Therefore, while the proportional burden of support for children will shrink and that for the elderly will grow for several decades, the total responsiblity that falls on productive adults won't be much heavier than it is now and will be far less weighty than it was a century ago. Nonetheless, inflation and other problems could turn the relatively stable statistical support burden into one that grows much heavier financially.

The number of elderly people for each 100 children aged 0-14 has increased astonishingly in the twentieth century and promises to rise even more in the twenty-first. Eventually, if birth and death rates stabilize and do not rise or fall significantly over long periods, the aged-child ratio and other indexes of the statistical relationships among various age groups also will not change. But because a given fertility situation continues to have a significant demographic impact for eight decades or more, such stability and the stationary population it would reflect may never occur. If it does, the proportions of children, workers, and elderly people will also approach a stable balance.

NOTES

1. Matilda White Riley, "Introduction: Life-Course Perspectives," in Matilda White Riley, ed., *Aging from Birth to Death*. Boulder, CO: Westview Press, 1979, p. 6.

2. Hubert O'Gorman, "False Consciousness of Kind," *Research on Aging* 1 (1980): 105.

3. *Ibid.,* p. 107.

4. Beth J. Soldo, "America's Elderly in the 1980s," *Population Bulletin* 35 (1980): 11.

5. Erdman Palmore, *Social Patterns in Normal Aging: Findings from the Duke Longitudinal Study.* Durham, NC: Duke University Press, 1981, p. 113.

6. *Ibid.,* pp. 4 and 109.

54

7. Matilda White Riley and Anne Foner, *Aging and Society*, v. 1, *An Inventory of Research Findings*. New York: Russell Sage Foundation, 1968, p. 25. Cf. Philip M. Hauser, "Aging and World-Wide Population Change," in Robert H. Binstock and Ethel Shanas, eds., *Handbook of Aging and the Social Sciences*. New York: Van Nostrand, 1976, p. 65.

8. Hauser, *ibid.*, pp. 64-65.

9. Riley and Foner, *op. cit.*, p. 27.

10. Hauser, *op. cit.*, p. 65.

11. For an account of some of these implications, see *ibid.*, pp. 81-83.

12. Peter Uhlenberg, "Demographic Change and Problems of the Aged, " in Riley, *Aging from Birth to Death, op. cit.*, pp. 157-158.

13. For a discussion of support burdens as a way to evaluate overpopulation, see David R. Kamerschen, "On an Operational Index of 'Overpopulation'," *Economic Development and Cultural Change*, 13 (1965): 169-187.

14. William Petersen, *Population*. 3rd ed. New York: Macmillan, 1975, p. 354.

15. U.S. Bureau of the Census, *Statistical Abstract of the United States: 1982-83*. Washington, DC: U.S. Government Printing Office, 1982, table 626.

16. For a discussion of how consumption norms and labor force participation bear on dependency ratios, see Ephraim Kleiman, "A Standardized Dependency Ratio," *Demography* 4 (1967): 876-893.

17. Jacob S. Siegel, "On the Demography of Aging," *Demography* 17 (1980): 357.

18. Discussions of the dependency ratio as an analytical device appear in Petersen, *op. cit.*, pp. 72-75; and John R. Weeks, *Population: An Introduction to Concepts and Issues*, 2nd ed. Belmont, CA: Wadsworth, 1981, pp. 188-189. See its use in Paul E. Zopf, Jr., "Variations in Support Burdens as Measured by the Dependency Ratio," *Greek Review of Social Research*, no. 19-20 (1974): 29-43.

19. Ansley J. Coale, "How a Population Ages or Grows Younger," in Ronald Freedman, ed., *Population: The Vital Revolution*. Garden City, NY: Doubleday, 1964, p. 54.

20. For a study of this matter in Indonesia, see Nathan Keyfitz, "Age Distribution as a Challenge to Development," *American Journal of Sociology* 70 (1965): 659-668.

21. Council on Environmental Quality and U.S. Department of State, *The Global 2000 Report to the President*, v. 2, *The Technical Report*. Washington, DC: U.S. Government Printing Office, 1980, pp. 16 and 18.

22. Hauser, *op. cit.*, p. 84. See also pp. 83-85 on the social and demographic impact of increases in the numbers of older people in the developing countries.

23. See Kingsley Davis, "Population and Welfare in Industrialized Societies," *Population Review*, 6 (1962): 27.

24. For data on this matter, see U.S. Bureau of the Census, "Persons of Spanish Origin in the United States: March 1980," (advance report), *Current Population Reports*, P-20, no. 361 (1981), table 3.

25. Siegel, *op. cit.*, pp. 356, 357.

26. Henry S. Shryock and Jacob S. Siegel, *The Methods and Materials of Demography*. v. 1. Washington, DC: U.S. Government Printing Office, 1973, p. 234.

27. *Ibid.*

Chapter 3

Sex Composition of the
Older Population

One of the most fundamental features of America's elderly population is its large majority of women, because the proportion of males typically declines through the age span, from a small excess of young boys to the massive deficit of men in the oldest ages.[1] In turn, these elements of the sex balance shape other social conditions at various stages in the age scale, for whether a person is male or female helps determine his/her attitudes, activities, and social and economic roles, though these things also are subject to change.

Moreover, the proportions of men and women in the older population affect the tempo of life in that group, particularly as they influence marital status and increase the difficulty older women have in finding male companionship. This reality is underscored by the large statistical surplus of elderly women who are single, divorced, and widowed. In 1980, for example, there were 8.4 million of them, compared with only 2.2 million men who were not married, which left a large surplus of 6.2 million women for whom marriage within their age group was statistically impossible. Translated into innumerable personal adjustments, chances for loneliness, and even individual tragedies, those data reflect one of the sensitive human dimensions of a severe sex imbalance in the older years.[2] The imbalance is especially acute among widows, for while there are less than twice as many single and divorced elderly women as elderly men in those categories, there are five times as many widows as widowers. At the same time, however, the worst problems of old age — poverty and poor health — have improved measurably,[3] so while the pains of widowhood and the problems of altered identity and loneliness do

56

confront part of our growing population of older women, some other difficulties have improved, especially among well-educated women. Moreover, there is a mounting body of evidence showing that large numbers
of elderly women not only retain but improve their ability to cope effectively with life, while dependence and passivity often decline as various
kinds of creative aggressiveness and adaptive capabilities grow.[4]

Measuring the Sex Balance

The index widely used to measure the sex composition of a population is
the *sex ratio,* which we will use in this chapter and which is computed as
follows:

$$\text{Sex ratio} = \frac{\text{Number of males}}{\text{Number of females}} \times 100$$

A figure over 100, which is rare among older groups, indicates more males
than females; a ratio below 100 reflects the reverse situation — more
females than males — which has become increasingly typical of the
elderly population during the twentieth century.

Factors Affecting the Sex Ratio

Mortality Differentials

The typical pattern of sex ratios in the United States is a general
decrease from birth through extreme old age as males become a progressively smaller share of each succeeding age group, females a larger
proportion. This pattern reflects the relatively high sex ratios at birth,
when there are about 105 male infants delivered for each 100 females,[5]
though even that figure is below the one at conception. But the sex ratio
begins its decline immediately, for even miscarriages take a higher toll of
male than female embryos and fetuses, resulting in the 105 sex ratio at
birth, at least in the nation's white population.[6] (See Figure 3-1.)

The reason for the continued reduction of the sex ratio with age is that
the death rates of males are substantially higher than those of females at
every level from infancy through the oldest years. Moreover, while death
rates have fallen dramatically in the United States over the last several
decades, females have benefited more than males, for their mortality
levels have dropped far faster than those of males. For example, in 1900

57

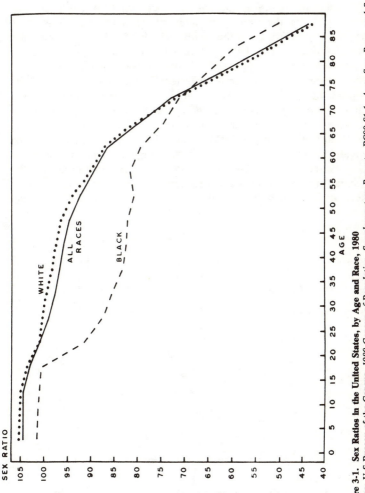

Figure 3-1. Sex Ratios in the United States, by Age and Race, 1980
Source: U.S.Bureau of the Census, *1980 Census of Population, Supplementary Reports*, PC80-S1-1, *Age, Sex, Race, and Spanish Origin of the Population by Regions, Divisions, and States: 1980* (1981), table 1.

58

the age-adjusted death rate of males was 9 per cent higher than that of females, but by 1980 the difference was 80 per cent. Consequently, while life expectancy at birth has increased substantially for both sexes, that for females has climbed far more rapidly, increasing the gap from only 2.9 years at the turn of the century to 7.5 years in 1980. Furthermore, the male-female ratio of age-adjusted rates rose from 1.1 in 1900 to 1.8 in 1980, though the figure did not increase between 1974 and 1980. (See Figure 3-2.) Thus, the growing mortality differential between the sexes, accelerated by reductions in the death rates due to childbirth and other causes that once claimed high proportions of women at younger ages, is the chief reason for the great sex imbalance among the elderly.[7]

The reasons for the lower death rates among women seem largely biological, though social causes, such as higher rates of smoking and greater involvement in dangerous occupations among men, also play a part. But even when we eliminate the deaths from accidents, violence, and other "external" causes that take an especially heavy toll of males, the survival advantage of females remains substantial in all except those few societies where childbirth continues to be particularly dangerous and the low status of women causes an inordinate neglect of females, especially infants. In an effort to uncover the causes of the differential, Madigan

Figure 3-2. Ratio of the Male to the Female Age-Adjusted Death Rate in the United States, 1900-1980

Sources: National Center for Health Statistics, *Vital Statistics of the United States, 1977,* v. 2, *Mortality,* part A (1981), Table 1-2; "Final Mortality Statistics, 1978," *Monthly Vital Statistics Report,* v. 29, no. 6 (1980), table 2; "Advance Report of Final Mortality Statistics, 1979," *Monthly Vital Statistics Report,* v. 31, no. 6 (1982), table 2; "Advance Report of Final Mortality Statistics, 1980," *Monthly Vital Statistics Report,* v. 32, no. 4 (1983), table 9.

learned that when the mortality rates of men teachers in Roman Catholic monasteries were compared with those of women teachers in Catholic convents — both controlled and relatively similar sociocultural environments — the men still had significantly higher death rates at all ages than the women. As a result, he concluded that biological factors have more influence than the exigencies of social life in producing the mortality differential by sex, whereas the social factors that do operate are comparatively minor contributors.[8] Therefore, while we don't know all aspects of the biological advantages that allow far more women than men to reach the older ages, it does seem clear that those factors are chiefly responsible for the great sex imbalance among people aged 65 and older.

One of the major reasons for the lower death rates of women is probably the fact that their extra X chromosome provides more resistance to certain illnesses. Moreover, women are biologically protected during their reproductive span, and because better nutrition and hygiene have lengthened that span, they are protected longer.[9] These factors and some not yet fully understood help produce the divergence in the death rates of the sexes, even while their life styles grow more similar and environmental factors converge to the point where they account for less of the differential. That is particularly apparent in the growing similarity of smoking behavior, for earlier in the century about two-thirds of the death rate differential was due to the fact that many men but few women smoked. The differential has also grown as deaths from infectious and parasitic diseases and childbearing have declined markedly and fatalities from heart disease, cancer, and other "degenerative" illnesses have increased. In the first group of causes the death rates of the sexes are not far apart, so decreases in those causes allow men no great advantage over women. In the group of degenerative causes, however, male death rates are far above those of females, so major increases in the relative importance of those causes strongly disfavor men and favor women. As a result, changes in the importance of certain causes of death have helped produce the large majority of women in the category 65 and over.[10]

In the future, the male-female mortality differential may decrease, for projections to 2050 suggest that the sex ratio of the elderly will stop falling and may even rise a little at times during the period. Some of that leveling will reflect events already past, but it may be that women who get caught up in the "work-or-perish" ethic that drives many men will incur some increases in mortality, or at least will not experience larger reductions than men.[11] Even so, the effect of the biological factors will probably remain largely as it is, and unless we reverse the present immigration pattern and receive large numbers of males, America's older population is unlikely to return to the earlier majority of men.

The steady decline in the sex ratio from birth to the oldest ages is typical of all developed countries, which have comparatively low birth and death

60

rates and mortality differentials that strongly favor the survival of women, though there are some departures from the pattern in the developing nations. Thus, table 3-1 indicates that during early childhood the sex ratios are nearly identical among the representative developed countries and that by age 65 the indexes have fallen well below 80, though the range is far wider then than in the first five years of life. The index for East Germany is particularly low because of the heavy losses of men during World War II. That situation is unusual, however, for even when war kills many men the losses have to be tremendous in youth in order to reduce the sex ratio very much in the older ages. Therefore, the sex differential in the "natural" causes of death is what gives women such a large numerical advantage over men; it is far more strategic than wars in reducing the sex ratio among elderly people in most countries at most times.[12]

Table 3-1. Sex Ratios at Several Ages, Selected Countries, 1980

Country	All Ages	0-4	40-44	65+
East Germany	88.3	105.5	99.7	53.6
West Germany	91.5	105.1	106.1	56.2
Finland	93.6	105.1	102.1	56.4
Austria	89.8	105.2	100.9	56.9
Scotland	92.8	105.8	96.4	60.8
France	96.1	104.8	104.3	64.2
England & Wales	95.0	105.6	102.9	64.5
Switzerland	94.8	104.6	101.1	66.9
UNITED STATES	94.5	104.7	95.8	67.6
Hungary	93.9	105.9	92.9	67.8
Netherlands	98.5	105.1	105.9	70.4
Italy	95.4	105.6	97.5	70.9
Denmark	97.5	105.2	102.0	73.2
Norway	98.3	105.5	102.5	73.8
Sweden	98.2	105.0	104.2	77.0

Sources: United Nations, Demographic Yearbook, 1980, table 7; 1981, table 7; U.S. Bureau of the Census, 1980 Census of Population, Supplementary Reports, PC80-S1-1, Age, Sex, Race, and Spanish Origin of the Population by Regions, Divisions, and States: 1980 (1981), table 1.

Effects of Migration

Immigration, which so greatly swelled the young-adult male population of the United States early in the twentieth century, now plays a less significant part statistically in the balance between older men and women; the role that the aging immigrant group does play affects the segment 75 and over more heavily than it does the one aged 65-74. Moreover, given the heavier representation of women in many recent immigrant groups, the sex ratio of the entire older foreign-born population is moving toward that of the elderly native-born group. A significant difference still remains, but it is diminishing as aged immigrants die and the younger ones with a more nearly even sex balance move into the older ages. In short, despite the impact of early twentieth-century immigration, the balance of males and females in the elderly segment is influenced most strongly by the sex differential in the death rate,[13] In the United States this factor has changed the balance markedly, from a slight surplus of elderly men in 1900 to the large surplus of elderly women at present.[14] This highly significant change and its social implications are yet another consequence of aging in America's population.

Variations in Sex Composition

The sex composition of the older population varies considerably among its component racial and ethnic groups, from state to state, and between rural and urban areas, and there are many significant departures from the average sex ratio. Despite their differences, however, the various groups are all alike in that the populations of women aged 65 and older have been growing much faster than those of men. As a result, between 1970 and 1980 the number of elderly women of all races and ethnic origins grew 31 per cent, while that of men increased only 22 per cent, thereby causing the sex ratio to fall from 72 to 68. This situation, which is most pronounced among whites, puts elderly men in great demand, alters the sex balance in some Sunbelt areas that attract significant groups of elderly migrants, and may even affect investment policy, political processes, and other social structures and dynamics.[15]

Differences by Race and Ethnicity

The proportions of men and women vary between the two major racial groups that make up the nation's elderly population. (See Figure 3-1.) For the most part, these differences result from significantly lower sex ratios at birth among blacks than among whites and from racial variations in mortality by sex.

The number of newborn male infants is closer to the number of females in the black than in the white population, and in 1980 the sex ratios at birth were 102.9 and 105.8, respectively. The black sex ratio at birth has risen faster in recent years, however, and so has that in early childhood, especially as infant mortality rates have fallen, but those ratios are still sufficiently lower than the ones for whites to help reduce the index for blacks at each age up to 70.

The sex ratio at birth isn't the only factor that contributes to the racial difference in the balance of males and females, however, for the death rates of black males and females are also more nearly alike at many ages than are those in the white population. For example, in 1980 the mortality differential between black men and women in all of the ages above 50 was less than in the white group. In addition, there are some distortions in the data, because black males get better coverage than females and the sex ratios recorded in the census reports are a bit higher than the actual ones, though the discrepancy is not great.

These factors interact to produce a sex balance among elderly black people that is more nearly even than the one among elderly whites. Thus, for the group 75 and over in 1980, the sex ratio was 60 for blacks but only 54 for whites. There is still a comparatively large number of widowed black women, however, for the proportion of those who remarry is considerably lower than in the white population; the percentage of black elderly divorced women who do not remarry is also larger than in the white group. Therefore, even though the sex ratio statistically favors remarriage for older black women more than it does for elderly whites, other factors stand in the way. As a result, in 1980 only 14 per cent of the black women 75 and over were classified as married with a husband present, compared with 23 per cent of the whites.

Elderly black women, especially those without mates, make up a "triple minority" insofar as disadvantages are concerned. They experience the social realities of being black, which tends to push their incomes and other indicators of material well-being below those of the white population; they are women, whose various level-of-living indexes compare poorly with those of men; and they are elderly, which intensifies their disadvantages over those suffered by younger people. Furthermore, elderly black women who have lost their mates or who never married tend to be even more seriously deprived than the ones with husbands, though higher percentages do live with other relatives than is true of whites. Older black women are also increasing faster in number than are their white counterparts, so their race will face particularly urgent future needs.

Even though the sex ratios of elderly blacks have been higher than those of whites for many decades, both indexes have also been on their way down for a long time. But the decline with age is less steep and less regular for blacks than it is for whites, producing the higher sex ratios among the black elderly. Even so, elderly people still make up a significantly smaller proportion of the black population than of the white, largely because the birth rates of black people are higher,[16] but also because black mortality historically has reduced the percentages who survive to 65 below those of whites who make it to that age.

The Spanish-origin population has a comparatively small share of elderly people and a relatively high birth rate, and the sex ratio for all ages collectively is fairly high. In 1980 that for elderly Hispanics was 76, contrasted with 67 in the population not of Spanish origin. Death rates and past birth rates play a part in this situation, but the selectivity of migration is a more significant component than in the American population as a whole. That is, men were heavily represented in the immigration from Latin America that brought many of today's elderly Spanish-origin people as young adults, especially from Mexico, Puerto Rico, and certain parts of Central and South America and the Caribbean. The Cuban-origin population, however, which is an aging one, has an unusually large deficiency of elderly men, partly because the post-revolutionary migration from Cuba consisted heavily of families whose elderly women have now outlived their men.

Women also tend to predominate in the recent immigrant population of all national origins collectively, and have done so for several decades. For example, the sex ratio of immigrants of all ages admitted in 1951-1960 was 85; in 1961-1970 it was 81, and in 1971-1979 it stood at 88. Men are still the majority in a few groups of immigrants, such as the refugees from Southeast Asia in the 1970s, but the large preponderance of young men among the earlier arrivals is generally not repeated among the new immigrant populations.[17] As those people age, therefore, the sex ratio of the elderly will fall well below the figure for native-born people and earlier immigrant groups, though presumably their descendants will produce a sex ratio at birth that approximates the national average, and the balance of older men and women in second and later generations will be like that in the total elderly population. In the meantime, however, the sex composition of recent immigrations will help intensify the great surplus of women that already exists among America's elderly, unless some new surge of male immigrants occurs.[18]

State-to-State Variations

All of America's elderly experienced particular historical events that gave them a base of common experiences and produced individual reactions that show up as collective behavior. Those formative events include childhood or young adulthood during World War I, the ravaging influenza epidemic of 1917-1918, the Great Depression, World War II, and the wars and political and economic crises since 1945. Moreover, large proportions of today's elderly have had small-town and farm experience, for in the few decades after 1900 about half the population was still classified as rural. Therefore, the experiences of the nation's elderly, like those of any age cohort, shaped their attitudes and skills, molded their economic pursuits, influenced the size of the families they produced and reared, and affected other patterns of behavior.[19]

The nature of these experiences, however, has varied widely from place to place throughout the nation, especially during the early decades of the century, when urbanization, the automobile, the mass media, and other forces had not yet diminished local and regional differences. The remnants of those differences show up in several forms, one of which is state-to-state variations in the balance of elderly men and women. Most significant is the fact that women substantially outnumber men in every state except Hawaii, where the sex ratio is 102, though Alaska's figure still stands near 100. Everywhere else the indexes range from a high of 85 in Nevada to a low of 58 in the District of Columbia, though it is significant that the elderly in about half the states have sex ratios in the narrow range from 65 to 70. (See Figure 3-3.)

The states that have lower sex ratios than the national average of 68 for all elderly people include several that are highly urbanized and industrialized along lines that attracted women workers who stayed put after retirement. Chief among those places are Washington, D.C., and the states of the Northeast. Many of the Southern states also have less than their fair shares of elderly men, partly because their older small towns and their newer urban centers have drawn elderly women, especially widows, or because those women didn't move when their husbands died. That is not true of Florida, however, partly because the elderly migration to that state consists so heavily of married couples. In addition, when husbands die in Florida, many widows move back to the places from which they came, often to be near adult offspring, though enough remain in Florida to help keep the sex ratio below 100.

Aging men are most heavily concentrated in the states that were still part of the old frontier early in the century, or whose largely "masculine" occupations attracted greater numbers of young men during those decades. Alaska — the last frontier — also has a relative abundance of elderly men, whose concentrations are also well above the national average in most of the Mountain and Pacific states, the Dakotas, and a few states in the South Central division. The last include Michigan and Wisconsin, where the work forces in automobile manufacturing, steel fabrication, dairying, and some other industries consist largely of men. Therefore, because the large majority of elderly people do not migrate after retirement, the present state-to-state variations in the sex balance of older citizens have been influenced by the particular functions that prompted

65

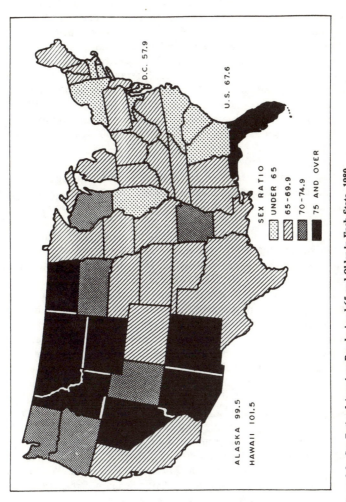

Figure 3-3. Sex Ratio of American People Aged 65 and Older in Each State, 1980
Source: U.S. Bureau of the Census, *1980 Census of Population, General Population Characteristics*, reports for states (1981), table 19.

earlier sex-selective migrations.

Certain sections of the country also have variable mortality differentials between males and females, and part of the variation in sex balance in some places is due to those differences in rates of survivorship. Overall, however, this factor is not very strategic, because in the 26 states collectively that have below-average sex ratios, life expectancy for women exceeds that for men to about the same degree as it does in the remaining states with above-average ratios. This similarity reflects the fact that the male-female discrepancy in mortality and life expectancy is almost always greater than are the variations within either sex from state to state or region to region. It is this nationwide differential between men and women that has shifted the sex balance of elderly people to a large predominance of women in every state except Alaska and Hawaii; even there the sex ratios have declined sharply in the twentieth century, just as they have in every other state.

Black-white differences in the states. In most states the sex balance is more nearly even for blacks than for whites, largely because the male-female mortality differential is greater for whites virtually everywhere in the country. Thus, in 1980 black people numbered at least 25,000 in the District of Columbia and 38 states, and 34 of them had significantly higher sex ratios among elderly blacks than elderly whites. For example, the sex ratio among older blacks in Washington, D.C., in 1980 was 63, whereas that for whites was only 51. The social and economic factors shaping the sex balance ordinarily work about the same for both racial groups, though, and those states that have relatively low or high sex ratios in one race usually show the same pattern in the other.

Given these similarities in most parts of the nation, the deficiencies of black and white elderly men are greatest in most of the Northeast and large parts of the South, including the District of Columbia. On the other hand, the smallest deficiencies of men among the elderly of both races are found in the Mountain and Pacific states, some of the industrialized sections of the North Central region, and a few of the Southern states. Older black men are particularly abundant in the places that attracted so many in the heavy migration from the South after 1910, and once drawn by the jobs in industry during both world wars, large numbers of older black men now remain in Ohio, Indiana, Michigan, Wisconsin, Washington, Oregon, and other places that witnessed significant influxes earlier in the century. They are also relatively abundant in Arkansas, Louisiana, and Mississippi, though earlier heavy migratory losses of women help explain those relatively high sex ratios. Furthermore, a sizable share of the small black farm population still lives in those states and elderly men are relatively abundant in that group, though the nation's black farm group has shrunk even more rapidly than the white segment during the last several decades. In fact, while 3 per cent of the nation's white people still lived on farms in 1980, that was true of less than 1 per cent of its blacks,[20] and the average age of the blacks was about four years higher than that of whites.

Rural-Urban Differences in Sex Composition

Elderly women outnumber older men most heavily in the urban parts of the country, especially the central cities, whereas men are relatively abundant in the rural portions, particularly on the farms. Moreover, the comparative abundance of women diminishes and that of men rises from the central cities of metropolitan areas to their suburbs, to small cities outside metropolitan areas, to villages and hamlets, and finally into the open countryside. In part, the sex ratios in the areas outside central cities have fallen because of the aging of the suburban populations that began to move from large cities to outlying districts several decades ago. But even on farms the relative abundance of men has dropped sharply, for the sex ratio of the elderly fell from 134 in 1940 to 112 in 1980. The figure would be considerably lower if many older women did not leave after the death of a spouse, for in the farm population as everywhere else in the nation, death rates are significantly higher for men than for women.[21] But those widows who do stay in farming communities still have a far better chance for remarriage than do their urban sisters.

The two major races differ markedly in the way elderly men and women are distributed among the rural and urban categories. Because they are the large majority, whites follow the national pattern closely and their sex ratios are the lowest in central cities and then rise progressively in the suburbs, the small cities, the towns and villages, and the farming areas. For elderly blacks, however, the situation is almost completely reversed. That is, the highest sex ratios appear in the suburban portions of metropolitan areas, followed closely by the central cities, especially the ones with more than 1 million people. Those were the destinations of many black migrants earlier in the century, and that group contained huge numbers of men fleeing the South in search of better jobs, less punitive race relations, and opportunities of other kinds. Most who have now reached 65 stay put, for while a substantial number of blacks are moving back to the urban South, few of them are elderly men. On the other hand, the sex ratios of elderly blacks are well below the national average for their race in all of the nonmetropolitan sections except the farms, where elderly men still slightly outnumber the women.

The overall sex ratio among older Spanish-origin people is comparatively high in several residential categories. In fact, elderly men make up large majorities in central cities with fewer than 1 million people, nonmetropolitan counties with a city of 25,000 or more, those with no places of 2,500, and on farms. Those patterns are affected by the size of the population clusters than happen to exist in the sections where Hispanic people have settled most heavily, especially the Southwest, but they do represent a different sex balance by residence than is to be found in various other groups. The lowest sex ratios among Hispanics appear in the nation's largest central cities and its suburbs, where elderly women outnumber the men most heavily.

No matter what their race or ethnic background, elderly women living in rural areas often have more socioeconomic disadvantages than the ones in cities and suburbs, though there are many problems in those places, too. The rural women tend to have lower incomes, less education, fewer years of paid work to generate pensions, less access to services and facilities, and more chronic health problems than do the urban women.[22] In the case of whites, the higher rural sex ratio does improve the chance for remarriage and that may solve some of the problems for some women. Among blacks, however, the sex balance lowers the chance of remarriage, and the elderly black woman probably experiences more disadvantages and fewer life alternatives than any other group in American society. That is especially true of the ones living in tiny villages and hamlets and on farms, though the small-town population does not fare much better. Thus, elderly rural women, particularly blacks, often need better services, higher incomes, stronger social ties, and improved health facilities.[23] At present, they are one of the nation's "invisible" groups who share poorly in its affluence.

Trends in Sex Composition

The most striking long-term trend in the balance of older women and men is the extent to which it has tipped strongly toward an abundance of the former. Thus, in 1870, when the census data for people 65 and over were first reported separately by sex, there was a slight overabundance of elderly men and the sex ratio stood near 101. (See Figure 3-4.) It was a little higher in 1880, but lower in both years than it would have been if the Civil War had not taken such a high toll of men of all ages. Then, as the relatively large immigrant groups of the late 1840s and 1850s began to reach age 65, the sex ratio rose to its highest point in 1890 and then began the downward trend still underway, propelled by the growing mortality differential between males and females.

Therefore, the balance between the sexes was again about even in 1930 and dropped off by 1940. (See also Table 3-2.) In the following decades the decline accelerated, especially between 1960 and 1970, partly because so many in the huge immigrant populations admitted before World War II had already died. That group originally contained so many men that in 1910, for example, the sex ratio of the foreign-born population of all ages was a very high 131. By 1940, however, the index for that group had fallen to 112, and by 1960 so many foreign-born people had died that the survivors didn't have much effect on the overall sex ratio of elderly people. The vast majority of the present elderly population is native born and their low sex ratio now reflects earlier fertility patterns and the mortality differential by sex, rather than important results of the sex selectivity in earlier immigrations. Moreover, because recent immigrations from most places contain more women than men, those groups will depress the elderly sex ratio even more when they reach age 65.

Trends by Race

White and black elderly populations have followed roughly similar patterns in that women have increased from slightly less than half of the older group to a large majority. (See Table 3-2.) Thus, women became a majority of the older white population just after 1930 and of the black group shortly after 1940. In later decades that numerical predominance increased rapidly in both races, and while the sex ratios of blacks re-

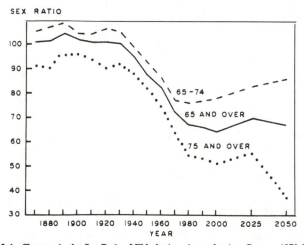

Figure 3-4. **Changes in the Sex Ratio of Elderly Americans, by Age Groups, 1870-2050**
Sources: U.S.Bureau of the Census, *Sixteenth Census of the United States: 1940, Characteristics of the Population, U.S. Summary* (1943), table 8; U.S. Census of Population: 1970, General Population Characteristics, U.S. Summary (1972), table 53; *1980 Census of Population, Supplementary Reports*, PC80-S1-1, *Age, Sex, Race, and Spanish Origin of the Population by Regions, Divisions, and States: 1980* (1981), table 1; "Projections of the Population of the United States: 1982 to 2050" (advance report), *Current Population Reports*, P-25, no. 922 (1982), table 2.

mained above those of whites, the amount of the difference declined. That suggests some convergence between the races in socioeconomic patterns, for when the factors that have historically separated them diminish and disappear, so do most of the major demographic differences.[24]

The sex balance of elderly people in the "other races" category, unlike the situations of blacks and whites, reflected a superabundance of men long before 1910, and until 1950 they became a larger majority with each

Table 3-2. Changes in the Sex Ratio of People 65 and Over, by Race, 1910-2050

Year	All Races	White	Black	Other Races
1910	101.1	100.6	107.7	118.3
1920	101.3	100.6	109.5	155.1
1930	100.5	100.2	103.4	155.4
1940	95.5	95.0	100.6	168.9
1950	87.9	89.2	90.7	191.4
1960	82.8	82.3	86.1	159.0
1970	72.2	71.6	76.5	123.8
1980	67.6	67.2	68.2	84.8
1990	66.1	66.4	61.7	72.9
2000	64.5	65.3	56.1	64.0
2025	70.3	71.8	60.8	65.3
2050	67.6	68.5	64.3	61.8

Sources: U.S. Bureau of the Census, Negroes in the United States, 1920-32 (1935), p. 90; Sixteenth Census of the United States: 1940, Characteristics of the Population, U.S. Summary (1943), table 7; U.S. Census of Population: 1950, Detailed Characteristics, U.S. Summary (1953), table 97; U.S. Census of Population: 1960, Characteristics of the Population, U.S. Summary (1964), table 158; U.S. Census of Population: 1970, General Population Characteristics, U.S. Summary (1972), table 52; 1980 Census of Population, Supplementary Reports, PC80-S1-1, Age, Sex, Race, and Spanish Origin of the Population by Regions, Divisions, and States: 1980 (1981), table 1; "Projections of the Population of the United States: 1982 to 2050" (advance report), Current Population Reports, P-25, no. 922 (1982), table 2.

decade. This reflected patterns of selectivity of immigration in the late nineteenth century, for many of the nonwhite and nonblack racial groups that entered the country consisted mostly of males. Men were an especially large part of the Japanese and Filipino groups and the Chinese contingent that came in the late 1800s to work as various kinds of laborers. Thus, in 1900 approximately 90 per cent of the nation's entire Chinese population of all ages was foreign born, and the sex ratio of that group was a lopsided 189. By 1950 they had grown old, but the sex ratio of Chinese people 65 and over still stood at 191 because of the initial predominance of men among the immigrants. Thirty years later, however, the large majority had died and the sex ratio among elderly Chinese had fallen to 103. Moreover, because most present Americans of Chinese ancestry were born in this country and because women outnumber men among the Chinese who still enter from abroad, the sex ratio of older people in that racial group will soon resemble that of the nation's total elderly population. Much the same is true of Japanese, Koreans, and other groups designated by the U.S. Census Bureau as races, though their initial immigrations also contained large majorities of men.

American Indians, who are also in the "other races" census category, include virtually no immigrants, so their sex ratio has been shaped by fertility and mortality, which have produced a more even balance of elderly Indian men and women than appears in the non-Indian population. Part of that balance results from the poverty in which so many native Americans have lived for so long, because childbirth and various causes of death that are well controlled in other groups have taken an unusually high toll of women. As a result, smaller proportions of Indian women reach old age than is true of blacks and whites. In 1980, for example, less than 6 per cent of all Indian women were 65 and over, compared with 9 per cent of the blacks and 14 per cent of the whites.

Trends by Regions, Divisions, and States

Since the turn of the century, the sex ratios among elderly people have fallen dramatically and the sex balance has become far more similar throughout the nation. (See Table 3-3.) But in 1900, when the sex ratio was 102 for all of the country's elderly people, the District of Columbia and 31 of the present 50 states ranked above that average. Elderly men made up the largest majority in Nevada, where there were 246 of them for each 100 elderly women, but the imbalances were also substantial in all but one of the other Western states, where most sex ratios were 130 or more. The only exception was Utah (sex ratio 98) because the sex balance of older people was still affected by the earlier plural marriage of Mormons — a practice which kept Utah from achieving statehood until 1896.

The majorities of elderly men were also substantial in the Great Plains states, for they, along with most of the West, still embodied many basic elements of the frontier, including an abundance of men. Males were also part of timbering in the Northwest, ranching in the grasslands, "sod busting" in the corn and wheat belts, and fighting in the tragic Indian wars in various parts of the West. Therefore, as the original settlers and adventurers aged, most of the elderly stayed in place and the original majorities of young men became majorities of elderly men.

In 1900 the lowest sex ratios appeared in the Northeast, because so many women had been drawn to the cities from more rural sections. The women, reflecting the historic preponderance of their sex in rural-to-urban migration, remained largely in place after they reached age 65 and caused elderly men to be a proportionately smaller part of the elderly population. In the South — at least the portions most destructively affected by the Civil War — the sex ratios were also relatively low, though they were higher in the border states and those closest to the old Western frontier. In a few cases, such as West Virginia, Mississippi, and Tennessee, elderly men made up slight majorities in 1900, partly because the lives of women had been so precarious that their death rates remained relatively high throughout the 1800s. That was especially true of black women. In addition, Florida had a significant majority of men (sex ratio 110), because it, too, had been a frontier area that attracted many more men than women, not merely in the 1800s but into the early twentieth century as well. The lowest sex ratio of all (84) was in the nation's capital, where governmental functions and related activities have long attracted disproportionately large numbers of young women who tend to remain in and around the city after they reach age 65. New England, however, was the division with the largest majority of elderly women.

By 1980 these early patterns had changed dramatically. The lingering effects of the frontier had virtually disappeared everywhere except Alaska, and the sex balance of the nation's elderly population was subject to certain homogenizing influences that caused the large proportions of women in one state to resemble those in most others. Those forces include a tendency for age-specific death rates to be roughly similar from state to state, the predisposition of most elderly people to stay put rather than to migrate, and the powerful standardizing influences that urbanization, the mass media, and other forces exert over behavior in any urban-industrial society, including much of its rural territory. As a result, the range of sex ratios from region to region and state to state was much narrower in 1980 than it had been in 1900, and the substantial predominance of women was a fact of life in the elderly population almost everywhere.

Some Projections

After 1970 the rate of decline in the proportion of elderly men diminished somewhat and seems likely to slow even more, though additional
small reductions are probable until 2000, followed by a series of slight
increases and decreases. (See Figure 3-4 and Table 3-2.) Those changes
mean that the rapid "feminization" of the nation's elderly population will
stop by 2000, though at a level that will make women close to 60 per cent
of the older group for at least the half century to follow. This is still a very
substantial imbalance, and while it may not intensify much from now on, it
will continue to have a profound social effect on the older population,
especially the women themselves.

Table 3-3. Sex Ratios in the Elderly Population,
            by Regions and Divisions, 1900 and
            1980

Region and Division	1900	1980
Northeast	88.5	64.0
New England	85.4	62.2
Middle Atlantic	89.9	64.7
North Central	109.9	67.1
East North Central	105.5	66.7
West North Central	118.6	67.8
South	101.1	68.4
South Atlantic	96.4	68.4
East South Central	102.2	67.7
West South Central	110.7	69.0
West	157.5	71.9
Mountain	141.1	76.4
Pacific[a]	164.9	70.4

Sources: U.S. Bureau of the Census, U.S. Census
of Population: 1970, General Population Characteristics, reports for states (1971), table 21;
1980 Census of Population, General Population
Characteristics, reports for states (1981),
table 19.

[a]Includes Alaska and Hawaii.

These patterns will vary some for blacks and whites as their elderly populations are shaped by earlier levels of fertility and mortality. (See Table 3-2.) But by the middle of the next century, the differences in the sex balances of whites, blacks, and other races should be relatively minor, particularly if those groups grow more alike according to various socio-economic criteria and their death rates continue to converge.

It also seems certain that the homogenizing trend of the last 70 or 80 years will continue into the next century, and that the balance of older men and women won't vary much from state to state, given a few exceptions. Most of the states with relatively high sex ratios in 1980 will witness some continuing reductions, whereas those with low indexes in 1980 either will change little or their sex ratios will rise slightly. Consequently, in 2000 most states will have somewhere between 60 and 70 elderly men for each 100 women, though a few states, such as Alaska, Hawaii, and Nevada, may have more. The patterns will also reflect a stabilizing tendency, for the majority of elderly women — already a large majority in nearly every state — won't increase markedly in most of them between now and the end of the century. This projected similarity among the states contrasts sharply with the situation in 1900, when sex ratios covered a range of 167 points. It means that certain demographic conditions that once distinguished one part of the country from another have diminished significantly, though the continuing imbalance of older men and women will produce or intensify certain problems.

Some Consequences of Sex Imbalance

The proportional abundance of women in the elderly population, owing to their greater average life expectancy, is a mixed blessing and even a crisis for many individuals. In particular, when women's greater longevity combines with their tendency to marry men a few years older, it means that large proportions have to expect a prolonged period of widowhood.[25] For that reason, only about a third of the older women are still living with their spouses, compared with about three-quarters of the men. Moreover, when the sex imbalance stabilizes there will be two elderly women for each elderly man, and some living arrangements will reflect that huge imbalance.

Living Alone

Even though most elderly people have adult children, relatively few live under the same roof with them. That fact, coupled with the high incidence of widowhood, means that a large share of America's elderly women live alone.[26] In fact, the likelihood of an elderly woman living by herself is now more than twice what it was in 1950, partly because improved finances make that arrangement possible for a larger percentage,[27] and partly because residence norms have changed in the direction of solitary living for more older people.[28] At present, about two of every three elderly women without a spouse live by themselves,[29] though largely by preference, for most older people choose to maintain residential independence at the same time they try to keep reasonably close social ties with their children and grandchildren. In addition, while the elderly population living in institutions of various sorts has been growing rapidly, that group is still a tiny percentage of all elderly.[30] All of this means that a disproportionately large share of the nation's older population consists of women living by themselves.

It is true that each succeeding generation of widows is somewhat less deprived economically on the average than the preceding one and that their levels of education and marketable skills also tend to be higher. Both improvements contribute to greater self-sufficiency for many older women attempting to acquire life's physical necessities. But those improvements may still leave a residue of stress and loneliness that come from being part of an increasingly large 'widowed majority, while the share of older men available for companionship and remarriage shrinks. For some older women accustomed to being homemakers and wives and whose fulfillment has been tied up with those activities, the prospect of a long widowhood with no one to care for helps convert the later years into a lonely wait for death. Even that may be made trivial by well-meaning others who attempt to contrive leisure activities and other types of behavior that simply intensify meaninglessness. Therefore, while the much greater life expectancy for women than for men does reflect the former's durability, it has a tragic side, too. Nonetheless, ample numbers of women do have the skills to deal with the death of a spouse, to adapt, and to endure, and most do cope adequately with the realities of widowhood. Whether or not specific ones can do so depends on a range of factors having to do with health, background experiences, emotional support in various social systems, finances, and the ability to find renewed meaning in other social niches. The task of the larger society is to find ways to encourage, sustain, and utilize those women who are unable to transform the tragic aspect of differential longevity into a final span of meaningful life.

Finances

The after-tax income per household member tends to rise gradually with the age of the householder until about age 60. Then it declines slightly for the group 60-64 and falls another 15 per cent or so for those 65

LIBRARY
OF
MOUNT ST. MARY'S
COLLEGE

and over.[*31*] Therefore, while elderly women living alone do fare worse financially than elderly men, it is too easy to stereotype the older woman as poor and lonely and to ignore the sizable numbers who are reasonably well off or even wealthy because of benefits received from their own years of work or inheritances from their husbands. Moreover, that group will grow proportionately, for more women now entering the elderly category are well educated and have held rewarding positions outside the home, though still at wages that average considerably below those of men. These women will probably grow as a force among corporate stockholders and will have a significant impact on investment decisions and other aspects of economic, social, and political life.

But many elderly people living alone still face poverty. In 1980, for example, 24 per cent of the men 65 and over who lived alone fell below the poverty line, as did 32 per cent of the women. Thus, even though the proportion in poverty declined steadily until about 1978, it has risen somewhat since then and still represents almost 2 million elderly women and 354,000 elderly men. Nor do those figures include the elderly who live with other relatives but who are still poor, though their incidence of poverty is below that of solitary individuals. Thus, in 1980 about 11 per cent of all elderly men and 19 per cent of all elderly women, irrespective of living arrangements, ranked below the official poverty line.[*32*] So even though these proportions are far below those just a few years earlier, the relative economic disadvantage of elderly women still stands out clearly. As expected, black women are at a particular disadvantage.

Part of the problem stems from discrimination against older women in the Social Security system, which, at this writing, still tends to reflect the old assumptions "that women marry once and do not work outside the home."[*33*] Therefore, a woman who divorces in less than 10 years after marriage cannot claim either a wife's or a widow's benefit, while a married woman who works must settle either for her own retirement benefits or half of her husband's. Ordinarily, the latter is greater because women's working years are generally fewer and their earnings are less, so most women get nothing for their own investment in Social Security.

Competent Older Women

We cannot leave our consideration of elderly women without some attention to the majority whose lives remain viable and who do manage to survive or even thrive financially and emotionally, even though aging is generally perceived more negatively among women than it is among men.[*34*] That perception, shared by many members of both sexes, tends to obscure the fact that women often enter the older years with skills that enable them to make better adjustments than men to changes wrought by the aging process, including its problems.[35] Indeed, many older women become not passive and dependent but more self-assured, while their husbands tend toward greater dependency, particularly after they retire and when they begin to experience serious health problems. Given the differential death rates by sex, the older woman is far more likely to have the care of an incapacitated mate, and that calls for strength and even aggressiveness that belie the common stereotypes about the older woman. In addition, women generally assume a large part or even all of the effort to survive on a reduced budget, and that, too, calls for inventiveness and competence. Therefore, increasing numbers of studies portray women in the older ages as confident, versatile, and in reasonable control of themselves and the destinies of their relationships.[36] After all, a lifetime of experiences is in place, which, along with the unique demands of the older years, often enhances a woman's ability to deal with life, including solitude. In addition, most older women still do not experience abrupt retirement from a salaried job, and the kinds of things they have been doing with competence tend to carry over without interruption to the later years. The housewife reaching age 65, for example, is apt to incur little of the trauma that may afflict the husband who was a full-time worker one day and a pensioner the next. That continuity of responsibility and role performance also tends to enhance the woman's competence, though the pattern could change as more women retire from salaried jobs in the future.[37]

Summary

Women make up the majority of the elderly population, basically because their death rates are so much lower than those of men, though in the past the large male majorities in immigrant populations offset much of the mortality differential, which was also smaller than it is now. In turn, the significant sex imbalance influences other conditions, including the roles of men and women, the options available to people who have lost their mates, and the kinds of coping mechanisms that widowed people — chiefly women — use to avoid passivity and dependence. In the future, the causal mortality differential, which seems more biological than environmental, will probably not change much and the sex ratio of older people is not likely to drop in the way it did after 1900. Nevertheless, it is unlikely to rise much either, which means that the great superabundance of women will be a permanent feature of America's elderly population.

Within the total elderly population the sex ratios are generally higher for blacks than for whites, though in a few states that isn't true. Moreover, the sex balance is more nearly even among Spanish-origin people than among blacks and whites, partly because men have been the majority in many recent immigrant populations from Spanish America.

The sex ratios of elderly people have become remarkably similar in most of the states, for the frontier conditions and other realities that attracted large majorities of men earlier in the twentieth century have disappeared almost everywhere except Alaska and Hawaii; they are declining there, too. In fact, the only group with more elderly men than women is the one living on farms, whereas the cities, the suburbs, and even the small towns have sizable majorities of women.

The long-term trends reflect a progressive decrease in the sex ratios of the elderly, but the projections suggest a leveling tendency that will leave about 65 or 70 men for each 100 women during the next half century or so. This points to prolonged widowhood for large numbers of women, and that experience, in turn, evokes coping mechanisms to deal with financial matters, solitude, and declining health. Most elderly women do rise to the challenge, however, and counter the stereotype of dependence and passivity, even becoming aggressive and more self-assured as they deal with aging, widowhood, adult children, and other aspects of later life in American society.

NOTES

1. U.S. Bureau of the Census, "Demographic Aspects of Aging and the Older Population in the United States," *Current Population Reports*, P-23, no. 59 (1978): 12.

2. For the data, see U.S. Bureau of the Census, "Marital Status and Living Arrangements: March 1980," *Current Population Reports*, P-20, no. 365 (1981), table 1.

3. Peter Uhlenberg, "Demographic Change and Problems of the Aged," in Matilda White Riley, ed., *Aging from Birth to Death*. Boulder, CO: Westview Press, 1979, p. 164.

4. Carol Boellhoff Giesen and Nancy Datan, "The Competent Older Woman," in Nancy Datan and Nancy Lohman, eds., *Transitions of Aging*. New York: Academic Press, 1980, pp. 59-60.

5. National Center for Health Statistics, "Advance Report of Final Natality Statistics, 1980," *Monthly Vital Statistics Report* 31 (1982), table 7. See the analysis of causes by Gerald E. Markle, "Sex Ratios at Birth: Values, Variance, and Some Determinants," *Demography* 11 (1974): 131-134.

6. I.M. Lerner, *Heredity, Evolution and Society*. San Francisco: Freeman, 1968, p. 120.

7. For an analysis of the differential, see Nathan Keyfitz and Antonio Golini, "Mortality Comparisons: The Male-Female Ratio," *Genus* 31 (1975): 1-33.

8. Francis C. Madigan, "Are Sex Mortality Differentials Biologically Caused?" *Milbank Memorial Fund Quarterly* 35 (1957): 202-223.

9. Jacob S. Siegel, "Prospective Trends in the Size and Structure of the Elderly Population, Impact of Mortality Trends, and Some Implications," in U.S. Bureau of the Census, *Current Population Reports*, P-23, no. 78 (1979): 11.

10. Parts of this analysis are adapted from *ibid.*, pp. 11-13.

11. Jacob S. Siegel, "On the Demography of Aging," *Demography* 17 (1980): 350.

12. For some other international examples, see Organisation for Economic Co-operation and Development, *Socio-economic Policies for the Elderly.* Paris: OECD, 1979, pp. 11-12.

13. Joseph A. Norland, "Measuring Change in Sex Composition," *Demography* 12 (1975): 84.

14. Henry D. Sheldon, *The Older Population of the United States.* New York: Wiley, 1958, p. 14.

15. J. John Palen, *Social Problems.* New York: McGraw-Hill, 1979, pp. 393-394.

16. U.S. Bureau of the Census, "Some Demographic Aspects of Aging in the United States," *Current Population Reports*, P-23, no. 43 (1973): 8-9.

17. The data are from U.S. Bureau of the Census, *Statistical Abstract of the United States: 1982-83.* Washington, DC: U.S. Government Printing Office, 1982, tables 132 and 134.

18. Sheldon, *op. cit.*, p. 14.

19. For this theme, see Beth J. Soldo, "America's Elderly in the 1980s," *Population Bulletin*, 35 (1980): 6.

20. U.S. Bureau of the Census, "Farm Population of the United States: 1980," *Current Population Reports*, P-27, no. 54 (1980), table B.

21. *Ibid.*, p. 2.

22. National Council on the Aging, *Perspective on Aging* 9 (1980): 24.

23. *Ibid.*

24. Paul E. Zopf, Jr., *Sociocultural Systems.* Washington, DC: University Press of Ameria, 1980, p. 423.

25. Uhlenberg, *op. cit.*, p. 161.

26. Siegel, "On the Demography of Aging," *op. cit.*, p. 355. Cf. Sheldon, *op. cit.*, pp. 101-102.

27. Robert T. Michael, Victor R. Fuchs and Sharon R. Scott, "Changes in the Propensity to Live Alone: 1950-1976," *Demography* 17 (1980): 39.

28. Frances E. Kobrin, "The Fall in Household Size and the Rise of the Primary Individual in the United States," *Demography* 13 (1976): 136.

29. Michael, Fuchs and Scott, *op. cit.*, p. 49.

30. Siegel, *op. cit.*, pp. 355-356.

31. For the data, see U.S. Bureau of the Census, "Estimating After-Tax Money Income Distribution Using Data from the March Current Population Survey," *Current Population Reports*, P-23, No. 126 (1983), table 1.

32. See U.S. Bureau of the Census, "Characteristics of the Population Below the Poverty Level: 1980," *Current Population Reports,* P-60, no. 133 (1982), table 15.

33. Soldo, *op. cit.,* p. 39.

34. Giesan and Datan, *op. cit.,* p. 57.

35. *Ibid.,* p. 58.

36. *Ibid.,* pp. 59-60.

37. *Ibid.,* p. 60.

Chapter 4

Marriage and Family Status
Of the Elderly

The personal situation of most older people, like that of most other adults, is strongly influenced by marital status, just as the nature of the whole elderly population is affected by the proportions who are single, married, widowed, and divorced. Beyond the demographic considerations, the marital situation of the elderly has important social ties with family processes, structures, and functions, and especially the roles that people perform. Moreover, the nature and composition of families has much to do with how well the needs of older people are met and with whether they reside in a family setting with a spouse, adult children, or other relatives; outside the family context in an institution or alone; or in some type of quasi-family.

Given these variations, we need to analyze the marital status of America's elderly population in a broad social and demographic context, for the family still has great importance in the lives of older people, including most of those who live alone. Moreover, the marital status and living arrangements of elderly men differ greatly from those of elderly women,[1] basically because of the huge statistical surplus of the latter and the unavoidable solitude of many. In turn, that is a consequence of the differential death rates by sex and the stronger tendency for widowers to remarry, often not just from among the pool of elderly widows, but from the group of younger unmarried women.[2] Therefore, we have to account for the variable marital patterns of the sexes and the consequences that follow. First, however, we need to consider how marital status varies from adolescence to extreme old age.

Age and Marital Status

Any person's marital situation depends so heavily on age, that the proportions of single, married, widowed, and divorced people in a total population are greatly affected by its age profile. Thus, Figure 4-1, which is for the male and female populations aged 14 and over, shows the abrupt decrease in the percentages of single people in young adulthood and the accompanying rise in the proportions married, followed by increases in widowhood with advancing age, especially among women. These general patterns reflect those of most industrialized societies and lead to several conclusions as a context in which to examine the marital characteristics of the elderly.

Married People

By age 15 a few people begin to marry, and from then on the percentage single falls dramatically and that of married people leaps upward, because the average age at first marriage is still in the early 20s. Women, following the tradition that helps prolong widowhood, continue to marry somewhat older men and the marriage curve for women rises sooner, though the time lag is only a couple of years. (See Table 4-1.) The difference has

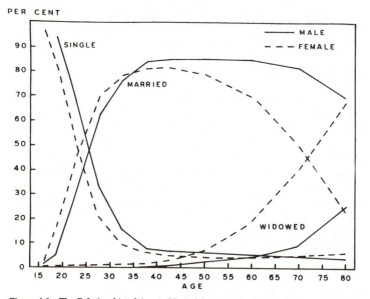

Figure 4-1. The Relationship of Age to Marital Status in the United States, by Sex, 1980
Source: U.S.Bureau of the Census, ''Marital Status and Living Arrangements: March 1980,'' *Current Population Reports,* P-20, no. 365 (1981), table 1.

actually diminished by almost two years since 1900, but the reduction has been accompanied by the wide divergence in the death rates of males and females, so the average woman who does marry a man a few years older simply adds to the time she can expect to live as a widow.

As the marriage curve rises with age, eventually it reaches a peak in middle age. Thus, the maximum proportion of women classified as married comes in the ages 35-39, when widowhood begins to increase substantially; the highest percentage of men who are married comes in the ages 45-49. After these peaks have been reached, the percentage married begins to fall off fairly rapidly for women and more slowly for men, and by the time women reach the ages 75 and over, only 23 per cent are still married, compared with 69 per cent of the men.

Widowed People

The proportion of those whose spouses have died are very low in adolescence and young adulthood, but even then more women than men lose their mates to accidents, violence, and other causes. The rate of widowhood among women climbs very significantly after age 45, when the number of widows exceeds that of single women, while a similar situation for men doesn't appear until age 65. Despite these losses for both sexes,

Table 4-1. Median Age at First Marriage, 1890-1980

Year	Male	Female	Difference, in Years
1890	26.1	22.0	4.1
1900	25.9	21.9	4.0
1910	25.1	21.6	3.5
1920	24.6	21.2	3.4
1930	24.3	21.3	3.0
1940	24.3	21.5	2.8
1950	22.8	20.3	2.5
1960	22.8	20.3	2.5
1970	23.2	20.8	2.4
1980	24.6	22.1	2.5

Source: U.S. Bureau of the Census, "Marital Status and Living Arrangements: March 1980," Current Population Reports, P-20, no. 365 (1981), table A.

however, fertility and mortality have changed in such a way that the average young couple who marry today and produce children can expect to live together 14 years longer than their parents could after the last child has left home, barring divorce or separation.[3] Those 14 years represent about a third of the 44 years that people with continuous first marriages can now expect to spend together.[4] Therefore, as tragic as widowhood may be for individuals, its present patterns do represent substantial improvements in longevity and they allow a couple to spend many older years together free of child care. At the same time, there is the huge imbalance between widowed older men and women. For example, among widowed people 65 and over, there are only 19 men per 100 women, and for those in the combined category of single, widowed, and divorced, the figure is just 26. Moreover, the average age of widowers is about three years above that of widows, so most elderly widows who do remarry can expect to become widows again.

Divorced People

Patterns of divorce also vary by age, basically in two ways. First, divorce is most likely to occur for those who marry in their teens, for whom the risk is well over twice as great as it is for those who marry in their 20s. Second, the proportion of people who have divorced and not remarried rises with age until the 30-39 range and then tapers off gradually. This suggests that people aged 30-39 became a pivotal group as divorce patterns changed, for their elders are products of times and circumstances in which divorce was less acceptable and less common, whereas their juniors experience higher divorce rates but are also more apt to remarry. Thus, the pivotal age group experienced a rapid increase in divorce rates when their marriages were new, but as those people grow older they are less and less likely to remarry, especially as the falling sex ratio works increasingly to the disadvantage of women. Therefore, the older women are when they divorce or become widowed or the longer they remain single, the less likely they are ever to marry.

Basic Marital Differences by Sex

A little over half the nation's total elderly people still have a spouse with whom they live and another 2 per cent have a living mate from whom they are separated. Since more women than men survive to the older ages, however, gender has an important bearing on the marital and family status of the elderly.[5] Therefore, we need to consider the circumstances of the sexes separately and account for their relative proportions in each of the marital categories.

Three-quarters of all elderly men are married and living with their spouses, but that is true for little more than a third of the older women, mostly because of widowhood, though somewhat larger shares of women than men are also classified as single. More than half the women are widows, whereas only 14 per cent of the men are widowers. Moreover, these sex differences intensify upward in the age scale, until well over two-thirds of the women aged 75 and older must contend with the realities of being left alone because of a husband's death, having very limited prospects to develop another relationship that will lead to remarriage. Even in those ages, however, more than two-thirds of the men are still married. (See Table 4-2.)

The United States is not alone in these patterns of marital status by age and sex, for the world's elderly populations all share the same general imbalance, though with some variations from country to country. That is, at age 65 and older the large majority of men are still married, usually amounting to three-quarters or more of the total and scarcely ever dropping below two-thirds, while the proportion of widowers is rarely above 25 per cent. Among women the relationship is reversed, for the percentage still married at age 65 and older is always a minority, usually around a third or less of the total, while widows are at least half the total in nearly all countries and over two-thirds in some. Therefore, no matter what the levels of development and despite the somewhat higher percentages of widows in most of the developing countries than in most of the ones already "developed," the large surplus of elderly unmarried women appears nearly everywhere, though the proportional significance of that surplus does vary.

Though the factor chiefly responsible for this pattern is the differential mortality by sex, marriage and remarriage rates also play a part. In turn, they vary according to a society's prevailing religious and cultural norms. But the tendency for women to outlive men is so pervasive that among the 150 or so countries for which the United Nations reported the expectation of life at birth in the late 1970s, there were only six — Bangladesh, Bhutan, India, Nepal, Pakistan, and Sabah in Malaysia — in which male infants could expect longer life than female infants. The greater longevity of women even holds in places where life expectancy at birth is still less than 50 years and women experience unusually high death rates in childbirth. And the phenomenon extends to the few places where the newborn have an average life expectancy of 40 years or less, such as Ethiopia and Yemen. Not one of the reporting countries has greater life expectancy at age 65 for men than for women. Therefore, they all have much higher percentages of widows than widowers in the older ages and far lower proportions of married women than married men, including the few countries where male life expectancy at birth still exceeds that of females.[6]

The patterns of divorce in the United States, unlike those of widowhood, are about the same for both sexes in the older years. People who have divorced and not remarried are found more commonly among the 65-74 age group than in the older ages, but that marital status is significantly less in evidence among all elderly people than it is among the other ages between 25 and 64.

The changes with age in the proportions of men and women who are single, married, widowed, and divorced are also related to the living arrangements of the elderly, for the death of a spouse not only leaves the mate living alone in most cases, but provokes the question of what to do

Table 4-2. Percentages of Older People in the Marital Status Categories, by Age and Race, 1980

Race and Marital Status	65-74		75+	
	Male	Female	Male	Female
All races	100.0	100.0	100.0	100.0
Single	5.4	5.6	4.4	6.4
Married[a]	79.4	48.1	67.7	22.1
Spouse Absent	2.2	2.0	1.7	1.2
Widowed	8.5	40.3	24.0	68.0
Divorced	4.4	4.0	2.2	2.3
White	100.0	100.0	100.0	100.0
Single	5.3	5.8	4.3	6.5
Married[a]	81.1	49.5	69.2	22.6
Spouse Absent	1.5	1.6	1.1	0.9
Widowed	7.9	39.2	23.5	67.7
Divorced	4.3	3.9	1.9	2.2
Black	100.0	100.0	100.0	100.0
Single	6.1	4.2	5.3	5.1
Married[a]	64.2	35.1	53.1	13.8
Spouse Absent	9.2	5.7	5.8	4.9
Widowed	14.9	49.9	30.4	71.9
Divorced	5.5	5.2	5.4	4.3

Source: U.S. Bureau of the Census, "Marital Status and Living Arrangements: March 1980," Current Population Reports, P-20, no. 365 (1981), table 1.

[a]Spouse present.

after one's marriage has disintegrated. In fact, "the trend in the percentage married as age increases is perhaps the best single index of the cycle of family formation and dissolution."[7] Coming as it does several years after the average couple's last child has left home, the sad occasion of widowhood causes the survivor, usually the wife, to decide in most cases to remain in the home, ordinarily alone, because the vast majority of elderly people do not reside with their children, other relatives, or in institutions. In fact, the last decade or so has seen a decrease in the percentage of elderly people who live in families and an increase in the proportion who maintain their own households, though sometimes with nonrelatives who may help constitute a quasi-family.[8] Therefore, the concept of the three-generation family living under one roof is more fiction than reality, though the family form that does prevail is a logical result of the American tendency to separate the nuclear unit from the larger extended family, at least residentially. Thus, in 1980 about 15 per cent of all American men aged 65 and older and 42 per cent of the women were living by themselves or with nonrelatives, and were designated as "nonfamily householders" (formerly "primary individuals") by the U.S. Bureau of the Census. The percentages are especially high in the groups above age 74. Furthermore, 95 per cent of all nonfamily householders occupied their own house or apartment alone, which points to the nation's substantial share of widows and widowers and its smaller single and divorced elderly populations that carry on their lives in relative solitude.

Variations by Race and Nativity

Race and ethnicity often have strong associations with differences in marital status and familial patterns, largely because of the socioeconomic variations attached to race and nativitiy, particularly when today's elderly people were young and their marital patterns were evolving under the onus of racism and segregation.[9] Therefore, black and white older people differ substantially in the percentages who are single, married, widowed, and divorced, and also in their living arrangements, though none of the variations is as great as in the past.

In general, elderly black men are less likely to be married than are white men but are more apt to be single, widowed, or divorced. (See Table 4-2.) At the same time, however, black men are more likely to be separated from their wives while still legally married to them. Most of the same relationships by race obtain for women, in that smaller percentages of black than white women are married, while higher percentages of blacks are widowed, divorced, or separated. The proportion single is below that among white women, however, and not only are the marriages of blacks dissolved more frequently, but their rates of remarriage are lower than those of whites. As a result, while 61 per cent of the white women aged

65 and older are not living with a spouse for one reason or another, that is true of 72 per cent of the black women. As expected, these conditions intensify with age.

The marital status of elderly Spanish-origin people varies some from those of blacks and whites. Men 65 and over are more likely than black and white men to be single or divorced, while they are intermediate between the two races in the proportions married or separated. Hispanic men are as likely as white elderly men to be widowers, but the proportions in both groups are much smaller than they are in the black segment. Spanish-origin women are intermediate between black and white women in the proportions single, married, or separated, but rank highest in the shares who are widowed or divorced. There are some differences in these patterns, however, between the two age groups that comprise the category 65 and over. There are also several variations among the nationality groups that constitute the Spanish-origin population. Thus, the proportions of single men and women are comparatively low in the Cuban population, relatively high among people with Puerto Rican backgrounds, and a bit above average in the Mexican group. The proportions of married men and women are relatively high in the Cuban group and low among Puerto Ricans, while Cuban and Puerto Rican women are especially likely to be widowed, finding themselves unable to remarry in an unusually large share of cases.

In addition to the rise in the proportion of widowed people in all elderly racial and ethnic categories, the percentages who are divorced or separated are growing in all of the groups, rapidly in some. Therefore, increasing proportions of older people will face living alone or with others who are not spouses or children, for the percentages who live in familes are declining, especially among women. Other things contribute to this tendency as well, such as improved pensions that facilitate independence, various public assistance programs, housing that tends to segregate the elderly from other age groups, and the wish of most adult children to live near but not with their aging parents.[10]

Both blacks and whites contribute to the tendency for elderly people to live alone, for the older members of each race seem to prefer independent arrangements as long as they are physically and economically able. In fact, some people in all racial groups pursue this independence because they cannot always rely on the extended family even when it appears strong, despite the myths about unwavering concern for the elderly in certain ethnic groups, especially the Japanese and Chinese.[11] Moreover, even when financial and other material assistance is available from families, it does not guarantee companionship and emotional support for the elderly, and each race and ethnic group has its minority of elderly parents whose children help provide the former but little or none of the latter, though it is easy to overestimate this problem. In some cases, the children's obligation to supply material assistance may even produce resentments that diminish the more affective types of support, especially as more people come to believe that high Social Security taxes give government the responsiblity for the elderly.

Farm-Nonfarm Variations

In general, city populations contain unusually large percentages of single women, widows and widowers, and divorced men and women, while farm areas have significantly more than their fair share of married people and single men, but relatively low proportions in the other marital categories. Among the elderly population living on farms, these patterns are strongly influenced by the surplus of men. Their group also contains a larger proportion of bachelors than appears in the nonfarm population, for even young men have a poorer statistical chance to marry than do those in cities, because rural-urban migration has taken away large numbers of young women. As these single men age, their statistical marriage prospects do improve somewhat, because the sex ratio declines, though at age 65 and older it is back to 112 in the farm population as compared with one of 68 in the older nonfarm group.

The proportions of widowed people are much lower on farms than they are in the nonfarm group. That isn't because of any mortality advantage in farm populations or because the death rates of men are any closer to those of women than they are in cities. Instead, the woman who becomes a widow in the farm population stands a far better chance of remarriage than her urban sister, owing to the supply of elderly men without wives, though the advantage diminishes fairly rapidly after age 65. In addition, rural norms tend to favor remarriage more strongly than is true in the cities as a whole, and various economic necessities, including the operation of a farm, often pressure a widow toward remarriage. Some of those factors also account for the low proportion of elderly farm people classified as divorced, though the initial divorce rate is also much lower than it is for urbanites.

Sex Ratios and Remarriage Prospects

Just what statistical chances do the elderly have for the remarriage mentioned in the preceding section? How many would actually remarry if the demographic situation allowed it? In order to address the first question we need to consider the categories of men and women who are single, widowed, and divorced, and who are statistical prospects for marriage. The index that allows such an analysis is the familiar sex ratio, which varies significantly by race, residence, and age in the 65-and-over group. The great bulk of this eligible group consists of widowed people, who are 61 per cent of the men who could marry and 85 per cent of the eligible women. Table 4-3 provides the basic data.

The fundamental fact affecting the prospects for marriage and remarriage of elderly people is the great sex imbalance, for as we saw in Chapter 3, in 1980 there was a surplus of 6.2 million women who could not find mates in their age bracket. Moreover, the imbalance intensifies with age. It is also more severe among whites than blacks, for while elderly unmarried white women outnumber men by four to one, black women predominate by just three to one, though the discrepancy is even less in the Spanish-origin population. Partly as a consequence of the sex imbalance among elderly unmarried people, about 18 of each 1,000 men actually do remarry, compared with only two of the women,[12] though unwillingness to establish a new marriage is also a factor for a large number of people. Therefore, the attitudes and the nine-to-one difference in the remarriage rate make remarriage among the nation's elderly people relatively rare.[13] Widowed people make up the majority of those who do remarry, but only because they are such a large share of the unmarried group. Divorced people actually have higher remarriage rates than widows and widowers at all ages including 65 and over. If one is going to remarry at all, it generally happens fairly soon after the first marriage ends, for the status of widowed or divorced person soon becomes part of one's way of life and is not easily relinquished in many cases.

Table 4-3. Sex Ratios of Elderly People Classified as Single, Widowed, and Divorced, by Race and Spanish Origin, 1980

Race and Ethnicity	65+	65-74	75+
All Races	26.1	28.2	23.8
White	25.2	27.3	23.1
Black	33.3	34.8	31.2
Spanish Origin[a]	42.1	43.2	40.3

Source: U.S. Bureau of the Census, "Marital Status and Living Arrangements: March 1980," Current Population Reports, P-20, no. 365 (1981), table 1.

[a]May be of any race.

Because their experiences bear little resemblance to those of divorced people, widows and widowers tend to marry each other, though they have to choose within a fairly narrow age range due to the rigid norms that still keep women from marrying much younger men. Those constraints further limit a widow's choices and discourage many women from marrying no matter what the statistical situation. Many don't want to repeat previous problems, care for another invalid husband, or suffer bereavement once again. Others cherish their independence and guard their finances against loss. Still others are concerned about the impact of remarriage on their children, who may be opposed for various reasons. Some believe the original marriage was so good and the first husband so saintly that neither could possibly be duplicated.[14] Furthermore, the older a woman is when she becomes a widow, the less her chances of remarriage, because the demographic and social factors both conspire against that possibility. Conversely, younger women are the best candidates to remarry, especially if they have worked for wages, are adept at making significant personal adjustments, and had deeply satisfying emotional relationships with their first husbands.[15] Many of these factors help reduce the numbers of elderly people who would remarry even if the sex ratio were closer to 100, so the 6.2 million "surplus" women do not constitute an eager throng who would all choose new husbands if only there were enough to go around.

Remarriage, even when it occurs, also presents certain problems, partly because American culture still includes remnants of the myth that there is only one love for each person, and thereby creates certain conflicts and hazards for the new marriage. In turn, a widowed person who idealizes the first spouse may cause the new mate to feel he/she is second choice, while friends, relatives, and in-laws from the first marriage may make the new relationship difficult to manage.[16] Nonetheless, most widowed people who do marry seem to succeed, partly because the marriage represents an escape from loneliness and other problems and thereby encourages people to adjust to a new mate who may be less than ideal.[17]

The Experience of Widowhood

Inasmuch as the vast majority of elderly people without mates are widows who don't remarry, we can consider some of the aspects of widowhood, though widowers deserve attention as well.

Widowhood is fundamentally different from other ways of ending a marriage, for it is involuntary, it provides the survivor with recognizable status, and it evokes sympathy from friends and relatives, at least for a time. Nor is widowhood perceived as failure in the same sense as divorce, though the widowed person may become a pariah with whom others feel uneasy for different reasons. Despite the more positive attitude toward widowed people, loneliness is still often a major problem, especially among women, for they are even less likely now than in the past to move in with adult children.[18] Therefore, the widow faces a social world oriented to couples and from which she is suddenly excluded, and her status is further complicated by the fact she is elderly in a society that prizes youth; many of the oldest ones also have health and financial problems. These conditions diminish the chances that a widow can find a mate in the small pool of widowers, and they contribute to the problems that can accompany solitude.

Widows and widowers differ in certain respects that make some adjustments more difficult for one group than for the other, though they also have many problems in common. Some elderly women find marriage the primary source of status, and the end of a marriage leaves a major gap in a woman's life. This is not to say, of course, that men are necessarily less dependent on their marriages, particularly those men who are retired and lack the occupational status to which they had been accustomed. Moreover, most men and women have other relationships and interests in their lives, and while the death of a spouse may alter some of them, it rarely destroys or even changes all of them. Despite these protections, however, there is a strong tendency for widowed people to feel shunned by friends and relatives who follow the American tendency to deny death and who may even assess a kind of blame for it. Therefore, the surviving spouse — man or woman — generally endures "the pain over being deserted, of losing a love object, and at least a significant other, of grief and loneliness,"[19] and must often struggle with these things in the absence of continuing support from friends and relatives. The problems are intensified because the nuclear family is the functioning domestic unit in the United States, while the potentially supportive network of the extended family is at least partly fragmented by residence arrangements that discourage the three- or four-generation household. Thus, widowed people of both sexes have in common the death crisis itself, the loss of someone to share household responsibilities and emotional ties, and the role-disorganization that may follow.

Widows and widowers can also experience financial problems as the result of the death, though on the average the women are less well off than the men, and they may either have to seek public assistance or help from children or see their levels of living decline. But even that fact fails to account for the economic loss sustained by a widower when his wife dies, whether or not she earned wages. Furthermore, widowers seem to suffer more severe problems of adjustment than widows and are more likely to be in poor health. Many widowers also appear to have poorer adaptive skills and find it more difficult to adjust to solitude and to the status of single in a world of couples. In any case, they suffer from higher rates of mental illness and suicide than do widows,[20] though their situations are also affected by class standing, level of education, and other factors. In short, even though some problems affect individual widows or widowers differently, the death of a spouse provokes many more common difficulties and adjustments. Therefore, many of the socioeconomic differences between elderly widows and widowers pale beside the fact that the former outnumber the latter by more than five to one.

The living arrangements of widowed people tend to reinforce the problems that some of them face, especially loneliness and the lack of material support. Thus, in 1980 over 64 per cent of the elderly widowers and 67 per cent of the widows were classified as nonfamily householders living alone. Most of the remainder were living in families headed by relatives, principally adult children; but even many of those elderly are there because of financial constraints and would actually prefer to reside independently. The elderly widowed people most likely to live alone are white, especially women, while less than half of the blacks reside by themselves, more often finding homes with relatives or friends. The percentage of widowed people living alone declines somewhat with age, because the oldest people are more likely to be incapacitated and in need of constant companionship, but in their case, too, solitude is more common among whites than blacks.

Living alone has increased markedly in the past several decades, partly because of changes in family relationships. In numerous earlier cases, especially in farming areas, parents accepted a newly married couple into an established household. The aging woman gradually turned its management over to the younger one but continued to reside in the home. Now an elderly widow who wishes to live with adult children must break up her original home and move in with a daughter or daughter-in-law. Because neither she nor the younger woman may really want that relationship, the elderly widow is more apt to remain in and control her own home, even though it may mean solitude. That solitude, however, tends to produce a lower level of life satisfaction for both rural and urban widows than does living with adult children,[21] though it is often modified by continuing contacts with the children.

Families of the Elderly

The older man or woman usually has numerous family roles as spouse, parent, grandparent, relative of other kinds, and more frequently than in the past, even child of a very old parent.[22] These roles cluster into a complex but changing set of relationships that affect the composition of the elderly person's family.[23] Moreover, while the older man or woman finally must adapt to the death of a spouse, for most people aged 65 and older the demanding adjustments to a new marriage, the acquisition of small children, and even the departure of the last child are far in the past. In place of those adjustments are such things as the husband's and perhaps the wife's retirement from a salaried job, reduced income, the appearance of grandchildren, eventual bereavement, and adjustment to the prospect of one's own death. The social network necessary for dealing with these changes is curtailed by the propensity of most older people to live alone or only with their spouses, while a small and declining minority live with their children. Nonetheless, many elderly people do come to depend emotionally, financially, and in other ways on the offspring who once depended on them, and a comparatively large majority do live *near* at least one of their children and visit often. Assistance during illness or incapacity is an especially significant factor in these relationships. In fact, one of the most persistent fictions about the elderly in contemporary American society is that they are largely abandoned by their adult children. That myth has evolved largely from the fact that the vast majority of elderly people do not reside with their children and are assumed, therefore, to be ignored or neglected. The abandonment myth is further sustained by the many elderly who do not receive the attention they would like, by the mistaken notion that the nuclear family is emotionally isolated from the larger kin network, by other beliefs about intergenerational relationships,[24] and by the role that government at many levels has assumed in meeting certain needs of the elderly. In fact, however, significant and productive ties still exist between most elderly people and their families, even though they don't all live under one roof.[25] The more common tendency is for the elderly and their offspring to work out mutually productive and fulfilling contacts that reflect the *modified extended family,* which holds together and provides in certain ways for its members, even though they may be geographically separated. It is a unit typical of urban-industrial societies whose members change residence frequently.[26] Moreover, the modified extended family reflects the persistence of parent-child relationships throughout life, partly because people share certain values and a sense of duty and obligation toward each other.

Family Functions

Aging does alter the nature of the older person's family and the contributions he/she makes to it. But the durability of family relations in some form is largely due to the functions that the family performs for older people and the contributions they make to it.

The elderly may help socialize children and thereby teach them certain elements of the society and create some dimensions of personality and the self-concept, though present-day older people are less likely to serve as authority figures than as benign baby-sitters. Moreover, since the family helps blend one generation into the next, elderly people give children apprenticeship with the oldest group, though that function is compromised when young offspring regard their parents as the older generation and their grandparents as ancient curiosities with little to offer.

The family remains a source of emotional security for many older people, largely because those relationships provide some caring and uncritical acceptance which, in turn, helps people deal with isolation, tension, and stress, and which constitutes the principal protective function of contemporary families that no longer have to overcome natural dangers. But the family also generates conflict and the opportunity for conflict management. The ability to control conflict and to interact productively with elderly members may be a skill that carries over into other relationships. Those functions may be limited, however, by the fact that more than two generations rarely live together, because the geographic separation of the elderly from young family members, even if only by a block or two, keeps many contacts between youth and the elderly artificial and weakly integrative. Nevertheless, the type of interaction in today's modified extended family is better than none at all in helping to moderate the prevailing stereotypes about older people. Even when conflict does occur, it may have a less devastating effect on the elderly than simply being ignored.

Finally, the family provides some links with other social institutions the older person can use, and it provides patterns and mechanisms for property inheritance when the older person dies. For many elderly, the family is an economic support unit and a convenient final step in the economic distribution system of the larger society. As such, it provides a context in which some elderly still operate as producers and all function as consumers of goods and services. Its form and level of income even help determine the nature and amount of those goods and services, especially the ones supplied by government.

These and other fundamental functions suggest that the family, flaws and all, still does strategic things for most of the elderly and that they contribute to the institution, though not always in the same ways or as well as before. Therefore, while changes in family relationships may make it seem that older people are largely isolated from kin contacts, a functional analysis actually indicates that families play vital roles for most elderly.[27]

Composition of Elderly Households and Families

The large majority of elderly men are householders (formerly called heads of households), and each unit usually consists of the man and his wife without children. (See Table 4-4.) Thus, in 1980 three-quarters of the men aged 65 and older headed families that included at least one other person, though the proportion dropped off progressively in the years past 65. The rest either lived alone or in domestic units headed by someone else. Most of the last group were living with middle-aged children and their offspring, though only a small fraction of elderly men actually take up residence with children.

About half the women 65 and over also are householders, but mainly because they are living alone, not because they are heads of families containing at least two people. In turn, that high proportion reflects the large percentages of women who are only reported in the census data as householders after their husbands have died. In 1980 about two-fifths of the elderly women were solitary householders, and the proportion increases with age. At the same time, almost half were living in a family setting with at least one relative, usually an elderly husband or adult offspring. The latter arrangement tends to be created, however, only when the elderly person is incapacitated or too old to manage independently, and then the usual host is a middle-aged daughter or daughter-in-law who carries the principal responsibility for the aged person's care. It is far more common for the elderly person to live near that relative and to receive attention and emotional support while maintaining a separate household, generally by preference, though adult children may also hesitate to take an elderly person into the home and thereby sacrifice potential employment and income, social activities, and privacy.[28] The least likely arrangement of all is for the elderly person to live with nonrelatives.

Blacks and whites differ some in the family settings of older people, though the general patterns are the same. Thus, black men are less likely than white men to be householders and are more likely to live alone or with adult children. Black men are also more apt to be living with friends or other nonrelatives, though the incidence is not great for either race. Black women are more likely than white women to be householders but less likely to be living alone or in families they do not head.

Thus, the living arrangements of the nation's elderly are quite varied — probably more so than in any other age group. Nonetheless, the large majority of elderly men and about half the women can still be found in family groups of one kind or another.[29] No matter what the living arrangements, however, it is clear that Americans don't generally abandon their older people, but instead provide emotional support routinely and money and other help when it is needed. Indeed, about 80 per cent of the home care required by elderly people is given by family members and much of the remainder is supplied by friends. Ignored though these contributions may be, they greatly exceed the assistance provided by public funds and personnel. Moreover, the support role of middle-aged offspring will become increasingly important as the proportion of very old people grows, and it will not be unusual for women who are elderly themselves to be looking after an extremely aged parent. Even now about a fourth of the people who have reached age 60 still have one surviving parent,[30] and given the patterns of mortality and the content of social roles, that situation produces a substantial number of elderly women looking after even older women, usually both of them widows. That type of care will probably grow more difficult, however, because an increasing

Table 4-4. Percentages of People 65 and Over With Various Living Arrangements, by Race and Sex, 1980

Living Arrangement	Male	Female
All Races	100.0	100.0
Householder	90.4	52.3
Family Householder	75.0	10.5
Living Alone	14.6	40.8
Living with Nonrelatives	0.8	1.0
Not Householder	9.6	47.7
Living in Families	8.0	46.6
Not in Families	1.6	1.1
White	100.0	100.0
Householder	91.4	51.8
Family Householder	76.5	9.3
Living Alone	14.2	41.6
Living with Nonrelatives	0.7	0.9
Not Householder	8.6	48.2
Living in Families	7.3	47.1
Not in Families	1.3	1.1
Black	100.0	100.0
Householder	83.4	60.0
Family Householder	61.9	22.6
Living Alone	19.5	35.3
Living with Nonrelatives	2.0	2.1
Not Householder	16.6	40.0
Living in Families	13.1	38.4
Not in Families	3.5	1.6

Source: U.S. Bureau of the Census, "Marital Status and Living Arrangements: March 1980," Current Population Reports, P-20, no. 365 (1981), table 6.

share of the women who look after an aged parent are also in the labor force and are responsible for more than one time-consuming commitment. Furthermore, when the baby-boom cohort is quite elderly, the number of adult offspring to look after them will be relatively small, and the problems of dependency will intensify. Therefore, the realities call for more imaginative governmental participation in meeting the needs of the very old, including more workable Medicare provisions, though the major responsibility seems likely to remain with family members.

These dependency patterns ought not to obscure the fact that husbands and wives have longer lives together than ever before and that dependency comes at a later age than in the past. For more than a century the rate at which marriages are dissolved by death has been declining, and despite the large mortality differential between the sexes, much higher percentages of people live longer as couples and delay entry into widowhood.[31] Therefore, the intact family is subject to aging in the same sense that the nation's whole population is aging, and in a growing percentage of American kin relationships adult children have joined their surviving parents in the 65-and-over group.[32]

Sexual Relations

The sexual interests and behavior of the elderly have been studied since the first Kinsey reports,[33] but many of the studies had various methodological problems that tended to obscure the actual sexual behavior of the elderly. The investigations often relied on voluntary reporting and were scarcely representative of the older population. Until the Duke Longitudinal Study, none of the research on sexuality followed the same subjects over time; most of the studies did not control for marital status and, therefore, for the availability of a partner with whom to have sex.[34] For these reasons and because stereotypes die hard, many Americans still assume that older people lack sexual interest or are vulgar, ridiculous, or even dangerous if they retain it. We often perceive sexuality to be an attribute of the young, to diminish sharply in middle age, and to have virtually disappeared when one reaches age 65 or 70. The biases in advertising and the mass media have much to do with that perception, but it is also perpetuated by adult children who can scarcely visualize their parents in a sexual relationship, let alone one parent in a lover relationship with a new mate or a date. Consequently, the myths that surround sexuality among the elderly help to aggravate the lack of intimacy that already troubles many, and some elderly are denied not only sexual relationships, but other expressions of intimacy as well.[35]

The facts about elderly sexuality indicate that many enjoy marital sex well into old age, even the more advanced years, and that good sex in the younger years can become good sex in the later ones. Deteriorating health certainly inhibits the sexuality of some older people, but even in many of those cases medical corrections are possible. Moreover, sexual fulfillment is more constrained by the loss of one's partner and by social pressures and psychological barriers than it is by physical infirmities. It is especially handicapped by the widespread failure to recognize "that sexuality and sexual expression are integral to the integrity of the personality from infancy through old age."[36] In addition, the sexual capability of elderly men seems to wane more than that of elderly women, but partly because of boredom and the fear of failure and not just from physical decline. Moreover, the men seem to regard sexual performance as a basic factor in their well-being, while the women consider it less central to self-confidence and tend to separate it from other aspects of the self.[37] These attitudes do generate considerable anxiety among elderly men about their sexuality, whereas elderly women are more likely to deny and suppress theirs. Both orientations are also strongly influenced by the social expectations and taboos that were attached to sex when today's elderly were young. As a result of these and other factors, many older people do have less interest in intercourse and get less satisfaction from it than when they were younger, and many simply lack the opportunity; thus far, few seem inclined to seek reconditioning to improve sexuality.[38]

Though it is easy to carry these generalizations too far and to ignore the individuals and couples who remain sexually interested and active well beyond age 65, the Duke studies do show that sexual interest, activity, and enjoyment tend to decrease gradually with advancing age, even among people who are still married. The studies also show, however, that about half the men are still sexually active through their mid-70s, half the women are active through their mid-60s, and the bulk of married couples are certainly not asexual, even until their 80s in many cases. For some older people, sexual activity even increases temporarily after age 65, though with advancing age sexual behavior becomes less variable and more homogeneous in the older population, and its frequency declines. Furthermore, among older people who have the opportunity to be sexually active, the level of health has much to do with actual performance. So does socioeconomic status, because those who rank higher on the social class scale tend to be more sexually active than those who place lower,[39] generally because of the better health, greater longevity, and other advantages that accompany higher social status.

Nonfamily Institutionalization

Despite the common notion that throngs of elderly Americans reside in nursing homes and similar nonfamily settings, less than 6 per cent of all people aged 65 and older actually live in institutions. Moreover, certain age groups are disproportionately represented and most are there because they have no spouse, children, siblings, or other intimates who could help look after their daily needs in the community.[40] Thus, the Census Bureau's 1976 study of the nation's institutional population showed that there were about 1 million elderly people in long-term care institutions, well over nine-tenths of them in nursing homes of various sorts. The remainder — less than 40,000 — were in facilities for the physically or psychiatrically impaired or the mentally handicapped, and in other settings besides nursing homes.[41] By 1980 the number in nursing homes had risen to about 1.4 million.[42] Some 60 per cent of the institutionalized elderly reside in private establishments run for profit, another 30 per cent are in private nonprofit places, and the remaining 10 per cent live in publicly supported institutions, most operated by state and local governments.

Characteristics of the Institutionalized Elderly

The people in nursing homes and other institutions are not a cross-section of the total population aged 65 and older, but a group with special characteristics that led to their institutionalization initially. The very old are heavily represented among this group. In 1976 about 62 per cent were at least 80 years of age, whereas people in those advanced years represented only 20 per cent of the total elderly population. Moreover, women make up more than two-thirds of the elderly institutional population. The group also has a very high rate of physical or mental disability that requires constant attention to meet even basic needs and perform routine tasks on a daily basis; perhaps as many as half the residents of nursing homes suffer from mental impairments of various kinds, many of them potentially correctable.[43] That argues for more research on such problems as Alzheimer's Disease in order to return many older people to the community and reduce the cost of their care and the severity of their problems.

The elderly institutional population is also characterized by a substantial scarcity of family members or others to look after them in the community, which means that those living in institutions are quite likely to be unmarried. In fact, about 64 per cent of the institutionalized elderly are widowed, 15 per cent are single, and 5 per cent are divorced or separated, whereas only 15 per cent are married. Furthermore, at least half have no adult children who could help them, and that group accounts for a large share of the older people who admit themselves to institutions. This suggests that the other half do have children who could be of assistance, but in most cases the offspring have already provided help to the older parent and have chosen the nursing home as a last resort, often when care at home has become impossible.

Some older people in institutions could reside with children if the latter wanted them, but they represent a small minority. In the greater number of cases elderly people are institutionalized because they have no family members left or because those members have exhausted their own emotional and physical resources and use institutionalization when they have no alternative. Often they are forced to accept that choice by the older person's degree of impairment and by the type and intensity of care required, for almost 80 per cent of all admissions are for medical conditions, most no longer manageable at home. Furthermore, about 82 per cent of the elderly admitted to nursing homes previously had no access to services, such as food delivery, housekeeping, home health care, and transportation. Given these factors, there is scant support for the assumption that large numbers of adults "dump" their aged parents into nursing homes simply to be rid of them. In fact, about two-thirds of the residents have visitors weekly and less than a tenth have none at all,[44] and visitation is so important that the majority of people cite location as the principal reason for selecting a particular institution.

Future Nursing Home Needs

The size of the elderly institutional population has been increasing rapidly, because both the numbers and proportions of older people have been growing, while the average number of younger relatives to care for each elderly family member has been declining. The increase in the institutional group will continue for a time, because the cohorts born in the Great Depression of the 1930s are relatively small compared with those of the preceding generation. Therefore, people who reach their 50s and 60s in the 1980s and 1990s will have a comparatively heavy burden of support for older people, many with only one adult child or even none to look after them. So a larger share of the elderly, especially as they reach very old age, will have to enter nursing homes and other institutions. Some will have needs that cannot be met at home; others will be only mildly impaired, but will have no one at home to help with daily tasks. Even now, however, there is a shortage of nursing homes, because their numbers and capacity are not growing and their waiting lists are long. Moreover, high interest rates and uncertainty about the future of Medicare and Medicaid funds have delayed needed construction.

As the small cohort of the Depression years enters the older ages, they will have the comparatively large baby-boom cohorts of 1945-1960 to help see to their needs, and each elderly person will have a larger average number of middle-aged children to help provide physical, emotional, and financial support. Therefore, other things being equal, it should be possible for a larger percentage of the elderly to remain at home and part of the community. In turn, it is likely that, briefly, the population admitted to nursing homes and other institutions will grow less rapidly that it has, though it will still grow. Presumably, in the future as now, it will be "the lack of a spouse, adult child, or other relative to help with routine daily tasks and not medical reasons per se that sends many slightly inform older persons to nursing homes."[45]

The longer term future, however, will produce another increase in the need for institutional care. In 2010 the first of the baby-boom people will reach age 65 but will have a comparatively small cohort of adult children to help provide for them, because the birth rate declined significantly after 1960 and reached an all-time low in the mid-1970s. Therefore, the two decades after 2010 will again see a sizable number of the elderly with one child or none to help with daily tasks and routine support. As a result, the population that will have to seek out institutions for care not available in the community will increase, perhaps dramatically.

Before that happens, however, there will be still another group of elderly people who will draw more heavily on resources, including institutions. They are the veterans of World War II and for whom the Veterans Administration already operates a huge, costly health care system. At present, there are about 3.3 million veterans aged 65 and older, but by 1990 there will be 7.6 million,[46] and they will be increasingly in need of medical and other care as they age. Moreover, since 1971, federal law has guaranteed free medical care to veterans 65 and over no matter what their financial condition and whether or not their health problems are service-related.[47] The coming task of caring for these veterans is further complicated by uncertainty about the areas in which they will be living and where the services should be concentrated, though the groups are likely to grow the fastest in the areas with large net in-migration in general. As a result of this impending growth, the needs related to it, and governmental financial commitments already made, the size of the veteran population using governmentally subsidized institutions will increase rapidly and soon, placing a much larger burden on Veterans Administration hospitals, out-patient clinics, nursing homes, and institutional residences. These places will be especially attractive because the quality of care is often superior to that available in other institutional settings.

By 2010, when the new crush of elderly begins, we may have learned that it is cheaper to keep all but the most severely impaired at home and will provide more public assistance to private caregivers — spouses and middle-aged offspring — in order to lessen their personal burdens and the need for expensive institutional care. At present, the large majority of elderly in families are cared for with no agency help, and much of their sustenance costs the public far less per person than does the process of institutionalization. Consequently, there is room for government at various levels to help families sustain the dependent elderly and to make the effort cost-effective. Without such help, more families will have to place the burden of support for their elderly upon public caregivers, and the costs to taxpayers will escalate accordingly.

The objectives of the Older Americans Act of 1965 certainly provide the basis for the necessary federal efforts. Perhaps those endeavors only require more versatile application, better coordination, less duplication, and greater simplicity. One problem now is that the older person must identify the various services needed, search them out in a maze of federal, state, and local agencies, and somehow put together a program that meets his/her needs, so it is hardly surprising that many impaired older people have no real access to the programs that do exist.[48] Some of those people enter nursing homes because it is a simpler, more comprehensible process, even though readily available public aid might allow them to remain in the community. Ideally, the institutional population would consist only of those impaired people who have no friends or others to help them, the ones whose families have too many disabilities or other problems to provide care, and those who are so severely disabled that the emotional and financial costs of care are less in an institution than at home. Such a population would consist even more heavily than it does now of the very old, the chronically ill, and the solitary.

Quality of Care

The growing nursing home population and large governmental subsidies have increased opportunities for promoters and exploiters to enter the business of looking after the elderly in an institutional setting, though the care provided in many homes run by churches, private operators, and others is quite decent. At present there are about 23,000 nursing homes in the United States to house over a million elderly people, most with substantial assistance from taxation of various kinds,[49] and some of the facilities are substandard. In certain cases, conscientious operators are forced to provide less than adequate care because of financial constraints, while others simply exploit the elderly for the highest possible income at the lowest possible cost. A large share of those older people have no one to look after their interests and are at the mercy of profiteering caregivers, which often means inadequate nutrition, poorly paid and incompetent employees, and various deals with physicians and others to maximize income at the expense of the elderly patients. Therefore, while many homes are scrupulously run, many others represent a national scandal that governmental agencies fail to stop.

Trends in Marital Status

During all of the last 100 years, elderly women have been far less likely than elderly men to be married but far more likely to be widowed. Therefore, the high incidence of widowhood is not solely a consequence of medical miracles performed in the last few decades, but a persistent feature in American history. In fact, as shown in Figure 4-2, the fluctuations in the percentages of men and women classified as married have been small since 1890, with only about half as many women as men reporting themselves as married, though the difference between the sexes is a little greater now than in most years since the turn of the century. Furthermore, the proportions of widows and widowers both generally have fallen, though the decline was much faster for the men than for the

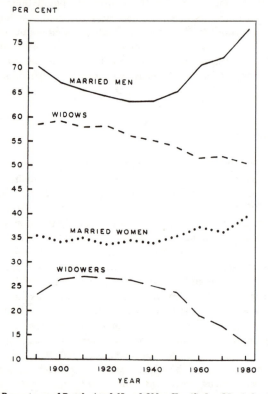

Figure 4-2. Percentages of People Aged 65 and Older Classified as Married or Widowed, by Sex, 1890-1980

Sources: U.S.Bureau of the Census, *U.S. Census of Population: 1960, Characteristics of the Population, U.S. Summary* (1964), table 177; *U.S. Census of Population: 1970, Detailed Characteristics, U.S. Summary* (1973), table 203; "Marital Status and Living Arrangements: March 1980," *Current Population Reports,* P-20, no. 365 (1981), table 1.

women. As a result, while the percentages of widowed people of both sexes are lower than ever, the superabundance of widows relative to the supply of widowers is also greater: In 1890 there were 2.5 widows for each widower, but in 1980 there were 3.8.

Some changes have also occurred in the percentages of elderly men and women classified as single and divorced, though taken together those categories have never accounted for more than 11 per cent of either sex. (See Figure 4-3.) After 1890 the proportions of elderly single people rose steadily until 1940 and then declined because of long-term increases in the marriage rate. It was more likely that those who reached age 65 around 1980 had married than was true of those who became 65 in the 1930s, 1940s, and 1950s. The proportions of elderly men and women classified as divorced (and not remarried) have risen steadily since 1890, and by 1980 the figure for men was more than nine times what it had been at the turn of the century, while that for women was 11 times greater. Those changes reflect radical alterations in the divorce rate in the twentieth century, and the proportions would be significantly higher if the remarriage rate were not much greater for divorced people than for widows and widowers. The incidence of remarriage is greater because divorce generally takes place

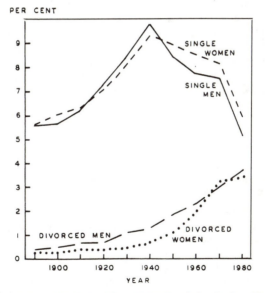

Figure 4-3. Percentages of People Aged 65 and Older Classified as Single or Divorced, by Sex, 1890-1980
Sources: U.S. Bureau of the Census, *U.S. Census of Population: 1960, Characteristics of the Population, U.S. Summary* (1964), table 177; *U.S. Census of Population: 1970, Detailed Characteristics, U.S. Summary* (1973), table 203; "Marital Status and Living Arrangements: March 1980," *Current Population Reports,* P-20, no. 365 (1981), table 1.

much younger than widowhood, and given the prejudice that aging men are more attractive than aging women, the younger divorced woman has a greater competitive advantage in finding a new mate. Furthermore, the many social and psychological barriers to remarriage, discussed earlier, either do not operate at all or are less formidable for many divorced women than for widows. No matter what the specific patterns, however, the steady increase in the percentages of divorced people reflects some of the basic changes in marriage and family during the last several decades, though the higher divorce rate is offset considerably by the relatively high remarriage rate among divorced persons.

Most of these trends apply to both white and black elderly people. Thus, since 1940 the proportions married have increased for both sexes and races, while the percentages widowed have decreased. Moreover, the percentages classified as divorced have risen markedly in all four groups, but especially among black men and women. In the category of single people, however, the races part company: The proportions of white men and women who have never married are considerably lower now than in 1940, while those of black men and women have increased somewhat. It is more significant, though, that the black and white populations are aging in many fundamentally similar ways, including the higher incidence of marriage now than in 1940, the widening mortality differential that produces many more widows than widowers, the higher rate of remarriage among people whose mates have died, and the greater tendency to be divorced. Most of the variations between elderly blacks and whites are a matter of degree rather than of kind, and the demographic similarities, in turn, suggest that the aging populations of both races have more in common socioeconomically than they did in the past.

Summary

Marital status, family relationships, and living arrangements help determine the content of the older years, so one highly significant fact for those reaching age 65 is the rapid decline in the proportion married and the concomitant increase in the percentage widowed, though the pattern varies greatly for men and women. Consequently, the large majority of elderly men are married and living with their wives, whereas the bulk of elderly women are widows with relatively poor statistical chances for remarriage, even when the social and psychological barriers are surmountable. As expected, these demographic realities become more exaggerated in the oldest age groups, though they also vary between blacks and whites, Hispanics and other ethnic groups, and rural and urban inhabitants.

Widowhood, which affects so many elderly women, is a social and psychological phenomenon that persists for most until they die, for remarriage is limited to a small minority. But even though the remarriage rate is far higher in the group of elderly widowers, there are still certain problems owing to the prevailing myths about love, mate selection, and the desirability of the elderly. Nevertheless, most elderly remarriages do seem to succeed, partly because they help people grapple with the experiences of death and isolation. Despite the incidence of widowhood, however, most couples have far more years of life together after the last child leaves home than did their parents and grandparents.

The functions of a family change with time and the older person comes to relate to them differently, but family ties remain significant for most elderly. Contrary to popular myth, the majority are neither isolated from a family context nor abandoned by family members, though it is not usual for an older person to reside with an adult offspring. That is true even for those whose mates have died and who face living alone, for the norm of independence in American society is a powerful one which, along with other factors, militates against the three- or four-generation family living in one household. But residential separation does not necessarily mean abandonment or emotional isolation, and various family bonds do help most elderly persons contend with the realities of the later years. So do sustained sexual interest and dating among some whose mates are gone.

Institutionalization, chiefly in nursing homes, involves no more than 6 per cent of the elderly population — a proportion that also belies the myth of widespread abandonment by adult children. In fact, the institutional population consists largely of people who are disabled to some degree and have no one to help them with daily tasks. They tend to be extremely old and female. Even the ones with children have not been wantonly abandoned to nursing homes, for most are institutionalized as a last resort after continuing their care at home becomes impossible. That often happens because the caregiver — usually a daughter or daughter-in-law — also is elderly and unable to provide what is necessary. For this and other reasons the institutional population can be expected to increase rapidly, at least for a few decades, although better governmental assistance for home care could slow that increase and help contain its costs.

108

NOTES

1. U.S. Bureau of the Census, "Demographic Aspects of Aging and the Older Population in the United States," *Current Population Reports*, P-23, no. 59 (1978): 45.

2. *Ibid.*, pp. 45; 47.

3. Paul C. Glick, "The Future of the American Family," in U.S. Bureau of the Census, *Current Population Reports*, P-23, no. 78 (1979): 1.

4. *Ibid.*

5. Matilda White Riley and Anne Foner, *Aging and Society*, v. 1, *An Inventory of Research Findings*. New York: Russell Sage Foundation, 1968, p. 158.

6. For the data, see United Nations, *Demographic Yearbook, 1980*, table 34.

7. Henry A. Sheldon, *The Older Population of the United States*. New York: Wiley, 1958, p. 90.

8. U.S. Bureau of the Census, "Demographic Aspects of Aging," *op. cit.*, p. 49.

9. Jacquelyne Johnson Jackson, *Minorities and Aging*. Belmont, CA: Wadsworth, 1980, p. 125.

10. *Ibid.*, p. 136.

11. *Ibid.*, p. 137.

12. National Center for Health Statistics, *Vital Statistics of the United States, 1977*, v. 3, *Marriage and Divorce* (1981), table 1-7.

13. U.S. Bureau of the Census, *op. cit.*, p. 47.

14. Helena Znaniecki Lopata, "The Widowed Family Member," in Nancy Datan and Nancy Lohman, eds., *Transitions of Aging*. New York: Academic Press, 1980, p. 107.

15. Lopata, *ibid.*, p. 108.

16. Lucile Duberman, *Marriage and Its Alternatives*. New York: Praeger, 1974, pp. 200-201.

17. Jessie Bernard, *Remarriage*. New York: Dryden Press, 1956, p. 64.

18. Helena Znaniecki Lopata, "Loneliness: Forms and Components," *Social Problems* 17 (1969): 249.

19. Lopata, "The Widowed Family Member," *op. cit.*, p. 95.

20. *Ibid.*, pp. 98-99. Cf. Richard A. Kalish, "Death and Survivorship: The Final Transition," *Annals of American Academy of Political and Social Science*, 464 (1982): 172-173.

21. Alfred P. Fengler and Nicholas Danigelis, "Residence, the Elderly Widow, and Life Satisfaction," *Research on Aging* 4 (1982): 113.

22. Richard A. Kalish, *Late Adulthood: Perspectives on Human Development*. Monterey, CA: Brooks/Cole, 1975, p. 76.

23. Herman J. Loether, *Problems of Aging*. 2nd ed. Belmont, CA: Dickenson, 1975, p. 16.

24. Elaine M. Brody, "The Aging of the Family," *Annals of American Academy of Political and Social Science*, 438 (1978): 23-24. Cf. Ethel Shanas and Marvin B. Sussman, eds., *Family, Bureaucracy, and the Elderly*. Durham, NC: Duke University Press, 1977.

25. See the work on this matter by Ethel Shanas and Gordon F. Streib, eds., *Social Structure and the Family: Generational Relations.* Englewood Cliffs, NJ: Prentice-Hall, 1965.

26. John E. Dono, Cecilia M. Falbe, Barbara L. Kail, Eugene Litwak, Roger H. Sherman and David Siegel, "Primary Groups in Old Age," *Research on Aging* 1 (1979): 405-406.

27. For studies of this matter, see Timothy H. Brubaker, ed., *Family Relationships in Later Life.* Beverly Hills, CA: Sage, 1983.

28. Mary Barberis, "America's Elderly: Policy Implications," *Population Bulletin* 35 (1981): 12. Cf. Fred C. Pampel, "Changes in the Propensity to Live Alone: Evidence from Consecutive Cross-Sectional Surveys," *Demography* 20 (1983): 433-447.

29. Beth J. Soldo, "America's Elderly in the 1980s," *Population Bulletin* 35 (1980): 26.

30. Elaine M. Brody, statement in House Select Committee on Aging, June 4, 1980, "Families: Aging and Changing," p. 56.

31. Riley and Foner, *op. cit.,* pp. 157 and 162.

32. Brody, "The Aging of the Family," *op. cit.,* p. 14.

33. Alfred Kinsey, Wardell Pomeroy and Clyde Martin, *Sexual Behavior in the Human Male.* Philadelphia: Saunders, 1953.

34. Erdman Palmore, *Social Patterns in Normal Aging: Findings from the Duke Longitudinal Study.* Durham, NC: Duke University Press, 1981, pp. 83-84.

35. For a treatment of this matter, see Mary S. Calderone, "Sex and the Aging," in Ronald Gross, Beatrice Gross and Sylvia Seidman, eds., *The New Old: Struggling for Decent Aging.* Garden City, NY: Doubleday, 1978, pp. 205-208.

36. *Ibid.,* p. 206.

37. Ardyth Stimson, Jane F. Wise and John Stimson, "Sexuality and Self-Esteem Among the Aged," *Research on Aging* 3 (1981): 235-236, 237.

38. Fred Cottrell, *Aging and the Aged.* Dubuque, IA: Wm. C. Brown, 1974, p. 47.

39. Palmore, *op. cit.,* pp. 93-94.

40. Soldo, *op. cit.,* pp. 26-27.

41. For the data, see U.S. Bureau of the Census, "1976 Survey of Institutionalized Persons: A Study of Persons Receiving Long-Term Care," *Current Population Reports,* P-23, no. 69 (1978), table II-6.

42. Al Sirroco, "An Overview of the 1980 National Master Facility Inventory Survey of Nursing and Related Care Homes," in National Center for Health Statistics, *Advance Data from Vital and Health Statistics,* no. 91 (1983).

43. Robert N. Butler, "Ageism," in Kurt Finsterbusch, ed., *Social Problems 82/83.* Guilford, CT: Dushkin, 1982, p. 130.

44. U.S. Bureau of the Census, "1976 Survey of Institutionalized Persons," *op. cit.,* p. 268.

45. Soldo, *op. cit.,* p. 27.

46. Paul R. Voss, "The Increasing Ranks of Elderly Veterans: Where They Will Be in 1990," paper presented to the Southern Regional Demographic Group, Greensboro, NC., October 6-8, 1982.

110

47. *Ibid.,* p. 4.

48. Soldo, *op. cit.,* p. 32.

49. Paul B. Horton and Gerald R. Leslie, *The Sociology of Social Problems.* 7th ed. Englewood Cliffs, NJ: Prentice-Hall, 1981, p. 179.

Chapter 5

The Educational Status of the Older Population

When today's elderly people were young, long years of schooling were a less compelling necessity than they are now and more people left school at an earlier age for a variety of reasons. A sizable part of the older population grew up on farms, where the informal apprenticeship system was a major element in one's education, and other people were diverted from additional schooling by World War I. Still others received inadequate formal education because strained family finances caused them to enter the labor force as soon as possible, especially during the Great Depression in the 1930s, or because the quality of teachers and education was comparatively low in many places, especially the rural areas. Consequently, each succeeding cohort has had more educational opportunities than the one preceding, corresponding to the rise in socioeconomic status of the American population, and each has aspired to and actually achieved higher levels of formal education. This has left the present elderly population with a significantly lower level of educational attainment than exists in the adult population as a whole,[1] and has imposed certain disadvantages on many older people.

Immigration also played a part in the relatively low educational standing of elderly people, though its effect is waning significantly. The huge populations of immigrants who came early in the century averaged less schooling than the native-born population and often didn't acquire much more after they arrived. Instead, they had to find unskilled and semiskilled jobs to support themselves and their families, though many did obtain some "night-school" training, mostly to learn English and achieve citizenship. A few even went farther up the educational ladder. As these large groups of foreign-born people became age 65, their higher rates of

111

illiteracy and lower educational attainment helped depress the average educational status of the elderly population, especially the group that is now 75 and over, while that of the younger population was rising rapidly. The disappearance of the old immigrants now, however, helps account for the rapid increase in the level of educational attainment among the elderly, as does the entry into that group of cohorts who are increasingly better schooled. Most of the latter are native born, but even many in the new groups of immigrants are better educated than their predecessors and tend to enter better jobs. Nonetheless, comparatively low levels of formal schooling are still a major characteristic of the nation's older population. In turn, those levels affect the older person's values, his/her views of the economy and the political system, and the way he/she interacts with intimates; it has much to do with one's ability to keep a job or find new work if necessary.[2]

Levels of Educational Attainment

There are several ways to report the educational accomplishments of a population, including the percentages who cannot read or write, the proportions who have acquired some schooling but too little to master basic skills, and the percentages who have completed various higher grades. Ordinarily, the national data on these matters are provided for people who presumably have completed their formal educations — usually those aged 25 and older — and for various groups beyond that age. If we were to study a whole population rather than merely the elderly, we would also be concerned with school enrollment, retention and dropout rates, and other matters applicable to children, teenagers, and traditional college-age people. But an assessment of the older population and how it compares with other adults needs to focus on outputs from the educational process several decades in the past, and requires that we emphasize educational attainment. Therefore, we will consider the proportions of people who have had no schooling and the ones who are illiterate, those who are functional illiterates, and the groups who are eighth-grade, high school, and college graduates. The median level of education also helps differentiate the various groups within the older population.

Median Years of Schooling Completed

The relatively poor educational showing that elderly people make in comparison with younger groups is illustrated in Table 5-1, which uses the amounts of formal schooling attained by men and women in several age categories. In 1982 the total population aged 25 and older had completed an average of 12.6 years of schooling, which made the average person a high school graduate with a few months of college work. But the average person aged 70-74 had finished only 10.9 years of formal education, and the level dropped progressively into the older years. This comparatively poor showing is the culmination of progressive decreases in formal education at each successive level in the age scale from 25 upward. The oldest people are at a particular disadvantage, however, for in 1982 even the average person 65-69 was a high school graduate.

These patterns apply to both major races, though the average educational levels of the black elderly are substantially below those of whites. There are differences between men and women, too, to be discussed later, but in the older years the gender differential within any one race is usually smaller than the variation between the races.

Table 5-1. Percentages of People with Specified Years of Schooling, by Sex and Age, 1982

Sex and Age	Per Cent Completing			Median Years Completed
	8 Years or Less	High School, 4 or More Years	College, 4 or More Years	
Male				
25+	15.7	71.7	21.9	12.6
55-59	18.6	64.4	19.7	12.4
60-64	24.0	59.9	13.7	12.3
65-69	30.9	51.7	13.2	12.1
70-74	40.1	43.0	12.0	10.9
75+	53.1	33.9	10.3	9.4
Female				
25+	15.6	70.3	14.0	12.5
55-59	16.3	67.1	9.5	12.4
60-64	22.6	61.5	8.3	12.3
65-69	27.8	54.2	8.0	12.1
70-74	36.7	46.0	7.9	10.9
75+	47.7	36.1	6.7	9.4

Source: U.S. Bureau of the Census, "America in Transition: An Aging Society," Current Population Reports, P-23, no. 128 (1983), table 10.

Literacy and Illiteracy

The percentages of people who cannot read or write in any language are supposedly so low in the industrialized countries, that data on illiteracy have not been collected in the decennial census of the United States since 1930. The estimates that do exist place about 0.5 per cent of all people aged 14 and older and 1.4 per cent of those aged 65 and older in the illiterate category, although the official data on the matter undoubtedly underestimate the actual magnitude of the problem among all age groups. At the turn of the century, however, about 17 per cent of the people 65 and over were illiterate, with significantly higher rates for women than for men. That compares with only about 11 per cent in the total population aged 15 and over, and indicates that the lower educational standing of the elderly is no recent phenomenon, though the data may also be distorted by deliberate misreporting of illiteracy by persons who are ashamed of their deficiencies,[3] and by assuming that all people who attend high school become literate. In fact, many do not.

Many of today's illiterate elderly have never attended school, but the illiterate population is not the same as the group that has completed no years of schooling. A considerable share of the latter have learned to read and write on their own or in various special programs that are not included in the reports on school grades completed. That is especially true of many foreign-born people, who did use means other than typical schooling to acquire the language skills necessary to function in jobs that facilitated their move up the social scale or at least provided a living. On the other hand, many illiterate people attended some years of school, but either did not learn to read and write or lost the ability they once had.[4] Therefore, while the percentage of elderly people with no formal schooling is similar to the percentage of illiterates, the two groups are not the same. In fact, among all elderly people who have completed no years of schooling, only about half are classified as illiterate.[5]

Functional Illiteracy

The concept of *functional illiteracy* was first used by the Civilian Conservation Corps in the 1930s and by the army during World War II, and now refers to people who have had less than five years of formal schooling.[6] The concept implies that a person has not had even the minimal formal training in basic language and conceptual skills necessary to manage well in a highly complex and sophisticated society, though in this case, too, some people with less than five years of formal schooling are adequately self-educated. Nonetheless, many functional illiterates of all ages appear near the bottom of the social scale, and they usually lack the ability to command even average incomes or occupy any but the most menial jobs.

Functional illiteracy still afflicts just under 10 per cent of the nation's elderly population, compared with less than a third of that percentage in the whole population aged 25 and older. Moreover, the percentage of functional illiterates rises with age, until it is one-eighth of the group aged 75 and older. In fact, the functionally illiterate population is so heavily concentrated among the elderly that nearly half of all people in that educational class are aged 65 and older, even though elderly people make up only 19 per cent of the population aged 25 and over. A substantial part of the functionally illiterate group has had no schooling at all, amounting to well over a half million older people, or nearly 3 per cent of the entire elderly population.

An Eighth-Grade Education

During the years when today's elderly people were young, an elementary school education was regarded much the same way a high school education is viewed now — the minimum amount of schooling necessary for a reasonably informed person. Therefore, in the face of urgent needs to enter the labor force, a very large proportion of the oldest people completed their formal schooling with graduation from the eighth grade, though that level of achievement is now seriously inadequate and very few young people stop their schooling there. (See Table 5-1.) When those eighth-grade graduates are added to the people who left school in even lower grades, it means that well over a third of the elderly population finished their schooling without ever having gone to high school, contrast-with less than 5 per cent of those aged 25-29. In fact, a high school education was so uncommon for today's oldest people, that half those past age 74 acquired only eighth-grade educations or less. The young-old fare better, but even in that group nearly a third did not go past the eighth grade.

High School and College Graduates

If a relatively small proportion of today's elderly entered high school as young people, even smaller shares graduated and only a tiny minority were able to obtain a college education. Thus, less than half the older population managed to graduate from high school, compared with almost nine-tenths of the 25-29 age group, for whom some college training is now the norm. Once again, the old-old are at the greatest disadvantage, for only a third of the group aged 75 and older graduated from high school. The proportion of the nation's oldest people who graduated from college is less than half the percentage among the total population aged 25 and

116

older, and little more than half that among people aged 55-59. The latter comparison shows how rapidly the educational status of the elderly is changing and illustrates the dramatic increases in the share of college graduates among even the young-old. Elderly people are especially unlikely to have post-graduate educations, although that situation also is changing rather quickly.

Summary

Irrespective of the index, the nation's elderly people have lower levels of schooling than cohorts just behind them, and much lower levels than young adults. The wide discrepancies reflect major changes in attitudes about education and the amount of formal training necessary for entry into the jobs that typify post-industrial America. The variations also mirror the nature of education in the United States, for it is seen largely as a tool to enter the labor force and to advance once in it, rather than as a means to intellectual development for its own sake. Therefore, many of today's elderly acquired only the schooling necessary to hold the semiskilled jobs that awaited them, and they could not afford to invest additional time in their educations. Consequently, many of our least educated elderly people have been by-passed by the knowledge explosion of the last few decades, and some are easily exploited because of their relatively unsophisticated formal educations. Quite a few scrape by on inadequate pensions because they lacked the education to obtain high salaried jobs that would have provided larger retirement incomes. Others are able to cope adequately with the realities of a complex society, but sometimes even they must struggle hard because of educational handicaps.

Educational Differentials

Though the elderly population of the United States ranks far below younger groups in their levels of education, it also has some variations internally, including that between men and women, but especially the discrepancy between blacks and whites. The variations reflect distinct differences in socioeconomic advantages and disadvantages, both in the past and at present, for the level of education is one major indicator of social status. They also reflect the historical definitions of social roles performed by the sexes and the races, because each group encountered differences in the expectations about the value of education, the degree of access to schooling, and the quality of the education provided.

Differences Between Men and Women

Elderly women have somewhat higher average levels of education than elderly men, particularly in the oldest ages. (See Table 5-1.) As a consequence, the men are more likely to be functional illiterates or to have finished their formal schooling with the eighth grade, whereas the women are more apt to have graduated from high school, though they are considerably less likely to be college graduates or to have post-graduate educations. On the average, therefore, elderly men are more heavily represented in the lowest and the highest levels of schooling, whereas women are more heavily concentrated among high school graduates. The net result is a somewhat higher average level of schooling for the women.

These patterns reflect several social conditions when today's elderly were in the traditional school ages. Males were more likely to leave school early or never to enter at all, because of the demands placed on many of them as youngsters to find jobs or to help with farm tasks. Girls were more likely to be excused from those necessities, though some were hurried through their educations to marry and fill the traditional roles of women. Moreover, given the social context in which they were reared, the girls often accepted the discipline of schooling more passively than did the boys and were less likely to drop out. The world wars also kept many young men from finishing their schooling, while more young women were able to continue, at least through high school. At the same time, a four-year college education was thought to be more crucial for men than for women, so a much higher proportion of the men who went to college actually graduated, many of them encouraged by governmental subsidies after World War II. The women, on the other hand, more often found husbands in the first few years of college and dropped out to help support their husbands and to start homes and families, partly because the professional opportunities for college-educated women were relatively limited.

Racial Differences

The educational variations between elderly men and women are far smaller than those between the two major races, because the education of today's elderly black people still bears the mark of "separate-but-equal" schools, in which the quality of education was vastly unequal for the races. (See Table 5-2.) The lower levels attained by blacks also show the results of discrimination in a broader sense, for education was available to fewer blacks than whites; it had less relevance to the immediate needs and future orientations of many enmeshed in Southern agriculture; and it required a large investment of time that many blacks could ill afford to let their children make, given the demands of survival. It is not surprising, therefore, that while the average elderly white person has obtained some high school training, the average elderly black was never able to complete the eighth grade, despite the premium that blacks have long placed on education.

The differential disabilities by race are so great that almost a third of the nation's elderly blacks are functional illiterates, compared with only 7 per cent of the whites. Moreover, while a third of the elderly whites never went beyond elementary school, that is true of two-thirds of the older blacks. Conversely, almost half of the whites but less than a fifth of the blacks are high school graduates. Among college graduates the black-white ratio is even more distorted, for 10 per cent of the whites but only 4 per cent of the blacks have finished at least four years.[7] No matter what the index, the black population suffers very profound disadvantages in its levels of schooling when compared with the white group, and the difference is closely tied to broad income differentials between the races and other components of socioeconomic status. The lower levels of education also make older blacks more vulnerable to exploiters and less able to deal with the social system in ways that are to their advantage. Their retirement years are more apt to be economically deprived, because as workers they lacked the education and the "right" skin color to get the better jobs and had to settle for those that paid low wages and accrued very small retirement benefits, if any. Therefore, many in the elderly black population still suffer the consequences of low educational levels, coupled with other results of the punitive racial discrimination of earlier times.

Most of the educational differences by sex appear in both the white and black populations in that elderly women in both groups have higher average levels of schooling than elderly men. But unlike the case among whites, the percentage of college graduates is higher for black women than for black men, though the latter are more likely to have obtained post-graduate degrees. The higher proportion of female college graduates is related to their use of an elementary or secondary teaching career to climb the social ladder, for that was one of the few channels of upward mobility open when today's elderly black women were young. Since that profession called for some higher education, almost always at a black college or university, black women were somewhat more likely than the men to continue their schooling past the secondary level. Many blacks of both sexes, however, have long felt education to be a way out of various social and economic disadvantages,[8] which helps explain the similar proportions of college graduates among black men and women aged 25-29, and the fact that black college enrollments have been rising faster than those of whites. Eventually the results will appear in the educational status of the elderly black population, and the sexes and both major races are likely to converge in average levels of education.

Education and Marital Status

Levels of education differ substantially by marital status and the patterns vary widely for men and women. Thus, among elderly men the lowest average amount of schooling was obtained by those who are widowed, though single and divorced men also have comparatively low levels. In all three groups the average man has completed only the ninth grade or less. Married men, on the other hand, have substantially greater average amounts of formal schooling, though educationally the men still rank significantly below the women in each marital status category. Among women, those who are single have substantially more schooling than any other marital status group, and the average single woman is a

Table 5-2. Percentages of People With Specified Years of Schooling, by Race and Age, 1982

Race and Age	Per Cent Completing			Median Years Completed
	8 Years or Less	High School, 4 or More Years	College, 4 or More Years	
White				
25+	14.7	72.8	18.5	12.6
55-59	14.9	69.1	15.2	12.5
60-64	20.9	63.6	11.4	12.3
65-69	25.9	56.5	10.8	12.2
70-74	35.2	47.6	10.3	11.3
75+	47.3	37.2	8.5	9.4
Black				
25+	24.8	54.9	8.8	12.2
55-59	38.8	35.9	4.9	10.3
60-64	45.4	33.2	3.8	9.7
65-69	59.0	21.0	4.7	8.4
70-74	65.9	18.9	3.0	7.9
75+	74.0	15.4	3.4	6.6

Source: U.S. Bureau of the Census, "America in Transition: An Aging Society," Current Population Reports, P-23, no. 128 (1983), table 10.

high school graduate with a few months of college study. Widows have the lowest levels of education, while married women and those who are divorced share the same level, intermediate between those who are single and those who are widowed.

What are some of the reasons for these differences, especially the relatively high educational levels of single women? When today's elderly people were young, marriage usually ended a woman's formal schooling as she assumed home duties and family roles on a full-time basis. Therefore, the woman who did not marry had a better chance to continue in school. At the same time, the wish for more education also caused some women to postpone marriage, and a share of them never married at all. In both cases, however, education and marriage proved mutually exclusive for many of today's elderly women, and schooling usually stopped in the same year that marriage took place. Men were not quite as likely to terminate their educations after marriage, so the highest levels of education are found not among single men, but those who are married and whose wives often worked to help them through college. Furthermore, the higher average age at first marriage among men allowed them about two additional years in which to continue with schooling before assuming domestic responsibilities. Not many people of either sex, though, seem to have been permanently deterred from marriage by having a particular level of schooling, for the percentages of men and women who eventually married vary only a little from one educational level to another.

The low levels of education in the elderly widowed populations of both sexes are closely associated with general socioeconomic status. The older people who are poor or who come from poor backgrounds generally received the smallest amounts of schooling when they were young, either because it seemed unrelated to their needs or because they had to seek jobs as soon as possible, though for some it simply was not available. In many cases, the quality of education was low anyway and did little to encourage continued attendance, particularly if families didn't see much value in it. Now many of those same people are still relatively poor and they have higher rates of widowhood at earlier ages than the more affluent members of the older population. Therefore, widows and widowers of both races are the most poorly educated of the marital status categories. In addition, the proportions of widowed people are much higher in the oldest ages than in those just past 65, and the older the group, the lower its average level of education.

Trends in Education

The educational attainment of elderly Americans is rising quite rapidly, just as it has been for the total population, because younger people with more schooling are aging into the 65-and-over group and the older ones with less education are dying.[9] Moreover, the various age groups will become more alike in educational achievement, for the rate of improvement among people under age 65 is slowing down and the more rapid advances among the elderly will allow the schooling gap to close, perhaps in 10 years or so. Graduation from high school and some college training is the median level of attainment now for people between age 65 and 69, and within a decade or so it will probably be so far those aged 70 and older as well. It is necessary to remember, though, that the median figure divides the population in half and that many in the lower half will still be poorly educated, some of them in the ranks of functional illiterates, premature dropouts, and unlearned victims of "social promotion." In that sense, there will still be ample challenge to educate many adults.

The progress that is occurring represents dramatic reductions in illiteracy among the elderly population, from 17 per cent in 1900 to 1.4 per cent now. This seems to portend its virtual elimination, because those unable to read and write are more heavily concentrated than ever before among the oldest people, who will soon die. But there are still substantial numbers of illiterates to replace them, despite educational improvements in the population as a whole, and significant numbers if not percentages of the future elderly population will be illiterate if there are not improvements in educational achievement among younger people.

The rapid rise in educational standing among older people is also reflected in all of the other indexes that are used to measure attainment. For example, the median years of schooling of the population aged 65-69 rose from 8.2 in 1940 to 12.1 at present as a result of substantial increases among blacks and whites and men and women, though the four groups improved at different rates. Furthermore, people aged 65-69 experienced greater improvement than their elders, especially between 1970 and 1982. (See Table 5-3.) Much of that rapid change is due to better-educated younger people entering the 65-69 age range and to losses of the more poorly schooled old immigrants, people with farm backgrounds, and unskilled and semiskilled workers in early twentieth-century industries. The improvements are showing up in the age groups above 70 as well, basically for the same reasons, though the rate of change is slower than among people aged 65-69. The trends suggest that all groups of older people will soon have far higher average levels of schooling than their predecessors, but also that the rate of improvement will slow down considerably, because that has already happened in much of the population under age 65.

122

Trends by Sex

The rates of educational improvement during much of the 1940-1982 period were greater for women than for men, but by the latter year the only significant difference in median years of schooling was that between the oldest men and women. In the ages 65-69 there was no variation, and as the present oldest groups disappear, so will the sex discrepancy in levels of education. (See Table 5-3.) Nevertheless, women are still less likely than men to be functional illiterates or merely eighth-grade graduates, while they are more likely to be high school graduates or to have attained one to three years of college. Older men are still significantly

Table 5-3. Changes in the Median Years of School Completed, by Sex and Age, 1940-1982

Sex and Age	1940	1950	1960	1970	1982
Male					
25+	8.6	9.0	10.3	12.1	12.6
55-59	8.2	8.4	8.7	10.7	12.4
60-64	8.2	8.3	8.5	9.6	12.3
65-69	8.1	8.1	8.3	8.8	12.1
70-74	8.0	8.0	8.1	8.6	10.5
75+	7.7	7.9	8.0	8.3	8.9
Female					
25+	8.7	9.6	10.7	12.1	12.5
55-59	8.4	8.6	9.0	11.1	12.4
60-64	8.3	8.4	8.7	10.4	12.3
65-69	8.2	8.3	8.5	9.1	12.1
70-74	8.2	8.3	8.4	8.8	10.9
75+	8.1	8.2	8.3	8.6	9.4

Sources: U.S. Bureau of the Census, U.S. Census of Population: 1950, Detailed Characteristics, U.S. Summary (1953), table 115; U.S. Census of Population: 1960, Detailed Characteristics, U.S. Summary (1964), table 173; U.S. Census of Population: 1970, Detailed Characteristics, U.S. Summary (1973), table 199; "America in Transition: An Aging Society," Current Population Reports, P-23, no. 128 (1983), table 10.

more likely to be college graduates, but that gap between the sexes is diminishing. It will widen again, however, at least for awhile, because the proportion of women aged 40-59 with four or more years of college is scarcely more than half that of men. In the age group under 40 the proportions of college graduates in both sexes are more nearly alike, and in the ages 25-29 about a quarter of the men and a fifth of the women have completed four or more years of college. Therefore, when those people eventually reach 65, the male-female gap at the highest level of schooling will narrow again, though men will still have some advantage. By that time the average man and woman aged 65-69 will be a high school graduate with at least one year of college.

Trends by Race

The huge educational disadvantage experienced by elderly black people in the United States has been diminishing rapidly and their average levels of education are more like those of whites than they were in 1940. In that year, for example, the median years of schooling completed by blacks aged 65-69 was far less than half that for whites, but by 1982 the difference had been reduced to less than a third. (See Table 5-4.) Black women experienced an especially rapid rate of improvement, making their pace of increase in median years of schooling the greatest of the four race and sex categories. Elderly black people were not able to overcome functional illiteracy at the same rate as white people, however, owing to the great educational disadvantages when the former were young. Moreover, while the percentage of older whites who completed their eductions with the eighth grade dropped between 1940 and 1982, that of blacks rose, because even that modest level of educational attainment represents an improvement over the high rates of illiteracy and functional illiteracy that prevailed in 1940. Beyond the eighth-grade level, older blacks have also moved ahead rapidly, for the percentage of high school graduates has increased faster for blacks than for whites, as has that of college graduates, including people who go on to post-graduate education. Thus, every index shows that the elderly black population has progressed faster than the white segment in raising the level of education, though blacks had a far greater initial disadvantage to overcome.

As a result of these improvements, the older members of both races have converged some in educational standing, though the blacks still rank substantially below the whites on every measure. Furthermore, black women have been making faster progress than black men, thereby adding to their initial educational advantage over the men. Thus, at each census since 1940, elderly black women have been less represented than black men in the group of functional illiterates and they are rising out of that low status at a faster rate. The women are more likely to have gone to college and to have finished four years than are the men; the women are even enjoying more rapid increases in the percentages who obtain college and post-graduate degrees. Therefore, given these changes, elderly black men remain the least well-educated group in American society, and while their levels are rising faster than those of whites, who are already much better educated on the average, they are not keeping pace with the improvements among black women.

Table 5-4. Changes in the Median Years of School Completed, by Race and Age, 1940-1982

Race and Age	1940	1950	1960	1970	1982
White					
25+	8.8	9.6	10.8	12.1	12.6
55-59	8.4	8.6	9.0	11.3	12.5
60-64	8.3	8.4	8.7	10.4	12.3
65-69	8.2	8.3	8.5	9.3	12.2
70-74	8.2	8.3	8.4	8.9	11.3
75+	8.1	8.2	8.3	8.6	9.4
Black					
25+	5.8	6.9	8.3	9.8	12.2
55-59	4.7	5.5	6.5	8.1	10.3
60-64	4.4	5.1	6.0	7.5	9.7
65-69	3.8	4.3	5.2	6.6	8.4
70-74	2.8	4.1	5.2	6.0	7.9
75+	1.2	3.3	4.9	5.7	6.6

Sources: U.S. Bureau of the Census, U.S. Census of Population: 1950, Detailed Characteristics, U.S. Summary (1953), table 115; U.S. Census of Population: 1960, Detailed Characteristics, U.S. Summary (1964), table 173; U.S. Census of Population: 1970, Detailed Characteristics, U.S. Summary (1973), table 199; "America in Transition: An Aging Society," Current Population Reports, P-23, no. 128 (1983), table 10.

Some Projections

As each younger cohort with its higher level of education moves into the elderly group, the overall average in the older population will continue to rise dramatically, though not indefinitely. At the same time, the rise in educational attainment will slow considerably among people under age 65, because some age groups are already getting about all the formal schooling it is practical to obtain, and that fact will help narrow the educational gap between older and younger Americans.

All of the people who will reach age 65 in the first several decades of the twenty-first century are now alive, and most of those 25 and over have obtained the bulk of formal education they will ever receive. Therefore, as each cohort enters the older category in the future, the average levels of education in that older group will be approximately the one which exists now in the several younger cohorts. In fact, it will even be a little higher, because the people with the poorest educations also tend to have the highest death rates and are least likely to seek more schooling as adults. These realities make it possible to project the median years of schooling among elderly people until 2020, when the group aged 25-29 in 1980 will have reached the ages 65-69. Table 5-5 provides the data on this matter.

The deficiencies in education among older people will continue to decrease through the period and the medians will rise, but not at the rates that prevailed between 1960 and 1980. Therefore, by 1990 the educational gap between people aged 65-69 and all those who are younger will have narrowed very significantly, though the elderly will still remain somewhat behind the younger population and the oldest groups will lag most severely. Moreover, the educational differential between the sexes will decrease and men may even hold a slight advantage, largely because they are still more likely than women to complete college and to seek postgraduate educations. By 2020, however, the average person aged 65-69 of each sex will be a high school graduate with a year or so of college education.

Black and white elderly people also will grow more alike in levels of schooling, as the oldest blacks with the severest educational handicaps are replaced by younger ones whose formal schooling has increased greatly in the past couple of decades. It will be at least 2000, though, before the average black person aged 65-69 will be a high school graduate. White men and women will become more similar in average levels of schooling, as will blacks of both sexes, though white men are apt to hold a slight lead over white women, while black women will probably retain a slight edge over black men.

All of the trends and projections suggest that the huge educational disadvantage of elderly people relative to younger ones will diminish sharply and that the large proportions of poorly schooled older Americans will not be duplicated in future generations. Nonetheless, even though serious educational deficiencies among the elderly may not be permanent, they will still affect a sizable share of that group, especially people 75 and over, for several years, while some in all of the elderly ages will continue to need additional education. But even if better continuing education were provided for those people, it would come too late for many because their ability to contend with reality was shaped long ago, and some will be unable to overcome many of the educational deficiencies of that time. Many also lack the self-confidence that would enable them to capitalize on additional education, tending instead to accept current constraints as inevitable. But there is a significant population of older people who can stretch their intellects, learn new skills and ideas, and expand their ability to manipulate their immediate environments. For them, adult education is a large-scale need not being fully met, and it remains for colleges and universities to compensate for the decling pool of traditional-age students by providing more useful and attractive services to older adults. That will long be so.

Table 5-5. Projections of Median Years of School Completed by Cohorts Reaching Age 65-69 in Specified Years, by Race and Sex

Race and Sex	1990	2000	2010	2020
All Races				
Male	12.4	12.5	12.8	13.0
Female	12.3	12.4	12.6	12.8
White				
Male	12.5	12.6	12.8	13.2
Female	12.4	12.5	12.6	12.9
Black				
Male	8.9	11.8	12.5	12.5
Female	9.7	11.7	12.3	12.6

Source: U.S. Bureau of the Census, "Educational Attainment in the United States: March 1979 and 1978," Current Population Reports, P-20, no. 356 (1980), table 1.

Educational Needs of the Elderly

The relationship betwen aging and education really involves three aspects: (1) education of people at all ages about the process of aging; (2) education of specialists who will work closely with the elderly and their needs; and (3) education of older people themselves, especially continuing education through all of the later years.[10] Important as the first two are, in this section we will focus on the educational needs of the elderly themselves.

Why Educate the Elderly?

It is too easy to regard the progress in educational levels among older people as an excuse to write off the present group of poorly schooled elderly. In fact, many of those inadequately educated people will be around for a decade or more and some will be replaced by other elderly with educational deficiences, for not all younger people are receiving adequate educations. Consequently, insufficient schooling will continue to work to the disadvantage of many older *individuals* even in the time when *average* levels come to resemble those of the total population. Those for whom levels of education remain low are heir to various social problems, because they are the most likely to suffer from poor health, improper nutrition, inadequate housing, fear of crime, exploitation, and loneliness, though the cause-and-effect relationships of these factors are very complex. Moreover, the deficient educational standing of many elderly persons originally forced them into unskilled and semiskilled jobs that later produced very small or even no retirement benefits, and there is every reason to re-educate at least some of them for jobs that will supplement incomes and diminish that initial handicap. Low levels of education even reduce the ability of older people to seek help with their problems, because it is difficult for the least educated to find out about assistance and to contend with the agencies that supply it.[11] In short, the social, technical, and financial resources of many older people are insufficient to meet the demands of a complex society,[12] and education is one fundamental way to enhance those resources. Moreover, as the proportion of workers in their 50s and beyond increases, the society will need to modernize their skills if those people are to maintain their productivity or switch to new jobs in order to help maintain a healthy economy.[13]

Low levels of education also contribute to inadequate self-confidence for many older people, whereas the better-educated ones tend to be more positive about themselves and to have greater confidence in their mental and physical abilities.[14] Many of the poorly educated have little faith in their ability to make decisions and they become cautious and even withdrawn, partly because they lack the information and skills necessary to function in a contemporary culture that requires many sophisticated decisions. In fact, a substantial part of the aging process for many elderly people is progressive social disengagement,[15] in which a lack of confidence in one's ability to interact productively plays a large part, though not all older people succumb to it. Considering that more than a third of today's elderly never got past the eighth grade, it isn't surprising that many lack confidence in their own abilities, despite decades of experience and productivity.

Few of the learning problems that elderly people encounter seem to result from decreases in the level of intelligence, for the ability to learn declines less with aging than was formerly thought and fewer specific areas are subject to such reductions.[16] The declines that do occur tend to come very late in life and often as a result of illness, such as Alzheimer's Disease. Therefore, the limited skill level of many elderly people, which reduces their ability to make productive use of their innate intelligence, is largely a consequence of the social rather than the physiological process of aging.

Some older people with those limitations need new skills to cope with life, while others require more satisfactory ways to use the skills they have, along with additional opportunities to be useful. The potential in this area is so great that some of the gradual wasting that often accompanies aging could be reduced or even largely undone if adequate education were available for the elderly.[17] Even the physiological declines associated with aging, such as those involving sensory abilities and physical mobility, need not reduce the motivation or ability to learn new things, to remember, and to respond intelligently, for those are the real keys to educational success among older people.[18] Consequently, education for the elderly can provide better skills to cope with daily living, create new ways to employ the skills one has, and overcome some of the psychological constraints that may accompany the aging process. Additional education is particularly useful to the individual if he/she believes it will improve status or ability, whereas those who feel they can achieve no higher level generally lose much of the incentive for additional learning as they age.[19] Thus, the prospect of a tangible payoff is strategic if the older person is to seek additional education.

Education is also one way to deal with the personal tragedies that come to most elderly people. When a spouse is seriously ill or dies, new activities may produce some relief and solace, and the very involvement in an educational program can be one of those new activities, regardless of the precise things one learns. But some educational experiences also provide coping skills directly, and can be far more than just a way to stay busy.

Responses to the Need for Education

To deal with some of these needs, there is a relatively new movement in education that has impelled one of every five colleges and universities toward education for older adults.[20] Most of the programs, which are free of grades and formal degrees as credentials to enter the labor force, involve learning for its own sake. In that respect, the adult programs have a basic component that has been uncommon in American education,[21] for they encourage learning as a process rather than as the expedient accumulation of information.[22] They also help older adults overcome the obsolescence of some of their early education, obtained when the content of schooling differed markedly from what it is now. In fact, not only are older adults poorly educated relative to younger groups, but some aspects of their educations are so remote in time as to be irrelevant.[23] Moreover, not all of what one needs for a lifetime can possibly be learned in 12 or 16 years of schooling, recent or not. Therefore, adult education programs can also streamline the knowledge that elderly people are using, thereby supplementing rich experiences that facilitate interpretation and adaptation, and encouraging the concept of lifetime learning. The growth of such programs also tends to accelerate as the average level of schooling of the elderly rises, because the more education a person has, the more likely he/she is to seek additional training,[24] whether in formal schooling, self-education, or other endeavors. Thus, because each successive cohort has more education than the one just before it, each is also more apt to get involved in adult education programs, and there is every prospect the latter will grow substantially.

In order to provide a rationale for the emerging programs and especially to articulate specific needs, in 1980 the National Council on the Aging formulated several recommendations for educators and governments, based on the assumption that the elderly will become increasingly interested in educational opportunities.[25] They are intended to do the following:

1. Promote the concept of lifelong learning.
2. Create opportunities specifically suited to older people that educate them not merely in tangible skills, but in "the arts and humanities, self-development, retirement-related skills and knowledge, civic issues and advocacy techniques, and career education in human services (particularly services to the elderly)."[26]
3. Provide education for the elderly at little or no cost in order to compensate for the fixed incomes on which many live.
4. Use settings apart from the normal classroom in order to bring education to the places where elderly people congregate, such as churches and senior centers.
5. Encourage school systems to use specialists in education for older people.

6. Promote research on the variable educational needs of older people in different ethnic groups and classes.

7. Introduce into high school and college curricula, courses on the aging of persons and the whole population.

If these recommendations are followed, many of the needs and interests of the elderly will be met by offerings that help overcome their educational liabilities, and knowledge of the aging process will become a sufficiently pervasive part of the whole educational system for the community to grow more aware of the needs of elderly people.[27] Both accomplishments would reduce substantially the educational gap that now separates much of the older population from many younger groups. The formal educational levels among younger people might still remain higher than those among the elderly, but the absolute deficiencies of many older people would diminish significantly and the two groups would have a better basis for communication to minimize the age clash that may well accompany the rising burden of support for the growing elderly population. Comprehensive adult education has a role to play in these areas, especially in a rapidly changing society where time renders the formal education of any generation partly obsolete long before that generation dies, no matter how effective the schooling may have been initially. In that sense, adult education will be necessary not just for the present group of elderly who were relatively poorly educated as youth, but for upcoming generations of older people who received much better schooling but who will need to remain current. That will be especially important for older workers who wish to stay in the labor force, though timeliness is a significant social skill for others as well.[28]

For the elderly or any other group, education needs to be continuous in order to hone intellectual skills. Given the tendency to perceive schooling only as a tool one acquires to enter the labor force, education is often viewed as something to be "done with," and many elderly see themselves beyond the time when education can be "useful." Therefore, education for them needs to be a lifelong process that provides not employment primarily, but insight into the aging process itself and the equipment necessary to carry on a range of activities in the older years. Moreover, if older people are to seek and use continuing education, they need a high chance of success in those endeavors, partly because failure would further shake the self-confidence of many and discourage them from additional educational efforts.[29]

They must also perceive a need for the education. That is more common among better-educated older people than among the poorly educated who actually have the greatest need. The latter often feel useless and unwanted, and while education might help restore their sense of personal worth, they are the ones least motivated to return to school. Therefore, continuing education should provide not just classes, but also a way to catch the interest and imagination of the elderly and to give them a clear picture of the benefits to be obtained from re-entry into the educational process. Once that is accomplished, continuing education can teach the skills and insights to help make the elderly feel more needed, useful, and positive about themselves, and can improve the chances that their new skills and interests actually will produce suitable rewards.[30] The elderly are too valuable a resource to be wasted because of inadequate education and the disabilities it imposes, and much of that waste can be reduced with appropriate motivation, educational programs that meet real needs, and satisfying rewards for educational pursuits.[31]

Summary

Elderly people have significantly lower average levels of education than younger ones, because they bear the imprint of a time when education was less available, less valued, and less important than the need to earn wages. In addition, the large immigrant population of the early twentieth century usually had little schooling, and they still affect the educational standing of the oldest people. In turn, deficient education tends to aggravate other problems, and many elderly lack the basic skills to cope successfully with a complex society and even the aging process itself. Consequently, even though the level of education is rising rapidly as better-educated cohorts age into the elderly category, there are still large numbers of older Americans whose lives are seriously constrained by their poor educational levels.

The elderly make a relatively poor showing on all of the measures of educational status: They average fewer years of schooling completed than do younger people; they are more likely to be illiterates or functional illiterates; they are less likely to have completed the eighth grade or to have graduated from high school or college. As a result, the vast expansion of knowledge, computerization, and robotics has by-passed many, while others have educations that are too obsolete to allow them useful access to these changes. Some are disengaged from all but the narrowest of social interaction and lack even the social, psychological, and technical skills to resist exploiters, understand available services, or plan meaningful activities. That group is at once most in need of continuing education and least likely to obtain it, partly because the better-educated elderly are the ones who seek even more training.

Within the older population, women have somewhat higher average levels of education than men because fewer women have eighth-grade educations or less, while more are high school graduates and have attended college. The men, however, are more likely to have finished college. Blacks have far lower educational levels than whites, owing largely to the old segregated, low-quality school systems and to the lesser relevance that education had for blacks in the rural South.

The level of formal schooling among America's elderly is rising very rapidly as younger, better-educated cohorts reach age 65. Consequently, the gap between the various age groups has narrowed substantially and will nearly disappear within a decade or so. This progress represents major reductions of illiteracy, a dramatic decline in functional illiteracy, and a significant increase in the proportions of older people with high school and college educations. The improvements were especially marked after 1960 as younger people became 65 and the oldest groups, containing many with immigrant or farm backgrounds, lost members. Furthermore, the rate of improvement has been greater for blacks than for whites, which is gradually decreasing the educational gap between these races. In the first two decades of the next century, most of the great educational differences between them may well become minor, though elderly whites will still have a slight advantage.

Despite the improvements, many older persons still have important needs that can be met by continuing education, provided it is geared to those needs and the elderly can be motivated to use it. If so, education can help older people overcome various social problems that often accompany aging and can contribute to a stronger self-image. In fact, part of the presumed process of aging itself, including indecisiveness, caution, withdrawal, and a feeling of uselessness, can be moderated by meaningful education that provides new skills and helps the older person understand the aging process. Too many older people have wasted away intellectually, not because of declines in their native intelligence, but because they have become obsolete. In a society that deplores obsolescence and readily affixes that label, continuing education has a high mission to save many of the elderly for a better fate.

NOTES

1. U.S. Bureau of the Census, "America in Transition: An Aging Society," *Current Population Reports*, P-23, no. 128 (1983): 21.

2. Lowell Eklund, "Aging and the Field of Education," in Matilda White Riley, John W. Riley, Jr. and Marilyn E. Johnson, eds., *Aging and Society*, v. 2, *Aging and the Professions*. New York: Russell Sage Foundation, 1969, p. 325.

3. John K. Folger and Charles B. Nam, *Education of the American Population*. Washington, DC: U.S. Government Printing Office, 1967, p. 122.

4. *Ibid.*, pp. 125-126.

5. U.S. Bureau of the Census, "Illiteracy in the United States: November 1969," *Current Population Reports*, P-20, no. 217 (1971): 9.

6. Folger and Nam, *op. cit.,* p. 126.

7. U.S. Bureau of the Census, "America in Transition...," *op. cit.,* pp. 21-22.

8. Paul E. Zopf, Jr., *Population: An Introduction to Social Demography.* Palo Alto, CA: Mayfield, 1984, p. 376.

9. U.S. Bureau of the Census, "America in Transition...," *loc. cit.*

10. Irving L. Webber, "The Educable Aged," in J.C. Dixon, ed., *Continuing Education in the Later Years.* Gainesville, FL: University of Florida Press, 1963, p. 14.

11. Beth J. Soldo, "America's Elderly in the 1980s," *Population Bulletin* 35 (1980): 19.

12. Webber, *op. cit.,* p. 15.

13. Robert L. Clark, Juanita Kreps and Joseph J. Spengler, "Aging Population: United States," in John A. Ross, ed., *International Encyclopedia of Population.* v. 1. New York: Free Press, 1982, p. 38.

14. Louis Harris & Associates, "Myths About Life for Older Americans," in Ronald Gross, Beatrice Gross and Sylvia Seidman, eds., *The New Old: Struggling for Decent Aging.* Garden City, NY: Doubleday, 1978, p. 103.

15. Kurt W. Back and Kenneth J. Gergen, "Cognitive Constriction in Aging and Attitudes Toward International Issues," in Ida Harper Simpson and John C. McKinney, eds., *Social Aspects of Aging.* Durham, NC: Duke University Press, 1966, p. 323. Cf. Elaine Cumming and William E. Henry, *Growing Old: The Process of Disengagement.* New York: Basic Books, 1961.

16. Robert N. Butler, "Ageism," in Kurt Finsterbusch, ed., *Social Problems 82/83.* Guilford, CT: Dushkin, 1982, p. 128.

17. Eklund, *op. cit.,* p. 324.

18. *Ibid.,* pp. 331; 333.

19. Matilda White Riley and Anne Foner, *Aging and Society.* v. 1, *An Inventory of Research Findings.* New York: Russell Sage Foundation, 1968, p. 440.

20. Ronald Gross, "I Am Still Learning," in Gross, Gross and Seidman, *op. cit.,* p. 364.

21. *Ibid.*

22. Eklund, *op. cit.,* p. 327.

23. Riley and Foner, *op. cit.,* p. 116.

24. *Ibid.,* p. 117.

25. The recommendations are adapted from National Council on the Aging, "NCOA Public Policy Agenda," *Perspective on Aging* 9 (1980): 28-29.

26. *Ibid.,* p. 29.

27. Joseph Drake, *The Aged in American Society.* New York: Ronald Press, 1958, p. 397.

28. Joseph J. Spengler, "Some Economic and Related Determinants Affecting the Older Worker's Occupational Role," in Simpson and McKinney, *op. cit.,* p. 13.

29. Eklund, *op. cit.,* pp. 335-336.

30. *Ibid.,* pp. 338-339.

31. One approach to education for older people is Patricia Harper Apt and Roger Heimstra, "A Model for Learning Resource Networks for Senior Adults," *Educational Gerontology* 5 (1980): 163-173.

Chapter 6

Work Characteristics
Of the Elderly

The work roles of elderly people, especially men, have changed substantially in the twentieth century, and the large majority have become a non-working population. In 1900, for example, more than two-thirds of the men aged 65 and older were still in the labor force, because both the economic system and their families needed them to be producers and there were few alternatives, while at present less than one-fifth are in the work force. Moreover, older people make up a steadily declining proportion of the whole working population and now account for less than 4 per cent of all employed. At the same time, the opportunity and pressure to retire have both increased, and large numbers leave the labor force because they want and can afford more leisure, while others are forced out by mandatory retirement provisions.[1] Some others suffer health problems that cause them to stop working. Furthermore, there is some pressure from younger workers for older ones to make way and it contributes to the substantial increase in the retired population; that pressure is often a factor in the mandatory retirement provisions negotiated by industries and unions. Despite various negative consequences and the need to make adjustments, however, the elderly generally have positive attitudes about retirement, unless income is a significant problem, and a sense of job deprivation seems less common than popular myth would have it.[2]

As a result of the rapidly growing retired population, including many who have not yet reached age 65, there is a heavy financial load on pension systems and the people who must underwrite them now and in the future, sometimes creating crises in those systems, including Social

Security.[3] It is a burden the society imposes on itself because of forced retirement policies, but one we may be unable to afford much longer as a financial constraint, a waste of skills and experience, and a form of discrimination against those elderly persons who need jobs to earn adequate incomes.

This situation is currently under close scrutiny, partly in light of the limited job opportunities for young workers who also need to be accommodated in the labor force, and partly as a result of the Social Security crisis. Certainly a more rational sorting process is needed in which those older people who are able and wish to work can continue without stigma, penalty, or pressure to retire; change in the mandatory retirement age is a step in that direction. At the same time, larger proportions of workers are choosing to retire early, mostly at age 62 but sometimes earlier, although that trend was slowed by the recession and inflation of the late 1970s and early 1980s. If the trend picks up again, however, it may precipitate substantial increases in the minimum age to receive Social Security benefits in order to keep the older worker on the job, perhaps until age 68 or 70, not just 67 as now projected for 2027. But such a change would be contrary to the preferences of workers who wish to retire earlier and would reduce the job opportunities for younger people, especially first-time entrants into the work force and those whose lack of seniority makes them the first fired during layoffs. Some of these dilemmas have come about because the work ethic has relaxed for many people and because retirement programs make it financially attractive to retire early, while changes in birth and death rates have enlarged the numbers and proportions of older workers available to claim retirement benefits.

Thus, even though work roles no longer have the same meaning they had when today's elderly entered the labor force, a large share of older people must survive on significantly lower incomes than the wages they earned, many because they have been cut off involuntarily from the opportunity to work. For some that severance causes feelings of uselessness, a decline in self-confidence, and uncertainty as they are converted from producers to pensioners. Their problems also tend to be reinforced by the larger society, which assumes that the aging process makes a person an ineffective or a hazardous employee, even though the older worker is usually able to meet existing occupational demands and adapt to new ones, provided he/she is appropriately rewarded. Furthermore, there is a tendency to overestimate the problems of retired people and to underestimate their successful adjustments, and to ignore the large proportions who prefer retirement to employment, including many who were forced out of their jobs.

Older People in the Labor Force

Participation Rates

A nation's potential labor force, or economically active population, includes all people who are available by age or other criteria to be employed in organized economic endeavors,[4] whether or not they are actually working. The actual labor force is the proportion of that group who are employed and the ones who are unemployed but actively seeking work. In the United States the labor force consists of all people aged 16 and over who are employed in civilian jobs, those who are unemployed but available for work, and members of the armed services,[5] though we will focus on civilians. Within that group, the elderly labor force consists of people aged 65 and older who meet the other criteria, though part of our analysis will also refer to people aged 55-64, because changes in work roles often take place during those years.

Moreover, the *labor force participation rate* of the elderly is a ratio of the number actually in the labor force to the total population aged 65 and over. In 1981, for example, 3 million of the 25 million noninstitutionalized elderly were still in the labor force, producing a rate of 12 per cent. That figure represents a steady decline from the younger ages. Among men, labor force participation reaches a peak of 95 per cent in the ages 35-44 and then drops steadily, while among women in those ages it rises to 70 per cent and then declines, though the patterns do differ by race. (See Figure 6-1.) Until the mid-1970s, women's participation fell during the childrearing years and then rose to another peak in the late 30s and early 40s,[6] but those fluctuations have now diminished and the rate remains relatively steady in the ages 20-44 and then begins to decline. For men, the participation rate remains relatively high through their 50s and then begins its downward plunge, largely because of voluntary retirements, though some men are unable to work for various reasons. (See Table 6-1.) For women, the participation rate falls significantly by age 60. In 1981 these changes left 1.8 million elderly men and 1.2 elderly women in the labor force, but the participation rates of both sexes were quite low compared with those of younger people. Many elderly of both sexes who are still working are employed in low-paying, low-status jobs, mostly because they need the income,[7] though some are also self-employed or high-salaried people of considerable value to their employers, and who work beyond the age when most others retire.

The official participation rates actually underestimate the numbers and proportions of older people who work for wages during the year. The data on labor force involvement reflect the number of jobs filled at the time the surveys are taken, but they leave out the people who are not working then

138

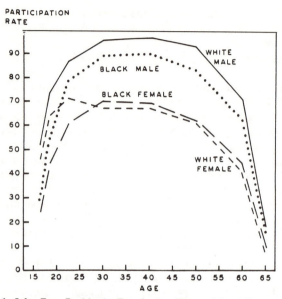

PARTICIPATION
RATE

Figure 6-1. Labor Force Participation Rate, by Age, Race, and Sex, 1981
Source: U.S.Bureau of Labor Statistics, *Labor Force Statistics Derived from the Current Population Survey: A Databook*, v. 1 (1982), tables A-3; A-4.

but who have worked at some time during the 12-month period. That is a particularly significant omission among older people, because sizable numbers are employed on a part-time or part-year basis, often to earn the maximum amount before Social Security benefits are reduced, and those workers do not usually figure in the data.[8] Therefore, perhaps as many as a quarter or more of the older people who have worked during a year are not represented in the official participation rates. Moreover, the rates would be higher if all older people who wanted jobs could get them.[9]

Leaving the Labor Force

The age variations in labor force participation rates reflect the complex social process by which elderly people vacate work roles, whether or not by choice, and assume others. In certain respects, the older person now separates from the role of worker more abruptly than in the past, when larger proportions were self-employed in agriculture and other fields and could remain partially productive longer. Now more workers are employed in large corporations that specify a uniform retirement age that makes the change from worker to pensioner relatively abrupt and, for some, traumatic.[10]

The process of removal from the labor force has subtle dynamics that actually begin in the 40s and 50s and push the worker toward retirement in the early to mid-60s. For example, the worker may find that after a certain age promotions are less likely, either because he/she has attained the maximum level or is passed over in favor of a younger person. In addition, the revolutionary technological changes in some industries make it difficult for some older workers to keep pace and thus make retirement a welcome relief from a frustrating struggle. The aging employee's salary also may not rise as rapidly as those of younger workers, often because supervisors accept the stereotype of lower performance levels among older workers.

Whatever the specific reasons, however, retirement is frequently preceded by a certain amount of disengagement for the worker in his/her 50s and early 60s, when the rewards go to younger people who can be hired more cheaply. Then, actual retirement simply culminates several antecedent events.[11] Many of them are unrelated to the older worker's actual performance or capacity, but reflect the beliefs and attitudes in America's occupational structure, though many people approaching retirement welcome progressive separation from work roles. Moreover, the mass exodus of older workers from the labor force occurs in the early to mid-60s, despite the Age Discrimination in Employment Act of 1967 and other legal

Table 6-1. Labor Force Participation Rates, by Age, Race, and Sex, 1981

Race and Sex	55-59	60-64	65+
All Races			
Male	81.2	58.5	18.4
Female	49.3	32.6	8.0
White			
Male	82.3	59.1	18.5
Female	49.1	32.0	7.9
Other Races			
Male	72.0	52.6	16.7
Female	50.7	37.8	9.1

Source: U.S. Bureau of the Census, "America in Transition: An Aging Society," Current Population Reports, P-23, no. 128 (1983), table 12.

protections, because the separation process is often too subtle to be detected or thwarted by the law, well-intentioned employers, or the workers themselves. The process is also a reciprocal one, however, because people are not merely ejected from the work force, but are attracted into retirement by adequate pensions, useful alternative roles, persuasive family members and previous retirees, and other influences. Moreover, some workers have no choice but to retire because of health problems.

In considering the situation of the older worker who is retired involuntarily, it is easy to overestimate the pervasiveness and the negative effects of the disengagement process, and even to see virtually the whole retired population as a tragic mass expelled from useful social activity and plagued by numerous problems. In fact, a large majority of workers look forward to retirement, hasten the process if they can afford it, and adapt well when they actually do retire, though the proportions who can retire vary as inflation and other problems change in intensity. Nor do most former workers slow down very significantly, withdraw into solitude, or sever major social contacts with family, friends, or even former co-workers,[12] though many experience these consequences in a mild form and a minority suffer them acutely. People whose incomes, educations, and health are good incur few or none of the negative results attributed to disengagement from the labor force, and they remain full social participants during retirement; for a time they may even increase their social activity.[13] Almost all elderly people, however, do tend to disengage gradually from social interaction as they age, partly because friends and spouses die, health deteriorates, and other changes occur as one moves toward the oldest years. Therefore, some degree of disengagement is a reality for most even beyond the question of employment, but its intensity varies greatly and it only creates serious difficulties for a fairly small number.

Once the older person has left the labor force it is relatively difficult to return because of hiring practices, the lower levels of formal education that many older workers have, the periodic recessions that reduce the demand for elderly job seekers, and the frequent glut of applicants for those jobs. Consequently, some of the 65-and-over group outside the labor force simply give up trying to return and settle for whatever retirement income they can get. Even labor unions, as they negotiate pension plans with employers, accept age limits that help push older workers out of the work force and hamper their return. The age requirements of the Social Security system and other governmental programs for the elderly have much the same effect. Therefore, to a certain degree the pension is "a formal reward for waiving the right to work,"[14] in order that the elderly can be removed from the labor force. But no matter how one assesses these various elements, they do reduce labor force participation rates rapidly after age 55 or 60.

Perhaps the major problem is a categorical view of the elderly that doesn't account for individual variations. Productivity does decline among some older workers, but many compete successfully with younger ones, and others substitute accuracy and dependability for high rates of productivity.[15] Furthermore, experience is often a strong compensation for certain decrements of aging, especially in sensory abilities; experience helps the older worker produce more consistently than many younger counterparts and still maintain as high a quality of work. Despite some chronic absentees, the average attendance record of elderly workers also is as good as that of younger ones, even when the older employees are bothered by certain health problems. Thus, removing workers from jobs at a uniform age is inconsistent with variations in their skills and performance, though the raising of the mandatory retirement age to 70 and the trend toward earlier voluntary retirement are modifying this artificial uniformity.

Some International Comparisons

Older people in most societies tend to withdraw from the labor force, but they are much more likely to do so in the industrialized nations than in the so-called developing countries, where poverty and subsistence labors are part of the way of life of many people. Moreover, even though longer life expectancy in the developed countries increases the average number of working years, those years represent a smaller percentage of life than is true in the developing nations, especially the more agrarian ones. Thus, Table 6-2 shows lower participation rates among elderly men in the representative developed countries than in the developing ones, though Japan is something of an exception because of its unique industrial situation. But it is rare in most developed countries for more than a quarter of the older men to be in the labor force, whereas the proportions are half, two-thirds, or more in the less developed ones.

The participation rates of elderly women also tend to be somewhat greater in many of the developing nations, though the pattern is less consistent than it is for men, because religion, the status of women, and other factors influence the proportions. In Pakistan, for example, only 3 per cent of the older women are in the labor force, partly because of restrictions imposed by Islam, which also helps account for women's low participation rates in Iran and some countries not listed in Table 6-2, including Bangladesh. Moreover, the work that women do in many developing countries, especially in agriculture, is substantially underreported in the official statistics on the economically active population. In fact, the ways of conceptualizing who is and is not in the work force in the developing countries differ considerably from the procedures used in the developed ones.[16]

The countries with the lowest participation rates for men and women are those with comprehensive services for elderly workers who retire, for they make retirement attractive and mandatory for large percentages of the work force. Most are European countries. Some provide better benefits for the elderly than does the United States, which helps account for our relatively high participation rates among older people, both men and women.[17] But retirement benefits are only one of the factors that affect labor force participation rates of the elderly. In Japan, for example, early in the twentieth century industries introduced the concept of lifetime employment with one firm, along with increases in income according to

Table 6-2. Percentages of People 65 and Over Classified as Economically Active in Selected Countries, by Sex

Country	Year	Per Cent	
		Male	Female
Japan	1978	41.5	15.8
Denmark	1978	20.9	5.6
UNITED STATES	1978	19.7	7.8
Spain	1978	17.1	6.1
Australia	1976	16.8	5.1
New Zealand	1976	16.2	2.8
Italy	1978	13.4	3.7
Finland	1976	10.8	3.1
West Germany	1978	8.4	3.4
Netherlands	1977	6.3	1.4
Bolivia	1976	80.5	14.1
Ethiopia	1977	68.1	14.2
Honduras	1977	67.2	6.5
Jamaica	1978	65.6	30.7
Cameroon	1976	62.8	31.2
Zambia	1977	61.3	30.2
Mexico	1979	60.3	8.9
Pakistan	1978	59.7	3.2
Iran	1976	56.6	4.2
Venezuela	1977	53.1	8.3

Source: International Labour Office, Year Book of Labour Statistics, 1979 (1979), table 1.

length of service. But because that tenure system is expensive, most firms require retirement at age 55 but begin paying benefits at age 60. In addition, the governmental social security plan is a recent one and its benefits are relatively small, even after age 60. Therefore, the older Japanese worker is often forced to seek employment after forced retirement, often in a poorly paid, low-status, part-time job, though the government, industries, and unions are now promoting measures to make older workers more employable. These several circumstances account for a considerable part of the high labor force participation rates of the elderly in Japan.[18]

Labor Force Participation Differentials in the United States

Participation Differences by Sex

Labor force participation has changed dramatically for American men and women under age 65, especially since 1970, because women are much more likely to be in the work force than they were previously, whereas the participation rates of men have declined. Despite the job and wage discrimination they still encounter, women have been increasingly available and motivated to work outside the home, partly because their child-care responsibilities have been diminished by more childlessness and smaller family size. Other significant factors include expanded job opportunities, higher levels of education that qualify women to work at better jobs, the wish for a level of living that only two salaries can provide,[19] the increase in one-parent families supported by women, and especially the high inflation rates of recent years. As a result, the proportions of men and women working for wages have grown much more alike.

In the elderly group, however, only some of this change has occurred, for although older men are now far less likely to be in the labor force than were those in 1900, the participation rate for women has dropped very little. Thus, while the rates of the nation's elderly men and women differed by 59 percentage points in 1900, in 1981 the two groups were separated by only 10 percentage points. During the period, the participation rate of elderly women has fluctuated a little, but now, at 8 per cent, it is not much below the 9 per cent of 1900 or even the 10 per cent of the 1950s and 1960s. Older men, on the other hand, are less than a third as likely to be in the labor force as they were in 1900. The factors chiefly responsible are pension plans that encourage voluntary retirement, age restrictions imposed by industries and unions, reductions in the rate of self-employment,[20] and the difficulty of finding work after age 65. For both sexes, however, older people are far less likely than younger ones to remain in the labor force, and the rates for men and women aged 65 and over are far below those of the group aged 60-64. (See Table 6-1 and Figure 6-1.)

The tendency for participation rates of older women to change relatively little since 1900 doesn't mean that the women are immune to the forces that reduced the rates among older men. Many elderly female workers are also motivated to leave the labor force because of improved retirement benefits and other incentives, or are forced to withdraw because of formal age limits, subtle age discrimination, stationary salaries, stereotypes about physical attractiveness, and other disincentives that favor younger women over older ones. Their separation from work roles may be concealed, however, by the greatly increased flow of women of all ages into the labor force, especially during the 1970s,[21] and the aging of many into the elderly category where they replace most who retire.

Like the men, women workers also tend to remain in the labor force in large numbers until age 62 or 65, especially if they are single or divorced and self-supporting, though many widows also must seek employment for financial reasons, sometimes at relatively old ages. That group is particularly likely to end up in low-paying service and white-collar jobs, partly because the widow whose income is so low that she must work is also apt to have a relatively poor education and limited job skills. Often she has spent much of her life engaged in housework, which has little negotiating value when she seeks paid employment, unfair though that may be.

The variable work force particpation rates of elderly men and women also reflect the different ways in which the sexes have viewed work historically. When today's elderly were young adults, paid work was far more central to a man's overall role than to a woman's, because it tied him to the larger social system and provided a major part of his self-concept.[22] Typically, the man was judged less as a husband and father than as a worker, and it was often difficult for him to relinquish the work role. That was true even for many who had no serious financial constraints, though pension plans were much poorer then than now. When elderly women were young adults, on the other hand, a woman's role was bound up with housekeeping and childrearing; she was identified chiefly as a wife and mother and part of her status simply reflected that of her husband. Paid employment was pursued by a comparatively small minority. Therefore, the present low labor force participation rates of elderly women and the higher ones of men are partly a residue of those earlier social realities.

The ways in which the sexes related to work are changing markedly, however, for the labor force participation rates of women in all age groups under 65 have risen sharply, while those of men have fallen somewhat. Therefore, paid work has become an important if not central feature in the lives of at least half the nation's women aged 18-54, and for a sizable minority it is just as basic as it has been for men. When these women reach age 65, many will carry with them the same attitudes about work and retirement held by many men, and future populations of older women will have far more versatile work experience than housekeeping and childrearing. In fact, a sizable share of women now reaching age 65 already have had long careers and face the same questions about role definitions, retirement and its meaning, and use of time that many men have had to resolve when their working years were over. That change is part of the fundamental convergence in the work histories of more and more elderly men and women, and is another of the dynamics involved in the aging of America's population.

Participation Differences by Race

Labor force participation rates among older people do not vary tremendously by race, though they are slightly higher for white men than for blacks and somewhat higher for black women than for whites.[23] (See Table 6-1 and Figure 6-1.) These patterns represent some changes, however, for as recently as 1950 the participation rates of elderly black men were significantly higher than those of white men; older black women, though, have long had higher rates than white women. In recent decades, the labor force involvement of older black men has declined somewhat more rapidly than that of any other elderly group,[24] but even at all of the ages under 65 the participation rates of black men have dropped substantially below those of white men. If the pattern doesn't change for those reaching age 65, blacks will continue to be less represented than whites in the elderly work force.

The labor force participation rate of elderly women of both races has been more nearly constant than that of men, owing to the sizable number of younger women who enter the work force, reach age 65, and replace the ones able to retire. White women of all ages have been entering the labor force at an especially rapid pace, but at age 65 and older their participation rates are still below those of black women, partly because larger proportions of the latter hold low-paying service jobs from which they cannot afford to retire. On the other hand, the percentage of elderly black women unable to work because of physical disability and other problems is more than twice that of white women; the same proportion holds among men.

Participation Differences by Other Characteristics

Rural-urban residence. Elderly men in the rural-farm population are more likely to remain in the labor force than are men in the urban and rural-nonfarm groups. Many of the farm men continue working in agriculture, either for themselves or for an adult child who has taken over principal responsibility for the business, or they are employed in other enterprises related to agriculture. Elderly women, on the other hand, are most likely to continue in the labor force if they reside in cities, where there are higher proportions of unmarried women who must support themselves.

Marital status. The labor force participation rates are highest for elderly married men (20% in 1981) and a little lower for those who are divorced (19%). The rates are still lower for single men (14%) and lowest of all for widowers (12%). Most of the married men still help support an aging spouse, which would be more difficult on a small retirement income, and they also tend to have better average health than widowers and are more able to work. In addition, widowers tend to be considerably older than 65 and less able to get or hold jobs because of advanced age. Elderly women are far less likely to be in the labor force if they are married than if they are single or divorced. Many in the last two groups are essentially on their own financially and must work to survive, particularly if their jobs are at the low end of the status scale and promise only small retirement incomes. Widows have participation rates nearly as low as those of married women, for while some must work to support themselves, many others have adequate incomes because of their late husbands' pension plans, survivor benefits, and other advantages. Moreover, considering that the soaring increase in the divorce rate is relatively recent, divorced and separated women tend to cluster closer to age 65 than do widows, so the former are often better able to work.

Educational attainment. Labor force participation rates are generally lowest for elderly people with the poorest educational attainment, highest for those who have the most schooling, because many of the latter hold jobs or practice professions that are less susceptible to mandatory retirement, and frequently they are doing things they enjoy and prefer to continue. Furthermore, the best-educated people have better average levels of health than the poorly educated and are more able to hold jobs, and they also have an advantage should they wish to return to work. At the same time, older workers as a group have less schooling than younger ones, are less likely to have the occupational training that equips them with valued skills, and are found less often in government-sponsored retraining programs.[25] Some of those discrepancies are diminishing, however, as better-educated younger workers age into the older labor force and as some elderly workers recognize the need to hone old job skills or learn new ones. But well-educated people also generally have attractive pension options that favor early retirement and keep their labor force participation rates from being higher than they are.

Part-Time and Part-Year Work

Elderly workers are especially likely to be employed part time, and the older one becomes, the greater the likelihood.[26] Thus, in 1981 about 48 per cent of the men aged 65 and older who were still working and 60 per cent of the working women were employed on a part-time basis. These figures compare with 30 per cent and 42 per cent, respectively, in 1960. Consequently, as the participation rate has declined among the elderly, part-time work has become an increasingly important source of employment for the minority who remain in the labor force.[27] In addition, elderly workers are far more likely than younger ones to work only part of each year, though more than half put in at least some hours during 50-52 weeks a year. Elderly women are slightly more likely than elderly men to be part-year workers, but the difference is small. Therefore, when older men and women do work, somewhat over half of each group are employed on a 50-52 week basis, but the women are significantly more likely to work less than 35 hours per week.

Although some elderly people work part-time because they cannot get more regular jobs, most prefer part-time work as a way to supplement their retirement incomes. Some, especially at the higher educational levels, get pleasure from the work itself but prefer to avoid the demands and commitments of full-time employment. Thus, the less regular employment of many elderly persons reflects the mix of activities with which they fill their older years, and while work supplements income and adds variety to life, it is not usually demanding enough to interfere seriously with other things that people want to do. In that sense, part-time and part-year work represents a tapering off in economic activity to avoid abrupt or even traumatic separation from the working world. Therefore, given the choice to work, many elderly people prefer to do so on a less rigorous schedule than their regular jobs previously required, though the limitation on earnings for Social Security recipients also plays a major role in the amount of work the older person chooses to do. In addition, many of the part-time jobs available to older people pay poorly and provide only a meager supplement to Social Security income. Thus, while fairly large numbers of older people hold part-time jobs, most do so out of economic necessity and most of the jobs pay only modest wages.[28]

The reasons for part-time rather than full-time employment also vary by sex. The most frequent reason women workers remain on a part-time basis is because of housekeeping responsibilities, whereas two-thirds of the men give retirement as their principal reason. Ill health or disability is an equally important reason for both sexes and is fairly minor, though it is, of course, a much more significant factor among the elderly who do not work at all.

Occupations of Older Workers

Older workers are concentrated rather heavily in the occupations that are declining in proportional importance in the economy, such as farm work, certain service jobs, and some types of manufacturing, though they are also heavily represented in occupations that require long years of experience. Young workers, on the other hand, are more likely to appear in the newer occupations, the ones that are expanding in importance, those that are physically demanding, the professions, and the jobs that are stepping stones to better positions.[29]

Occupational Differences by Sex

Reflecting these differences between age groups, the data in Table 6-3 on occupations show that elderly men are far more likely than younger ones to be employed in farming, especially as private operators, and in nonhousehold service jobs of various kinds, such as guards or janitors. Moreover, the older men are somewhat overrepresented in white-collar jobs, chiefly as managers and administrators, sales workers, and clerical employees; they are underrepresented in professional and technical occupations and greatly so in blue-collar jobs with mandatory retirement. In large companies particularly, persons who reach age 65 as blue-collar workers are more likely to retire than are older workers in small companies. Far more elderly men are employed in white-collar jobs than in any other category, whereas blue-collar occupations account for 45 per cent of all jobs held by men aged 16-64.

Elderly women workers are very heavily concentrated in white-collar positions and service jobs. In 1981 those two job categories accounted for 87 per cent of the female work force aged 65 and older. Even so, elderly women are less represented in many specific white-collar jobs than are younger ones, including professional and technical work, managerial positions, and sales and clerical jobs, partly because prejudices still favor young women in some of those categories. The unusually large share of elderly women in service jobs includes a significant number of household workers and baby-sitters, for many of the older women, especially those past age 70, still have to work for whatever wages they can get in the only positions they can get. Many of their situations represent an accumulation of low levels of education, limited job skills, modest or no retirement income from private pensions, and subsistence wages that help stave off the more serious deprivation they would suffer if they depended on Social Security or Supplemental Security Income (SSI) alone. Not all women in those jobs are poor, however, and some do the work because they enjoy the activity and the contacts it provides.

Older women have lower rates of participation than younger ones in all of the blue-collar jobs, but much higher rates in farm work, especially as operators. Some of these women are the widows of farmers and are still working to hold onto a family farm, though nearly half of them are laborers working for wages or other remuneration. The group of farm laborers, however, is limited largely to women under age 70, for very few past that age could meet the physical demands of such work.

It is clear that older workers of both sexes appear disproportionately in the more menial and poorly paid occupations and those that demand lesser skills, while they are underrepresented in the jobs that provide relatively high income and status. Consequently, many of the nation's older workers hold the least coveted white-collar positions and service jobs,[30] laboring as janitors, guards, household employees, and similar workers. Job status does not decline much for some after they reach age

Table 6-3. Percentages of Workers Employed in Various Occupation Groups, by Age and Sex, 1981

Occupation Group	Male		Female	
	16-64	65+	16-64	65+
White-Collar Workers	42.7	47.3	66.2	56.7
Professional & Technical	15.9	13.7	17.2	11.1
Managers & Administrators	14.5	17.5	7.3	9.3
Sales	6.0	9.3	6.7	11.5
Clerical	6.3	6.8	35.0	24.8
Blue-Collar Workers	45.0	25.7	13.6	10.2
Crafts	21.0	11.8	1.9	1.1
Nontransport Operatives	11.3	4.5	9.8	7.9
Transport Operatives	5.6	3.4	0.7	0.2
Nonfarm Laborers	7.1	6.0	1.2	1.0
Service Workers	8.7	13.2	19.1	30.5
Farm Workers	3.6	13.8	1.1	2.6

Source: U.S. Bureau of Labor Statistics, Labor Force Statistics Derived from the Current Population Survey: A Databook, vol. 1 (1982), p. 648.

65, however, and they simply continue in the relatively menial positions they held before age 65,[31] while for others the low-level jobs are a tolerable way to supplement income.

But education, not age, is the variable that determines occupational placement for most older workers. For example, the large majority of elderly working men with college educations are white-collar employees in the professions, technical fields, administrative positions, and other situations with relatively high status, whereas the men with less than eighth-grade educations are heavily represented in farm jobs and service occupations.[32] Moreover, the proportions of older and younger workers engaged in most occupations do not vary a great deal if the level of education is held constant. Therefore, poor educational attainment tends to dog elderly people throughout their lives and to diminish their chances of high-status employment in the older years, just as it did when they were younger. It can also reduce the elderly person's confidence to be able to do a job and can erode his/her self-concept after retirement.[33]

Inadequate education also prevents older workers from having much occupational mobility, either upward in the social scale or from one job to another at the same level, although job security, pension investments, and other factors also reduce mobility. Many are reluctant to attempt a move because they know the prospects to find a better position diminish sharply after age 45 or 50, and unless forced out, older workers rarely leave one position to find another. Even when they do, relatively large shares remain unemployed for long periods or even permanently, or they end up taking part-time work. In addition, with the relocation of many plants to other parts of the country in the last few decades, often from the Snowbelt to the Sunbelt, many older workers were left behind by their companies or were unwilling to move. The least skilled have often been unable to find new jobs, particularly if the economy of an area is in general decline and its unemployment rate for all ages is relatively high. On the other hand, older people with the highest levels of education and job status continue working the longest, particularly if they are self-employed,[34] and though they often choose not to move to new jobs, many could do so if they wished.

Occupational Difference by Race

Many of the occupational variations between elderly men and women apply to both blacks and whites, but there are some differences between the sexes by race and major ones between the races for each sex. Thus, elderly white women are more likely than men to be white-collar workers, whereas the proportions are about the same in the older black group, partly because the percentage of female professional and technical workers, many of them teachers, is higher than that of men; so is that of clerical workers. (See Table 6-4.) But in the blue-collar and farm categories, men predominate in both racial groups, whereas higher proportions of women of both races are service workers.

There are large variations between the races, however, that reflect long-term advantages and disadvantages in employment status. Thus, black men are far less likely than white men to be white-collar workers in all of the sub-categories but much more apt to be blue-collar workers, especially laborers. Black men are also more than twice as likely to be service workers, but somewhat less apt to be farm workers. Elderly black

Table 6-4. Percentages of Workers 65 and Over Employed in Various Occupation Groups, by Race and Sex, 1981

Occupation Group	White		Other Races	
	Male	Female	Male	Female
White-Collar Workers	49.6	60.8	22.1	22.3
Professional & Technical	14.5	11.6	5.4	7.4
Managers & Administrators	18.4	9.9	8.6	5.0
Sales	9.8	12.5	2.7	2.5
Clerical	6.9	26.8	5.4	7.4
Blue-Collar Workers	24.5	10.6	38.3	6.6
Crafts	12.0	1.1	8.9	0.8
Nontransport Operatives	4.3	8.4	6.9	5.0
Transport Operatives	3.3	0.2	4.8	a
Nonfarm Laborers	4.9	0.9	17.7	0.8
Service Workers	12.0	26.0	26.8	68.6
Farm Workers	13.9	2.6	12.8	2.5

Source: U.S. Bureau of Labor Statistics, Labor Force Statistics Derived from the Current Population Survey: A Databook, vol. 1 (1982), p. 649.

[a]Less than 0.1 per cent.

women who work are heavily concentrated in service occupations, which employ more than two-thirds of them. They are proportionately less abundant than white women in all of the white-collar and blue-collar categories, though they are about equally likely to be farm workers. It is clear, though, that the status profile of jobs held by elderly blacks is significantly poorer than that of older whites, and that the occupational choices of the elderly black woman are especially limited.

Industries of Older Workers

Because of these occupational patterns among older workers, the largest proportions of them are employed in service industries, especially education, personal services, business and repair services, and various kinds of welfare, religious, and medical services. Trade also employs a large share of older workers, particularly as retail store clerks. Together, service industries and trade provide the jobs for about two-thirds of all elderly workers, and for a much larger percentage of the women than of the men.

Manufacturing is the third most important industrial category employing older workers, but after age 65 the percentage engaged in it drops substantially. Part of the decrease is due to the pension plans and mandatory retirement provisions enacted as the labor movement gained strength and wrested concessions from factory owners and managers, though the physical demands of some jobs and the routine nature of others also help reduce the employment of the elderly in manufacturing. For some, health problems play a major part, but often the worker on the assembly line or in other forms of manufacturing has had enough of the factory and simply wants to retire as soon as possible. The job prospects for older people in manufacturing and other industries are also reduced by product competition from abroad, robotics and other rapid advances in computer technology, and increases in the educational sophistication expected of many employees. Those changes have forced out some who would like to work after age 65 and have reduced new employment opportunities for many people who have reached that age or are even in the 40s and 50s. The changes also help concentrate older workers in the service industries and trade, because they are the only areas in which many elderly can hope to find jobs. And whenever the economy slides into a recession, their prospects are poor even in those industries, especially with younger people and undocumented alien immigrants competing for the same jobs. Many manufacturing industries also have no provisions for part-time or part-year employment, which many older workers must have if they are to maintain a tolerable level of living; the service industries and trade are the most likely to provide those opportunities.

The only other industry in which there is a heavier proportional concentration of workers age 65 and over than of those 55-64 is finance, insurance, and real estate, though that is true only for men. Within that category of industries older workers are especially drawn to real estate, and many continue in that field after "normal" retirement age, while others enter it for the first time. Even there, however, when high interest rates and other conditions inhibit the real estate market, the older worker is apt to have fewer opportunies than the younger one.

Older workers are relatively scarce in mining, transportation and public utilities, construction, and public administration. Moreover, all but the last category represent "male" occupations that provide jobs for very few elderly women. The latter are at a disadvantage even in public administration, though the discrepancy is not as great.

Employment and Unemployment

In one sense, the elderly are less susceptible to unemployment than are younger people, especially teenages, because the labor force participation rates of older people are so much lower.[35] Thus, in 1981 the unemployment rates for workers generally declined with age, until only 2.9 per cent of the men and 3.6 per cent of the women aged 65 and older were reported as seeking work but unable to find it. (See Table 6-5.) Elderly whites were especially unlikely to be classified as unemployed, while members of other races, chiefly blacks, had substantially higher rates. Nonetheless, the unemployment figures for the elderly, whether male or female, black or white, are less than half those of workers aged 16 and over, except for black women. It might seem, therefore, that the employment situation of elderly job-seekers is a relatively favorable one and that the youngest people in the labor force are far worse off.

But the situation of the elderly is actually poorer than it appears, for the data refer to unemployment among people classified as being *in the labor force*. Very sizable numbers of the elderly population, especially men, are classified as retired and thus not in the work force, even though a significant share of that group would take work if they could get it.[36] In fact, when economic growth slows and general unemployment rates rise, the elderly are especially unlikely to find the work they would like and often need. Many abandon the search, accept the designation "retired," and are not reported in the unemployment figures. A person out of work must be actively seeking a job to be considered officially unemployed, and for some elderly people it is less degrading to be retired than unemployed, and they report themselves accordingly.[37] People aged 65-69 are especially affected, because they are the large majority of older people who do work or would like to, and men are still more affected than women, because the majority of today's elderly women never worked for wages outside the home. That, of course, may change dramatically with future generations of elderly women who held paying jobs in their younger years.

Competition with younger workers is a key factor in the unemployment patterns of older workers, for even though the older person offers more experience than the younger one, the job is more likely to go to the latter, especially if it calls for a type and level of training the older worker lacks. Frequently, the younger worker is also thought to need the job more in order to support a growing family, whereas the older worker is felt to have at least some retirement income, fewer financial responsibilities, and more governmental protection from the costs of illness and accident. Older workers have been particularly hard pressed by this competition during the 1970s and 1980s, because their numbers and proportions have been increasing rapidly at the same time the large baby-boom generation has entered the labor force and worked its way into the industrial structure. Complicated by periodic recessions, this means there are more younger applicants for the jobs that older people might have been able to get or retain in the past.

Table 6-5. Percentages of the Labor Force Unemployed, by Age, Race, and Sex, 1981

Age	All Races		White		Other Races	
	Male	Female	Male	Female	Male	Female
16+	7.4	7.9	6.5	6.9	14.1	14.3
16-17	22.0	20.7	19.9	18.4	40.1	41.4
18-19	18.8	17.9	16.4	15.3	36.0	36.5
20-24	13.2	11.2	11.6	9.1	24.4	24.2
25-34	6.9	7.7	6.1	6.6	12.6	13.9
35-44	4.5	5.7	4.0	5.1	8.3	8.9
45-54	4.0	4.6	3.6	4.2	7.1	6.7
55-64	3.6	3.8	3.4	3.7	6.2	4.6
65+	2.9	3.6	2.4	3.4	7.0	8.0

Source: U.S. Bureau of Labor Statistics, Labor Force Statistics Derived from the Current Population Survey: A Databook, vol. 1 (1982), table A-28.

Thus, incentives and pressures for elderly people to leave the labor force have pushed their actual unemployment rates substantially above the official rates. Furthermore, when older job-seekers do find employment, much of it offers less prestige and income than the jobs people held before they were aged 60 or 65. Even the exceptions among professional, technical, and other highly skilled workers do not negate the general pattern. And when the older worker does look for a job, the search takes much longer than it does for the average younger worker,[38] increasing the likelihood the elderly job-seeker will become discouraged and retire. Sometimes the problems of the search are worsened by employers who choose younger workers even when they are compelled by law to interview older ones, because employers often expect to train younger people more cheaply and to get a longer period of productivity.[39] Perhaps the prospects of older workers will improve when the low birth rates since the late 1960s reduce the proportions of very young job-seekers, but at present the prospects are limited and will grow worse as the baby-boom people reach age 65. In addition, the indebtedness and reduced purchasing power of many developing countries, such as Mexico and Brazil, have reduced the demand for American products, eliminated jobs, and made the elderly job-seeker's quest even more difficult. So has product competition from other nations.

Finally, the unemployment situation of older people is no longer ameliorated as it once was by a relatively high incidence of self-employment. In particular, farming has declined as an employer of older people who could continue working as long as they were able and then reduce their activity gradually rather than abruptly. Much of the same is true of small shopkeepers, grocers, and others who could not compete with chain and discount stores, and self-employment has also decreased in those businesses, especially among the elderly.

Some Trends and Projections

Labor Force Participation Trends

The labor force participation rates of older people have declined substantially over the past several decades, principally because of very significant decreases in the proportions of older men who work, though the employment rate of older women is also declining slowly. At the turn of the present century, nearly two-thirds of the men aged 65 and older were "gainful workers" (participants in the labor force),[40] but by 1950 fewer than half were so classified. The proportion declined steadily up to the present and promises to drop even more in the 1990s.[41] (See Table 6-6).) Moreover, while the participation rates of men aged 65 and older have fallen the most rapidly, those of men aged 55-64 have also dropped since 1970. As a consequence, although the whole labor force aged 16 and over will probably increase from 105 million in 1980 to 128 million by 1995, the group 65 and over is likely to remain at about 3 million throughout the period.[42] That will make elderly workers an even smaller percentage of the total work force and of the whole elderly population, unless significant changes take place in employment policies and opportunities, economic pressures on the elderly, or other conditions that affect labor force participation.

The reasons why the labor force participation rates of older men have declined so dramatically are complex, but five factors help to explain this drop:[43]

1. As work has shifted away from agriculture and self-employment and toward bureaucratized forms, more men have come under mandatory retirement rules designed by industries to enhance efficiency and favor younger workers, who can often be hired at lower wages than people with long seniority. This has forced out many workers at various ages from 55 to 75, though especially at 65, and in the future it will eject many at age 70. But status also enters the picture, because people in menial jobs are more likely than those in prestigious ones to retire, even on fairly low incomes if they must, though the retirement rates of various status groups are converging.

2. The increase in pension plans, both public and private, has made retirement more attractive to many workers, and to others the plans represent welcome relief from an unhappy work situation. The private plans are often part of a system that mandates retirement at a given age, so the worker is both drawn and pushed out of the work force. Moreover, the maximum-earnings test in the Social Security system and the prospect to receive some benefits as early as age 62 help to reduce labor force participation, while the meaning of retirement has also changed so much that some people prefer leisure to full-time work even if they must get it at considerable sacrifice of income. Therefore, some persons retire even under relatively poor pension plans or with Social Security alone, though many must then resort to part-time employment. Even for them, however, the pension does prevent the late-life destitution that many unemployed elderly experienced in earlier generations.[44] Retirement has also come to be defined as appropriate for older Americans, while non-work has lost its stigma and is even reinforced, both financially and normatively.[45]

3. When jobs are difficult to find because general unemployment rates are high, the older unemployed male is apt to become discouraged in his search for work and to stop looking. Furthermore, once unemployed he is more likely than the younger worker to remain out of the labor force, partly because he can qualify for retirement benefits the younger man cannot yet claim, but also because of barriers to re-employment. Those

circumstances have helped lower the labor force participation rates of older men, including those aged 55-64.

4. Ill health and disability also drive some older men from the labor force, while improved disability benefits enable them to survive financially if they must stop working. The proportion who claim disability as a reason for leaving the work force is a small fraction of those who credit retirement, however, though the latter may be an excuse for the former. The percentage of older men who claim poor health or disability is also smaller than in the past, so more could work if they wished and if suitable jobs were available.

Table 6-6. Labor Force Participation Rates in Two Major Age Groups, by Sex, 1890-1995

Year	Male		Female	
	55-64	65+	55-64	65+
1890	89.0	68.3	11.4	7.6
1920	86.3	55.6	14.3	7.3
1950	87.0	45.8	27.0	9.7
1955	86.4	38.5	32.2	10.3
1960	86.8	33.1	37.2	10.8
1965	84.6	27.9	41.1	10.0
1970	83.0	26.8	43.0	9.7
1975	75.8	21.7	41.0	8.3
1980	72.3	19.1	41.5	8.1
1985	69.7	17.5	41.6	7.7
1990	67.5	15.8	41.7	7.3
1995	66.5	14.3	42.3	6.8

Sources: U.S. Bureau of the Census, Statistical Abstract of the United States: 1960, tables 16, 262, and 264; 1981, table 636; Kingsley Davis and Pietronella van den Oever, "Age Relations and Public Policy in Advanced Industrial Societies," Population and Development Review, vol. 7 (1981), table 1; Howard N. Fullerton, "The 1995 Labor Force: A First Look," in U.S. Bureau of Labor Statistics, Economic Projections to 1990, Bulletin 2121 (1982), p. 52.

5. Employers still discriminate covertly against the older job-seeker, despite protective legislation. Often relying on stereotypes, many employers assume that older workers are less efficient than younger ones, less capable physically and even mentally, and less adaptable, though obsolete skills in a time of rapid technological change are a genuine problem. Moreover, many employers fear that hiring or even retaining older workers would increase insurance and pension costs. Newly hired older workers would also be unable to work long enough to participate in existing pension plans, and employers often assume they are less trainable than young ones and more likely to fall ill.

As noted earlier, the labor force participation rates of elderly women have fluctuated far less than those of men, basically because the larger proportion of younger women who entered the labor force in recent decades and then aged into the 65-and-over group tends to compensate for the growing number of those aged 65 and older who retire. Therefore, the participation rates of women are declining only slowly and will probably continue to fall gradually into the 1990s. The factors that have reduced the labor force involvement of older men are increasingly at play for women as well, however, although other forces encourage many women to enter or remain in the labor force during middle age and to stay in it past age 65.

As a consequence of various socioeconomic changes in the twentieth century, including improvements in retirement income, the falling labor force participation rates of the elderly have caused older workers to become a smaller share of the total work force. Their proportions have risen at times because of national emergencies that kept them at their jobs after age 65, but those were only temporary reversals in the long-term trend. Moreover, the tendency for the elderly to be less and less represented in the work force seems likely to continue, although new crises in the Social Security system and other financial problems could alter that trend and cause more older people to seek work or keep the jobs they have. That likelihood should decrease for awhile, however, because from 1985 to 2000 the baby-boom people will be in their prime working years, whereas the small group born during the Depression will be retiring; the pressure on retirement systems should ease, though only until the baby-boom group itself reaches retirement age.

Occupational Trends

Employed men aged 65 and older. Since 1950 the male labor force of all ages has grown most rapidly in the service occupations, followed by white-collar positions and blue-collar categories. (See Table 6-7.) Their participation in farming has been cut by nearly two-thirds. Within the broad occupational groups, professional and technical workers have increased at the greatest rate, followed by nonhousehold service workers, managers and administrators, craft workers, clerical people, sales workers, nonfarm laborers, and operatives. The number of private household workers has fallen substantially.

Elderly employed men show some of these same patterns, though others differ markedly. Most significant is the 19 per cent decline in the older employed labor force between 1950 and 1981, compared with an increase of 48 per cent in the male labor force aged 16-64. Moreover, the numbers of older men have decreased significantly in all of the blue-collar categories, in the group of private household workers, and in the class of farm workers. On the other hand, the older white-collar group grew,

Table 6-7. Percentage Change in Major Occupation Groups, by Age and Sex, 1950-1981

Occupation Group	Male		Female	
	16-64	65+	16-64	65+
All Groups	48.3	-19.3	182.1	148.3
White-Collar Workers	101.7	29.8	244.2	265.2
Professional & Technical	213.6	70.6	282.8	116.1
Managers & Administrators	98.5	37.2	380.0	173.4
Sales	39.1	29.1	116.8	267.2
Clerical	40.5	17.4	245.3	543.0
Blue-Collar Workers	37.2	-35.2	73.1	49.1
Crafts	61.2	-35.8	246.5	64.4
Operatives	18.8	-34.9	49.4	37.3
Nonfarm Laborers	27.2	-34.9	320.2	214.3
Service Workers	122.0	1.8	163.5	103.2
Farm Workers	-62.6	-60.4	-10.0	-7.4

Sources: U.S. Bureau of the Census, U.S. Census of Population: 1950, Detailed Characteristics, U.S. Summary (1953), table 127; U.S. Bureau of Labor Statistics, Labor Force Statistics Derived from the Current Population Survey: A Databook, vol. 1 (1982), p. 648.

particularly because of a large increase in the number of professional and technical workers and a smaller one among managers and administrators, whose jobs are often attractive enough for them to continue working and who are less subject to mandatory retirement than are blue-collar workers. Sales and clerical workers, who are usually farther down the social scale, also registered increases, as did nonhousehold service workers.

These changes suggest that the older men who do remain in the labor force have become more concentrated in a small number of occupations, largely white collar, though they are also getting out of farming at a slower pace than younger men. At the same time, the proportion of older workers in the blue-collar jobs has declined while that of younger ones has risen, though rather slowly. The percentage of workers aged 16-64 engaged in service occupations has risen significantly since 1950, while that of elderly men has scarcely changed. That is the net result, however, of a two-thirds reduction of elderly workers in private households and a 23 per cent increase in other service jobs. In no occupational category has the male labor force aged 65 and older increased nearly as fast as that aged 16-64, so the former continue to fall as a proportion in each category.

Employed women aged 65 and older. Since 1950 the female labor force of all ages has grown much faster than the male group in every occupational category except farm labor, and even there the number of women declined more slowly than that of men. These changes reflect the large influx of women workers into the work force in the past three decades and the tendency for some younger women to replace older men in the jobs that can be done by either sex.[46] Moreover, white-collar occupations as a whole attracted women faster than any other large category, followed by service jobs outside private households and blue-collar positions, particularly as laborers and craft workers. The growth in specific occupations in the white-collar category shows women rapidly becoming professional and technical workers and managers and administrators, though the more traditional clerical jobs have also attracted large numbers. Nonhousehold service jobs have also shown very substantial growth.

The number of elderly women employed has grown somewhat slower than that of all women, but the large increase in the elderly group contrasts dramatically with the decrease among older men. Given the rapid growth of the female population aged 65 and older, however, even this large increase in labor force participants has not raised the participation rate of elderly women.

The numbers of elderly women have grown faster than those of younger ones in the white-collar category, but only because of extremely large increases in the sales and clerical subgroups. In the blue-collar category and service occupations the numbers of older women grew more slowly than those of younger ones in every subgroup; the number of older women in farming fell, but more slowly than that of younger ones.

By 1990 women will probably be about 40 per cent of the elderly work force, up from 17 per cent in 1950, because some of the many employed women aged 55-64 will keep their jobs after age 65 and the number of older male workers will probably continue to shrink.[47] Older workers of both sexes will tend to concentrate even more heavily in nonhousehold service jobs and clerical and sales positions, though growth in the higher status professional and technical occupations also will be important. At least for a time, older women will increase quite substantially in the blue-collar jobs that elderly men are leaving in large numbers. These trends also suggest that while the percentage of older women who work probably won't rise or fall much, the *number* who work will be substantially greater, largely because of inadequate retirement incomes. Heavily represented in that group will be single and divorced women and widows.

The nation will also need more occupational opportunities for the elderly, because some who are retired or unemployed would like to work. In addition, the financial difficulties of the Social Security system are not over and may cause other cutbacks that will make Social Security alone a less adequate source of income, while inflation, even at a decreasing rate, will reduce buying power, and periodic high unemployment will make jobs especially scarce for the elderly. Mandatory retirement policies also are being challenged in the courts as discrimination, and may either fall or undergo additional change. Older people are also increasingly well educated and healthy and are able to hold more sophisticated occupations longer, while the self-images of some are changing to include continued work as a viable option. Finally, the social services needed by older people, especially in the advanced ages, have grown so costly that the elderly and their families are having to bear more of those costs. Work for wages over a longer period is one way to help solve this problem.[48] and may prove a necessity for people aged 65-70 who are caring for even older parents.

Summary

The proportion of elderly people who work has declined sharply in recent decades, and those who do hold jobs tend to be concentrated in relatively low-status, low-paying occupations. Older men have been particularly likely to leave the labor force, though the participation rates of older women also are declining gradually. Perhaps as many as half the elderly workers who leave the work force are pushed out by mandatory retirement policies, and while pension plans and Social Security make that practice palatable financially, it is still discriminatory and expels some older persons who would like to work. Moreover, most who do retire, whether voluntarily or involuntarily, find their incomes cut substantially. Many poorer ones are forced to seek re-employment, usually part time at the lower end of the status scale.

Despite these problems, more workers than ever choose early retirement, often several years before age 65. Thus, the aging work force consists of some workers who will have to retire but prefer to continue working and others who want to leave their jobs as early as possible. Income is the critical factor for many, though the nature of the work, the satisfaction it provides, the types of post-retirement activities available, the worker's self-image, and many other factors influence the complex process of leaving the labor force. Once out, however, it is relatively difficult for the older person to find another job, and the low official unemployment rates among the elderly fail to account for those who get discouraged and stop seeking work and for the long periods of unemployment faced by many of those who do eventually find jobs.

The labor force participation rates of older people will probably continue to decline, despite the increase to 70 of the mandatory retirement age. Yet each cohort that enters the older population is better educated than its predecessors and more able to do the sophisticated work in the evolving occupational-industrial system. Employers are also increasingly likely to look at individual abilities and preferences, and the nation may be moving slowly toward a job pattern that is more responsive to those older persons who want to work, as well as to those under age 65 who want to retire. Court challenges to mandatory retirement are partly responsible, as is the tendency for the elderly to consolidate their voices in opposition to age discrimination in the work-place and other parts of the American social system. Genuine cohesion in any age cohort is difficult to foster, for while people remain male or female, white or black, all their lives, they soon pass from one age group to another and common interests are diluted by that passage and by individual variations.[49] Even now, however, it is clear that older people as a group are not really expected to provide for themselves by working and that large numbers do prefer retirement, while they are also becoming an increasing financial burden for the employed population. That paradox may well become a major intergenerational crisis.

NOTES

1. Fred C. Pampel, *Social Change and the Aged.* Lexington, Ma: Heath, (1981), p. 61.

2. Beth J. Soldo, "America's Elderly in the 1980s," *Population Bulletin* 35 (1981): 21.

3. Robert N. Butler, "Ageism," in Kurt Finsterbusch, ed., *Social Problems 82/83.* Guilford, CT: Dushkin, 1982, p. 127.

163

4. Judah Matras, *Introduction to Population.* Englewood Cliffs, NJ: Prentice-Hall, 1977, p. 301.

5. For the detailed definition, see U.S. Bureau of the Census, *Statistical Abstract of the United States: 1982-83.* Washington, DC: U.S. Government Printing Office, 1982, p. 372.

6. Herman J. Loether, *Problems of Aging.* 2nd ed. Belmont, CA: Dickenson, 1975, pp. 61-62.

7. Soldo, *op. cit.,* p. 19.

8. Harold L. Sheppard, "Aging and Manpower Development," in Matilda White Riley, John W. Riley, Jr. and Marilyn E. Johnson, eds., *Aging and Society.* v. 2, *Aging and the Professions.* New York: Russell Sage Foundation, 1969, pp. 186-187.

9. Charles S. Harris, *Fact Book on Aging: A Profile of America's Older Population.* Washington, DC: National Council on the Aging, 1978, p. 74.

10. Matilda White Riley, Marilyn E. Johnson and Anne Foner, eds., *Aging and Society.* v. 3, *A Sociology of Age Stratification.* New York: Russell Sage Foundation, 1972, pp. 165-166.

11. *Ibid.,* pp. 173-174.

12. Erdman Palmore, *Social Patterns in Normal Aging: Findings from the Duke Longitudinal Study.* Durham, NC: Duke University Press, 1981, pp. 3-4; 108-109.

13. *Ibid.,* pp. 52; 61.

14. Riley, Johnson and Foner, *op. cit.,* p. 179.

15. Matilda White Riley and Anne Foner, *Aging and Society,* v. 1, *An Inventory of Research Findings.* New York: Russell Sage Foundation, 1968, pp. 427-428.

16. Henry S. Shryock and Jacob S. Siegel, *The Methods and Materials of Demography.* v. 1. Washington, DC: U.S. Government Printing Office, 1973, p. 353.

17. United States data are for 1978 in order to keep the countries in Table 6-2 as close together in time as possible.

18. Organisation for Economic Co-operation and Development, *Socio-economic Policies for the Elderly.* Paris: OECD, 1979, pp. 57-58.

19. Harold L. Sheppard, "Work and Retirement," in Robert N. Binstock and Ethel Shanas, eds., *Handbook of Aging and the Social Sciences.* New York: Van Nostrand, 1976, p. 291.

20. U.S. Bureau of the Census, "Some Demographic Aspects of Aging in the United States," *Current Population Reports,* P-23, no. 43 (1973): 27.

21. Riley and Foner, *op. cit.,* p. 44.

22. Loether, *op. cit.,* p. 51. Cf. Kurt W. Back and Carleton S. Guptill, "Retirement and Self Ratings," in Ida Harper Simpson and John C. McKinney, eds., *Social Aspects of Aging.* Durham, NC: Duke University Press, 1966, p. 120.

23. Riley and Foner, *op. cit.,* p. 51. Cf. Harris, *op. cit.,* p. 75.

24. U.S. Bureau of the Census, "The Social and Economic Status of the Black Population in the United States: An Historical View, 1790-1978," *Current Population Reports,* P-23, no. 80 (1979): 60.

25. Riley and Foner, *op. cit.,* pp. 58-59.

26. Harris, *op. cit.,* p. 80.

164

27. U.S. Bureau of the Census, "America in Transition: An Aging Society," *Current Population Reports*, P-23, no. 128 (1983): 23.

28. Harris, *loc. cit.*

29. John A. Priebe, "Occupation," in U.S. Bureau of the Census, "Population of the United States, Trends and Prospects: 1950-1990," *Current Population Reports*, P-23, no. 49 (1974): 155. See also Ida Harper Simpson, Richard L. Simpson, Mark Evers and Sharon Sandomirsky Poss, "Occupational Recruitment, Retention, and Labor Force Cohort Representation," *American Journal of Sociology* 87 (1982): 1305.

30. Mary Barberis, "America's Elderly: Policy Implications," *Population Bulletin* 35 (1981): 7.

31. Palmore, *op. cit.*, p. 15.

32. Sheppard, *op. cit.*, p. 197.

33. Ida Harper Simpson, Kurt W. Back and John C. McKinney, "Work and Retirement," in Simpson and McKinney, *op. cit.*, p. 59.

34. Riley and Foner, *op. cit.*, p. 50.

35. Juanita M. Kreps, "The Economy and the Aged," in Binstock and Shanas, *op. cit.*, p. 272.

36. *Ibid.*, p. 278.

37. Loether, *op. cit.*, pp. 65-66.

38. Soldo, *op. cit.*, p. 20.

39. Fred Cottrell, *Aging and the Aged*. Dubuque, IA: Wm. C. Brown, 1974, p. 31.

40. Riley, Johnson and Foner, *op. cit.*, p. 164. Cf. Harris, *op. cit.*, p. 75.

41. The projections assume moderate rather than high or low growth in the labor force as a whole. See Howard N. Fullerton, Jr., "The 1995 Labor Force: A First Look," in U.S. Bureau of Labor Statistics, *Economic Projections to 1990*, Bulletin 2121 (1982): 48-58.

42. Congressional Budget Office, *Work and Retirement: Options for Continued Employment for Older Workers*. Washington, DC: U.S. Government Printing Office, 1982, p. 10.

43. Parts of the first three reasons are adapted from Pampel, *op. cit.*, pp. 24-25; 60-61.

44. Judith Treas and Vern L. Bengston, "The Demography of Mid- and Late-Life Transitions," *Annals of American Academy of Political and Social Science*, 464 (1982): 17-18.

45. Melissa A. Hardy, "Social Policy and Determinants of Retirement: A Longitudinal Analysis of Older White Males," *Social Forces* 60 (1982): 1119.

46. Paula J. Schneider and Thomas J. Palumbo, "Social and Demographic Characteristics of the Labor Force," in U.S. Bureau of the Census, "Population of the United States...," *op. cit.*, p. 144.

47. Sheppard, *op. cit.*, p. 292.

48. For a summary of these factors, see Harris, *op. cit.*, p. 774.

49. Kingsley Davis and Pietronella van den Oever, "Age Relations and Public Policy in Advanced Industrial Societies," *Population and Development Review* 7 (1981): 2.

Chapter 7

Retirement

The vast majority of America's elderly are retired, and the amount, sources, and adequacy of their incomes have caused much popular debate and misunderstanding. The perceptions range from masses of older people huddled in rundown tenements and rural shacks and eating dog food, to a huge group of nonproducers who generally live very comfortably because of the heavy financial support burden that falls on the producing population. There are questions, too, about why people retire, what meaning retirement has for them, and how well they adjust to it. Do most desire retirement because it is an attractive alternative life style, or because they are thrown out of their jobs by uncaring employers obsessed with derogatory stereotypes about the abilities and productivity of older workers? Would most retired people rather work or not? Are most of them poor or aren't they? This chapter addresses these and other related questions.

Views of Retirement

Much has been written about the retirement patterns of older people, especially men, the reasons why they leave the labor force, and what they do afterwards.[1] Chapter 6 has already alluded to several aspects of the subject, and in this section it is possible only to summarize some significant findings about retirement — voluntary or involuntary — as a reality in the lives of older people, though the reader needs to know that some of the literature on the retired population is characterized by stereotyping, over-generalizing, and contradictory findings. Too often retired people have been pictured as poorly adjusted and desperate to return to jobs they never wanted to leave in the first place. Some of the apparent contradictions, however, also reflect changes in attitudes among retired people over the past couple of decades, especially as financial opportunities to retire have improved.

Analytically, retirement is simply the withdrawal of a person from the work force and entitlement to an income based on previous employment,[2] and is a process that has many forms and effects. One of the most strategic characteristics of retirement is that it need not be destructive or the beginning of a meaningless existence, any more than it is forced on all those who do leave the labor force. At the same time, negative images of retirement abound among people of all ages, and for some elderly it does symbolize the end of youth, vigor, usefulness, and social involvement, particularly if ill health forces them to retire.

In part, these views exist because some older persons are not prepared to retire *to* something rather than just *from* something, and because retirement often does connote "old age,"[3] even though most people who are forced to retire make reasonably good adjustments after a time. It is easy to miss the tremendous individual variability among retired people, including their different levels of satisfaction, the many ways they use their time, the highly variable amounts of money they have available, their diffences in health, the degrees of satisfaction and happiness they expect, and other variations that keep the retired population from being homogeneous. Thus, one of the complex issues that a discussion of retirement must address is the extent to which the event really is a crisis for retired persons and their spouses. Another issue is why they retire in the first place, for while many leave the labor force involuntarily because of illness or mandatory provisions, many others choose to retire, often before age 65. That trend toward early retirement began in the 1950s and was accelerated by a 1961 Social Security provision that granted reduced benefits at age 62.[4] In the late 1970s, however, inflationary pressures tended to slow this trend, and many people who would have retired early actually had to postpone moving into that phase of the life cycle. Even so, for many retired people the adjustments are successful, and finances, physical and mental health, and outlook seem adequate for the bulk of the retired population to adjust satisfactorily.[5]

The Retired Population

The retired group is more difficult to identify than it might seem, for there are various ways to classify them. Some do not work at all in a given year; others are not at work or in the labor force during the week they are surveyed; some hold only part-time or part-year jobs, though they may have retired from full-time positions. The last group experiences a certain degree of retirement, but not complete disengagement from the workplace. One can define retired people as those who receive retirement benefits, even though some of them also work, many up to the earnings-limit allowed by the Social Security system. Perhaps the most inclusive definition involves that group who hold less than full-time, year-round jobs, for under that designation about 90 per cent of the men and 95 per cent of the women aged 65 and older are retired.[6]

If the receipt of Social Security retirement benefits is used as a criterion, in 1980 almost 20 million Americans aged 62 and older were drawing such benefits, but only about a third that number received full benefits, which begin at age 65. Thus, 4.6 million men and 2.8 million women fell into the latter category, which means that about 64 per cent of the men and 31 per cent of the women were full beneficiaries. But women often do not receive full benefits because of their work histories and the way the Social Security system has classified them relative to their husbands. Many people of both sexes still work at part-time jobs while they receive benefits, so these data do not really reflect the retired population either.

If retirement is gauged by the proportions not in the labor force, then in 1980 about 81 per cent of the men and 92 per cent of the women 65 and over were classified as retired. (See Table 7-1.) But these data are strongly influenced by what people were doing during the survey week, the number of hours worked by those who were employed, whether or not unemployed people were seeking work, and other factors that prevent non-involvement in the work force from being a perfect measure of the nation's retired population. Nonetheless, the materials available do show that between the ages of 55 and 64 the retirement rate rises significantly, that at age 65 the vast majority of workers of both sexes are retired, and that in the 10 years after age 65 virtually all remaining workers retire from the labor force. For the society at large those proportions represent two opposing trends: (1) reductions in the death rate and increases in life expectancy raise the number of years the average person could work; while (2) the tendency for virtually all elderly people to retire and for many to do so before age 65 reduces the number of years one actually works and increases the time he/she is a dependent.[7] Those trends have basic implications for the productivity of the older population and for the financial costs borne by the younger group.

Men and Women

The patterns of retirement have changed quite dramatically over the past few decades, and have done so differently for men and women. For example, even among men aged 45-54 the retirement rate appears to have increased since 1950, though more than 90 per cent of that age group is still in the labor force. A sizable share of those who do retire in their 40s or early 50s are military personnel and people who worked in police and fire departments or were otherwise occupied as civil servants;[8] others are forced to stop working because of poor health. In the 55-64 age group the retirement rate doubled between 1950 and 1980, largely because retirement at age 62 or even earlier has caught on with a quarter or more of the men in the 55-64 age range. The proportion of men aged 65 and older who are retired is also much higher than in any past decade, largely due to improvements in benefits that allow an older couple sufficient money to live on, though the income is usually considerably lower than their last pre-retirement wage.

Mandatory retirement provisions have also helped push the proportion of retired men aged 65 and older to more than 80 per cent of the total. But even with the mandatory retirement age now at 70, the trends suggest that other forces favoring early retirement are far more powerful than the legal right to work until that age. One of those forces is the recent relatively high unemployment rates which have caused large groups of workers to be laid off despite seniority, and which make it difficult for elderly workers to find new jobs.

At the same time, continued inflation has forced some older workers to

Table 7-1. Percentages of People Not in the Labor Force, by Sex and Age, 1900-1990

Year	Male			Female		
	45-54	55-64	65+	45-54	55-64	65+
1900	4.5	10.0	31.6	85.3	86.8	91.9
1930	3.5	9.8	41.7	79.6	83.9	92.0
1940	7.9	16.2	58.5	87.9	83.6	94.1
1950	4.2	13.0	54.2	62.0	73.0	90.3
1960	4.3	13.2	66.9	50.2	62.8	89.2
1970	5.8	17.0	73.2	45.6	57.0	90.3
1980	8.8	27.7	80.9	40.1	58.5	91.9
1990	9.2	32.5	84.2	35.7	58.3	92.7

Sources: U.S. Bureau of the Census, Sixteenth Census of the United States: 1940, The Labor Force, U.S. Summary (1943), table 8; Statistical Abstract of the United States: 1981, table 636; U.S. Bureau of Labor Statistics, Handbook of Labor Statistics: 1980, table 2; Howard N. Fullerton, "The 1995 Labor Force," in U.S. Bureau of Labor Statistics, Economic Projections to 1990, Bulletin 2121 (1982), table 4.

169

continue until age 70 and caused others who did retire to seek part-time employment. But it probably isn't realistic to expect that any large number of older people can return to the work force during times of relatively high unemployment.[9] The jobs are simply too scarce and younger people have too much of an edge in obtaining and holding the ones that are available. Moreover, each new recession tends to start with a higher unemployment rate than did the previous one, and that reduces the older person's job prospects.

As we have seen, the involvement of women in the labor force has increased substantially since 1950, and the percentages of participants aged 45-64 are now much higher. For those aged 65 and older, however, there has been little change, and women seem more likely than men to retire. The Duke Longitudinal Study suggests that even when the women who list themselves as "housewife" and who are not in the official labor force are omitted from consideration, women workers are still more likely than men to retire early, having a substantially higher retirement rate in their 50s and beyond.[10] In part, this difference comes about because the work role is still more important to today's older men than it is to older women, given their earlier socialization, their lower average wages, persistent negative stereotypes about elderly women, and other disincentives to remain in the labor force after age 62 or 65. Furthermore, married women have far higher retirement rates than single women and somewhat higher ones than divorced women, partly because the married ones are less compelled by economic necessity to continue in the work force.

But the sex differences in retirement patterns are diminishing because of the gradual shift toward equality of men and women in the work-place. More women than ever are in the labor force and more are working full time without long interruptions for childrearing or other reasons. In addition, men's attitudes toward working women have been changing, as have those of the women themselves, and they are now less likely to end up in the relatively few categories of "female" jobs available to earlier generations. Therefore, women are apt to work for wages longer and more continuously than their mothers did, and to do so in better jobs and at higher wages, though the income differential between the sexes remains a persistent problem. Given these conditions, more women tend to have longer tenure in the work force than did earlier cohorts, and their retirement patterns by age are becoming more like those of men.[11 At the same time, more men are retiring earlier and their retirement rate is pushing toward that of women.[12]

Reasons for Retirement

People retire from the work force for many reasons, some of which were discussed in Chapter 6, but as the data in Table 7-1 suggest, advancing age is the principal one; the older one gets, the more likely one is to retire. Therefore, the general aging of the population will create a growing retired segment to be supported by a proportionately smaller working group, unless the basic trends reverse and larger percentages of older workers remain in or return to the labor force. That seems unlikely in the near future, though over a longer period the economic system may have to be fundamentally restructured so they can, because older workers will still need jobs, some employers will need their services, and they will be too large a population to be supported adequately if they are all retired. Of course, other things go along with advancing age, such as discrimination, the general expectation that older people should retire, increased financial benefits, and, for some, disability.[13]

Therefore, retirement is not just an individual matter, for it serves many purposes and has many motivations. For the person it may represent relief from a difficult, unpleasant, or boring job, and it is now a socially accepted way to stop working in a work-oriented society and do other things. In that sense, the person usually feels he/she has earned the right to live as much on his/her own terms as allowed by health, finances, family considerations, and other realities. Retirement also allows flexibility in the work force, so that employers can replace people they deem undesirable and can reduce the number of employees in tight economic times, often by not filling jobs vacated by retirees. Retirement helps lower the rate of unemployment and admits more young people to the labor force, while it also protects those elderly covered by pensions from the abject poverty that the loss of a job would otherwise impose. This is especially significant in times of high unemployment when labor is abundant. Even unions agree to mandatory retirement in order to extract concessions from employers, including pensions.[14]

Given these forces and factors, involuntary and voluntary retirement need to be considered separately, though they overlap substantially in many actual cases, especially when the worker who is pushed out of the labor force is also provided advantages that pull him/her out.

Involuntary Retirement

Given the impact of aging and other forces on retirement, it is clear that involuntary reasons loom large in causing people to retire after age 65, and that mandatory provisions adopted by industries are the most important cause of involuntary retirement. Thus, the Duke Longitudinal Study, whose findings agree with a 1963 survey done by the Social Security Administration, found that about 40 per cent of the older retired male workers and 35 per cent of the females left the work force because of mandatory retirement or layoffs, while another significant share cited poor health or disability.[*15*] Therefore, considerably more than half the retired workers of both sexes left their jobs involuntarily, although much mandatory retirement does allow sufficient benefits for the retirees to live reasonably comfortably, and thereby merges an incentive with the necessity to retire. In fact, that combination raises serious questions for the future, when the number of older workers forced to retire and the strains on public and private pension plans both will increase.

The issue of discrimination is also inherent in forcing people out of work at any age no matter what income is provided, for mandatory retirement does fail to account for individual differences in productivity, ambition, and occupational usefulness. Moreover, about half the working population is not covered by private pension plans, and the financial problems many face after forced retirement do discriminate against the group that must rely only on Social Security and other governmental programs, savings,[*16*] help from family members, and other sources that are sometimes insufficient or unpredictable.

But given the sizable proportions who live reasonably comfortable, well-adjusted lives after retirement and the benefits still needed by those whose incomes are inadequate, the most basic question is this: Can the economic system afford to force more workers out because of age and still provide the income that makes retirement humane?[*17*] Mandatory retirement at a uniform age well below average life expectancy of the elderly is a rite of passage that the society may be unable to subsidize in the future, especially if the cost of maintaining the average retired worker continues to escalate beyond his/her contributions to the Social Security system, and if the ratio of workers to retirees continues to drop.

Despite its problems, mandatory retirement is a more humane alternative than dismissing older workers for inadequate performance, although the latter practice would better reflect individual variations. Moreover, mandatory retirement gives workers a "target" date toward which they must plan, while younger workers know when certain positions will open up. As those younger workers move up, presumably more entry-level jobs also become available for people just completing their educations. This is especially critical in times of high unemployment, such as the early 1980s, though some of those jobs are also being eliminated by more sophisticated technology. Finally, given the tendency for white men to dominate the ranks of upper-level senior employees in most industries, mandatory retirement gives employers the opportunity to recruit additional women, blacks, Hispanics, and others whose chances would otherwise be more limited.[*18*]

Mandatory retirement is certainly a complex issue, but it does appear that moving the age limit from 65 to 70 will solve some problems while it intensifies others. If the change keeps more older workers in the labor force, it will shorten the time during which they receive benefits from the hard-pressed Social Security system and from private pension plans, most of which are not growing and provide no cost-of-living increases, and many of which are also under severe financial strains. Furthermore, a few extra years in the labor force will make the worker a continuing contributor to Social Security and might provide some additional private savings for retirement, though high rates of inflation and interest on purchases would erode some of those gains. Finally, longer years in the labor force would partially offset the fact that the elderly population is growing faster than the group aged 20-64, and would relieve some of the burden on the latter.

But because the forces that result in retirement are so complex, even if all people were allowed to work longer, it is uncertain how many would choose to do so. The average age of retirement is already substantially below the old mandatory age of 65, and many people still find retirement so attractive that they are willing to take substantial cuts in income to achieve it, though the relative adequacy of that income after retirement is often better than the dollar losses might imply. If many people continue to want retirement in their early 60s or at age 65, it seems useful to encourage the wider development of private pension plans that will allow earlier voluntary retirement and help relieve unemployment and other problems, while they also help the Social Security system preserve the long-term solvency intended by the 1983 reforms, one of which is a gradual increase in the minimum age at which workers can claim full benefits. The system was never meant to be the sole source of income for retired persons anyway.

Voluntary Retirement

Though about 40 per cent of all retired workers leave the labor force involuntarily because of compulsory provisions and another 15 per cent quit because of disability, the other 45 per cent are not subject to mandatory retirement, are in good health, and yet choose to leave the work force for a variety of reasons. For men, the wish to enjoy more leisure and recreation is a major incentive, as is the availability of an adequate pension or other financial resources that allow a decent retirement income. For women, family considerations seem the most important, because they either wish to spend more time at home or are needed to do so. In many cases, the woman worker in her late 50s or her 60s becomes the chief caregiver for an aged parent, usually a mother or mother-in-law, and that role takes precedence over her job.

In addition, a substantial number of women prefer more leisure and recreational opportunities, often with husbands who have also retired.

This helps account for the higher retirement rates among women who are married than among those who are not, as does the availability and adequacy of the husband's retirement income. It is also significant, therefore, that the proportion of women who choose to retire because they personally have good pensions is far lower than the percentage of men who cite that reason.[19] Many of the older women who continue to work are sole wage-earners in a household; not a few live alone, and some have had long work experiences that encourage them to continue working. Thus, given the tendency for fewer women to be covered by adequate pension plans and the lower wages on which their retirement benefits are computed, it is not surprising that financial incentives are a less attractive reason for women to choose retirement than they are for men.

The level of education and type of job also affect voluntary retirement rates, for people with the highest levels of schooling tend to retire relatively late and at a lower rate. Many of them are doing work that demands little physical exertion and are not as overwhelmed by the energy demands of their jobs as a laborer might be, though some may be too sedentary. In addition, well-educated people are more likely to hold interesting and rewarding occupations they are reluctant to leave, and are more apt to have skills that make them less easy to replace or power that makes them difficult to expel. They are also more likely to be self-employed and unaffected by mandatory retirement, and some are able to scale down their activities gradually while partners or heirs take on more responsibility, such as in a law or medical practice. The well-educated are also less subject to the age discrimination that often forces the poorly educated out of their low-status jobs.

Conversely, people whose educations and opportunities have caused them to be laborers all of their working lives are apt to retire as soon as they can afford to do so, thus escaping the arduous physical demands of their jobs. Other blue-collar workers, especially in manufacturing, must depart at the mandatory age and their retirement rate is relatively high, though many are also glad to leave the work force. At the same time, older people in service positions have a fairly low rate of retirement, basically because they cannot afford to leave their jobs, but also because those jobs don't make impossible physical demands on the elderly worker. In fact, many older workers who do retire from other occupations take service jobs as a way to supplement their incomes, which might otherwise come exclusively from Social Security, though the jobs tend to be relatively low in the status hierarchy. Finally, workers in middle management also tend to have relatively high retirement rates, often because their chances for promotion decline sharply after age 45 or 50 and they tend to be "stuck" at the same level for many years,[20] some because of obsolete skills and educations.

In general, then, the retirement rates are lowest at the extremes of the income and job-status range: Professional and technical workers and senior management personnel tend to work past age 65 because of high rewards and their value as workers or because they are self-employed. Service workers tend to hold on to jobs which pay relatively little and which they may even dislike, but which supply small supplements to Social Security payments and are not too difficult physically for the older person to perform. Workers between these extremes tend to have higher retirement rates because of adequate pensions, mandatory provisions, or "dead-end" jobs that are not an inspiring alternative to leisure; the rates are also comparatively high for laborers.

In the retired population of all ages, voluntary reasons seem responsible for the fact that the average worker now has a 30 per cent greater chance of retirement than one with the same job and nonwork income had in 1950. Much of this increase is due to early retirement that is unaffected by mandatory provisions, and that helps account for the rapid growth in the total retired population. And most of the people who are subject to mandatory retirement appear to leave willingly at the specified age, or at least to adjust eventually to the nonwork role. Therefore, the workers who have been forced out of jobs they really wanted to keep are only a minority, whereas those who have chosen or adjusted readily to retirement are the majority. The former group is enlarged some by the people who must retire because of disability, the latter by the increasing numbers who can count on reasonable pensions after they retire, though certain numbers choose to retire on low incomes because retirement has significant attractions for many people even when it creates financial strains; the retirement choice is at least partly independent of income and the effects of inflation.[21]

Nevertheless, there remains a sizable number of retirement resisters, perhaps 4 million or more retired people age 65 and older who do not like their situations and want to work for wages. Once again, however, the state of health and the adequacy of income play major roles in whether or not a person resists or accepts retirement, as do the nature of the job, the strains it imposes, how the person perceives his/her degree of autonomy in the job, and other factors that may be quite subjective.[22]

Adjusting to Retirement

Retirement calls for more adjustment by some people than others, but as in most phases of the life cycle, the large majority deal with it as smoothly as possible and go on with their lives. In fact, most who retire find the event and subsequent accommodations far less traumatic than the popular wisdom suggests. The process does not appear to create unbearable poverty, serious mental or physical problems, idle boredom, or grim unhappiness for the great majority; for many people it has the opposite effects. It is crucial, however, for retirement to allow people continued self-respect, no matter how they may construe it, and a reasonable measure of social responsibility and usefulness, partly to offset the negative status that Americans still tend to assign persons who are retired.[23] In a society that is strongly youth-oriented and where one's worth is still tied partly to work, retirement signifies the loss of two socially desirable traits and the concomitant acquisition of two less desirable ones. Therefore, even though retirement doesn't shatter many lives unless it plunges people into extreme poverty, it does necessitate adjustments and redefinitions, some of them painful, others easy and pleasurable. On the whole, however, retirement doesn't seem to reduce life satisfaction for most people, and "very few suffer severe poverty, illness, inactivity, or depression as a result."[24]

In contrast to some earlier studies, the recent ones cited herein show that people's attitudes toward impending retirement are generally favorable, and that the number of years a person has to go before retirement or the years already spent in it have little relationship to how he/she assesses retirement. The two factors that do strongly affect attitudes are health and projected or actual income, because they influence the person's options during retirement.[25] Both of these factors have improved markedly for the older population in the past few decades, so that many who might have feared retirement in the 1950s and 1960s do not do so now. Therefore, while the findings of some earlier studies on the matter are inconsistent with those of later investigations, the apparent contradictions actually reflect significant shifts in the attitudes of the elderly themselves,[26] and those, in turn, mirror important financial improvements for the elderly population as a whole.

Some caution is necessary, however, as one interprets the results of surveys that attempt to gauge the life satisfaction of older people, especially those who are retired. Some may report that they are genuinely satisfied with conditions that other age groups would reject or which the elderly themselves would have deplored when they were younger, whereas their favorable responses may represent an ego-defense. Even if elderly respondents truly believe they are deprived and less happy than other groups, they may still report themselves in more optimistic terms as a way to deny the feeling that they have failed, are poor, and are otherwise unable to live up to the life-satisfaction norms they think prevail.[27] Such a phenomenon is closely related to the tendency for the elderly to see themselves as a more homogeneous group than they are, as discussed in Chapter 2.[28]

176

Income

When most persons retire, income does go down substantially and they must get by on the much-discussed smaller "fixed income," though cost-of-living increases in Social Security benefits have provided some flexibility. But lingering fears about income insufficiency are often exaggerated, for despite the inflationary spiral the proportion of elderly people living in families below the official poverty line declined from 27 per cent in 1959 to 8 per cent in 1981, while the proportion among unrelated individuals (essentially the people living alone) fell from 62 per cent to 29 per cent. Moreover, most of the elderly who live in poverty did so when they were younger, though it is noteworthy that even the lower percentage of elderly poor in 1981 meant there were still 4 million people, or 15 per cent of the entire older population, below the official poverty line. Obviously, those people need more of the help an affluent society can provide, whether privately or publicly.

The decrease that retired people experience in *actual* income is generally far more than the decrease in the *adequacy* of income, because most retired people no longer pay home mortgages, while they have small or no responsibilities to rear and educate children and are less burdened by certain other expenses carried by younger adults, including the bulk of Social Security taxes. Retired people also have the protection of medical care that is partly publicly financed, increases in Social Security benefits to counter cost-of-living changes, discounts on many purchases, and other offsetting advantages,[29] though some of these were reduced as the federal government attempted to restore the financial health of the Social Security system. In general, the spectacle of a class of elderly persons forced into poverty by mandatory retirement is a myth for all but a relatively small minority, though they do need attention and some are truly destitute. In addition, retirees report they miss money more than any other aspects of the job, while comparatively few miss the work itself,[30] which means that older people's assumption of widespread poverty in their age group may be a problem no matter what the realities.

Chapter 8 to follow deals more fully with the elderly who are truly poor and with the larger matter of income received by various groups of older people.

Health

Almost everyone seems to know at least one older person who retired and died soon afterward, appearing to languish and waste away in the interim. Such cases have created the assumption that retirement causes a decline in health, both physical and mental. It may do so for those whose lives were consumed by a job and who became totally inactive after retirement. But the principal reasons retired people have higher rates of illness and death than other groups is because existing health problems forced more of them to retire, and because advancing age increases the likelihood of illness irrespective of employment status.

Moreover, while some retirees report poorer health after retirement, equal numbers experience improvements, especially those who worked in hazardous or unusually stressful jobs, and the ones who became more active physically after retirement.[31] As expected, most of those whose health is poor tend to be less satisfied with retirement than people who have few disabilities, largely because illness keeps the former from living life as they please, including the choice to keep on working. But retirement also allows the unhealthy person to lay down the burden of a job, and his/her level of satisfaction with life may rise as a result. Nonetheless, health and income are the two most strategic predictors of how well a person adapts to retirement, though the decision to retire in the first place seems to be influenced much more strongly by the availability of retirement income than by the level of health, unless the latter is severely incapacitating.[32]

Personal Adaptation

Retirement does not cause depression or unhappiness for the great majority of elderly people, though a small minority with limited interests and the compulsion to continue working do suffer such problems. Furthermore, some of those who resist retirement are often able to keep their jobs, at least in certain occupations, while others can sometimes find new ones to offset forced retirement. Altogether, therefore, perhaps 80 or 90 per cent of the retired population seem no less happy than when they worked, and the great majority do not slip into extreme loneliness, depression, isolation, and inactivity.[33] although those difficulties were probably more severe in the 1950s and 1960s than they are now. Nevertheless, there is a tendency toward greater solitude among many retirees, for not all of the hours one formerly worked are necessarily filled with other social activity, and one's productivity in the conventional sense does decrease; nor does the person have a work role around which to orient other activities.

Retirement also has some unfavorable social meanings the person must confront, and status may fall because the society still assigns rather negative meanings to a person's departure from work, and because his/her income will probably decrease.[34] Even worse, the drop in income does force some retirees to experience poverty or near poverty for the first time in their lives.[35] Nearly all retirees tend to be labeled "old," which also has negative connotations despite individual differences in chronological and physiological age, mental and physical states, and levels of activity. Therefore, some retired workers must struggle to preserve a decent level of living, self-respect, and a sense of usefulness in the face of these realities and their meanings, especially if significant associates believe that retirement is "the end of things." The task is particularly difficult for those who lack an adequate network of integrative relationships to replace the work role.

But new retirees begin to give more effort to activities for which they once had little time, such as recreation with a spouse or friends who have also left the labor force. Many people who had hobbies spend more time on them and obtain a feeling of productivity from those efforts or from part-time employment, volunteer work, home maintenance, religious involvement, new educational experiences, and other activities. Consequently, most of the negative effects of retirement that do occur, including disengagement from full-time work, lower incomes, and the change from "middle aged" to "old," seem to be temporary and manageable for most retired persons. Their successes, however, should not belittle the adjustments that virtually all retirees must make, or the substantial strains experienced by a minority who do not progress smoothly into that phase of the life cycle and who suffer once in it. Some of them are too poor to afford activities that would enhance social integration. But no matter what the cause, social activity for the elderly can be improved by public and private efforts to create centers for the elderly, group dining arrangements, and other activities that enhance social integration and adaptation.[36]

Changes in the Nature of Retirement

A New Institution

In assessing the ways people adapt to retirement, it is useful to recognize that it is a relatively new institution in American society, other industrialized societies, and the socialist countries, while it scarcely exists for the great majority of people in most of the developing nations. As suggested by the data in Table 7-1, only in the last few decades has any group but a wealthy minority been able to afford retirement, while the majority either died while still employed or were forced out by disability or employment policies, usually without pensions or much other financial security. Many didn't have to retire at all because they were self-employed, mainly in farming, and in those farm households that did include three generations the elderly continued to contribute what they could, being neither forced by age alone to give up productive work nor protected by pensions from sharing any deprivations experienced by the rest of the family. As noted in Chapter 4, however, the three-generation family was never as common as often assumed; nor are most modern families indifferent to elderly members and their needs, though the task of caring for very old retired members may fall on offspring who are retired themselves.[37]

The newness of the retirement process means, therefore, that American society is just now developing mechanisms and attitudes to smooth the transition from work to nonwork and to make retirement a fully respectable and satisfying stage in the life cycle. Moreover, the great variation in the post-retirement incomes received by individuals means that financial comfort for some people in the older years contrasts sharply with deprivation for others. Consequently, before older people can adapt more easily and productively to retirement, the society must complete the process of creating institutions that provide adequate incomes, medical care, housing, and other aspects of retirement that are still not as thoroughly incorporated into the American system as is work. Only then will retirement become a fully acceptable status in a reasonably ordered period of life for virtually all individuals, rather than the last struggle after an earlier ordered period of life is over.[38]

Supporting the Retired Population

There is another side to this matter. It involves the increasing burden of support for the elderly that falls on the working population, for that situation has also changed significantly. Chapter 2 dealt with the statistical relationship between producers and the elderly and pointed out that the *combined* youth and elderly dependency ratio is no greater now than it has been, but that the relative importance of the two components has changed significantly. This section considers the financial implications of a growing, non-producing elderly population, including the degree to which the working population will continue to accept the rising costs of supporting that group.

The burden of support for the elderly has passed increasingly from the family to public responsibility, though the working population still carries the burden. Several factors, including rapid social change, geographic movement, vertical social mobility, and high divorce rates, have broadened the social distance between many elderly persons and their children, and in many cases they have reduced the direct care that offspring provide their elderly parents. Simultaneously, these and other factors have increased the dependence of the elderly on pension plans, Social Security, Medicare, community agencies, and other formal public programs and agencies.

Moreover, despite the family relationships that still pervade the care that large numbers of older people receive, the elderly have come to expect less from children directly and more from the society, which is to say more from the working population indirectly through taxation and various transfer payments. And because this expectation has been institutionalized, the small population of wealthy elderly whose family resources allowed them to retire in earlier generations has been joined by the large majority of all people aged 65 and older, for they can now call on the resources of the whole society. In the process, the cost for support of the retired population has risen astronomically.[39] As a result, the older person who retires now recoups his/her total Social Security investment in a few years and then draws from funds paid by current workers, whereas young people may never receive the full amount they will contribute during their working lives.

This situation raises several questions: How high can taxation for support of the elderly go before it is counterproductive? How long will the working population be willing to pay for such support, balancing costs against genuine benevolence for older people and the knowledge that they, the younger people, will eventually become recipients rather than contributors? What additional reforms are needed in the Social Security and Medicare systems to keep them solvent indefinitely and yet allow us to meet the costs of other necessary services? How can the elderly come to rely more heavily on wages generated by their own efforts, and how can attitudes be changed to encourage work as a way to reduce the strains on public finances? Can the economy accommodate a larger population of working elderly and still provide "full employment" for younger people, including teenagers? Can we head off a serious intergenerational conflict over these matters?

American society is struggling with these questions now and will need to deal with them more intensively in the future. In the meantime, it is undeniable that the elderly whose support derives from nonwork income, use but do not produce goods and services, no matter how much they may have earned that privilege and no matter what other useful things they may do. In turn, the burden on those who do produce grows, because the numbers and proportions of retired people have increased rapidly, the ratio of workers to retired people has fallen sharply, and the relative incomes of the elderly have risen.[40] All of this represents an unprecedented burden on producing adults, no matter how much the support burden for children may have declined, and is a major social change that has made care for the elderly much more a public matter with major political implications. There is no escaping the fact that fertility fluctuations in the twentieth century, along with mortality reductions, have greatly increased the elderly population, and that the retirement of the great majority of older people has made them a dependent group for an increasingly long period.[41] With the average age of retirement falling and life expectancy increasing, more elderly are drawing more heavily from both public and private pension plans financed by a working population that is growing at a slower rate than is the older group. That is another basic feature in the aging of America's population, and is a major dilemma.

Summary

Most Americans aged 65 and older are retired, though numerous misperceptions stereotype them as poor or as an overwhelming burden on the working population; as with most stereotypes, there is *some* truth in both views. The "retired" population is actually very diverse, because some people work part-time or part-year; others retire on comfortable pensions but have difficulty in adjusting to income reductions; still others continue to be just as poor as they always were or become even poorer. Therefore, it is difficult to identify who is retired and the nature of their circumstances.

People retire for many reasons, but one large group is forced to do so by mandatory provisions or poor health, while the other large segment chooses retirement willingly, usually because they can afford it and look forward to a financially tolerable future. Moreover, much voluntary retirement is accompanied by a package of Social Security benefits and private pension income, so that many people are simultaneously forced and attracted out of the labor force. Those who must retire early because of serious disabilities, however, often have limited resources and large expenses. Those who retire voluntarily because they can afford to and want more leisure account for the bulk of early retirees, and they have helped lower the average age at retirement significantly.

How well people accept and adjust to retirement is subject to conflicting findings, but largely because adjustment seems to have been more difficult in the recent past than it is now. The critical factors in adjustment are the adequacy of one's income, the state of one's health, and the kinds of activities that one experiences in the older years. But most retirees appear to adjust well and relatively easily and to go on with their lives fairly smoothly. Those who really miss work itself are a comparatively small and declining minority, though most people do miss the higher income that work provided. Large-scale retirement is a relatively new phenomenon, however, confined to the industrialized countries and the socialist nations, and many questions remain about its impact on the retired population and the support burden that the working population must carry for the rapidly growing retired group.

182

NOTES

1. See, for example, Gordon F. Streib and Clement J. Schneider, *Retirement and American Society.* Ithaca, NY: Cornell University Press, 1971; Frances M. Carp, ed., *Retirement.* New York: Behavioral Publications, 1972; Robert C. Atchley, *The Sociology of Retirement.* Cambridge, MA: Schenkman, 1976; Anne Foner and Karen Schwab, *Aging and Retirement.* Monterey, CA: Brooks/Cole, 1981; Neil G. McCluskey and Edgar F. Borgatta, eds., *Aging and Retirement: Prospects, Planning, and Policy.* Beverly Hills, CA: Sage, 1981; Erdman Palmore, *Social Patterns in Normal Aging: Findings from the Duke Longitudinal Study.* Durham, NC: Duke University Press, 1981, chapter 3; and Robert C. Atchley, "Retirement: Leaving the World of Work," *Annals of American Academy of Political and Social Science* 464 (1982): 120-131.

2. Atchley, *op. cit.,* p. 120.

3. Marvin B. Sussman, "An Analytical Model for the Sociological Study of Retirement," in Carp, *op. cit.,* pp. 32; 36.

4. Judith Treas and Vern L. Bengston, "The Demography of Mid- and Late-Life Transitions," *Annals,* p. 19.

5. Palmore, *op. cit.,* p. 36.

6. For the various definitions, see *ibid.,* p. 32.

7. Trudy B. Anderson, "The Dependent Elderly Population: A Function of Retirement," *Research on Aging* 3 (1981): 314.

8. Richard A. Kalish, *Late Adulthood: Perspectives on Human Development.* Monterey, CA: Brooks/Cole, 1975, p. 111.

9. Juanita M. Kreps, "The Economy and the Aged," in Robert H. Binstock and Ethel Shanas, eds., *Handbook of Aging and the Social Sciences.* New York: Van Nostrand, 1976, p. 282.

10. Palmore, *op. cit.,* p. 34. Cf. Fred C. Pampel, *Social Change and the Aged.* Lexington, MA: Heath, 1981, p. 69.

11. Jacob S. Siegel, "On the Demography of Aging," *Demography* 17 (1980): 358.

12. For a treatment of this matter, see Robert C. Atchley, "The Process of Retirement: Comparing Women and Men," in Maximiliane Szinovacz, ed., *Women's Retirement.* Beverly Hills, CA: Sage, 1982, chapter 10.

13. Palmore, *op. cit.,* pp. 34-35.

14. For several of these points, see Atchley, "Retirement," *op. cit.,* p. 121.

15. Palmore, *op. cit.,* pp. 37-39.

16. Harrison Givens, Jr., "An Evaluation of Mandatory Retirement," *Annals of American Academy of Political and Social Science,* 438 (1978): 51-52.

17. Harold L. Sheppard, "The Issue of Mandatory Retirement," *Annals* 438 (1978): 48-49.

18. Givens, *op. cit.,* p. 51.

19. Palmore, *op. cit.,* pp. 37-38.

20. Organisation for Economic Co-operation and Development, *Socio-economic Policies for the Elderly.* Paris: OECD, 1979, pp. 82-83.

21. Pampel, *op. cit.,* pp. 60-61.

22. Harold L. Sheppard, "Work and Retirement," in Binstock and Shanas, *op. cit.,* p. 302. Cf. National Council on the Aging, *The Myth and Reality of Aging in America.* Washington, DC: NCOA, 1975.

23. Carp, *op. cit.,* pp. 40-41.

24. Palmore, *op. cit.,* pp. 45-46.

25. Robert C. Atchley and Judith L. Robinson, "Attitudes Toward Retirement and Distance from the Event," *Research on Aging* 4 (1982): 311.

26. On this matter, see Nancy Lohman, "Life Satisfaction Research in Aging: Implications for Policy Development," in Nancy Datan and Nancy Lohman, eds., *Transitions of Aging.* New York: Academic Press, 1980, chapter 2, especially pp. 31-32; 35.

27. For a treatment of this methodological problem, see Frances M. Carp and Abraham Carp, "It May Not Be the Answer, It May Be the Question," *Research on Aging* 3 (1981): 85-100, especially pp. 97-98.

28. Hubert J. O'Gorman, "False Consciousness of Kind," *Research on Aging* 2 (1980): 105-128.

29. Palmore, *op. cit.,* p. 40.

30. Kalish, *op. cit.,* pp. 108; 109.

31. Palmore, *op. cit.,* pp. 40-41.

32. Willis J. Goudy, "Antecedent Factors Related to Changing Work Expectations," *Research on Aging* 4 (1982): 153-154.

33. Palmore, *op. cit.,* p 41. Cf. Atchley and Robinson, *op. cit.,* pp. 301-303.

34. Sussman, *op. cit.,* pp. 40-41.

35. Beth J. Soldo, "America's Elderly in the 1980s," *Population Bulletin* 35 (1980): 21.

36. Lohman, *op. cit.,* pp. 34-35.

37. Elaine M. Brody, "The Aging of the Family," *Annals* 438 (1978): 17.

38. Sussman, *op. cit.,* p. 34.

39. Kingsley Davis and Pietronella van den Oever, "Age Relations and Public Policy in Advanced Industrial Societies," *Population and Development Review* 7 (1981): 4-6.

40. *Ibid.,* pp. 8-9.

41. Anderson, *op. cit.,* pp. 311; 314.

Chapter 8

Income and Poverty Status
Of the Elderly

Popular attitudes and literature tend to portray older people as poor or close to it, because most of the elderly experience such large cuts in their money incomes when they retire. Since 1960 their incomes have averaged only about half to two-thirds those of younger people,[1] and that drop is a severe blow to many, even those whose reduced resources are still adequate.[2] In addition, many people now reaching retirement age have worked at low-paying jobs, and the base on which their retirement benefits are computed is small, their incomes even less adequate when they do retire. Therefore, it would be cruel to minimize the plight of those older persons who encounter poverty for the first time when they leave work and of those who can't afford a decent level of living. Such groups include many sick and disabled people, widows, members of minority groups, and persons covered only by minimum Social Security benefits.

Despite these real problems, however, governmental programs and other forces have helped protect increasing proportions of the elderly from severe deprivation. Those forces include transfer payments, Medicare and other governmental health programs, the smaller number of dependents supported by older than by younger people, double tax exemptions, discounts on certain purchases, help from family members, and other advantages that partly offset the smaller cash incomes received by many elderly. These things are difficult to measure and rarely show up in the reports on financial resources, but even a few refinements in assessing the data on income show most older persons to be better off relative to younger ones than we often assume.

Income

Indexes of Income

This study relies principally on two indexes of income and focuses on the large majority of elderly who are not in the labor force or receiving full wages. The indexes are *family income* and *personal income*.

Family Income. The U.S. Census Bureau, through its Current Population Survey, regularly provides data on family income and household income, but unless those materials are used as carefully as they are recorded, they can support the impression of pervasive poverty among the elderly.[3] In 1980, for example, the mean income for all American families, unweighted by the number of family members or by age, was $23,974, while the unweighted mean for families with householders aged 65 and older was only $16,918, or about 71 per cent of the figure for all families.[4] But if family incomes are calculated on a per capita basis, the situation of older people seems far less dire, because most elderly householders need use the income only for themselves and a spouse; they are no longer responsible for high childrearing costs. Consequently, Table 8-1 shows how differently the elderly fare when per capita family income is substituted for overall family income, and that in 1980 the per capita income of families with a householder aged 65 or older was 99 per cent of the per capita amount received by all families.

Clearly, elderly families are about as well off on the average by this index as is the population as a whole, and they fare better than the families with a householder aged 15-24, 25-34, or 35-44. The last two groups are likely to have dependent children who impose a financial strain that most elderly no longer have to endure. In 1980, for example, while the average family with a householder aged 35-44 had 1.86 children and that with a householder aged 25-34 had 1.52, elderly families averaged a mere 0.10, while those with householders aged 15-24 averaged 0.87. Even the ones with householders aged 55-64 were down to an average of 0.28. Thus, while the elderly family had a smaller number of earners and less total income than most other age groups, it also had the fewest dependents.

If the per capita income data are further refined to reflect income before and after taxes, the elderly make an especially good showing. In 1980, for instance, all households collectively had a per capita income after taxes of $5,964, but those with an elderly householder had one of $6,299, so the elderly actually fared better on this index. All households paid nearly 23 per cent of their total money income in taxes, but the elderly paid only 13 per cent, which significantly improves their financial situation. In fact, the per cent of income that people aged 65 and older lost to taxes was only half that paid by households with a head aged 55-59, because of the progressive nature of the income tax, "bracket creep" created by inflation, and increases in Social Security taxes. Clearly, an assessment of the relative income situation of older people depends heavily on the type of index used.[5]

The usefulness of the per capita income index is also demonstrated by the wide variations in elderly household income according to the number of members. Thus, in 1980 one-person units with a householder aged 65 or over had a median income of $5,134, while two-person units received $12,134, three-person households obtained $17,436, and those with four persons had an average income of $20,485. But these figures also show how drastically the position of the elderly householder can change if one income receiver is lost, particularly if a spouse in a two-person household dies.[6]

Income of persons. The Census Bureau also reports personal income by age, cross-classified by sex and race, which allows an analysis of how well elderly individuals fare relative to younger ones in those categories. This index allows us to compute *relative income* for each age group, males and females, and blacks and whites. But more so than in the case of family income, the use of personal income as an index does support the conclusion that the elderly income receiver is at a substantial disadvantage

Table 8-1. Mean, Per Capita, and Relative Family Income, by Age of Householder, 1980

Age	Mean Family Income (Dollars)		Per Cent of Mean	
	Total	Per Capita	Total	Per Capita
15+	23,974	7,341	100.0	100.0
15-24	14,696	5,376	61.3	73.2
25-34	21,394	6,291	89.2	85.7
35-44	26,927	6,719	112.3	91.5
45-54	30,279	8,287	126.3	112.9
55-64	27,319	9,874	114.0	134.5
65+	16,918	7,275	70.6	99.1

Source: U.S. Bureau of the Census, "Money Income of Households, Families, and Persons in the United States: 1980," Current Population Reports, P-60, no. 132 (1982), table 21.

relative to most other groups, because personal income data include many older people living alone. In 1980, for example, persons aged 65-69 received a median income of $6,150, which was 77 per cent of that for all ages, while people aged 70 and over received $4,872, or only 61 per cent of the figure for all ages.

Recall, however, that elderly income receivers have fewer dependents than most other age groups, which improves the adequacy of their income. Moreover, the data on personal income do not account separately for people who have no income of their own but who live with relatives who do have income, and the census data tend to underestimate the overall resources available to the elderly.[7] That still does not justify the situation of those who really do live in or near poverty and whose lives are unreasonably constrained by inadequate incomes. Their cases provide ample room for improvement, though the degree of income inequality between the elderly and other groups has diminished because of changes in income distribution techniques. For those who no longer work, income generally comes from Social Security, earlier savings and investments, public and private pension plans, and private charity, and the mix of those things has changed in recent years so that income discrimination against the elderly as a whole has declined, though there are still wide discrepancies among individuals. Nor do the income indexes include indirect or non-money income, which can be quite significant for many people of all ages, including the elderly.[8] That group benefits from government programs; from the fact that mortgages are paid off, although property taxes continue to rise; and from shifts of money from younger people to older ones.[9]

Many types of income constitute the data from which the family and personal income indexes are computed. They include wages and salaries, net receipts from farm and nonfarm self-employment, Social Security (but not Medicare reimbursement), and Supplemental Security Income (SSI) from various levels of government for low-income people who are aged, blind, or disabled. Also included are welfare payments; dividends, interest, rents, royalties, and related payments; unemployment compensation, veterans' payments, and worker's compensation; and private and government pensions. Incomes also include annuities, alimony, and regular contributions from persons outside the household, as well as government transfer payments.[10] Thus, official "income" is a very broad category, and yet because not everything that people actually receive gets reported any place, the dollar amounts that are officially recorded still underrepresent total income. Moreover, the data omit money from the sale of property (e.g., stocks or a house), withdrawals of bank deposits, money borrowed, tax refunds, gifts, and lump-sum inheritances or insurance payments. These sources contribute to actual financial well-being and their omission also helps underestimate the real incomes of many elderly people. Nevertheless, the available data do facilitate various comparisons of the elderly with other age groups and among different groups within the older category.[11]

Incomes of Older and Younger People

The percentages of elderly people who have some income are greater than those for every other age group in the population. As a result, in the 1980 population of 25 million elderly people in the United States, only 333,000 had no income at all. Nevertheless, the median income received by persons aged 65 and older is significantly below that in all but the 15-19 age group and is especially low compared with those of middle-aged persons in their peak earning years. (See Table 8-2.)

People aged 65 and older are also very heavily concentrated in the $2,000-$4,999 category, and only somewhat less so in the $5,000-$9,999 range; even most of the latter cluster near the lower end. In fact, 63 per

Table 8-2. Median and Relative Income of Persons, by Age and Sex, 1980

Age	Median Income (Dollars)			Per Cent of Median		
	Both Sexes	Male	Female	Both Sexes	Male	Female
15+	7,944	12,530	4,920	100.0	100.0	100.0
15-19	1,736	1,801	1,673	21.9	14.4	34.0
20-24	6,612	7,923	5,286	83.2	63.2	107.4
25-34	11,173	15,580	6,973	140.6	124.3	141.7
35-44	12,254	20,037	6,465	154.3	159.9	131.4
45-54	11,927	19,974	6,403	150.1	159.4	130.1
55-64	9,420	15,914	4,926	118.6	127.0	100.1
65-69	6,150	8,953	4,379	77.4	71.5	89.0
70+	4,872	6,545	4,168	61.3	52.2	84.7

Source: U.S. Bureau of the Census, "Money Income of Households, Families, and Persons in the United States: 1980," Current Population Reports, P-60, no. 132 (1982), table 50.

cent of the persons aged 65-69 and 76 per cent of those aged 70 and older had incomes between $2,000 and $10,000 in 1980, compared with only 38 per cent of those aged 55-64 and even smaller proportions of people in their 30s and 40s. In addition, almost half the people 65 and over had incomes below $5,000. That amount scarcely provides survival for those living alone, though couples in which each member has an income fare better.

These concentrations of older people at the lower end of the scale reflect the abrupt income shifts most incur when they retire, for the proportion receiving more than $10,000 falls significantly, while the percentage receiving over $15,000 drops to a third or less of the proportion among middle-aged groups. Part of this age discrepancy occurs not just because of retirement, but also because any age group tends to have a lower average income than younger ones who move into that group, for each new cohort joins the labor force with higher entry salaries. Moreover, younger cohorts often receive larger salary increases than older ones, despite the escalating rewards of seniority, and the younger people have higher average levels of education that produce higher incomes. The younger workers also appear more frequently in high-paying growth industries, whereas many older people retire from low-paying industries on the decline.[12] Nonetheless, income inequality has been decreasing and the elderly as a group are in an improved position relative to other age groups, although the incomes of the oldest people have not risen as rapidly as those for people nearer 65, so that gap has widened some.[13]

For these and other reasons, including discrimination, the income of the average older person is lower than that in all other age groups, except for young people still in school or who have just entered the labor force. The elderly seem especially poor relative to people aged 35-44, but the latter also have the largest average child support burdens, because most have already produced as many children as they will have while they are still paying the high costs of rearing those children through adolescence and college. Thus, like people aged 15-19, the incomes of the elderly can be devoted almost entirely to supporting themselves, and the relative income position of many is better than dollar comparisons might suggest.

This is why it is important to study per capita income, discussed in connection with the data in Table 8-1. That index shows that the income situation of the elderly is often better than we assume, but it also allows us to pinpoint those older people, often solitary individuals, who really are desperately poor. That approach helps explain why families with a householder aged 55-64 are better off on a per capita basis than those with one aged 45-54, even though the latter group has the highest dollar income. By the time the householder reaches 55-64, most or all of the children have left home and the smaller income goes further. At the same time, however, costs for food, fuel, rents and property taxes, and health have risen rapidly and older people tend to spend a larger percentage of their incomes on those items than do younger ones.[14]

This may diminish the amounts available for things that make life more pleasant. Therefore, there are limits to the advantages older people gain by having fewer dependents to support, and some can hardly support themselves. For them, "the greatest destroyer of old-age security is inflation,"[15] because it erodes the income for which the elderly have planned and compromises the efforts society has made to improve pension plans, health care, and other supports. Therefore, many of the elderly may hold their own because of cost-of-living adjustments in Social Security and other increases in income, but most do not improve their positions measurably; many even have to draw principal from savings accounts, sell property, and otherwise diminish the assets from which they derive part of their income.[16]

Finally, the decline in income that most elderly persons experience when they retire has different meanings to different individuals, and many people whom a demographer might place below an arbitrary poverty line do not feel their status has fallen. Conversely, a middle-class wage earner plunged into poverty because a pension didn't materialize or was smaller than expected might experience an acute sense of deprivation and severe adjustment problems. So might a pensioner whose savings and fixed income are reduced by inflation, which has actually happened to many people on pensions that don't provide cost-of-living increases.[17] Similarly, a relatively wealthy person whose retirement income drops below previous earnings may feel deprived, even though he/she has a fully adequate income by less subjective standards.[18] Therefore, while the data on income provide a reasonably objective view of how the resources of different age groups compare, they cannot tell much about how people perceive those resources.

Elderly full-time workers. So far the discussion of income by age has dealt with the entire group of elderly people, the large majority of them retired and living on reduced incomes. But some people 65 and over still work full-time and their incomes are relatively high. Thus, in 1980 the group of workers aged 65-69 had a median personal income of $15,647, compared to that of $15,836 for full-time workers of all ages; and even working people aged 70 and older earned $14,963. The *mean* incomes of both elderly groups were actually above the national average because the older contingent includes a relatively large share of high-salaried persons who choose to continue working. The elderly group working full time is relatively small, however, for in 1980 it included only 15 per cent of all men aged 65-69 and 4 per cent of those 70 and over. The female contingent was even smaller. Therefore, this group has comparatively little statistical impact on the income situation of the whole elderly population.

Income Differences by Sex

At all ages the percentage of women receiving any income at all is smaller than that of men, though the difference declines in the 65-and-over group, especially for whites. Moreover, no matter what the age bracket, the median personal income of women is still significantly below that of men, though the discrepancy is less in the ages past 65 than it is for people between 25 and 64. (See Table 8-2.) Even so, in 1980 the median personal income of women aged 65-69 was only 49 per cent of that received by the men, and the income of women 70 and over was 64 per cent of that obtained by men. But the sex discrepancy for the elderly is less than it is for younger people, because women of all ages had a median personal income that was only 39 per cent of that received by men. That wide variation reflects the fact that the incomes of women are more likely to be based on part-time work, but it also shows that large numbers of women are still confined to typical "female" jobs that pay relatively poorly.

Furthermore, the persistent wage discrimination against women, even in the same jobs or in different jobs that ought to provide comparable rewards, is still a serious problem. For retired women, these circumstances mean that the lower earnings on which their pensions are based extend the discrimination into the older years as well. As a result, women aged 65 and older who reported themselves as retired in 1980 had a median personal income of $6,393, whereas the retired men had a median of $8,620.[19] However, the *relative income* of elderly women is fairly close to that of all women, while the relative income of elderly men is far below that of all men. With much higher pre-retirement incomes than women, the men experience a larger proportional drop when they leave the labor force, though the reduced incomes they do receive are still higher than those of elderly women.

When the personal incomes of the average elderly woman and man are combined into a family income that must support only two people, the elderly do not fare badly. When people live alone or with nonrelatives, however, their incomes are apt to be quite small compared with those of elderly families, and elderly women are at a considerable disadvantage relative to older men. A comparison of their circumstances uses the concept of *unrelated individuals,* who are people not living with any relative and who either reside alone, in group quarters, such as a rooming house, or with other nonrelatives. A large number of elderly women fall into this category, and in 1980 women accounted for 79 per cent of all unrelated individuals aged 65 and older.

Table 8-3 shows that the incomes of women classified as unrelated individuals fall below those of men in every age group, except in the case of blacks aged 25-34; but the sex discrepancy is also lower for whites in those ages than in any other bracket up to age 65. The reduced sex inequality among people aged 25-34 reflects the changes that are finally occurring for young women who have not been in the labor force very long, and who may be pursuing serious and rewarding careers in addition to or instead of marriage. As those people age and if new labor force entrants come close to income equitability, the present income discrepancy between men and women aged 35-64 may diminish significantly, though thus far that has been a slow process.

The sex disparity in the incomes of unrelated individuals aged 65 and older is still less than that of any other age group, not because women's retirement incomes are so high, but because those of men plunge more dramatically after age 65. Thus, in 1980 women aged 65 and older received 67 per cent of the income of women aged 55-64, whereas the figure for men was only 58 per cent. In fact, the sex disparity decreases after 55, when men begin to retire early, and it declines even more after age 62.

No matter what the index, elderly women have smaller average incomes than elderly men. Their personal incomes are lower, as are those of female householders (family heads), widows, and other women living alone. The

Table 8-3. Median Income of Unrelated Individuals, by Age, Race, and Sex, 1980

Age	Median Income (Dollars)					
	All Races		White		Black	
	Male	Female	Male	Female	Male	Female
15+	10,929	6,668	11,679	6,932	7,196	4,011
15-24	8,444	6,599	8,767	6,824	6,099	4,623
23-34	14,082	11,884	15,040	12,060	9,432	9,958
35-44	15,505	12,300	17,584	13,246	10,067	8,391
45-54	13,131	9,046	15,828	9,534	8,092	5,044
55-64	9,913	7,376	11,167	8,137	4,848	3,618
65+	5,746	4,957	6,161	5,186	4,219	3,558

Source: U.S. Bureau of the Census, "Money Income of Households, Families, and Persons in the United States: 1980," Current Population Reports, P-60, no. 132 (1982), table 27.

women without husbands but still supporting dependents who have little or no income, such as abandoned grandchildren or disabled parents, are especially badly off, even though they may have certain governmental assistance available. Despite the income inequality by sex among the elderly, however, the gap is narrowing gradually, for in 1970 women aged 65-69 had only 43 per cent of the personal income received by the men, whereas by 1980 women were receiving 49 per cent. In the 70-and-over group, the change was from 57 to 64 per cent. Therefore, elderly women are a little less disadvantaged relative to elderly men than they were, and all elderly are moving a bit closer to parity with other age groups. The latter change is facilitated by the movement of better-educated cohorts into the elderly group, for lifetime and retirement incomes both rise dramatically as the level of education improves.[20]

Until recently, women have suffered at least one other injustice because of their greater life expectancy. Almost all pension plans have paid women lower monthly benefits because they are expected to outlive men and to receive the payments over a longer period. Thus, even in those cases where their total benefits during the retirement years were comparable to those of men, their average monthly benefits were significantly less. In 1983, however, the Justice Department won a test case involving 3,400 colleges and universities and 650,000 employees that should eliminate the disparity, though the impact of the Supreme Court's findings of sex discrimination will take some time to accommodate.

Income Differences by Race

By every index, elderly black people have far lower average incomes than elderly whites, and Hispanic people also trail whites significantly. For example, in 1980 the per capita income in families headed by blacks aged 65 and older was only 47 per cent of that in elderly white families, while Hispanic families received 57 per cent of the white figure. (See Table 8-4.) Elderly white families also have per capita incomes that are virtually the same as those for all white families, whereas the ones headed by elderly blacks have significantly lower per capita incomes than do all black families collectively.

Irrespective of race, however, nearly all elderly people do receive *some* income, small though it may be for most minority elderly and for many whites as well. Important, too, is the greater tendency for elderly blacks to live with adult children, for while black per capita household income is low relative to that of whites, the black elderly person, especially a widow, is more apt to be accepted within a younger household, which helps in the struggle against a higher poverty rate. Moreover, a black grandmother is often useful in caring for children while one or both parents work, and she often enjoys greater family respect than her white counterpart, sharing more fully in whatever resources the family has and contributing more work.[21]

Poverty is also more evenly distributed among age groups in the black population, which means it may come as a considerably greater shock for elderly whites than for blacks,[22] though we do need to be careful not to assume that either group is homogeneous. Nonetheless, the data on family and household income imply that the black elderly population contains an abnormally large percentage of poorly educated people who were the victims of blatant job discrimination that forced them into menial jobs at low wages. As a result, those jobs provided minimal retirement incomes, savings, home ownership, and job skills with which to seek part-time work after age 65. That set of problems will not disappear quickly, for more middle-aged blacks than whites still suffer from them and will have higher rates of poverty in their older years.[23]

Table 8-4. Mean and Relative Per Capita Family Income, by Age of Householder, Race, and Spanish Origin, 1980

Age	Mean Per Capita Family Income (Dollars)			Per Cent of Mean Per Capita Family Income		
	White	Black	Spanish Origin	White	Black	Spanish Origin
15+	7,787	4,321	4,549	100.0	100.0	100.0
15-24	5,764	3,503	3,960	74.0	81.1	87.1
25-34	6,608	4,204	4,247	84.9	97.3	93.4
35-44	7,029	4,444	4,158	90.3	102.8	91.4
45-54	8,834	4,649	5,339	113.4	107.6	117.4
55-64	10,573	4,845	5,731	135.8	112.1	126.0
65+	7,745	3,639	4,382	99.5	84.0	96.3

Source: U.S. Bureau of the Census, "Money Income of Households, Families, and Persons in the United States: 1980," Current Population Reports, P-60, no. 132 (1982), table 21.

These realities also pertain when personal income is used as an index, and at every age level the incomes of blacks are below those of whites, while women of both races fare considerably worse than men. The least favorable comparison, therefore, is between black women and white men, for in the ages 65-69 the former receive only 35 per cent as much income as the latter; at age 70 they receive 45 per cent as much. But unfair as they are, these great disparities are softened somewhat by the greater proportional loss of income experienced by the more affluent groups in the population when they retire, either fully or partially. Thus, white men, with the highest incomes of all, sustain a drop of 44 per cent between the age groups 55-64 and 65-69, whereas black men, with the second highest average incomes in the 55-64 ages, experience a 36 per cent decline. The incomes of white women fall 10 per cent and those of black women decrease 15 per cent. Similar changes are also apparent in the incomes of unrelated individuals. In a limited sense, therefore, some status differences tend to level a bit after age 65, and the older people get, the more leveling takes place.[24] Even so, while the leveling phenomenon may someday reduce the income inequality that results from being black and female, it is still a long way from producing black-white or male-female equality in the older ages, let alone between the elderly and all of the other age groups over 20.

Spanish-origin persons have median incomes that are a little above those of elderly blacks as a whole, but both groups rank far below non-Hispanic whites. In addition, Hispanic men fare somewhat better than black men, while Hispanic women have slightly lower average incomes than black women.

Sources of Income

Most elderly people have several sources of income, though Social Security and other transfer payments are major sources for almost all. Those other transfers include railroad retirement, public assistance or welfare, Supplemental Security Income (SSI), pensions and annuities, veteran's payments, and unemployment and worker's compensation. Thus, Table 8-5 shows that well over 90 per cent of the elderly men and women receive various combinations of these transfers, though only a quarter of all older people depend on them exclusively. Therefore, the large majority also have other sources of income, including earnings from wages, salaries, and self-employment, and returns from property of various kinds. Moreover, elderly women rely more heavily than men on government transfer payments and welfare, but are only half as likely to have earnings and income from property. This places them even more at the mercy of "public" funds. Among all sources, Social Security is the single most important one for both men and women.[25]

Only about 5 per cent of all elderly families rely exclusively on Social Security, and in that sense the program meets the intent of its creators that it be only a supplement to other income. But many older people derive a much larger share of their income from it than was intended, and to that degree Social Security is more than just a protective supplement to savings and other sources. The system's creators did not envision its significant cost-of-living increases or its proliferation into other areas, such as SSI. Nor did President Franklin Roosevelt and the other founders foresee the present conflict between the insurance and welfare functions

Table 8-5. Percentages of Persons Aged 25-64 and 65 and Over Receiving Various Types of Income, by Sex, 1980

Type of Income	25-64		65+	
	Male	Female	Male	Female
Earnings	92.4	72.2	25.1	11.1
Earnings & Property Income	61.0	46.1	19.6	8.1
Government Transfer Payments	21.9	20.2	94.4	96.1
Government Transfer Payments Only	3.3	6.2	19.6	28.8
Public Assistance, SSI, or Both[a]	2.2	6.4	5.7	10.7
Social Security, Pensions, or Both	9.2	9.7	93.7	93.7
Social Security, SSI, or Both[a]	5.8	9.3	92.0	94.7

Source: U.S. Bureau of the Census, "Money Income of Households, Families, and Persons in the United States: 1980," Current Population Reports, P-60, no. 132 (1982), table 54.

[a]SSI refers to Supplemental Security Income, i.e., payments made by federal, state, and local welfare agencies to low-income persons who are 65 or over, blind, or disabled.

of the system,[26] though they did hope it would eventually provide many kinds of protection for all segments of society. In fact, the expanded role of the system is reflected in its actual name: The Old-Age, Survivors', Disability and Health Insurance Program. These and other expansions helped generate the financial difficulties of the 1980s and the reforms of 1983 to guarantee the system's long-range solvency and protections for the elderly. Those changes, which represent a compromise among proponents of various solutions to the problems, temporarily postponed one cost-of-living increase; raised Social Security taxes; increased the age for full benefits from 65 to 67 over a 27-year period beginning in 2000; brought new federal employees into the system; subjected high-income recipients to partial taxation of benefits; and changed the taxation system for self-employed persons. Even those measures may prove inadequate, however, as the numbers and proportions of elderly people grow and the burden on workers increases. Nor did these steps address the costly problems in Medicare and other programs for the aged.

About 17 per cent of all older people still do have some earnings from work, much of it part-time. Men are more than twice as likely as women to have this source, though the figures for both contrast sharply with the 81 per cent of persons aged 25-64 who receive earnings. Conversely, only 21 per cent of the younger group receive income from public sources, compared with 95 per cent of those aged 65 and older. Therefore, one of the basic difficulties is that the incomes of more and more elderly depend less on earnings than they do on non-work income, and deserved though the unearned income may be, the huge costs threaten the survival of various retirement systems and still leave a significant share of the elderly in poverty or near-poverty. Even with its escalating benefits, Social Security alone does not provide an adequate retirement for most elderly, and nearly a third of the people who rely on that source fall below the poverty threshold,[27] though the number of elderly poor would probably triple if the system did not exist.

All of the emotional and humanitarian considerations aside, the older person who could work but doesn't imposes a cost that we have not yet learned to manage adequately, either for the elderly recipients of non-work income or for those who must provide it,[28 though it is often difficult for those older people who want jobs to find them. Moreover, pension coverage from all sources combined is quite uneven and many elderly receive too little to live comfortably. Despite its large costs, even the Social Security system has gaps and flaws, while at least half of all elderly Americans are not covered by private pension plans, some of which pay only small benefits anyway.[29] Therefore, income sources vary widely within the older group, as does the relative adequacy of the total amount provide by those sources. Consequently, while some elderly are wealthy and others are desperately poor, as a whole the older group does not fare as well financially as the rest of us, and while their relative incomes are better than their absolute incomes would suggest, many still need help, especially those in their late 70s and beyond.

In view of these circumstances, it isn't surprising that the financial *satisfaction* of elderly people hasn't changed much since the 1960s, basically because most feel their income situations haven't improved enough relative to their costs. Some of this attitude reflects their expectations, which can never be fully satisfied as long as they continue to rise. Significant, too, are misperceptions among older people about their real situations relative to other members of the population.[*30*] But part of the financial dissatisfaction expressed by many elderly also reflects real deprivation, especially for the group living in poverty.

Income Trends

The incomes of the elderly have risen substantially for many decades, as have those of younger people. Moreover, because of improvements in the Social Security system and other sources of retirement income, the proportion of desperately poor elderly has fallen significantly, especially since 1970, though it began to rise again in the 1980s. Much of this means that the money incomes of elderly households have risen a little faster than those of all ages combined, and considerably faster than several other specific age groups.[*31*] (See Table 8-6.) The same is true when personal income is used as the index. Although the average elderly household does sustain a considerable drop in income when the householder and his/her spouse retire, the decline is not quite as great as it was. In 1970, for example, elderly households had 69 per cent of the incomes of those headed by people aged 55-64, while in 1980 they had 72 per cent. Some of that change is due to the early retirements of more people in the 55-64 age group, but part of it is also due to improvements in the absolute and relative income situations of those aged 65 and older. Furthermore, the rise in elderly household per capita income from $2,960 in 1970 to $7,243 in 1980 represents an increase in real income (1980 constant dollars) of about 43 per cent, compared with an increase of roughly 39 per cent for all ages. In addition, the ratio of per capita income in households with elderly heads to that in all households moved up from 72 per cent in 1970 to 94 per cent in 1980. Thus, the elderly are pushing slowly toward greater equality of income with younger people, at least by this measure.

These changes in the relative per capita income situation in the older family continue a longer trend, because for several decades the incomes of elderly families have risen faster than those of all other age groups combined, although the older ones did start with a significant disadvantage, especially during the Great Depression, when large proportions of the elderly were utterly destitute. In addition, not only are the incomes of the elderly increasing faster than those of the total population, but the proportion now protected from destitution by one or more income sources also has increased. So both income and coverage have expanded significantly.[32] The elderly have also probably been helped more than other age groups by non-cash benefits not reflected in the income data. As a result of these factors, the elderly also tend to grow somewhat more homogeneous in income and assets, despite major differences between elderly men and women and blacks and whites.

The old racial discrepancy remains a particular problem, for in 1970 older black men had 59 per cent of the median personal income of elderly white men, while in 1980 they had 58 per cent. Among elderly women the ratio of black to white personal income fell from 75 per cent in 1970 to 72 per cent in 1980. Those figures do not account for non-cash income or for

Table 8-6. Per Capita Family Income, by Age of Householder, and Percentage Change, 1970-1980

Age	Per Capita Income (Dollars)		Per Cent Change, (1970-80)
	1970	1980	
15+[a]	3,200	7,713	141.0
15-19[b]	2,743	6,327	130.7
25-35	2,798	7,082	153.1
35-44	2,736	7,131	160.6
45-54	3,660	8,527	133.0
55-64	4,305	9,969	131.6
65+	2,960	7,243	144.7

Sources: U.S. Bureau of the Census, Statistical Abstract of the United States: 1979, table 752; "Money Income of Households, Families, and Persons in the United States: 1980," Current Population Reports, P-60, no. 132 (1982), table 4.

[a] Unweighted average of the means of the age groups.

[b] Aged 14-19 in 1970.

differences in family support, of course, and it is true that the cash incomes of people of both races have grown very substantially. Regardless, the degree of inequality between older white and black people has increased somewhat, whereas the discrepancy between the elderly and other age groups has decreased, as has that between older men and women.

The Elderly Poor

It hasn't been too many decades since nearly all older people were poor or close to it, so their present overall income situation is far better than in the past. Despite these improvements, however, a significant share of the elderly still must endure extreme poverty, either for the first time in their lives or as the continuation of lifetime poverty; they lack sufficient income for even the basic necessities, and they inhabit rural slums and the deteriorating areas of large cities, somehow managing to endure. They are the "hard-core" elderly poor whose situations have improved the least. Moreover, while SSI, cost-of-living increases in Social Security, and other measures significantly reduced the percentage living in poverty, after 1978 their proportion rose somewhat and there are still about 4 million persons aged 65 and older below the official poverty line.

Indexes of Poverty

The *poverty index* now used by the U.S. Bureau of the Census was first developed by the Social Security Administration in 1964 and revised in 1969 and 1980, though the first data on the matter were published for 1959. The index now provides several *poverty income thresholds* that vary according to family size, the age of the householder, and the number of children under age 18. The poverty index is also oriented to the Consumer Price Index and is, therefore, adjusted annually so that its dollar figure changes each year for the various groups mentioned above.[33] Because of these detailed refinements, the index is a sensitive measure of how the economic well-being of the elderly compares with that of other age groups, though the index does include only money income. Moreover, the data are provided separately for persons, unrelated individuals, and families, with the last identified according to the number of members.

Older and Younger People

In 1980 about 16 per cent of the nation's elderly people fell below the poverty threshold, compared with 13 per cent of those of all ages. But the proportion for the elderly was higher than that of all other categories except persons in the very youngest years. (See Table 8-7.) In fact, the proportion in poverty falls steadily until about age 55 and then rises until the percentage for the elderly is far higher than that for people in their late 40s and early 50s. There is even a considerable increase between the ages 55-59 and 60-64, because many who retire in their early 60s are forced to do so by disability, and their pension incomes, if any, are generally well below those of people who work until age 65. The percentage of those aged 60-64 who are in poverty would be even higher if it were not for the relatively affluent group that can easily afford to retire before age 65.

This pattern by age is virtually the same for whites, blacks, and Hispanics, except that for the last group the lowest percentage of poverty is in the ages 55-59, largely because the Cuban contingent is older and wealthier on the average than are people with other Spanish backgrounds. Moreover, males and females experience similar changes with age. Therefore, no matter how the data are cross-classified, the levels of poverty tend to be very high for children, to decline steadily until late middle age, to rise somewhat after age 60, and to increase sharply after age 65. The problem is the most severe for the nation's oldest people. Moreover, since more than half the elderly population is aged 72 and older and women exceed 60 per cent of that age group, the poverty population is fairly heavily concentrated among the nation's oldest women.

The near-poor elderly. The proportion of elderly people in poverty is about 21 per cent greater than that of people in all age groups, but when the near-poor are taken into account, the difference increases. Those people have incomes that are no more than 25 per cent above the poverty threshold, and while they are not quite poor by official standards, their incomes are still inadequate. Thus, in 1980 the upper limit of income for a near-poor family of two with a householder aged 65 or over was $6,222, while that for an elderly unrelated individual was $4,937. In that year about 2.5 million older people not below the poverty line were no more than 25 per cent above it, and they accounted for about 10 per cent of all elderly. In contrast, about 5 per cent of all age groups collectively fell into the near-poor category.

When the poor and near-poor are combined, about 26 per cent of the elderly are in poverty or just above it, compared with 18 per cent of all age groups. Furthermore, people in families with an elderly female householder and no husband present fare especially badly, for 43 per cent are in poverty or near it, although in most other age groups female-headed households without husbands do not do a great deal better. All of this means that in 1980 about 6.5 million elderly people did not have sufficient income to maintain an adequate level of living, or were having to scrape by with few luxuries.

Table 8-7. Percentages of Persons Below the Poverty
Level, by Age, Sex, Race, and Spanish
Origin, 1980

Age and Sex	All Races	White	Black	Spanish Origin[a]
Male	11.2	8.7	28.7	23.5
Under 15	19.0	14.5	43.6	33.6
15-17	14.1	10.3	35.8	29.1
18-21	10.9	8.5	24.4	21.9
22-24	9.8	8.4	17.6	16.4
25-34	7.5	6.2	17.2	14.9
35-44	7.6	6.2	18.4	16.0
45-54	6.5	5.4	15.2	15.2
55-59	6.4	4.8	22.3	12.7
60-64	7.8	6.2	24.6	19.1
65+	10.9	9.0	31.5	26.8
Female	14.7	11.6	35.7	27.7
Under 15	19.3	14.8	42.6	33.9
15-17	15.8	11.1	41.5	31.0
18-21	16.0	12.3	36.5	29.2
22-24	15.1	12.0	33.6	20.9
25-34	12.8	10.0	31.1	23.9
35-44	10.6	8.3	26.8	23.1
45-54	8.9	6.7	26.3	22.4
55-59	10.6	8.2	31.8	19.5
60-64	12.6	10.3	35.8	19.6
65+	19.0	16.8	42.6	34.4

Source: U.S. Bureau of the Census, "Characteristics
of the Population Below the Poverty Level: 1980,"
Current Population Reports, P-60, no. 133 (1982),
table 11.

[a]May be of any race.

Differences by Sex

Significantly higher proportions of older women than men fall below the poverty line, though their situations vary by marital status. Thus, in 1980 about 19 per cent of all women aged 65 and older were living in poverty, compared with only 11 per cent of the men, for a ratio of 174 women for each 100 men. The ratio is greater for whites (187) than for blacks (135) and Hispanics (128) (See Table 8-7.) The poverty difference between the sexes does tend to diminish in the oldest ages, for although both sexes aged 72 and over are more apt to be poor than are the young-old, the ratio of women to men in poverty falls somewhat. That reflects the tendency toward several forms of homogeneity as people move into their 70s and 80s.

Differences by Race

The incidence of poverty among elderly blacks is roughly three times that among elderly whites. (See Table 8-7.) Consequently, just under a quarter of the whites but well over half of the blacks are either living in poverty or hovering close to it. In addition, elderly Hispanics are far more likely than the white population as a whole to be poor, but somewhat less apt than blacks to be so.

The poorest people of all in American society are elderly black women, for their incidence of poverty is significantly higher than that of elderly black men and white women. Even though they may receive somewhat more protection through the efforts of family members than do older white women, who are more apt to live alone, the average incomes of older black women are so low that a large majority live in or near poverty. And for those who do live alone or with nonrelatives, the situation is truly appalling. In 1980, for instance, 82 per cent of the elderly black women classified as unrelated individuals were in poverty or close to it, compared with 62 per cent of the black men, 47 per cent of the white women, and 38 per cent of the white men. People living in families, even if there is no spouse present, are somewhat more fortunate, but even among them the incidence of poverty and near-poverty is especially high for elderly black women. Thus, unrelated individuals and female householders are the poorest of the elderly poor; among them blacks fare worse than whites and women are worse off than men.[34] Moreover, the rates of poverty still tend to be higher among blacks who live in the South than in any other region in the nation, and also among those who reside in nonmetropolitan places rather than in SMSAs.

Despite these obvious problems, however, it is well to recall that in 1980 less than 16 per cent of all people aged 65 and older were living in poverty, that the proportion has declined significantly since the first data were complied on the topic, and th~t the differences among several groups of elderly tend to diminish as they age. That "leveling" helps to offset some of the effects of being old, female, and black. The concept of poverty is also relative, for many of those now classified as "poor" still have goods and services that would have been available only to the wealthy a century ago. Also, the poorest people often deal better with their problems than do members of the middle class whose incomes may plunge when they retire and who feel an acute sense of deprivation.[35]

Effects of Other Characteristics

Marital status. Among elderly men, the highest incidence of poverty occurs for those who are separated or divorced, the lowest for those who are married and living with their wives. (See Table 8-8.) Single men and widowers are about equally likely to be poor, but their rates of poverty are well over twice those of married men. Among women, the incidence of poverty is highest among those who are separated, followed by those who are divorced and who are single, and lowest for the women who are

Table 8-8. Percentages of Elderly Persons Below the Poverty Level, by Sex and Marital Status, 1980

Marital Status	Both Sexes	Male	Female
All Classes	15.7	10.9	19.0
Single	21.4	19.0	22.7
Married[a]	8.2	8.3	8.1
Spouse Absent	32.9	22.2	43.5
Separated	37.8	29.5	45.7
Other	22.7	14.4	40.5
Widowed	24.1	18.8	25.1
Divorced	27.1	21.8	30.7

Source: U.S. Bureau of the Census, "Characteristics of the Population Below the Poverty Level: 1980," Current Population Reports, P-60, no. 133 (1982), table 15.

[a]Spouse present.

married. They have a slightly lower incidence of poverty than married men, but in every other marital status category the women fare much worse than the men.

Educational status. The incidence of poverty is closely related to the levels of education people have attained and what that schooling helped produce in the way of pre-retirement income and post-retirement pensions. Therefore, the high rates of poverty in some elderly groups can be explained partly by their low levels of education, though there are still significant discrepancies between the races and the sexes for other rea-

Table 8-9. Percentages of Elderly Persons Below the Poverty Level, by Amount of Schooling, Race, and Sex, 1980

Years of Schooling Completed	All Groups	White		Black	
		Male	Female	Male	Female
All Levels	15.7	9.0	16.8	31.5	42.6
None	36.3	33.2	34.3	a	a
Elementary					
1-5 Years	34.4	22.8	36.9	36.7	54.9
6 & 7 Years	25.5	16.8	28.1	33.1	44.5
8 Years	17.9	9.1	22.0	33.3	36.1
High School					
1-3 Years	13.8	6.4	16.3	32.4	36.7
4 Years	8.4	4.5	9.7	16.7	30.0
College					
1+ Years	6.1	4.3	6.9	a	a

Source: U.S. Bureau of the Census, "Characteristics of the Population Below the Poverty Level: 1980," Current Population Reports, P-60, no. 133 (1982), table 13.

[a]Population base too small to compute derived measure.

sons. In 1980, however, the proportion of all elderly living in poverty declined steadily as the level of education rose, and those with no schooling had a poverty rate six times that of people who had at least one year of college. (See Table 8-9.) Moreover, the same progressive decrease was apparent for men and women, blacks and whites. Nonetheless, at each of the educational levels, men had significantly lower rates of poverty than women, and whites had far lower rates than blacks, so those differentials are partly independent of education.

Table 8-10. Percentages of People 65 and Over Below
the Poverty Level, by Selected
Characteristics, 1959-1980

Characteristic	1959	1970	1978	1979	1980
All Persons 65+	35.2	24.5	14.0	15.2	15.7
White	33.1	22.5	12.1	13.3	13.6
Black	62.5	48.0	33.9	36.3	38.1
Spanish Origin[a]	....	....	23.2	26.8	30.9
Persons in Families	26.9	14.7	7.6	8.4	8.5
Householder	29.1	16.3	8.4	9.1	9.1
Male	29.1	15.6	7.7	8.4	8.2
Female	28.8	19.9	12.2	13.0	14.0
Unrelated Individuals	61.9	47.1	27.0	29.4	30.6
Male	59.0	38.9	20.7	25.3	24.4
White	56.8	36.0	17.4	22.3	21.1
Black	77.5	59.7	37.8	44.8	45.1
Female	63.3	49.7	28.8	30.5	32.3
White	61.8	47.5	25.9	27.6	29.3
Black	84.6	79.2	62.0	65.6	66.5

Source: U.S. Bureau of the Census, "Characteristics of the Population Below the Poverty Level: 1980," Current Population Reports, P-60, no. 133 (1982), table 3.

[a]May be of any race.

Trends in Poverty Status

The proportion of elderly people living below the poverty threshold dropped by more than half between 1959 and 1980 and even the number fell from 5.5 million to 4 million, despite the substantial increase in the size of the older population. (See Table 8-10.) Those decreases represent a considerably faster rate of reduction in poverty among the elderly than among all age groups collectively, largely because of such things as Medicare, SSI, food stamps, transfer payments of other kinds for older people, and significant increases in Social Security benefits after 1972.[36]

The proportion of near-poor elderly has also decreased, but not as rapidly, partly because many people who would have been classified as poor in the 1960s and early 1970s have now moved into the near-poor category, though this should not obscure the significantly larger share of older people whose improved incomes now place them above both categories.

The proportion below the poverty level fell especially rapidly for older people living in families, though the rate of reduction was far faster among families with a male than a female householder. In 1959 male householders even had a slightly higher incidence of poverty than the females, but by 1980 the proportion of men householders in poverty had fallen 72 per cent, while that of women had dropped only 51 per cent. The same patterns hold for persons and unrelated individuals; that is, the incidence of poverty declined significantly for both sexes, but more for men than for women.

The incidence of poverty among the elderly also dropped more drastically for whites than for blacks. Between 1959 and 1980 all elderly white persons witnessed a 59 per cent decrease in poverty, blacks only a 39 per cent drop. For those living in families and for unrelated individuals the proportion living below the poverty threshold also fell more slowly for blacks than for whites, who had the advantage to begin with.

When the situations of the sexes and the races are considered together, it is clear that the great financial disadvantage of elderly black women is a persistent one despite some improvements, and they are still more likely than black men and whites of both sexes to be poor. In addition, the rate of improvement has been slowest for those who were the poorest in 1959 — elderly black women living alone or with nonrelatives. Two-thirds of them are still below the poverty line, and while the poverty rate for all unrelated individuals was cut in half, their rate fell only 21 per cent.

Table 8-10 shows that there has been some tendency for the incidence of poverty to rise since about 1978. A small part of that increase is due to revisions in the definition of "poverty," but inflation and other factors are also involved. It is too early, however, to tell whether the economic constraints of the early 1980s will cause the percentage of poverty-stricken elderly persons to rise significantly, or whether the increases since 1978 will prove temporary. The data for 1982 and 1983, though, show that the proportion of elderly persons in poverty dropped slightly. Even so, in our attempt not to underestimate the economic well-being of the elderly, we don't want to overestimate it, because a significant share of older people who don't fall below the official poverty line don't live very comfortably either, and major improvements are still needed in some groups, especially that of older women living alone. Many of them are not quite poor enough to be eligible for Medicaid, which can prove a costly omission, and the problem is intensified by the tendency to eliminate hospitals that treat the poor and near-poor at subsidized rates.

Women have also suffered from the practice of reducing their benefits from private pension plans because of their greater longevity, even though benefits were not increased for groups with relatively short life expectancy such as black men.[37] Under the recent Supreme Court ruling, however, the situation for women should gradually improve. Even so, each race and sex category still has significant numbers in poverty and others above that level who lack an overall income in cash and other benefits to provide what the federal government defines as a moderate standard of retirement living (now about $6,500 for single people and $9,800 for couples).[38] At present, that situation includes well over half of all elderly persons and more than a third of the couples.

The great proportional decrease in poverty during the 1970s represents a unique combination of legislation and other advantages that we are unlikely to match in the 1980s. The elderly could even lose ground because of changes in the Social Security system to overcome its financial problems, other budgetary constraints, and the shift of priorities away from "social programs" in order to deal with budgetary deficits created by higher military spending and reduced revenues because of high unemployment. At the same time, prices for most of the things that use most of the funds of elderly people — food, fuel, utilities, and medical care — are still rising, and the elderly are more affected by the increases than are many younger people. Therefore, new millions of the elderly could become officially poor or at least poorer than they had expected. It simply is not true that the bulk of elderly Americans live well enough to withstand major cuts in benefits or rapid inflation and not suffer, for while that assumption might have some credibility if the income trends of the 1970s had continued, it had little during the economic reversals of the early 1980s.[39] For some elderly any failure to provide regular increases in Social Security benefits will produce hardships and perhaps even a class of new poor among them.

Summary

Most elderly are often thought to be poor, but while some are deep in poverty, most manage to get by and a minority live well. The actual income situation of elderly persons depends in part on whether they live in families or alone, for while the average income of elderly families is substantially below that of all families, the older ones have fewer members and their per capita income is relatively close to that received by all families. But the picture is far less favorable for those who live alone or with nonrelatives and for women who head households without a husband present. The incomes of the elderly in those categories are far below the ones received by people of all ages collectively, although virtually all older people have some source of income.

Typically, elderly women have significantly smaller incomes than elderly men, no matter what the living arrangements, and older blacks receive considerably less than older whites. Therefore, the poorest elderly poor in American society are black women, especially those who live alone or with nonrelatives. At the same time, more black than white women are apt to be taken into a family and to share in its resources, no matter how meager.

Income and poverty status are also heavily influenced by marital status and education. The incidence of poverty is far less for married people with a spouse present than for those in all of the nonmarried categories, especially the ones who are separated or divorced, and the women in those groups are much more likely than the men to be poor. Income also rises as the level of education rises, and the incidence of poverty decreases accordingly. Nevertheless, the income and poverty disparities between men and women and blacks and whites persist even at the same levels of schooling, thus reflecting pervasive patterns of discrimination that have affected the wages of those groups and still influence their retirement incomes.

Income and poverty trends have been quite favorable for the elderly, especially since the early 1970s when various kinds of government benefits were increased significantly. Therefore, the incomes of older people rose faster between 1970 and 1980 than did those of all other groups collectively, and the disparity between the elderly and younger wage earners decreased. At the same time, the incidence of poverty fell dramatically, though the greatest reductions took place before 1975 and it rose a little after 1978.

NOTES

1. Charles S. Harris, *Fact Book on Aging: A Profile of America's Older Population.* Washington, DC: National Council on the Aging, 1978, pp. 37-38. See also Beth J. Soldo, "America's Elderly in the 1980s," *Population Bulletin* 35 (1980): 21.

2. Fred C. Cottrell, *Aging and the Aged.* Dubuque, IA: Wm. C. Brown, 1974, pp. 23-24.

3. Kingsley Davis and Pietronella van den Oever, "Age Relations and Public Policy in Advanced Industrial Society," *Population and Development Review* 7 (1981): 9.

4. The term *householder* has replaced the designations *head of household* and *head of family.* See U.S. Bureau of the Census, "Money Income of Households, Families, and Persons in the United States: 1980," *Current Population Reports,* P-60, no. 132 (1982): 223.

5. For the data, see U.S. Bureau of the Census, "Estimating After-Tax Money Income Distributions Using Data from the March Current Population Survey," *Current Population Reports,* P-23, no. 126 (1983): 12.

6. Use of the per capita index is adapted from Davis and van den Oever, *op. cit.,* pp. 9-10. See also U.S. Bureau of the Census, "Demographic Aspects of Aging and the Older Population in the United States," *Current Population Reports,* P-23, no. 59 (1978): 53.

7. Fred C. Pampel, *Social Change and the Aged.* Lexington, MA: Heath, 1981, p. 18.

8. George F. Patterson, "Income," in U.S. Bureau of the Census, "Population of the United States, Trends and Prospects: 1950-1990," *Current Population Reports,* P-23, no. 49 (1974): 163.

9. Bernice L. Neugarten, "The Rise of the Young-Old," in Ronald Gross, Beatrice Gross and Sylvia Seidman, eds., *The New Old: Struggling for Decent Aging.* Garden City, NY: Doubleday, 1978, p. 48.

10. U.S. Bureau of the Census, "Money Income of Households...," *op. cit.,* pp. 221-222.

11. For an analysis of the problems in using income data, see Oskar Morgenstern, *National Income Statistics: A Critique of Macroeconomic Aggregation.* Washington, DC: Cato Institute, 1979.

12. James C. Schulz, "Income Distribution and the Aging," in Robert H. Binstock and Ethel Shanas, eds., *Handbook of Aging and the Social Sciences.* New York: Van Nostrand, 1976, p. 563. Cf. Juanita M. Kreps, "The Economy and the Aged," in Binstock and Shanas, *ibid.,* pp. 273-276.

13. Pampel, *op. cit.,* pp. 107-108; 122-123.

14. Soldo, *op. cit.,* pp. 23-24.

15. William C. Greenough and Francis P. King, *Pension Plans and Public Policy.* New York: Columbia University Press, 1976, p. 235.

16. Harris, *op. cit.,* pp. 63-64.

17. Soldo, *op. cit.,* p. 24.

18. Gordon F. Streib, "Social Stratification and Aging," in Binstock and Shanas, *op. cit.,* p. 163.

212

19. U.S. Bureau of the Census, "Money Income of Households...," *op. cit.*, table 61.

20. Patterson, *op. cit.*, pp. 170-171.

21. Nancy Hicks, "Life After 65," in Kurt Finsterbusch, ed., *Social Problems 81/82*. Guilford, CT: Dushkin, 1981, p. 161.

22. Jacquelyne Johnson Jackson, *Minorities and Aging*. Belmont, CA: Wadsworth, 1980, p. 144. For another analysis of coping networks and mechanisms, see Rose C. Gibson, "Blacks at Middle and Late Life: Resources and Coping," *Annals of American Academy of Political and Social Science* 464 (1982): 79-90. Cf. Ronald Angel and Marta Tienda, "Determinants of Extended Household Structure: Cultural Patterns or Economic Need?" *American Journal of Sociology* 87 (1982): 1360-1383.

23. National Caucus on the Black Aged, "A Generation of Black People," in Gross, Gross and Seidman, *op. cit.*, pp. 281-282.

24. Pampel, *op. cit.*, pp. 150-152.

25. Soldo, *op. cit.*, p. 21.

26. For an analysis, see Peter J. Ferrara, *Social Security: The Inherent Contradiction*. Washington, DC: Cato Institute, 1982.

27. Mary Barberis, "America's Elderly: Policy Implications," *Population Bulletin* 35 (1981): 6.

28. Davis and van den Oever, *op. cit.*, pp. 8-9.

29. Barberis, *op. cit.*, p. 7.

30. Pampel, *op. cit.*, p. 182.

31. Davis and van den Oever, *op. cit.*, p. 12.

32. R. Meredith Belbin, "Retirement Strategy in an Evolving Society," in Carp, *op. cit.*, p. 177.

33. For this description of the poverty index, see U.S. Bureau of the Census, *Statistical Abstract of the United States: 1982-83*. Washington, DC: U.S. Government Printing Office, 1982, p. 417. For the specific dollar variations among different groups in 1980, see U.S. Bureau of the Census, "Characteristics of the Population Below the Poverty Level: 1980," *Current Population Reports*, P-60, no. 133 (1982): 3-4.

34. For discussions of this matter, see Soldo, *op. cit.*, pp. 21-23; Jackson, *op. cit.*, pp. 166-169; and Philip Janson and Karen Frisbie Mueller, "Age, Ethnicity, and Well-Being," *Research on Aging* 5 (1983): 353-367.

35. Cottrell, *op. cit.*, pp. 23-24.

36. Harris, *op. cit.*, p. 51. Cf. U.S. Bureau of the Census, "The Social and Economic Status of the Black Population in the United States: An Historical View, 1790-1978," *Current Population Reports*, P-23, no. 80 (1979): 29.

37. Phyllis W. Berman and Estelle R. Ramey, eds., *Women: A Developmental Perspective*. Washington, DC: National Institutes of Health, 1982, p. 408.

38. Cyril F. Brickfield, "Rags to Riches — or Reality? Economic Prospects for the Elderly in the 1980s," in Kurt Finsterbusch, ed., *Social Problems 82/83*. Guilford, CT: Dushkin, 1982, p. 132.

39. *Ibid.*, p. 133.

Chapter 9

Mortality Levels, Differentials, and Trends

The first three chapters dealt with the ways in which mortality affects the growth of the older population, the distribution of people among the various elderly age categories, and the sex composition of the older population. Now, however, the analysis turns to mortality per se, and especially the ways in which it has changed for various groups in the elderly population, including its rates, differentials, and causes.

Measures of Mortality

Mortality can be gauged by a large variety of rates, ratios, and other indexes, but this study concentrates principally on three:

1. Age-specific death rates are mortality levels computed separately for persons in various age categories, usually five-year or 10-year ranges. This index is related to the *age-adjusted death rate,* which shows what the level of mortality would be if the age composition of a population remained unchanged from year to year, and which uses the age distribution for a given year as the standard.

2. Life expectancy is usually expressed in two ways. The expectation of life at birth is the average number of years a group of newborn infants would live if their survival were governed by the age-specific death rates that prevailed when they were born. The expectation of life at 50, 65, 80, or any other age is the average lifetime remaining to persons who have reached those ages, also assuming unchanging age-specific death rates.

3. Age-specific death rates by cause result from heart disease, cancer, stroke, accidents, and other causes, and are a way to report the relative importance of the events from which people actually die and the changes in their importance over time.

All of these indexes are also reported separately for men and women, blacks and whites, and other groups in the population.[*1*] The vital statistics registrations on which they and the long-term trends are based are available for as early as 1900-1902, but it was not until 1933, when the last state (Texas) was added to the registration area, that the data applied to the nation's total population. For that reason and because the quality of the data has improved greatly since the early decades, this chapter will trace most trends from 1940 to the early 1980s. It is worth noting, however, that since 1900 the death rates of all age, race, and sex groups dropped dramatically, though there were fluctuations, including increases, at various times.

Indexes of *morbidity* (illness, injury, and disability) are also available, though more difficult to create and use; the line between wellness and illness is often unclear, while specific older persons are often afflicted by several maladies at the same time. In addition, the information on this topic is generally less adequate than mortality data for earlier decades, partly because the morbidity materials depend on the person's own assessment of his/her state of physical well-being. Nonetheless, health surveys have improved greatly in recent years and do enable the use of *morbidity factors*, such as the number of days one is hospitalized or bedridden, the time during which one's activity is restricted by certain degrees, the number of sick days one suffers during a year, and the person's own report on illnesses and their severity. But morbidity is a large study in itself and beyond the scope of this book, though we will allude to it at points where it is inseparable from a consideration of mortality.

Differences in Age-Specific Death Rates

Death rates are relatively high for infants, but they drop to a low point for children aged 5-14 and then begin their virtually uninterrupted rise toward the oldest ages, though the change in the ages 20-34 is slight. (See Table 9-1.) It isn't until about age 60 or so, however, that the death rate again reaches the one for infants, so while the first year of life is still rather hazardous, the several decades that follow have very low death rates. In fact, disease control is so effective that until people reach their mid-30s, accidents are the chief cause of death, and the chances that a person in late middle-age will die from most of the major causes of death are not drastically greater than those of an infant.[*2*]

Despite that situation, however, after about age 40 the death rate rises by at least 50 per cent for each of the succeeding five-year age groups, and the climb is especially rapid in the 80s. As a result, the death rate of people aged 85 and older is more than six times that of people aged 65-69.

Table 9-1. Age-Specific Death Rates, by Race and
            Sex, 1980

Age	Deaths per 1,000			
	White		Black	
	Male	Female	Male	Female
All Ages	9.8	8.1	10.3	7.3
Age-Adjusted	7.5	4.1	11.1	6.3
Under 1	12.3	9.6	25.9	21.2
1-4	0.7	0.5	1.1	0.8
5-9	0.3	0.2	0.5	0.3
10-14	0.4	0.2	0.5	0.3
15-19	1.4	0.5	1.4	0.5
20-24	1.9	0.6	2.9	0.9
25-29	1.7	0.6	3.7	1.3
30-34	1.7	0.7	4.6	1.7
35-39	2.1	1.1	5.9	2.5
40-44	3.2	1.7	8.1	4.1
45-49	5.2	2.8	12.0	6.3
50-54	8.7	4.5	17.6	9.1
55-59	13.8	7.0	24.6	13.1
60-64	21.4	10.8	33.8	18.6
65-69	33.1	16.4	44.8	25.4
70-74	50.2	25.9	60.5	37.6
75-79	74.7	41.9	80.9	52.4
80-84	112.7	72.4	115.5	80.3
85+	191.0	149.8	161.0	123.7

Source: National Center for Health Statistics,
"Advance Report of Final Mortality Statistics,
1980," Monthly Vital Statistics Report, vol. 32,
no. 4 (1983), tables 1 and 9.

These patterns together mean that the median age of death is quite high and that the average young-old person enjoys reasonably good health and can anticipate several more years of life.

Even though the current death rates in the ages 60-64, 65-69, and 70-74 are much lower than those of earlier decades and large proportions of people reach the late 70s and the 80s, people eventually die of something. Therefore, the oldest population is faced with the paradox of declining death *rates* and a large *number* of deaths concentrated in their ages. For example, in 1980 people aged 80 and over accounted for 46 per cent of all deaths in the population aged 65 and older, even though they made up only 20 per cent of the elderly group. Consequently, the probability of dying has continued to shift upward in the age scale and has helped enlarge the population of the old-old faster than that of any other group, because far more of the young-old now survive to those oldest ages than was true in earlier generations.

Some International Comparisons

The death rates of America's elderly compare favorably with those in most other highly technological societies, including Japan and most European countries. Table 9-2 shows that the rates for American men and women both fall below the means and medians for the other nine representative countries collectively in all of the elderly age groups, except the 65-69 category. The rates in the United States are especially low for persons aged 75 and older, though those low figures are partly due to differences in the age structures of the 85-and-over group. Japan, Norway, and Sweden also have excellent overall records of low mortality among the elderly, and in the young-old categories those countries are superior to the United States. Moreover, those three countries, along with a few others, have higher life expectancy at birth than does the United States, both for males and females.

Other developed countries, for which the data are not quite as recent as those in Table 9-2, also have relatively low death rates among their various groups of elderly; they include Canada, Hong Kong, Israel, New Zealand, and several European nations. In each of them life expectancy at birth for males approaches or even exceeds 70 years, while for females it is in the upper 70s, just as is true of most countries in Table 9-2. In the developing nations, on the other hand, the often incomplete data that are available show substantially higher death rates among the elderly and life expectancy at birth that is many years below that in the industrialized countries. At the same time, the average expected years of life remaining to people who do reach age 65 is often only a few years less in the developing countries than in the developed ones.[3]

Table 9-2. Age-Specific Death Rates for the
            Elderly Populations of Selected
            Developed Countries, by Sex, 1980

Country and Sex	Deaths per 1,000				
	65-69	70-74	75-79	80-84	85+
Male					
Austria	36.1	58.3	94.7	146.8	225.1
Denmark	33.6	54.2	84.0	121.9	216.7
Finland	41.0	61.7	92.2	142.7	230.7
France	28.7	49.3	79.5	133.8	232.2
Germany, East	40.5	67.5	107.8	167.2	288.8
Germany, West	35.8	58.9	93.2	140.9	222.5
Japan	25.4	43.8	75.6	123.5	209.4
Norway	31.0	46.7	76.7	117.7	200.8
Sweden	28.4	47.0	75.9	123.7	222.0
UNITED STATES	33.9	50.8	74.8	112.4	188.0
Female					
Austria	17.6	32.1	60.0	109.1	207.0
Denmark	17.0	27.9	46.8	83.7	172.1
Finland	16.4	30.4	53.1	97.3	187.8
France	11.7	22.7	42.9	83.3	187.4
Germany, East	22.2	39.8	73.1	128.8	244.7
Germany, West	16.9	30.5	56.3	100.3	191.4
Japan	13.5	25.0	47.7	87.8	176.3
Norway	13.7	25.0	45.8	83.2	167.2
Sweden	14.0	24.7	46.0	84.2	173.9
UNITED STATES	17.2	26.7	42.6	72.6	147.5

Sources: United Nations, Demographic Yearbook,
1981, table 14; National Center for Health
Statistics, "Advance Report of Final Mortality
Statistics: 1980," Monthly Vital Statistics
Report, vol. 32, no. 4 (1983), table 1.

Sex Differences in the United States

At every age from birth to age 85 and older the death rates of males are significantly higher than those of females, just as they are in all other technologically advanced countries and most developing ones as well. These differences are apparent in Tables 9-1 and 9-2. Therefore, second only to age, sex is the most significant variable in mortality analyses, and age-specific death rates must also be made sex specific for even reasonable accuracy. Moreover, the lower the general death rate, the greater the difference between the sexes, so the gap is narrower in the developing countries than in the industrialized ones.[4] In turn, differences in the mortality sex ratio produce significant variations in the overall sex ratio, as we saw earlier.

But the death rates of the sexes still vary widely by age, for among infants and young children males are only about 25 per cent more likely than females to die, while in the ages 20-24 the difference is over 300 per cent. The gap then narrows somewhat, but from the middle 30s until the middle 70s the death rates of men remain nearly twice as high as those of women. Finally, in the oldest ages the difference declines, until at 85 the death rates of men are only about 27 per cent higher than those of women. The mortality sex ratio also declines into the oldest ages among the various racial and ethnic groups in the United States.[5]

Men also have higher mortality rates from the leading causes of death, though larger percentages of women are likely to be disabled when ill, perhaps because more are willing to seek treatment and take time to recuperate when illness strikes. Moreover, men appear more often in the morbidity categories that result in high death rates, whereas women show up more frequently in those that produce chronic illness.[6] Nor have the sexes shared equally in the mortality-reduction advances of the twentieth century, for in 1900 females had only a slight advantage over men in mortality rates, whereas now their advantage is considerable.[7]

The reasons for the male-female difference are not fully known, though both the environmental and biological explanations considered in Chapter 3 have credibility. Perhaps most convincing is the hypothesis that women have greater potential durability because of various biological advantages, and with the great reductions in death rates from infectious and parasitic diseases and childbirth, that biological superiority has become more fully manifest, though a range of environmental factors also operates.[8] No matter what the reasons, however, black and white females of all ages have far lower death rates than males, though the sex differential does diminish some in the oldest years and is not as great for blacks at most ages as it is for whites.[9] Furthermore, while the mortality sex ratio may decrease in the future as environmental factors grow more alike for males and females, it is likely that women's biological advantage will still keep the death rates of the sexes from becoming identical.[10]

Racial Differences in the United States

The death rates of blacks in all but the ages 15-19 and those 85 and over are significantly higher than the rates of whites, though the racial gap has been narrowing while that between the sexes in both racial groups has been widening.[11] Thus, Table 9-1 shows that the death rate of black infants is about twice as high as that of white infants, but that the black-white mortality ratio then declines steadily to 100 in the ages 15-19. That happens largely because the death rate from motor vehicle accidents is more than twice as high for whites in those ages as it is for blacks, and the higher black death rates from other causes are not sufficient to offset the large discrepancy in motor vehicle deaths. By age 20, however, the mortality disadvantage of blacks is again substantial, and from age 25 to 54 their death rates are at least twice those of whites. At the same time, of course, the death rates of members of both races rise significantly with age, especially after 50.

In the older years the racial differential does decline substantially, and among people in their 80s the "crossover" occurs, in which the reported death rates of blacks of both sexes fall below those of whites. The data for those oldest years are less than perfect, however, especially for blacks, and the census bases and the reported numbers of deaths contain enough errors to account for at least part of the crossover.[12] Medicare data, which substantiate the crossover, do seem more reliable and allow some revisions in the materials compiled by the National Center for Health Statistics, but they are not specific for causes of death and go back only to 1966. To complicate matters further, there are differences btween the races as a whole in education, income, and other aspects of socioeconomic status that affect mortality rates, though they generally work to the disadvantage of blacks; those factors would reduce their chances of reaching age 65 and diminish the crossover phenomenon.

Therefore, despite some data inaccuracies, perhaps the blacks who have made it to the older years in spite of more severe environmental stress "may be destinted by natural selection to live an especially long life,"[13] though it is easy to carry this Darwinian notion too far and thereby miss other possible explanations. Nonetheless, the racial mortality similarities in the older years probably do reflect greater similarities of other kinds among people who survive to those ages than exist among the cohorts at birth and in middle age, when the racial mortality discrepancies are the greatest.[14] In addition, larger proportions of elderly blacks than whites live with relatives instead of alone, and that probably contributes to longevity, though there is still much to be learned about the precise causes and actual magnitude of the crossover phenomenon.[15]

The longevity advantage that women have over men shows up in the racial comparisons long before the crossover in the 80s. Thus, the death rate of black females, which is substantially below that of black males at every age, also falls below that of white males in the ages 10-14 and remains lower until the early 30s. It then rises somewhat above the rate for white men until the late 50s, and thereafter it falls below and remains there through the ages 85 and older. That comparison further demonstrates that while the age-specific death rates of blacks and whites have tended to converge because the black rates have fallen faster than the whites, the differences between males and females of both races have increased substantially. As a result, the life expectancy at birth of black females now exceeds that of white males and is approaching that of white females, while the life expectancies of the sexes remain several years apart, even though black males are slowly nearing white males.[16] Some discrepancy between the races will persist as long as average socioeconomic levels differ, but the long-term racial convergence in death rates does imply significant improvements during the twentieth century. They are also reflected in the increasingly good data on morbidity, health care usage, levels and periods of disability, and similar indexes.

Differences by Socioeconomic Characteristics

The racial differentials in mortality reflect variations in average levels of education, especially of older people, and other aspects of socioeconomic status that were shaped by historical circumstances. Therefore, mortality variations by education, income, and occupation are also important, though space and the available data enable only a cursory look at these influences. Moreover, the situation of the elderly cannot easily be separated from that of the population as a whole according to these characteristics.

Education. The level of schooling attained is probably the single best socioeconomic variable to analyze mortality differentials between men and women, because it is applicable to all people and changes little in the older years. In general, there is a strong inverse relationship between the amount of schooling people receive and their age-specific death rates, though it is less consistent for elderly persons than for those aged 25-64. The relationship also pertains to both major races and to men and women. It is particularly strong for the sexes, though they are more alike in this respect after age 65 than they are in the younger ages.[17] Given these mortality differentials by education, as better-educated cohorts enter the older years, their death rates will probably decrease even more because of the various advantages that accompany higher levels of schooling. In fact, the significant drop in the age-specific death rates of the elderly after 1968 was related in part to the rapidly rising average level of education among that age group. As a result, they are better informed about health, nutrition, and other conditions that prolong life, though the impact of education is not that simple, for it also relates to the ability to afford medical care and to other variables.

Income. Age-specific death rates also fall as income rises, though this inverse relationship is closely tied to the one between mortality and education. The latter helps determine the level of income, and people in the higher income brackets are better able to afford good nutrition, housing, privately financed health care, rising Medicare premiums and deductibles, and other things that help prolong life. Therefore, significant improvements in Social Security coverage and the advent of cost-of-living increases also help account for the renewed downward trend in the elderly death rate after 1968, though the enactment of Medicare on July 1, 1965, was also a major part of that process. Its significance is reflected in the fact that between 1965 and 1970 health expenditures by people aged 65 and older almost doubled, while public payment of those costs rose from 30 per cent in 1965 to 61 per cent in 1970.[18] Furthermore, over nine-tenths of all elderly men and women discharged from short-stay hospitals expect Medicare to be the principal source of payment;[19] that also signifies the extent to which public funds have helped provide the better health care that lowers the death rate of the elderly.

Occupation. The death rates of elderly people are at least indirectly related to the occupations at which they worked, though levels of education and income are also part of that relationship. Some occupations produce relatively high rates of death from specific causes, such as "black lung" in coal mining, "brown lung" in textile manufacturing, and "asbestosis" in certain insulation jobs; many who do survive to 65 are apt to have serious chronic illnesses and abnormally short life expectancies. Other occupations, such as logging and mining, are unusually subject to accidents, and some elderly survivors may also succumb rather soon to disabilities incurred earlier. In general, however, the lowest mortality rates occur among elderly persons who had been professional and technical workers, the highest among laborers of various kinds, while other categories are intermediate.[20] As a result, though the occupations themselves probably play some part, they seem less directly related to mortality rates than are the levels of living they provide. Moreover, in some occupations the direct danger is partly offset by high levels of physical activity that may lower mortality rates, whereas the safer conditions of others may be partially countered by their sedentary nature, which tends to increase mortality indirectly. In fact, many apparent occupational differentials in mortality can be explained by other socioeconomic factors that affect the type of job one gets and the amount of income it pays.

Trends in Age-Specific Death Rates

The long-term decline in death rates throughout the world really began after the *age of pestilence and famine* brought high death rates and life expectancy of only 20 or 25 years. That era extended from prehistory to the eighteenth century in the developed countries and to the twentieth century in many developing ones. The next *age of receding pandemics* saw less massive decimation of populations and increases in life expectancy at birth to about 50 years. It was followed by the *age of degenerative and human-made diseases,* in which the death rate fell to a low and relatively stable level and life expectancy at birth reached 70 or more years. That stage prevails now in the developed countries.[21]

Over a much shorter time than this entire three-stage *epidemiologic transition,* mortality trends in the United States also followed three fairly distinct periods according to the pace at which the death rate fluctuated. From about the middle of the last century until 1954 the rate fell steadily, interrupted significantly only by the disastrous influenza epidemic of 1917-1918. Between 1954 and 1968, however, the death rate became so static that no further decline was expected; but from 1968 to the late 1970s it fell steadily once again.[22] Table 9-3 shows how various groups in the 65-and-over category were affected by these changes.

Between 1979 and 1980 the death rates for all age groups in the elderly category rose significantly because of new outbreaks of influenza, but in 1981 they began to move downward once again, especially among people aged 75-84. Despite the fluctuations, however, the substantial fall in the elderly age-specific death rates between 1940 and 1980 helps account for the rapid growth in the numbers of older people, particularly women, and for increases in their life expectancy. These changes, especially the re-newed mortality drop after 1968, represent improvements not only in the "quantity" of life, reflected in such things as greater longevity, but also in the "quality" of life, mirrored in decreased rates of illness, disability, and hospitalization.[23] Therefore, the changes are related to improvements in the delivery of health care services, such as Medicare and the programs developed to screen for high blood pressure, and to alterations in people's life styles. The significant reductions in deaths from heart disease are closely associated with these developments, although the precise causes of the swings in death rates from 1940 to the present are still not fully understood.[24] What is clear is that the death rates of the elderly in the United States are now declining faster than those in the other industrialized countries, except Japan.[25]

Despite the significant long-term decreases in the death rates among the elderly, the reductions among several other age groups have generally been greater, because young children have benefited most as deaths from infectious diseases have diminished, while the elderly, especially men, are the chief victims of the chronic and degenerative illnesses that have taken on greater proportional significance.[26] Thus, the death rates of people in the five age-groups that make up the 65-and-over age category have fallen more slowly than those of children and young adult women, and often they have not decreased as rapidly as the rates among middle-aged persons. The rates for elderly black men have even gone up, as have those of young adult males, whose mortality levels from motor vehicle accidents have grown significantly.

Table 9-3. Average Annual Percentage Change in the Death Rates of Elderly People, by Age and Sex, Selected Years

Sex and Age	1940-54	1955-67	1968-78	1979-80
Male 65+[a]	-1.1	+0.2	-1.5	+2.9
65-69	-0.7	+0.1	-2.2	+2.1
70-74	-1.0	+0.2	-1.5	+0.3
75-79	-1.1	+0.2	-0.9	+3.2
80-84	-1.3	-0.4	-1.2	+2.2
85+	-1.5	+0.9	-2.2	+6.8
Female 65+[a]	-2.0	-1.0	-2.3	+4.0
65-69	-2.3	-1.1	-2.6	+4.5
70-74	-2.2	-1.3	-2.0	+2.1
75-79	-1.9	-1.2	-1.7	+3.1
80-85	-1.9	-1.1	-2.3	+3.1
85+	-1.3	0.0	-3.0	+7.0

Sources: Lois A. Fingerhut and Harry M. Rosenberg, "Mortality Among the Elderly," in National Center for Health Statistics, Health, United States, 1981, PHS Pub. no. 82-1232 (1981), p. 17; National Center for Health Statistics, "Advance Report of Final Mortality Statistics, 1979," Monthly Vital Statistics Report, vol. 31, no. 6 (1982), table 1; "Advance Report of Final Mortality Statistics, 1980," Monthly Vital Statistics Report, vol. 32, no. 4 (1983), table 1.

[a]Age-adjusted rates.

On the other hand, data collected since 1980 show that the death rates of the elderly are falling a little faster than those of some middle-aged groups, but still not as rapidly as those of infants, children, or people in several other age groups. Therefore, while declining death rates of older people over several decades have added greatly to their numbers, the slower pace of reduction has actually retarded rather than accelerated the aging of the total population. That process, as we have seen, is due primarily to major reductions in the birth rate since 1960. Moreover, the average life expectancy of the whole population has increased significantly because larger percentages of infants can expect to reach the older ages, while life expectancy of the elderly themselves has increased more modestly, given the smaller reductions in their death rates.

Trends by sex. Reductions in the death rates of infants and very young children have not varied greatly by sex, but at most ages the death rates of females have fallen more than those of males. That is particularly true of the elderly, and the mortality sex ratio of people in all of the age groups over 65 has increased substantially. (See Table 9-4.) That ratio has risen most rapidly for people 70-74, followed by those 65-69 and people in the three oldest age ranges. The ratio among people age 85 and older has also increased, but the death rate of men in that group is still only 27 per cent higher than that of women, whereas among people 65-69 the male death rate is more than twice that of females.

But the rates at which the mortality sex ratio is rising in most age groups under 80 is less now than it was in earlier decades, and the white figure in the ages 65-69 has even fallen slightly. This deceleration suggests that the death rate differential between older men and women won't increase in the future as it has in the past. It will probably decrease, perhaps significantly, though there is little likelihood that the death rates of the sexes will again converge to the ratios of 1900 or 1940.[27] Moreover, even if the environmental differences between the sexes were eliminated, biological factors would still preserve a significant mortality difference between males and females, though a smaller one than exists now. But the largest increases in the mortality differential by sex seem about over for young-old whites, though not yet for the old-old. In the black group, however, the mortality sex ratio is still rising for all age groups 65 and over, and the rate of increase is also the greatest among the oldest people. It is likely, however, that for both races the pace of divergence in death rates by sex will slow and even give way to some convergence as elements in the socioeconomic environment become more similar for men and women.

Trends by race. Tracing the long-term mortality trends for blacks is discouraging methodologically, because even now many vital statistics are

Table 9-4. Male to Female Death Rate Ratios Among the Elderly, by Age and Race, 1940-1980

Race and Year	Death Rate Ratio, by Age				
	65-69	70-74	75-79	80-84	85+
All Races					
1940	1.34	1.25	1.20	1.15	1.08
1950	1.58	1.40	1.29	1.21	1.13
1960	1.83	1.62	1.42	1.26	1.11
1970	2.02	1.82	1.61	1.41	1.15
1980	1.98	1.90	1.76	1.55	1.27
White					
1940	1.36	1.26	1.19	1.14	1.07
1950	1.62	1.42	1.29	1.20	1.12
1960	1.88	1.65	1.43	1.27	1.12
1970	2.10	1.86	1.62	1.42	1.16
1980	2.02	1.94	1.78	1.56	1.27
Other Races					
1940	1.20	1.20	1.28	1.33	1.25
1950	1.28	1.23	1.28	1.30	1.20
1960	1.47	1.37	1.30	1.30	1.18
1970	1.52	1.46	1.47	1.33	1.12
1980	1.74	1.58	1.53	1.45	1.32

Sources: Robert D. Grove and Alice M. Hetzel, Vital Statistics Rates in the United States, 1940-1960 (Washington, D.C.: National Center for Health Statistics, 1968), table 55; National Center for Health Statistics, Vital Statistics of the United States, 1970, vol. 2, Mortality, part A (1974), table 1-8; "Advance Report of Final Mortality Statistics, 1980," Monthly Vital Statistics Report, vol. 32, no. 4 (1983), table 1.

226

compiled only for the categories *white* and *all other* or *other races*. That tends to obscure the actual situation of blacks, even though they are well over 90 per cent of the "other-races" group. In many earlier years, the designations were *white* and *nonwhite*, which were no more helpful and even implicitly racist.[28] Therefore, in order to trace trends only for the two major races, we have used data for 1960 and 1980, which do separate blacks from other races.

The age-adjusted death rates for the black population as a whole fell faster between 1960 and 1980 than did those of whites, but that was true only because of reductions in early childhood and several other ages up to 70, whereas the death rates of black infants and elderly people did not drop as fast as those of whites.[29] Nevertheless, the more rapid decreases in the death rates of blacks under age 70, especially women, significantly accelerated the proportions who entered the older years, and blacks rose from 7.2 per cent of the nation's elderly in 1960 to 8.2 per cent in 1980. At the same time, however, there is also a tendency for the mortality levels of the oldest whites to fall faster than those of the oldest blacks, so while the death rate crossover persists, the difference in favor of blacks is growing smaller. In fact, the death rate of black men aged 85 and older was 32 per cent lower than that of white men in 1960, but only 16 per cent lower in 1980; for women the difference declined from 33 per cent to 17 per cent. Some of the change, however, was due to improvements in the quality of the data.

Life Expectancy

At the turn of the century, when life expectancy at birth was only 49 years, relatively few Americans could expect to live to age 65. But the situation has changed so much that death is now primarily a phenomenon of those past age 65, rather than an event that occurs more evenly over the age span.[30] Moreover, deaths of the elderly are disproportionately concentrated in the oldest ages. These changes have occurred largely because greater proportions of the newborn survive to the older ages, but also because the life expectancy of older persons has increased, even if rather modestly. Thus, in 1981 the expectation of life at birth for the total population was 74.1 years, which was an all-time high and an increase of almost 25 years over 1900-1902, although there were periodic decreases for some groups during the 80-year period, especially in 1917-1918. (See Table 9-5.) In the 1980s the expectation of life at birth was still moving upward and represented a 57 per cent increase over 1900-1902. This spectacular progress has close parallels in the other industrialized countries. The increase in the United States indicates very significant progress in health status during the twentieth century, and while in 1900-1902 only

41 per cent of the newborn could expect to reach age 65, by 1981 about 77 per cent could anticipate surviving that long — a gain of 36 elderly people for each 100 infants.

Variations by Race and Sex

In the first 80 years of the century, life expectancy at birth increased by the largest percentage for white females, followed closely by black females. However, the latter actually added more years to their life expectancy because their situation was so much poorer in 1900-1902. Black males also added more years than white males to their life expectancy, and their proportional improvement was greater. Even so, the life expectancy at birth of black males is still well below that of the other three race and sex categories.[31]

Table 9-5. Years of Life Expectancy at Birth, by Race and Sex, 1900-02 to 1980-81

Years	All Groups	White		Other Races	
		Male	Female	Male	Female
1900-02[a]	49.2	48.2	51.1	32.5	35.0
1909-11[a]	51.6	50.3	53.7	34.2	37.7
1919-21[a]	56.5	56.6	58.6	47.2	47.0
1929-31	59.3	59.2	62.8	47.5	49.5
1939-41	63.8	63.3	67.2	52.4	55.4
1949-51	68.2	66.4	72.2	59.1	63.0
1959-61	68.9	67.6	74.2	61.5	66.5
1969-71	70.7	67.9	75.5	61.0	69.1
1980-81	73.9	70.8	78.4	65.7	74.8

Sources: National Center for Health Statistics, Vital Statistics of the United States, 1978, vol. 2, sec. 5, Life Tables (1980), tables 5-A and 5-5; "Annual Summary of Births, Deaths, Marriages, and Divorces: United States, 1981," Monthly Vital Statistics Report, vol. 30, no. 13 (1982), pp. 3-4 and 15.

[a]Death-registration states only.

The most spectacular change of all has been the divergence between males and females in life expectancy. In 1900-1902, white females already had an edge of 2.9 years over white males, but in 1980-1981 the difference was 7.6 years. This reflects the superior progress in mortality control that has accrued to white females as compared with any other group in the population, for their life expectancy still exceeds by 3.6 years that of their nearest competitor — black females — though the latter are moving up fast. But blacks also experienced an even more significant divergence between the sexes, and in 1900-1902 life expectancy for black females was 2.5 years higher than that for black males, while by 1980-1981 the gap had increased to 9.1 years. In fact, about 1965 the life expectancy of black females even surpassed that of white males, and by 1980-1981 the difference had grown to 4.0 years.

At the extremes, white females can now expect to live an average of 12.7 years longer than black males, though the discrepancy is not as great as it was in 1900-1902, when 18.6 years separated those groups. So despite the great divergence by sex, there are also certain convergences underway, and it is likely they will continue until the life expectancy of males and females and blacks and whites grow at least somewhat more alike.

Changes in Life Expectancy of the Elderly

The expectation of life at age 65 has changed much less than that at birth, because the most spectacular mortality reductions have occurred at the younger end of the age scale. Therefore, expectation of life at birth doesn't provide a true picture of what really happened to the average remaining lifetimes of older people, but shows, instead, that much larger percentages of infants survive to the older ages. Consequently, it is necessary to examine life expectancy for each of the age-groups in the elderly population.[32]

For all race and sex groups together, life expectancy at age 65 rose from 11.9 years in 1900-1902 to 16.7 years in 1980, for a difference of 4.8 years, which is a far smaller increase than the 24.7 years at birth in the same period. Furthermore, the life expectancy of elderly women of both races has increased significantly more than that of men in each of the five-year age groups that make up the 65-and-over age category, as shown in Table 9-6. White women registered the largest gains, followed by black women, black men, and white men, in that order. The only exception was the nearly equal increase among black and white women at age 65. There were even occasions during the 80-year period when the life expectancy of elderly white men dropped slightly, whereas in most instances that of the other three groups continued to rise, except in 1917-1918, when the influenza epidemic caused life expectancy to fall for all of the groups.

Early in the 80-year period, life expectancy tended to rise most rapidly for the young-old, but because of the dynamics of the last few decades, the rate of increase has become substantial for the old-old. As a result, the pace of increase during the twentieth century has been greater for men of both races at age 85 than for those aged 65. Life expectancy for the oldest white women has also increased slightly faster than that for the young-old, while the reverse is true for black women. In total, however, the elderly population is becoming increasingly concentrated in the oldest ages, which profoundly affects the kinds and costs of services that are necessary.

In summary, the life expectancy of Americans of all ages has increased dramatically since 1900, but while much of the change is due to rapid

Table 9-6. Years of Life Expectancy at Various Elderly Ages, 1900-02 and 1980

Year and Age	White		Black	
	Male	Female	Male	Female
1900-02[a]				
65	11.5	12.2	10.4	11.4
70	9.0	9.6	8.3	9.6
75	6.8	7.3	6.6	7.9
80	5.1	5.5	5.1	6.5
85	3.8	4.1	4.0	5.1
1980				
65	14.2	18.5	13.5	17.3
70	11.3	14.8	11.1	14.2
75	8.8	11.5	8.9	11.4
80	6.7	8.6	6.9	9.0
85	5.0	6.3	5.3	7.0

Sources: National Center for Health Statistics, Vital Statistics of the United States, 1978, vol. 2, sec. 5, Life Tables (1980), table 5-4; "Advance Report of Final Mortality Statistics, 1980," Monthly Vital Statistics Report, vol. 32, no. 4 (1983), table 2.

[a]Death-registration states only.

improvements in the survival potential of infants, the elderly have also experienced important if more modest increases in the expectation of life. The improvements have been particularly significant for women and for persons aged 75 and older. In Chapter 11 we will consider the impact on longevity of new technologies, especially those that may lengthen the life span, which has long been thought to be a fixed attribute of the human species, and will look at the prospective changes in life expectancy and the impact they will have on the future of American society.

Cause of Death

The three major causes of death of elderly people are heart disease, cancer, and stroke, though individual deaths often result from multiple causes and the average person suffers from more than one chronic illness. For example, pneumonia finally kills some patients disabled by strokes or bedridden with osteoporosis, because these and other chronic deteriorative diseases often reduce resistance to the point where people are susceptible to fatal infections, often of the lungs and blood.[33] Numerous victims of fatal heart attacks have also endured years of hypertension, emphysema, arthritis, or other maladies, and many suicides among the elderly are motivated at least partially by serious health problems. Thus, while the data on the eventual cause of death are useful, especially in tracing long-term changes in the importance of various causes, they do not reveal the several chronic maladies that may combine to bring about the deaths of specific individuals or cause suffering before death.

Age Differences

The causes of death vary greatly in importance by age, and those that claim most elderly lives are not the same ones that account for most deaths of infants, children, and young adults. For example, infants are most likely to die from birth defects, accidents, and pneumonia and influenza, but for children aged 1-14, accidents are the chief cause of death, followed by cancer, especially leukemia, and the lingering effects of birth defects. People aged 15-34 also succumb most often to accidents, especially those involving motor vehicles, but homicide and suicide are the second and third most important causes. Those aged 35-54 die most often from cancer, followed by heart disease and accidents. From there on, however, heart disease assumes first place, cancer second position, and cerebrovascular disease (stroke) third place. There is no change in that ranking with increasing age, except that stroke is in second place for people aged 85 and over, while cancer is third. Moreover, until the ages

55-64 heart disease and cancer are about equally important, but heart disease then pulls far ahead despite its declining rate in recent years, and by the ages 75-84 it kills well over twice as many people as cancer; at age 85 it takes more than three times as many lives as stroke, its nearest competitor.

It is also worth noting, however, that while accidents account for a larger *percentage* of deaths among young people than among any other age group, the *death rate* from that cause is highest for those aged 65 and older. The majority do not involve motor vehicles, whereas for young adults the reverse is true, and for people aged 85 and older the death rate from other accidents is 10 times that from vehicular accidents. Both men and women are especially likely to die from falls, though motor vehicle accidents are in second place, fires in third, and the inhalation or ingestion of food in fourth.[*34*] Since 1968-1969, however, the death rate from accidents among the elderly has declined by about a third, though older people still account for twice their fair share of all fatal accidents.

These and other major killers of elderly people appear in Table 9-7, which shows the 10 leading causes of death and the rates from each in 1980.[*35*] Those data emphasize the significant gap between the three top killers of the elderly and all of the other causes, for heart disease, cancer, and stroke account for 75 per cent of all deaths among persons aged 65 and older. The proportion is the same for those aged 65-84, but it drops to 73 per cent in the oldest ages, when people are somewhat more likely to succumb to a wider range of causes, especially pneumonia and influenza, atherosclerosis, accidents, and chronic pulmonary diseases, particularly emphysema.

The list of major causes of death among the elderly is also significant for what it does not include. Especially scarce are most of the infectious and parasitic diseases and the effects of nutritional deficiency, all of which were far more significant earlier in the century. For example, the death rates from tuberculosis, syphilis, intestinal infections, and hepatitis are a small fraction of what they were in 1940, and despite the 1980 influenza epidemic the death rates from that disease and pneumonia were less than half what they were in 1940. The death rates from other controllable maladies, such as appendicitis, also have fallen faster than the overall death rate of the elderly. Therefore, the major causes have become more heavily concentrated among the degenerative illnesses that are much more difficult to control than are infectious and parasitic diseases, and which are typical of any population with low overall mortality rates and a high percentage of elderly people.

Table 9-7. Death Rates of People 65 and Over for
the Ten Leading Causes, by Age, 1980

Cause of Death[a]	Deaths per 100,000			
	65+	65-74	75-84	85+
All Causes	5,253	2,995	6,693	15,980
Diseases of Heart	2,331	1,219	2,993	7,777
Malignant Neoplasms	1,012	818	1,232	1,595
Cerebrovascular Diseases	573	220	789	2,289
Pneumonia & Influenza	178	56	220	886
Chronic Obstructive Pulmonary Diseases	171	129	224	274
Atherosclerosis	110	24	126	657
Diabetes Mellitus	99	65	131	222
Accidents	97	58	120	293
Motor Vehicle	22	19	28	28
Other	75	39	92	265
Nephritis & Other Kidney Diseases	60	25	68	174
Chronic Liver Disease & Cirrhosis	37	43	31	20
All Other Causes	585	280	639	1,500

Sources: National Center for Health Statistics,
"Advance Report of Final Mortality Statistics:
1980," Monthly Vital Statistics Report, vol. 32,
no. 4 (1983), tables 4 and 5; U.S. Bureau of the
Census, 1980 Census of Population, Supplementary
Reports, PC80-S1-1, Age, Sex, Race, and Spanish
Origin of the Population by Regions, Divisions,
and States: 1980 (1981), table 1.

[a]Ninth International Classification, 1975.

Cause-of-Death Differences by Sex

The death rates for elderly men attributable to heart disease and cancer are far higher than those for elderly women, though the toll from hypertensive heart disease (associated with high blood pressure) is somewhat greater among women. Men are much more likely to die of ischemic (coronary) heart disease, though it also accounts for the great majority of heart disease deaths among women. Cancer, which is the only major cause of death for which the mortality rates among the elderly have continued to rise since 1900,[36] also takes a much higher toll of elderly men than women, particularly cancer of the digestive and urinary organs, the respiratory system, and the mouth, throat, and larynx, largely because of a higher incidence of long-term smoking among the men. Conversely, cancer of the breast is almost exclusive to women, and their death rates are also higher for cancer of the genital organs.

Men are also considerably more likely to die from influenza and pneumonia, accidents, and the chronic obstructive pulmonary diseases, principally bronchitis, emphysema, and asthma. The death rates from kidney diseases are also about twice as high among elderly men as among women, and so are those from liver diseases, partly because of long-established cultural differences between the sexes in the use of alcohol. Cerebrovascular disease also tends to produce higher rates among men close to age 65, but as people approach their 80s the gender differential diminishes substantially, and for the whole group 65 and over the death rate from this cause is somewhat higher for women than for men. The same is true for atherosclerosis. Women are also somewhat more likely to die of diabetes mellitus, but even that crossover doesn't occur until about age 70.

In short, most of the causes of death reflect the greater survival potential of women, as does the fact that their death rates from most of the major causes have declined faster than those of men. Even in the case of cancer, the death rates of men have gone up sharply and steadily, whereas the rates among women have escalated far less and only since the mid-1960s, particularly because of the change in their smoking habits.

Cause-of-Death Differences by Race

In the elderly population as a whole, the differences between the races in rates of death from the leading causes are generally smaller than those between the sexes, though certain causes are particularly hard on one race or the other. For example, elderly blacks have lower rates from bronchitis, emphysema, and asthma and from cirrhosis of the liver, and their suicide rate is far below that of whites. Conversely, the rates for blacks are considerably higher for diabetes and infections of the kidney, and especially homicide. But the races are fairly similar in their susceptibility to most of the major causes of death.

The relationship is strongly influenced by the age distributions within the 65-and-over group, however, and by differences in the sex ratio by race, and it is necessary to account for both of those variables. Thus, among men aged 65-74 the death rates are significantly higher for blacks than for whites from most of the major causes, except bronchitis, emphysema, and asthma, and cirrhosis and suicide, while the rate from cancer is somewhat higher for blacks and that from heart disease is a little lower. The black men are nearly six times as likely as whites to die from homicide, but less than a third as likely to take their own lives. Among women aged 65-74 most of the same relationships between the races apply, except that death rates of black women are much higher than those of white women from heart disease, cerebrovascular disease, and diabetes. But the black women are less often the victims of motor vehicle accidents and their suicide rate is especially low.

In the ages 75-84 the mortality levels for blacks from about half the causes drop below those of whites, though the differences are relatively small. These are the ages in which the death rate crossover appears. Thus, black men aged 75-84 are considerably less likely than whites to die of heart disease, bronchitis and related diseases, atherosclerosis, cirrhosis, and suicide, while their rates from kidney disease and homicide remain relatively high. At about age 80 the death rate from cancer among black men drops slightly below that among white men. Black women aged 75-84 follow many of the same patterns, except that their heart disease death rate is about the same as that of white women, while their rates from cerebrovascular disease, diabetes, and kidney problems remain relatively high. As with black men, the homicide rate of the women is far above that of whites.

In the ages 85 and older the reported data suggest that the death rates of blacks from virtually all causes have fallen well below those of whites, both for men and women. The only exception is the homicide rate of black men, which is still nearly four times that of white men. Moreover, the rates are about the same for blacks and whites of both sexes from kidney infections, while the women of both races have nearly similar rates from diabetes and homicide. Because of distortions in reporting, however, the comparisons in the oldest ages should be treated with caution.

In general, then, heart disease is the major cause of death for the elderly of both races and sexes, followed by cancer and cerebrovascular disease. Moreover, blacks and whites are gradually tending to succumb to more of the same causes at more similar rates, because the diseases associated with low levels of living and poor medical care have declined greatly during the twentieth century and no longer take the disproportionate toll of blacks they once did. But while blacks are increasingly like whites in the tendency to die from the major degenerative illnesses of old age, the changes have not totally obliterated the mortality differences between the races, and a few causes are still much more lethal for elderly people in one race or the other.

Cause-of-Death Trends

Since 1900 the infectious diseases have diminished greatly in importance as causes of death of Americans of all ages. In that year, influenza and pneumonia and tuberculosis led the list of killers and accounted for 23 per cent of all deaths, compared with less than 3 per cent in 1980. They were followed in order by diarrhea and enteritis, heart disease, stroke, nephritis, accidents, diseases of early infancy, cancer, and senility.[37] Other significant causes were syphilis, the death rate from which fell 98 per cent, and typhoid and paratyphoid, which have almost disappeared, as has diphtheria.

Changes in the causes of death among the elderly have paralleled those in the whole population, and in fact the changes are closely associated with the aging of the population and significant increases in life expectancy at birth. But the classification of causes of death has changed over time and record keeping has improved, so it seems best to look at changes in the causes of death that occurred among the elderly between 1950 and 1980. Even during that time the International Classification of Diseases has been revised, but the data are reasonably comparable or can be made so statistically. They show that by 1950 heart disease, cancer, and stroke already accounted for three of every four deaths of elderly people, just as they did in the 1980s, though the relative importance of these three major causes has changed during the period. Table 9-8 shows that while the death rates from heart disease and stroke have fallen significantly, that from cancer has risen, especially since 1970.

Heart disease. This cause is so significant that its trends greatly affect mortality trends in general. It was, of course, by far the leading cause of elderly deaths in 1950 as it is now, but it has been decreasing in importance since the mid-1960s, largely because of reductions in the death rate from coronary heart disease. Furthermore, while the rates have fallen for both sexes and races, they have generally done so fastest for white women, followed by black men and women, and trailed by white men. Between 1950 and 1980, however, the mortality sex ratio for heart disease deaths among the elderly rose significantly, so the advantage that women enjoy relative to men in deaths from this major cause is growing.

Malignant neoplasms. The death rate of the elderly for cancer has risen since 1900 and the increase continued at a substantial pace after 1950. But the situations of men and women are quite different: The former experienced virtually uninterrupted increases, while the rates for women fell until 1965 and then began to move upward. The cancer category includes many types of malignancies, however, and only a few are responsible for the overall increase in death rates from this cause. The dramatic increase in lung cancer is most at fault for both sexes in all of the older age categories, and cigarette smoking is now responsible for more than 80 per cent of the lung cancer deaths among the men and more than 40 per cent of those among the women.[38] In addition, death rates from cancer of the colon have risen among men but decreased among women. The relative significance of breast cancer also increased somewhat among women aged 65-74, but decreased in the older ages. As a result of these dynamics, the mortality sex ratio for cancer among the elderly rose significantly between 1950 and 1980, though the rate of increase slowed after the mid-1960s because of the rapidly increasing incidence of lung cancer among women. Those changes coincided with an increase in the percentage of women smokers and a decrease in the proportion of men who smoke, though the latter who continue tend to consume more cigarettes daily than they did.

Much progress has also been made in curing or arresting some malignant neoplasms, such as cervical cancer, and in increasing the average survival time of treated victims. But these advances have not yet been sufficient to offset the increases from other types of the disease, especially lung cancer, but also genital and colon cancer among men.

Cerebrovascular disease. Death rates for stroke among the elderly have decreased even faster than those for heart disease, especially since 1970 and among women aged 65-74, largely because of substantial improvements in the control of hypertension. In the two older age groups the 1970-1980 decrease has been nearly the same for men and women. As a result, strokes still take a somewhat higher toll of men than women in the ages 65-74, but the reverse is true above age 85.

Not only have the infectious, parasitic, and deficiency diseases become less significant as causes of death among the elderly while the degenerative illnesses have become more important proportionately, but the large majority of elderly people suffer from one or more chronic illnesses, especially arthritis, heart ailments, high blood pressure, and diabetes.[39] They are the price paid for long life expectancy, and while certain chronic diseases may be even better controlled in the future and death rates for them lowered further, they will remain the principal maladies of the older years, and the present major killers of elderly people are apt to be the same in the foreseeable future. Consequently, health-care efforts for the elderly require better daily care for people whose chronic illnesses, unlike the acute ones, are not very responsive to dramatic measures and sophisticated medical technology.[40]

Various chronic diseases will persist in the older population even if the three major killers are much better controlled. For example, Alzheimer's Disease, which produces progressive mental disability, is poorly understood and its cause still unknown. As the population ages, the incidence of that disease is likely to rise dramatically from the 1.5 million people who now suffer from it. It is also costly of a family's financial and emotional resources, because care for its increasingly disoriented victims can extend

Table 9-8. Changes in the Death Rates of Elderly People for the Three Leading Causes of Death, by Age and Sex, 1950-1980

Cause and Age	Per Cent Change		
	1950-60	1960-70	1970-80
Heart Disease			
65-74	-5.4	-10.5	-21.8
75-84	-5.1	-9.9	-18.8
85+	+1.8	-9.1	-8.2
Malignant Neoplasms			
65-74	+3.1	+5.6	+8.5
75-84	-2.2	+3.7	+5.4
85+	-0.1	-2.3	+12.6
Respiratory Cancer			
65-74	+69.1	+49.0	+39.9
75-84	+48.5	+70.2	+54.5
85+	+23.6	+54.0	+31.0
Cerebrovascular Diseases			
65-74	-14.6	-18.1	-42.7
75-84	-0.6	-15.9	-37.1
85+	+23.1	-12.1	-29.2

Sources: National Center for Health Statistics, Health, United States, 1982, PHS Pub. no. 82-1232 (1982), tables 16-19; "Advance Report of Final Mortality Statistics, 1980," Monthly Vital Statistics Report, vol. 32, no. 4 (1983), table 6.

over several years before death follows. Alzheimer's Disease will increase the need for nursing home facilities, although the large majority of victims are cared for at home and the total cost of that care will rise. Therefore, this one example illustrates the fact that even with better control of heart disease, cancer, and stroke, it will be a long while before the aging clock can be turned back and more years of *healthy and vigorous* existence added to the life span. In the meantime, the quality of life for the nation's elderly may even deteriorate in the sense that we will have larger numbers and percentages of people in the oldest ages suffering from the chronic illnesses, many of which develop over a long period, not just because of environmental conditions that could be controlled, but also because of less manipulable genetic factors. Therefore, the health and longevity of a rapidly growing population of old-old still pose perplexing questions.

Summary

In the 100 years from 1900 to 2000 America's elderly population will have grown from 3 million to 35 million, and while fertility changes are a principal reason, reductions in mortality have also played an equally significant part. Because of sophisticated mortality controls, the death rate among infants is not reached again until about age 60, and while the mortality levels of children and young adults haven't fallen to their absolute limits, they have come close to it. Furthermore, the mortality rates of elderly persons are quite low compared with those of earlier decades, and death is more a phenomenon of the very old. In that sense, the United States compares favorably with other urban-industrial societies, though the death rates of elderly women are significantly lower than those of elderly men, while the older black population still has higher rates than the older white group. Even so, the death rates of elderly black and white people have been converging, while those of men and women have been diverging. The racial convergence even results in the well-known cross-over effect, in which the reported death rates of blacks over age 80 are lower than those of whites, partly because of inaccuracies in the data, but also because blacks who do manage to reach the oldest ages seem to have a somewhat higher survival potential than whites in the advanced years. The mortality variations also reflect higher death rates among the most poorly educated Americans and those with the lowest incomes.

Given these differences in death rates, it is logical that vastly more people reach the older ages now than ever before, and that life expectancy is longer for women than for men and greater for whites than for blacks. Despite these variations, however, in 1981 Americans could expect an average lifetime at birth of 74.1 years, while people aged 65 could antici-pate an average of 16.7 more years of life (by 1984, the figures were 74.7

and 16.8, respectively). Both figures are record highs in longevity and both reflect the progress in saving lives at all ages, though the incremental increases in life expectancy are smaller among the elderly than the young, because life-saving technology has had more effect at the lower than the upper end of the age scale. Moreover, the increases in life expectancy are due more to the large proportions of the newborn who reach the older years than to prolongation of life among elderly persons, though the latter improvement has also occurred at a modest rate.

The question as to whether or not life expectancy of the elderly will increase at the rate it has in the past is still open, though medical advances now underway could increase it considerably. They could even expand the historically inexpansible life span — the biological potential for people to survive only a certain number of years, generally 100 or so.

The major causes of death have become fewer in the sense that infectious, parasitic, and nutritional diseases have diminished greatly as causes, leaving heart disease, cancer, and stroke as the major causes of death of the elderly. This is typical of an aging population, in which most people are cut down by the degenerative diseases. There are race and sex variations, but the basic causes of death of elderly Americans reflect a high degree of control over the contagious illnesses of earlier times. They also mirror the effects of excessive smoking, inadequate physical activity, and other contributing factors that could potentially be controlled.

NOTES

1. For detailed accounts of mortality measurement procedures, see Henry S. Shryock and Jacob S. Siegel, *The Methods and Materials of Demography.* v. 2. Washington, DC: U.S. Government Printing Office, 1973, chapters 14 and 15.

2. U.S. Bureau of the Census, "Some Demographic Aspects of Aging in the United States," *Current Population Reports,* P-23, no. 43 (1973): 20.

3. See the international comparisons in Lois A. Fingerhut and Harry M. Rosenberg, "Mortality Among the Elderly," in National Center for Health Statistics, *Health, United States, 1981.* PHS Pub. no. 82-1232 (1981), pp. 20-22.

4. Shryock and Siegel, *op. cit.,* p. 401.

5. Fingerhut and Rosenberg, *op. cit.,* pp. 21-22.

6. U.S. Bureau of the Census, "A Statistical Portrait of Women in the U.S.," *Current Population Reports,* P-23, no. 58 (1976): 8.

7. For a discussion of these points, see U.S. Bureau of the Census, "Demographic Aspects of Aging and the Older Population in the United States," *Current Population Reports,* P-23, no. 59 (1976): 28-29.

8. *Ibid.,* p. 30.

240

9. See the discussion by Estelle R. Ramey, "The Natural Capacity for Health in Women," in Phyllis W. Berman and Estelle R. Ramey, eds., *Women: A Developmental Perspective.* Washington, DC: National Institutes of Health, 1982, pp. 3-12, especially pp. 4-6.

10. Jacob S. Siegel, "On the Demography of Aging," *Demography* 17 (1980): 350.

11. Beth J. Soldo, "America's Elderly in the 1980s," *Population Bulletin* 35 (1980): 15.

12. Lois A. Fingerhut, "Changes in Mortality Among the Elderly: United States, 1940-78," *Vital and Health Statistics,* Analytical Studies, series 3, no. 22 (1982): 15-18.

13. U.S. Bureau of the Census, "Demographic Aspects of Aging...," *op. cit.,* p. 32.

14. Jacquelyne Johnson Jackson, *Minorities and Aging.* Belmont, CA: Wadsworth, 1980, p. 64.

15. For a discussion of the crossover phenomenon, see Charles B. Nam, Norman L. Weatherby and Kathleen A. Ockay, "Causes of Death Which Contribute to the Mortality Crossover Effect," *Social Biology* 25 (1978): 306-314.

16. John Reid, "Black America in the 1980s," *Population Bulletin* 37 (1982): 14-15.

17. Paul C. Glick, "Differential Mortality," in U.S. Bureau of the Census, "Population of the United States, Trends and Prospects: 1950-1990," *Current Population Reports,* P-23, no. 49 (1974): 45; 46-47.

18. National Center for Health Statistics, *Health..,* p. 210.

19. Edmund Graves and Robert Pokras, "Expected Principal Source of Payment for Hospital Discharges: United States, 1979," in National Center for Health Statistics, *Advance Data from Vital and Health Statistics,* no. 75 (1982): 3.

20. Shryock and Siegel, *op. cit.,* pp. 409-410.

21. Regina McNamara, "Mortality Trends," in John A. Ross, ed., *International Encyclopedia of Population.* v. 2. New York: Free Press, 1982, p. 461; adapted from Abdel R. Omran, "The Epidemiologic Transition: A Theory of the Epidemiology of Population Change," *Milbank Memorial Fund Quarterly* 49 (1971): 509-538.

22. Jean van der Tak, "U.S. Population: Where We Are; Where We're Going," *Population Bulletin* 37 (1982): 15.

23. U.S. Bureau of the Census, "Demographic Aspects...," *op. cit.,* p. 25.

24. Siegel, *op. cit.,* p. 348.

25. Lois A. Fingerhut, "Chartbook," in National Center for Health Statistics, *Health, United States, 1982,* PHS Pub. no. 83-1232 (1982): 34.

26. Soldo, *op. cit.,* p. 16.

27. For projections to 2000 that anticipate reductions in the mortality sex ratio, see Shryock and Siegel, *op. cit.,* p. 780, table 24-4. Cf. Siegel, *op. cit.,* p. 350.

28. For an effort to overcome some of this problem, see Jacquelyne Johnson Jackson, "Death Rate Trends of Black Females, United States, 1964-1978," in Berman and Ramey, *op. cit.,* pp. 23-35.

29. For the data, see National Center for Health Statistics, *Health, 1981, op. cit.,* table 8; and National Center for Health Statistics, "Advance Report of Final Mortality Statistics, 1980," *Monthly Vital Statistics Report* 32 (1983), table 1.

30. Richard A. Kalish, "Death and Dying in Social Context," in Robert H. Binstock and Ethel Shanas, eds., *Handbook of Aging and the Social Sciences.* New York: Van Nostrand, 1976, p. 484.

31. For a discussion, see Reid, *op. cit.,* pp. 14-15.

32. U.S. Bureau of the Census, "Demographic Aspects...," *op. cit.,* p. 27.

33. Kenneth G. Manton and Eric Stallard, "Temporal Trends in U.S. Multiple Cause of Death Mortality Data: 1968 to 1977," *Demography* 19 (1982): 539.

34. Metropolitan Life Foundation, *Statistical Bulletin* 63 (1982): 12.

35. Causes are from World Health Organization, *Manual of the International Statistical Classification of Diseases, Injuries, and Causes of Death, Ninth Revision.* Geneva: WHO, 1977.

36. National Center for Health Statistics, *Health, 1981, op. cit.,* p. 18.

37. van der Tak, *op. cit.,* p. 16.

38. American Cancer Society, *Cancer Facts and Figures.* New York: American Cancer Society, 1983.

39. Mary Barberis, "America's Elderly: Policy Implications," *Population Bulletin* 35 (1981): 8.

40. *Ibid.,* p. 12.

Chapter 10

Internal Migration of the Elderly

Migration within the United States is the third major population process that determines the size, proportional significance, and distribution of the elderly population in particular places, although movement from abroad also has some impact. Despite recent attention to the movement of older retired persons to Florida, California, and other Sunbelt areas, however, movements of the elderly are not new in industrial societies, for they have long altered the lives of millions, while they have helped re-distribute the older population in general.[1] Nevertheless, migration is mostly an activity of young adults, and older people are far more likely to stay where they are because of social ties, familiar settings, or prohibitive costs. Therefore, the focus on the minority who do migrate tends to divert attention from problems in the areas where most older people remain after they retire, especially the rural communities, the deteriorating urban areas, and some aging suburbs.[2] Some of these places have become elderly enclaves, not because of migratory influxes of old people, but because the exodus of younger ones has left behind a high concentration of the elderly.

There is a growing body of literature on the minority who do migrate, however, and it deals with their characteristics, the places they leave and those they enter, and the reasons they move. These studies, most done since 1960, show that elderly migrants are not representative of the entire older population, but rather that the process selects for certain kinds of people. Even most of those who do move don't go very far, because well over half remain in the same county, while only a fifth depart for another state. The young-old also tend to migrate for different reasons than the old-old; the former often seek better recreational opportunities and climate, whereas the latter frequently relocate for health reasons or to be with adult offspring, sometimes returning to an original home area.[3] In any case, elderly migration is now studied intensively, and while the phenomenon lacks an adequate explanatory theoretical framework, there are many specific contributions toward that end.[4]

Measuring Migration

Migration is assessed by counting either the number of people who move from place to place on a relatively permanent basis within a given period, or the number of moves specific persons make. Data for the United States better enable the first measurement than the second.[5]

Sources of Data

There are two basic sources of data on migration in the United States: the decennial census of population and the Current Population Survey, which has collected statistics on the spatial mobility of the population each year since 1948. Both sources provide information on the numbers of people who enter and leave various places, usually during periods of one year or five years. But these sources account for only one move per person during the specific period, and thus neglect multiple moves and seasonal shifts — a methodological problem created by the assumption that the person has a "usual place of residence."[6] Nevertheless, the materials do include considerable detail on movement by age, sex, marital status, and other characteristics. They also describe the migration of people between counties, states, and major regions, as well as more localized moves within counties and Standard Metropolitan Statistical Areas (SMSAs) and their components.

These data fail to reveal much about the social environments that people leave and enter, however, and while one can infer some things about the elderly who move from the Northeast to South Florida, what do shifts from North Carolina to South Carolina mean, or from one Iowa county to another? Therefore, while the data describe several types of physical movement, other kinds of studies must provide the information about changes in social settings and status, the reasons people move, the kinds of adjustments they and the receiving areas make, and other crucial matters. This is one reason why the last two decades have seen numerous investigations of elderly migration.[7]

Other more limited sources of migration data include sample surveys of changes in people's places of employment, taken by the Social Security Administration; the Health Interview Survey of the National Center for Health Statistics, which began to ascertain residential mobility in 1979; the Study of Housing Adjustments of Older People, conducted in a few areas as part of the Annual Housing Survey; and several surveys that determine the home areas of the institutionalized population.[8] These materials have specific usefulness as well as limitations in coverage, but used with censuses and Current Population Survey data, they help enlarge our view of elderly migration. In its diversity, that phenomenon includes the migration of older workers because of job relocation; retirement migration; residential changes necessitated by deteriorating health or other aspects of the aging process; shifts of the elderly poor who are evicted from rental housing; migration in pursuit of a better environment or to be near children; and temporary moves, usually on a seasonal basis because of climate.[9] Thus, while most elderly long-distance movers go to retirement areas, the whole phenomenon of migration is far more complex than that and has a qualitative dimension that is not easily detected in the quantitative data on who went where.[10]

Concepts and Indexes

The vocabulary of migration in the United States is quite specific, and because certain terms used in this chapter will have those specific meanings, it is well to clarify them briefly:

Mobility status is ascertained by comparing where people lived when they were surveyed with where they resided a given number of years earlier, usually one or five. *Nonmovers* are people who were living in the same residence at the beginning and the end of the period, though any who left and returned to the same house in the interim are classified as nonmovers. *Movers* are all persons who lived in a different house at the end of the period than at the beginning. They are classified further according to whether or not they were living in the same county, state, or region; had moved from abroad; lived in the same or a different central city or SMSA; or had made any other type of move.[11] Thus, people can be identified as intracounty movers, movers between counties in the same state, interstate migrants to contiguous or noncontiguous states, and interregional migrants.

In addition, *in-migrants* are people who enter an area, while *out-migrants* are those who leave, and the balance between them is *net migration. Migration streams* flow from one area to another, and each has a *counterstream,* either larger or smaller; the two produce the *net interchange* between the two areas, represented as a net gain for one and a net loss for the other. Finally, *return migration* refers to people who move back to their origins, though they are usually classified simply as movers.[12]

Differentials in Internal Migration

The elderly people who do move differ from those who do not according to several personal, social, and economic characteristics, which also vary by the distance covered, the reasons people move, and their destinations. Therefore, interstate migration and local movement are selective of different types of older persons. Specifically, migrants who cover relatively long distances tend to be the young-old, and to be married, affluent, and relatively well educated, whereas those who move locally are more apt to be poor and dependent.

The following sections consider the various characteristics of the elderly people who do move. The discussion of age compares their migration patterns with those of younger people, while the sections on selectivity by sex, race, and other characteristics focus only on the older population.

Differentials by Age

The demographic characteristic that most influences the rate of migration is age, and the elderly are far less likely than younger people to move from region to region, state to state, county to county, or even house to house within the same county.[13] Figure 10-1 shows that the migration rate of children aged 6 or 7 is relatively high, because they share the high rates of their parents, who are generally in their late 20s or early 30s. The rate falls off steadily from early childhood until age 18, when most people have finished high school and many leave home for college, new jobs, or their own marriages and households.[14] Thus, the proportion who moved between 1975 and 1980, added to those who came from abroad, reached a peak of 83 per cent at age 27. By age 35 the rate falls sharply, because adults become increasingly committed to particular jobs, homes, and social contacts, and because their older children are more likely to resist moving than are younger ones.[15]

The migration rate reaches a low point about age 61, but rises somewhat between 62 and 64, when some of the people who can afford early retirement move to better climates and recreational opportunities. There are additional increases among people in their late 60s, reflecting the movement of those who retire at age 65, some of whom migrate long distances in search of amenities or to be near children, while others move only within their home counties. Finally, people aged 75 and older also have higher rates of interstate migration than do those slightly younger, and people aged 85 and over have even higher rates, because many can no longer live alone and must migrate to be with adult children or to enter nursing homes near those children.[16] Much of the migration among people of any elderly age, however, represents an effort to find better living conditions, especially housing, and is far less affected by employment factors than is the movement of younger people.[17] In fact, involvement in the labor force is a minor influence in elderly migration, though some retired people might seek part-time jobs in their new locales.

Figure 10-2 shows the details of the various movements of people from age 55 to 75 and older, though these migration rates by single years of age refer to moves that people made at any time in the 1975-1980 period. Consequently, someone aged 65 who is classified as a mover could have made the shift at any age from 60 to 65 and could have moved more than once.

Almost four-fifths of the people aged 65 and older did not move at all between 1975 and 1980, though the ones who did represent 5 million individuals and the interstate migrants among them numbered 1 million. Furthermore, in every age category from 5 to 75 and over, smaller per-

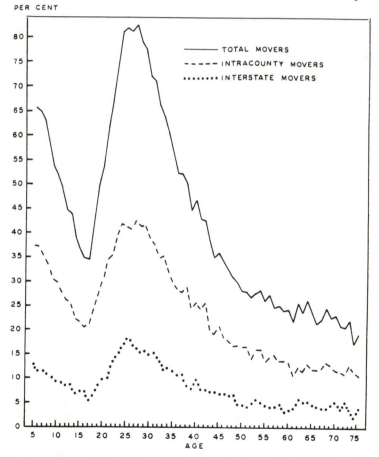

Figure 10-1. Percentages of American People Who Made Specified Moves Between 1975 and 1980, by Single Years of Age in 1980
Source: U.S. Bureau of the Census, "Geographical Mobility: March 1975 to March 1980," *Current Population Reports,* P-20, no. 368 (1981), table 5.

248

centages of people were intercounty and interstate movers combined than were intracounty movers. In the age group 65 and over, 57 per cent of those who moved stayed in the same county, while 20 per cent went to another state; but three-quarters of them went to noncontiguous states, often in the Sunbelt. In fact, the elderly began moving to the Sunbelt long before the large flow of younger people to those states got underway. They were also the harbingers of the reversal in metropolitan-

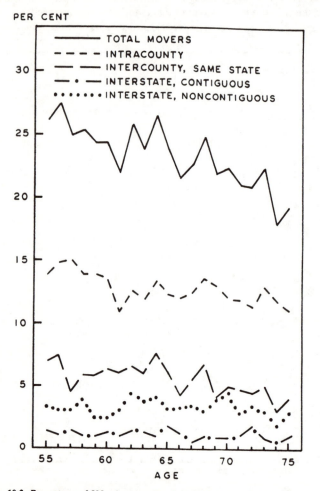

Figure 10-2. Percentages of Older American People Who Made Specified Moves Between 1975 and 1980, by Single Years of Age in 1980
Source: U.S.Bureau of the Census, "Geographical Mobility: March 1975 to March 1980," *Current Population Reports,* P-20, no. 368 (1981), table 5.

nonmetropolitan migration, for while large numbers in other age groups started moving to small towns and other nonmetropolitan areas after 1970, the elderly had begun that movement in the 1960s. Furthermore, although elderly interstate migrants tend to cover shorter distances than other age groups, those who move to Florida, Arizona, and California often come from quite far away.[18]

Actual rates of migration tell little about the elderly people who would like to move but cannot for various reasons, often financial. Therefore, low mobility rates are not evidence that all of the nonmovers are satisfied with their settings. On the contrary, many are not content and even hope to move, and when opportunities present themselves many older people actually do migrate. Fairly small percentages get those opportunities, however, and when people feel they have no alternatives, they may even say they are satisfied in unpleasant or even dangerous surroundings. Thus, actual movement is a poor indicator of people's satisfaction with their situations, just as expressed intentions about migration are a faulty way to predict actual movement, because the interplay of aspirations and circumstances, opportunities and constraints is very complex.[19]

Differentials by Sex

There is relatively little difference between the internal migration rates of men and women, including the elderly, though women have somewhat higher rates in their late teens and early twenties, and somewhat lower rates from then through their early 50s. (See Figure 10-3.) The peak age of probability for women to migrate is 24, while that for men is 26 or 27, though even that difference may reflect the persistent tendency for women to marry men who average a couple of years older and with whom they then migrate.[20]

In the ages 65 and over, there is also not much difference in mobility rates by sex, because 20 per cent of the men and 21 per cent of the women moved between 1975 and 1980. There are significant variations in the ages 70 and over, however, as the proportion of widows increases and many give up their homes and move to be with children, to enter retirement facilities or nursing homes, or to return to areas where they grew up. (See Table 10-1.) Those changes account for the higher rate of intracounty movement among women than men in the ages 70 and over, while the rates of interstate migration don't vary a great deal.

The *number* of elderly women who move, of course, is much greater than that of elderly men because of the low sex ratios in the older ages. Thus, between 1975 and 1980, about 2 million men aged 65 and older but 3 million of the women made a move of some kind. Therefore, the currents of movement within and between counties contain larger numbers of older

250

women than men, as does interstate migration, even though the mobility rates are quite similar for the sexes. That similarity does allow the use of a single "model of migration" for elderly men and women in the United States,[21] but it doesn't deny considerable differences in sex ratios in certain areas owing to sex selectivity in past migration. Because the elderly population is largely retired and their migration is not greatly affected by occupational considerations, it is less sex-selective than movement among younger people. In fact, economic factors of many kinds affect the migration of older people less than that of younger people, while non-economic factors such as climate and crime rates are more significant for the elderly.[22]

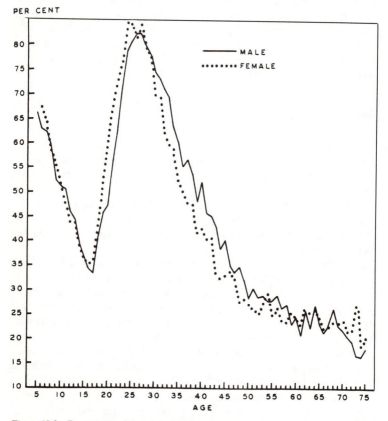

Figure 10-3. Percentages of American Males and Females Who Moved Between 1975 and 1980, by Single Years of Age in 1980
Source: U.S. Bureau of the Census, "Geographical Mobility: March 1975 to March 1980," *Current Population Reports,* P-20, no. 368 (1981), pp. 16; 17.

Differentials by Race

The migration of blacks out of the South, first to the industrial centers of the Northeast and North Central regions and later to the West, is legendary in the movement of Americans. It is also the background for considering the present migration of elderly black people.

The great movement actually began with the flight of slaves before the Civil War, picked up during the period of industrial expansion in the late

Table 10-1. Percentages of Persons Who Made Various Moves Between March 1975 and March 1980, by Sex and Selected Ages in 1980

Age and Sex	All Movers[a]	Same County	Different County, Same State	Different State
Male				
5+	45.7	25.8	10.4	9.5
20-24	59.6	32.7	14.6	12.3
25-29	76.3	40.2	18.9	17.2
55-59	25.9	14.5	6.7	4.7
60-64	23.5	12.6	6.0	4.9
65-69	22.7	12.7	5.4	4.6
70-74	18.9	9.9	4.8	4.2
75+	17.7	10.0	3.6	4.1
Female				
5+	44.4	25.7	9.9	8.8
20-24	69.7	39.6	16.6	13.5
25-29	78.1	42.6	19.1	16.4
55-59	24.2	14.2	5.8	4.2
60-64	24.2	12.4	7.0	4.8
65-69	22.5	12.6	5.4	4.5
70-74	22.2	13.6	4.2	4.4
75+	19.9	11.9	4.4	3.6

Source: U.S. Bureau of the Census, "Geographical Mobility: March 1975 to March 1980," Current Population Reports, P-20, no. 368 (1981), table 5.

[a]Includes movers from abroad.

1800s and early 1900s, and assumed large proportions when the Northern factories needed workers during World War I. (See Table 10-2.) The black migration from the South was slowed and finally stopped briefly by the Great Depression, which made poverty agriculture in the region a better survival alternative to industrial unemployment in the North. But the movement resumed after New Deal legislation in the early 1930s provided more relief provisions for urban populations than for farm people. A large share of Southern blacks fell into the latter category, and they migrated to urban centers in pursuit of the new if still meager assistance opportunities. So did great numbers of poor-white farm tenants, sharecroppers, wage laborers, marginal farm owners, and even some middle-class owners. Most of these groups contributed to the mass transfer of poverty from farms to cities, especially its shift from the South to other regions. The labor demands of World War II also swelled the movement out of the South and off the poorer farms elsewhere in the nation, and between 1933 and 1970, when movement from farms nearly exhausted the supply of potential migrants, about 55 million people left agriculture for the cities. Blacks were an unusually large share of that group.[23]

The exodus of blacks from the rural South resembled most other long-distance migrations, in that it consisted largely of young adults and their children, while people aged 65 and over were a very small share — probably less than 5 per cent. In 1949-1950, for example, which ended the decade of the largest black net migration from the South, 26 per cent of the blacks who left the region were aged 20-24 and 72 per cent were under age 35; only 3.5 per cent were 65 and over. But the blacks in the early exodus have now become an elderly population. Some of them are part of the new return migration to the South, though that movement consists largely of younger urban-born black people seeking economic opportunities away from the depressed industrial centers of the Northeast and North Central regions; even the West, which is still experiencing net gains of blacks by migration, is doing so at a decresing rate. Moreover, the migration to the South is a movement to metropolitan centers and suburbs, not a return to farms, and includes not just the poor and unemployed but also many highly paid and well-educated younger blacks as well as elderly persons returning home.

For many black elderly, who are a larger percentage of the return migration than elderly blacks were of the original exodus, a move to the South represents a move back to the extended family, which tends to be a more protective and integrative force in the lives of older blacks than of older whites. That is just now becoming apparent, however, because the strength and protective functions of the extended family, as well as the wide diversity of black family forms, have often been neglected by analysts who concentrated on the earlier mother-centered and frequently disrupted family of many blacks, especially the poor.[24] Therefore, the return to the security of the extended family by many elderly blacks helps modify the assumption of a single black family form and explains a significant share of the black movement back into the South. Other factors are at work, too, such as milder climate, nonfamily social contacts, occupational opportunities to supplement small pensions, better race relations, and the search for one's roots.

Nor are the patterns exclusive to blacks, for white people have also migrated to and from the South and other regions for many of the same reasons, and though whites were not the target of racial discrimination, many people of both races did share poverty as a motivation to leave originally. Therefore, the conditions that are drawing blacks to the South

Table 10-2. Net Migration of Blacks of All Ages, by Regions, 1870-1980

Period	Net Migration (1,000s)			
	South	Northeast	North Central	West
1870-1880	-60	+24	+36	....
1880-1890	-70	+46	+24	....
1890-1900	-168	+105	+63	....
1900-1910	-170	+95	+56	+20
1910-1920	-454	+182	+244	+28
1920-1930	-749	+349	+364	+36
1930-1940	-347	+171	+128	+49
1940-1950	-1,599	+463	+618	+339
1950-1960	-1,473	+496	+541	+293
1960-1970	-1,380	+612	+382	+301
1970-1975	+14	-64	-52	+102
1975-1980	+195	-175	-51	+30

Sources: U.S. Bureau of the Census, "The Social and Economic Status of the Black Population in the United States: An Historical View, 1790-1978," Current Population Reports, P-23, no. 80 (1979), table 8; "Mobility of the Population of the United States: March 1970 to March 1975," Current Population Reports, P-20, no. 285 (1975), table 28; "Geographical Mobility: March 1975 to March 1980," Current Population Reports, P-20, no. 368 (1981), table 42.

are also attracting whites, and in 1975-1980 that region gained more than 1.6 million whites of all ages by net migration, the West gained about half that number, and the Northeast and North Central regions each lost well over 1 million.

The overall migration rates of the races do not differ a great deal, for between 1975 and 1980 elderly blacks were only slightly less likely than older whites to have made a move of some kind. (See Table 10-3.) Furthermore, the moves that older blacks did make tended to be relatively short distance, because they were more inclined than whites to relocate within the same SMSA or same state. However, even though the rate of interstate migration among older blacks was only about two-thirds that of elderly whites, when blacks did change states they were much more likely to change regions as well, largely because of the movement back to the South. Thus, 83 per cent of the black interstate migrants went to another region in the process of moving, while only 60 per cent of the whites did so. Clearly, the regions that people felt offered the best opportunities earlier in the century seem less promising now, and to the extent net in-migration reveals the places where people feel their life chances are best, the South seems to offer more to elderly people of both races than do the other three regions.

Differentials by Marital Status

The choice to migrate is associated with marital status, though the presence or absence of children of particular ages is also a strategic variable in making that choice.[25] But while some elderly people may still have charge of older children or grandchildren, most lack that responsibility and the influence of marital status on their migration is little affected by children in the household. Even so, deciding whether or not to migrate is often influenced by the wish to be close to adult children who have established their own households, which is one reason why the migration rates of older people with offspring living nearby are especially low.

In general, elderly married people are less likely to move than are those who were never married or who are separated, widowed, or divorced. But there are some variations by sex, and marital status operates in the context of other personal, social, economic, and health circumstances that also promote or retard movement. Men are least likely to move if they are married, while single men are the most mobile, followed by those in the other marital categories. Women show similar but not identical migratory patterns by marital status: Married women are the least mobile, while those who are separated, widowed, or divorced are most likely to move. And since the nonmarried group consists largely of widows, the death of a husband affects many individual choices to move or stay put. For example, a great deal of elderly migration to the Sunbelt consists of married couples. But numerous husbands die after a few years in the new retirement areas and many of their widows then return to the communities they once left, while the Sunbelt populations are continually replenished by elderly married couples who migrate in. That helps explain why the 1980 sex ratio of elderly people was 76 in Florida and 79 in Arizona, compared with only 68 for the nation's older population as a whole, though the ratios in those states would be even higher if many women did not remain after being widowed.

Differentials by Level of Education

In the general population, educational attainment has a substantial effect on migration: Better-educated persons are most likely to change residence, while the poorly educated are considerably less mobile.[26]

Table 10-3. Percentages of Persons Aged 65 and Over in 1980 Who Made Specified Moves Between 1975 and 1980, by Race

Type of Move	White	Black
Same House (Nonmovers)	78.8	79.9
Total Movers within United States	20.9	20.1
Different House, Same SMSA	8.8	11.8
Different House, Different SMSA	3.3	2.0
Same State	16.6	17.2
Different State	4.3	2.9
Same Region	1.7	0.5
Different Region	2.6	2.4
Movers from Abroad	0.3	a

Source: U.S. Bureau of the Census, "Geographical Mobility: March 1975 to March 1980," Current Population Reports, P-20, no. 368 (1981), tables 36 and 40.

[a]Less than 0.1 per cent.

The same is true for the elderly, as shown in Table 10-4, though migration is affected by the interplay between education, occupation prior to retirement, and income. That is, the higher the level of one's education the better one's job is likely to have been, and the income and subsequent pension it produces make migration financially feasible.[27] In addition, new jobs are easier for well-educated people to find, and some older ones, especially men who retire relatively early, migrate to begin new careers.

Education also seems to have more impact than sex, race, and marital status on the distance older people move.[28] (See Table 10-4.) Thus, people with 0-8 years of schooling have the highest rates of movement from house to house within their counties, and the rates of local movement drop steadily as the level of schooling rises. This suggests that once they are established in a home or neighborhood, well-educated elderly people tend either to be more stable residentially or to go long distances if they move at all, while the poorly educated are more nomadic locally, mostly shifting between deteriorating sections of central cities in an effort to cope with high crime rates, frequent evictions, and other problems. Financial constraints keep most of them from escaping to another county or state or to the suburbs, and after retirement many even have to settle for worse conditions than they had known.

The people who move to another county within the same state and those who migrate to distant states tend to be relatively well educated. In fact, the rate of movement to noncontiguous states is more than two and a half times greater for people who attended college than it is for those who finished only eight grades or less. Long-distance movement is expensive and emotionally risky, and it is largely an activity of those whose educations and jobs provided them with enough income and psychological resources to move comfortably and safely. Long-distance migration is also dominated by the young-old, who are better educated as a group than are the old-old.

Finally, well educated or not, elderly people who are still in the labor force have significantly lower rates of migration than those who are retired, and when the working elderly of both sexes do move they tend to go short distances.[29] The basic reasons are the difficulty elderly people encounter in finding new jobs in new places and their reluctance to relinquish a present position for an uncertain employment future elsewhere. Even the wish to be employed part-time holds back some would-be migrants, though the need to work often reflects their inability to finance a move in the first place and the prospect of losing assistance from relatives, friends, and local agencies.

Table 10-4. Percentages of Persons Aged 65 and Over in 1980 Who Moved Within the United States Between 1975 and 1980, by School Years Completed

School Years	All Movers	Same County	Different County, Same State	Contiguous State	Noncontiguous State
All Levels	20.8	12.0	4.7	1.1	3.1
Elementary 0-8 Years	19.5	12.8	4.2	0.8	2.0
High School					
1-3 Years	21.3	12.7	4.4	1.5	2.7
4 Years	21.0	11.6	4.5	1.1	3.7
College					
1-3 Years	23.9	10.8	5.9	2.0	5.1
4 Years	22.2	9.1	5.5	1.4	6.2
5+ Years	22.0	7.5	7.9	1.3	5.1

Source: U.S. Bureau of the Census, "Geographical Mobility: March 1975 to March 1980," Current Population Reports, P-20, no. 368 (1981), table 24.

Metropolitan and Nonmetropolitan Migration

The Nonmetropolitan Revival

Since about 1960 the elderly have been part of the reverse spatial mobility that caused metropolitan areas to begin losing more people by migration than they gained, while nonmetropolitan places began to experience net gains.[30] Those older movers were joined later by many younger ones who were also fleeing central cities and even some suburbs for the towns, villages, and countrysides, some at considerable distance from the urban centers, though neither group moved back to agriculture. The nonmetropolitan movement was a revolutionary change, because virtually the entire history of the United States has been marked by greater urbanization and net migration gains in the cities, net losses in the rural areas.

We should be clear, however, that we are talking about *net gains and losses by migration,* for the reversal in metropolitan-nonmetropolitan growth rates by that process has not caused the absolute size of the metropolitan population to decrease. The opposite is true, because natural increase has so offset losses by net migration that in 1980 the 169.4 million Americans living in SMSAs were a larger number than ever before and their proportion (75 per cent) was also greater than at any prior time.[31] Even so, the populations in 29 of the 318 SMSAs identified in 1980 actually did decrease numerically during the 1970s. Moreover, Table 10-5 shows that the metropolitan population increased at a slower pace after 1960, while the nonmetropolitan segment grew at a faster rate, at least between 1960 and 1975; net migration losses by SMSAs and gains by nonmetropolitan areas were largely responsible. They almost caused the central cities collectively to stop growing in the 1970s, whereas the outlying parts of SMSAs — mostly suburbs — still increased, though at a slower rate than they had.

Just how long the movement to nonmetropolitan areas will last remains to be seen. Indeed, there is evidence that it reversed once again in the 1980s. But significant migration to the less urban sections is likely to continue until people perceive increases in the quality of urban life, or until the new attractions of the more rural areas stabilize or even wane; since 1978, for example, unemployment rates in those places have been higher than in the SMSAs.[32] As a result, the rate of net migration to nonmetropolitan places was lower between 1975 and 1980 than between 1970 and 1975, though it still produced significant gains there and substantial losses from the SMSAs (now called Metropolitan Statistical Areas - MSAs).

The participation of the elderly in these net gains and losses by migration during the 1970s is shown in Table 10-6, as is that of the population under age 65. For both groups, 1970-1975 was the peak period of net losses from metropolitan areas and net gains by the small towns and villages. In the following five years, the SMSAs still lost more migrants than they gained and the nonmetropolitan sections continued to gain, but the numbers and rates declined in both cases. Thus, between 1970 and 1975, nonmetropolitan areas gained 51 elderly perons for each 1,000 elderly nonmovers, but between 1975 and 1980 the ratio fell to 33. Conversely, the rate of loss from metroplitan areas slowed considerably and the ratio of elderly movers to nonmovers fell from 30 in 1970-1975 to 19 in the next half decade. As a result, the rate of net exodus from metropolitan areas, once higher for the elderly than for younger people, is now about the same for both groups, while older people are no more likely than younger ones to migrate to nonmetropolitan places. Some of the reasons include the higher costs of fuel to visit the cities, rising land prices and taxes in the less urbanized sections, reduced economic vigor and employment opportunities in many industries that located in rural areas, efforts by city governments to attract people back, and fewer of the recreational and "cultural" advantages to which urban people had grown accustomed.

Table 10-5. Percentage Increases in Metropolitan and Nonmetropolitan Populations of All Ages, 1950-1980

Area	1940 to 1950	1950 to 1960	1960 to 1970	1970 to 1980
United States	14.5	18.5	13.3	11.4
Metropolitan	22.0	26.4	16.6	10.2
In Central Cities	14.0	10.7	6.4	0.1
Outside Central Cities	35.5	48.6	26.8	18.2
Nonmetropolitan	6.1	7.1	6.8	15.1

Source: U.S. Bureau of the Census, 1980 Census of Population, Supplementary Reports, PC80-S1-5, Standard Metropolitan Statistical Areas and Standard Consolidated Statistical Areas: 1980 (1981), table B.

The combined effects of inflation and recession also make it financially impossible for some people to move, though the elderly are generally hurt more by inflation than by recession. Finally, when many elderly move to the Sunbelt, they seek out the SMSAs, not the more rural sections.

Though some elderly also move to nonmetropolitan parts of the Sunbelt, numerous others go to nonmetropolitan sections outside that band of states, seeking better environmental and recreational opportunities. Their destinations include the upper Great Lakes portions of several states, parts of the Ozarks and the Blue Ridge Mountains, some areas of the Rocky Mountains, and coastal parts of the Northeast and the Northwest.

Table 10-6. Metropolitan and Nonmetropolitan Migration of Persons in Two Age Groups, 1970-1980 (1,000s)

Area and Movement	5-64		65+	
	1970-75	1975-80	1970-75	1975-80
Metropolitan				
In-Migrants	4,928	5,736	198	257
Out-Migrants	6,229	6,857	492	481
Net Migration	-1,301	-1,121	-294	-224
Ratio to Nonmovers[a]	-22.8	-18.6	-30.1	-18.9
Nonmetropolitan				
In-Migrants	6,229	6,857	492	481
Out-Migrants	4,928	5,736	198	257
Net Migration	+1,301	+1,121	+294	+224
Ratio to Nonmovers[a]	+47.9	+39.3	+51.1	+32.6

Sources: U.S. Bureau of the Census, "Mobility of the Population of the United States: March 1970 to March 1975," Current Population Reports, P-20, no. 285 (1975), table 1; "Geographical Mobility: March 1975 to March 1980," Current Population Reports, P-20, no. 368 (1981), table 4.

[a]Number of net migrants per 1,000 nonmovers in each age group and residence area.

Many of these areas were long drained of rural people and have now been revitalized by the migration turnaround. Other sections, however, are still losing elderly people, including the Great Plains and central Midwest, large parts of Appalachia, sparsely settled areas of the West, and even some sections of the South, especially the Mississippi Delta.[33] It is important to recall, too, that most counties with the highest percentages of elderly have lost significant shares of their younger people, but have had little if any net in-migration of older persons.

Movement within SMSAs

Metropolitan movement includes more than just net losses to nonmetropolitan areas, because the shifts between central cities and suburbs within SMSAs are also substantial, as are movements inside the central cities. The bulk of the former migration is from the urban core to the outlying sections, but there is also a smaller reverse movement, and the elderly participate in both. The overall result is a slow increase in the segregation of the elderly in or near central cities, though it is still far less than the segregation of blacks of all ages in those areas.[34] At the same time, the numbers and proportions of older people are also increasing in the suburbs for several reasons: Suburban birth rates have fallen significantly; some younger people have moved to nonmetropolitan areas outside the suburban portions of SMSAs; original suburban populations are growing older; and more elderly persons are migrating to suburbs than are leaving them.

Because of these dynamics, the central cities of SMSAs are still losing people of all ages by net migration, including the elderly, while the outlying parts of SMSAs are gaining in the exchange within given SMSAs, between them, and between nonmetropolitan and metropolitan areas. Not all of the SMSA population outside central cities consists of suburbanites, but they do make up the large majority. Consequently, there is still a substantial flow of the elderly to suburbs from central cities, though as with any type of migration, their proportional representation is less than that of younger people; but the flow that does exist is helping to "age" some suburbs appreciably. That is particularly true of certain relatively low-density, low-cost ones in the more rural and often unincorporated parts of SMSAs.[35] Most of the elderly who move to these areas, as well as those who go to nonmetropolitan communities, are retired and free to seek places in which their reduced incomes will provide a more satisfactory quality of life or at least prevent its deterioration, and for them migration is an adjustment mechanism.[36]

There is also considerable movement of people within central cities and within outlying territory, and the elderly participate in those flows. Some of the shifts lead to further age segregation, basically because older people with similar social and economic backgrounds tend to be thrown together, not because they necessarily seek out each other. On the other hand, some older people do prefer housing especially for them, often at high rents in the urban fringe. Most elderly do not live in rigidly age-segregated neighborhoods, however, and those who do are often the residue of youthful out-migration; large proportions of them are relatively poor.

Interregional and Interstate Migration

Streams of Movement

Though local movement accounts for most of the spatial mobility among all age groups, significant numbers of people, including the elderly, do go from one major region to another. In the process they disperse in particular ways to states and counties, creating net migration gains in some and losses in others, while leaving still others virtually unchanged. The percentages of people of all ages who have relocated to another region in the process of interstate migration increased especially significantly after 1940, and even though the elderly are less likely than younger groups to migrate, the rates of increase in interregional migration have been about the same for both age groups.

Moreover, the elderly tend to concentrate at a smaller number of destinations, though they have a wide range of origins,[37] and they are particularly likely to seek areas that will make retirement more satisfying. That generally translates into the large movements from the Northeast and North Central regions to the South, as well as the smaller net flow to the West. Younger people also tend to be heading in most of the same general directions, though they go to a larger number of states and counties. Furthermore, blacks and whites follow many of the same migration routes, but between 1975 and 1980 older blacks produced net migration gains only in the South, whereas older whites did so there and in the West, largely because of their movement to California and Arizona. Elderly blacks and whites are deserting the North Central region at the highest rate and are leaving the Northeast, particularly the Middle Atlantic states and southern New England, at a pace that is only slightly slower.

The currents of interregional migration among the nation's elderly, as well as those aged 5-64, appear in Table 10-7, which shows the volume of migration to and from each major region. Together the streams that move in opposite directions are *gross migration*, while the difference between them is *net migration*. [38] The stream into the South is heavily dominated by the large-scale migration of elderly people to Florida, which is responsible for well over half of the total net gain of elderly people in all of the states with increases by migration. Within the South, sizable numbers also go to Texas, North Carolina, Mississippi, Tennessee, Arkansas, Alabama, Georgia, and South Carolina. Outside the South, Arizona and California acquire many more older people than they lose by migration, and there are also important net flows to some other parts of the West and

Table 10-7. Interregional Migration of Two Age Groups, by Race, 1975-1980 (1,000s)

Region and Movement	5-64		65+	
	White	Black	White	Black
Northeast				
In-Migrants	958	99	38	0
Out-Migrants	2,106	262	165	12
Net Migration	-1,148	-163	-127	-12
North Central				
In-Migrants	1,729	166	64	4
Out-Migrants	2,688	203	212	18
Net Migration	-959	-37	-148	-14
South				
In-Migrants	3,464	382	282	33
Out-Migrants	2,076	214	99	6
Net Migration	+1,388	+168	+193	+27
West				
In-Migrants	2,381	183	177	10
Out-Migrants	1,661	152	85	11
Net Migration	+720	+31	+92	-1

Sources: U.S. Bureau of the Census, "Geographical Mobility: March 1975 to March 1980," Current Population Reports, P-20, no. 368 (1981), table 40; 1980 Census of Population, Supplementary Reports, PC80-S1-1, Age, Sex, Race, and Spanish Origin of the Population by Regions, Divisions, and States: 1980 (1981), table 2; PHC80-S1-1, Provisional Estimates of Social, Economic, and Housing Characteristics (1982), table P-5.

264

even a few sections of New England. But no other state has more than a small fraction of Florida's proportional growth of elderly by net migration.

Characteristics of Sunbelt Migrants

Older people who migrate to the Sunbelt tend to be the young-old and are also likely to be married, to maintain independent households, to have relatively high incomes, and to derive those incomes from nonwork sources.[39] At least in the short run, therefore, the elderly migrants help the Sunbelt areas economically. If they don't return to the Snowbelt as they grow older, however, in the long run they tend to increase the demand for nursing homes, medical care, and other services for the old-old, though those functions also provide jobs and help boost local economies. But even if they do migrate back to where they grew up, the old-old join the poorer elderly they originally left behind, and the two groups together can impose relatively heavy demands on the public welfare services of their local areas,[40] for by the time they return to the Snowbelt, the migrants are apt to have lost a spouse and to be more dependent than they were at the time of the earlier move. Thus, not only are people who remain in the Snowbelt less advantaged on the average than those who move to the Sunbelt, but the ones among the latter who return to their old home areas tend to be less advantaged than the ones who remain in the Sunbelt. Because of these variations, services for the elderly have to account not just for their number in a state or local area, but also for their income, marital status, age, and the other characteristics that affect their level of dependence.[41]

Finally, the movement of elderly people to the Sunbelt includes not only those who seek permanent residence, but also many seasonal migrants. Some arrive in travel-trailers, spend the winter months, and drive home; others participate in time-sharing plans for a few weeks or months annually; still others rent rooms or other housing. The most affluent open their winter homes for "the season." Sometimes the seasonal move is a prelude to permanent migration after retirement, while for the wealthier elderly it is a way to enjoy the best of two climates. But most of the seasonal group is not included in the data on migration, so its size and specific destinations are not fully known. As part of the Sunbelt phenomenon, however, these elderly "snowbirds" deserve mention, for their numbers seem considerable even though their impact on the receiving areas is known only impressionistically.[42]

Some Reasons for Migration

Elderly people do not migrate for most of the same reasons that motivate younger ones. Job-related factors are less important to most elderly, and while some who migrate are still in the labor force,[43] retirement frees the large majority from having to live where work opportunities are the best. Instead, the decisions that older people make about moving are influenced by family and other social attachments, housing, climate, recreational facilities, present and prospective social environments, and levels of income and education.[44] For the elderly, migration generally represents a reduction in responsiblities, not a search for new ones, though some of it is motivated by tragedy, as in the case of widows who move closer to adult children when their husbands die. In short, a significant change in one's life situation, such as retirement, loss of a spouse, or illness, often precipitates migration,[45] which suggests that the reasons elderly people move are highly diverse. Even so, those reasons can be aggregated into a few categories that represent the characteristics of the migrants and the events on which they base their migration decisions.[46] Such a synopsis needs to distinguish between local and long-distance moves, because the two groups decide to change residence for some but not all of the same reasons.

The Decision-making Process

Like anyone else, elderly persons have variable needs and their lives are shaped by certain constraints, and these realities all influence the decision to move. They have to combine into a relatively powerful force, however, in which "push" factors encourage the decision to leave one place and "pull" factors influence the decision to enter another. Otherwise, sheer inertia will tend to prevent migration. Other things also stand in its way, such as poor health or poverty that force people to stay where they are, but for them the question of whether or not to move isn't debatable. In addition, most elderly are reasonably satisfied with their surroundings and choose not to leave, though that is also a decision. For those individuals and couples who do consider migration a possibility, however, the decision-making process has the following components:

1. Precipitating factors. These include retirement or other changes that free people to move as they enter a new stage of the life cycle; dissatisfaction with housing, climate, crime rates, and other conditions that tend to push people out; and the vision of better conditions elsewhere that pulls them toward particular areas. Other push factors are personal tragedies, especially the loss of a spouse, and the decline of financial and physical independence, while other pull factors include the wish to be nearer family and friends, and favorable reports from others who migrated.

2. Variables that help people decide whether or not a move is possible and desirable. These include levels of income, the strength of local social ties, any prior experience with migration, and judgments about how a move is likely to turn out. Other influential factors are the cost of housing at the destination and the consequences of leaving present housing, the overall cost of living in the new area, and the social networks that seem available.

3. Alternatives a prospective migrant has in choosing how far to go and whether to move permanently or seasonally. By this stage the elderly person or couple must decide that the first two groups of components either favor a move or do not. Having contemplated the matter means that either choice will have advantages and disadvantages, or there would be no decision to make — they would go or stay.

4. Variables that affect the choice of a destination after the decision to move has been made. That part of the larger decision-making process is influenced by people's knowledge of prospective destinations, perhaps from prior visits, what they hope to find, and the presence of friends who can ease the adjustment. As was true of foreign immigration, prior migration to a particular place by acquaintances is a powerful pull factor for others; it helps account for the large flows to Florida and the Southwest, and so do the promotional efforts of local governments and other recruiters.

5. Various consequences of migration. These include the housing that one can actually find and afford, the extent to which the overall dream becomes real, the degree to which the move has severed old connections, and the problems that arise in the new area. In turn, these factors affect people's degree of satisfaction with their original choice and their decision to stay, return home, or move elsewhere.[47]

These components of the decision-making process may be involved no matter how far people move, but they are particularly strategic for long-distance migrants, especially the young-old who are most likely to move just after they retire. Those people must account for various amenities at the point of destination, the kinship bonds and other things they will have to leave behind, the prospect of being able to return to the place where one grew up after a spouse has died, and other factors. Widowhood produces considerable return migration, especially among very elderly women.[48]

Local Movers

Elderly people who move from house to house in the same county may also seek amenities in the form of better or cheaper housing, a safer neighborhood, improved social contacts, and a leisure life style that can be found locally. Some also want smaller homes after they retire. Along with these pull factors are those that push people out, especially a stressful environment caused by high crime rates or juvenile harassment, or eviction by landlords who are often quick to expel people for nonpayment of rent but slow to make repairs that would encourage them to pay promptly and to help look after the property. Moreover, most elderly people leaving such conditions are poor, and while they may escape the original stress, they often have to move into similar dwellings and neighborhoods with the same problems.

Some local movers must shift in order to obtain assistance from kin, nursing homes, or other sources, because their incomes are too low or their health is too poor for them to remain alone. Widows make up a large part of this group, but elderly local movers in general are poorer than interstate migrants and tend to become more dependent on other people. Finally, some poorer elderly people are simply forced to move because tenements and other housing are destroyed as cities attempt to regenerate their centers, usually replacing low-cost housing and rundown hotels with high-cost apartments, condominiums, and offices. For these and other reasons, some elderly become chronic movers, shifting from rental to rental and often continuing a pattern begun much earlier.[49] Thus, residential satisfaction is crucial in much elderly movement, whether long-distance or local, and it is also a factor for those older people who would like to move but cannot.[50] Within the broad category of residential satisfaction, housing is by far the single most important component. But one could infer from the relatively small percentages of the elderly who do move locally and the even smaller proportions who migrate long distances that older people are generally satisfied with their housing, social bonds, and familiar settings. In fact, many cannot afford to move, and some elderly who claim to be satisfied with a poor residential situation are merely expressing their adjustment to a hopeless situation, while others actually do want to stay put because the compensations outweigh the problems.[51]

Trends in Elderly Migration

The migration rate of people aged 65 and older appears to have been declining since the mid-1950s, because the proportions who changed residences during a five-year period fell from 30 per cent in 1955-1960 to 21 per cent in 1975-1980. (See Table 10-8.) Moreover, the mobility rate decreased for each of the single years of age that make up the elderly group, and for the ones aged 55-64 as well. The decreases are especially significant before age 62, when people tend to hang onto the jobs they have and to stay in one place, but the rates have even dropped for people who reach the retirement ages.

Table 10-8. Percentages of Persons 65 and Over Who Made Specified Moves, 1955-1960 to 1975-1980[a]

Mobility Status	1955 to 1960	1965 to 1970	1975 to 1980
Total Population	100.0	100.0	100.0
Same House (Nonmovers)	70.1	71.9	78.7
Different House	29.7	27.7	20.9
Same County	20.7	17.9	12.0
Different County	9.0	9.8	8.9
Same State	4.8	5.3	4.7
Different State	4.2	4.5	4.2
Contiguous	1.4	1.4	1.1
Noncontiguous	2.8	3.1	3.1
Movers from Abroad	0.2	0.4	0.4

Sources: U.S. Bureau of the Census, U.S. Census of Population: 1960, Subject Reports, Mobility for States and State Economic Areas (1963), table 3; U.S. Census of Population: 1970, Subject Reports, Mobility for States and the Nation (1973), table 2; "Geographical Mobility: March 1975 to March 1980," Current Population Reports, P-20, no. 368 (1981), table 5.

[a]Age designated for the latter year of each five-year period.

Table 10-8 also shows that the overall rate of elderly migration fell because of a significant decrease in the proportion of local movers, while the percentages of people who made long-distance moves of various kinds changed far less. In particular, the rate of migration to noncontiguous states rose somewhat between 1955-1960 and 1965-1970, and held at the same level in 1975-1980. Thus, among people who actually did move, migration to a distant state increased in popularity, not just for the whole group aged 65 and over, but for each single year of age as well. At the same time, the percentage of movers who shift from house to house in the same county has continued to fall. These two patterns represent a sorting mechanism in the movement of elderly people, for while the whole group is not as mobile as it was, those who do move consist even more heavily than ever of affluent and well-educated people better able to leave their home states for distant attractions. Their movement reflects the trend toward earlier retirement and the ability of many early retirees to change both life style and residence.

Several reasons seem to account for the decrease in local movement, though all need further study. (1) Much of the flurry of urban renewal that destroyed old tenements and other low-cost housing is over and the large displacement of elderly residents has decreased. Some of these places are also being rehabilitated while people continue to inhabit them. (2) Supplement Security Income and cost-of-living increases in Social Security payments may enable more urban people to pay their rents and avoid the ceaseless trek from one place to another, while others are better able to keep and pay taxes on the homes they bought much earlier. (3) The decreasing proportion of elderly people below the poverty level may allow more of those who want to move to go longer distances in search of a whole group of amenities, and thus may increase the relative importance of interstate migration while that of local movement falls. For example, this helps account for the groups of elderly people in many of Florida's cities who live very modestly but who still migrate from elsewhere. (4) More of the withdrawal from the labor force of people over age 50 may be involuntary because of unemployment rates, poor health, and retirement practices; more of those people may remain in local areas hoping for re-employment.[52] It is possible, though, that the high unemployment rates of the early 1980s also prompted moves by some of the elderly who had to continue working, just as it caused many younger job-seekers to leave the older industrial centers for high-technology opportunities in the South and West. (5) Some elderly people who would like to move are simply too poor to do so.

Whatever the reasons, the overall spatial mobility rate of the elderly has decreased, while long-distance migrants have become a larger percentage of those who do move, local ones a smaller share. The former make up a significant part of the movement to the Sunbelt, attractive nonmetropolitan places, and other areas that promise substantial amenities, while many of the latter remain behind in central cities, aging suburbs, and poor rural areas. Sometimes the two groups mix, as in the case of the Blue Ridge Mountains where affluent migrants enter the same counties as the elderly poor whose families have lived there for generations. In addition, a portion of the interstate migration of the oldest people represents a return to the areas where they grew up, and in the late 70s and 80s the rate of movement exceeds that of the young-old.

Summary

The migration of elderly people is not new, though their rate of movement is far below that of young adults, because most elderly have formed bonds and established roots they don't wish to dislodge, but also because many cannot afford to move. Moreover, while some elderly migrants shift between counties in the same state and between states and major regions, the great bulk of internal migration is local and only about a fifth of those who move go to another state. Therefore, despite its publicity, the elderly movement to Sunbelt areas is comparatively small, and the older one gets the less likely one is to leave home. There are some temporary increases, however, at the customary retirement ages and again at the oldest ages when some people, especially widows, return home.

Elderly men and women move at about the same rates, partly because much interstate migration occurs among married couples, though the rate for women does rise after age 70, when many new widows move to be near adult children or to nursing homes. Older black women are especially likely to migrate to the extended family, and many are returning to the South for that reason. In general, though, blacks tend to mover shorter distances than whites. For both races, marital status is significantly associated with migration rates, and both men and women who are unattached are the most mobile. Married people, however, move less than other groups over short distances, but more over long ones, especially between noncontiguous states. Those long-distance moves also reflect the flows of affluent, relatively well-educated elderly people to popular retirement areas, especially Florida, Arizona, and California. Conversely, the elderly poor, with low average levels of schooling, tend to stay put or to shift from house to house in the same county.

The elderly were in the vanguard of the migration from metropolitan to nonmetropolitan areas, especially villages and small towns. That movement was greater between 1970 and 1975 than in the following five years, however, and is partly countered by continuing movements to SMSAs, especially suburbs.

The various interstate exchanges result in significant gains and losses of older people by the nation's four major regions. In the 1970s the South, which was a long-time net loser of migrants, led the four in net gains, followed by the West. Conversely, the Northeast and North Central regions lost heavily by net migration of all age groups, including the elderly. Many of the latter headed toward the Sunbelt states in the South and West, though they tended to concentrate at just a few destinations. Moreover, other places, such as the upper Great Lakes and coastal parts of the Northeast and Northwest, also gained. In fact, elderly migration is a complex social, psychological, and economic phenomenon that reflects many individual reasons, especially the search for climatic and recreational amenities, financial and emotional support from kin, safety from crime, and the wish to return to the place where they grew up. Its motivations also vary according to the distance covered.

Finally, the overall movement rate of elderly people is declining, but only because of significant decreases in short-distance relocations. Among those who do move, intracounty movers are a decreasing percentage, though still the majority, while migrants to noncontiguous states are a growing share. Many of them are well-educated, affluent people who can afford the luxuries of retirement areas, though others of modest means also move to those places. Many of the elderly poor left behind, however, still have serious problems they cannot afford to escape by migrating.

NOTES

1. Francoise Cribier, "A European Assessment of Aged Migration," in Charles F. Longino, Jr. and David J. Jackson, eds., *Migration and the Aged,* special issue of *Research on Aging,* 2 (1980): 255.

2. Jacob S. Siegel, "On the Demography of Aging," *Demography* 17 (1980): 354.

3. Beth J. Soldo, "America's Elderly in the 1980s," *Population Bulletin* 35 (1980): 13.

4. Some representative studies are Charles R. Manley, "The Migration of Older People," *American Journal of Sociology* 59 (1954): 324-331; Henry S. Shryock, *Population Mobility Within the United States.* Chicago: Community and Family Study Center, University of Chicago, 1964, chapter 11; Larry H. Long, "Migration Differentials by Education and Occupation: Trends and Variations," *Demography* 10 (1973): 243-258; Steve L. Barsby and Dennis R. Cox, *Interstate Migration of the Elderly.* Lexington, MA: Heath, 1975; and Longino and Jackson, *op. cit.*

5. Regina McNamara, "Migration Measurement," in John A. Ross, ed., *International Encyclopedia of Population.* v. 2. New York: Free Press, 1982, p. 448.

6. Deborah Sullivan and Sylvia A. Stevens, "Snowbirds: Seasonal Migrants to the Sunbelt," *Research on Aging* 4 (1982): 160.

272

7. For a discussion of the usefulness and limitations of migration data, see Henry S. Shryock and Jacob S. Siegel, *The Methods and Materials of Demography*. v. 2. Washington, DC: U.S. Government Printing Office, 1973, pp. 616-617. Cf. McNamara, *op. cit.*, pp. 448-450.

8. Norfleet W. Rives, Jr., "Researching the Migration of the Elderly," in Longino and Jackson, *op. cit.*, pp. 160-161.

9. Cribier, *op. cit.*, pp. 257-259.

10. For proposed investigations in these areas, see Stephen M. Golant, "Future Directions for Elderly Migration Research," in Longino and Jackson, *op. cit.*, pp. 271-278.

11. U.S. Bureau of the Census, "Geographical Mobility: March 1975 to March 1980," *Current Population Reports*, P-20, no. 368 (1981): 131.

12. For several of these definitions, see Shryock and Siegel, *op. cit.*, p. 618.

13. See R. Paul Shaw, *Migration Theory and Fact: A Review and Bibliography of Current Literature*. Philadelphia: Regional Science Research Institute, 1975, pp. 18-19.

14. Larry H. Long, "Migration Differentials," in U.S. Bureau of the Census, "Population of the United States, Trends and Prospects: 1950-1990," *Current Population Reports*, P-23, no. 49 (1974): 133.

15. Jean van der Tak, "U.S. Population: Where We Are; Where We're Going," *Population Bulletin* 37 (1982): 26.

16. Shryock, *Population Mobility...*, *op. cit.*, p. 352, Figure 11.1.

17. James M. Brockway, Tanya K. Brockway and Marcia A. Steinhauer, *Kentucky Demographics: Migration Patterns of Kentucky's Older Population*. Louisville, KY: Urban Studies Center, University of Louisville, 1980, p. 4. Cf. Calvin Goldscheider, "Differential Residential Mobility of the Older Population," *Journal of Gerontology* 21 (1981): 103-108.

18. Cynthia B. Flynn, "General versus Aged Interstate Migration, 1965-1970," in Longino and Jackson, *op. cit.*, p. 175.

19. Frances M. Carp, "Housing and Living Arrangements of Older People," in Robert H. Binstock and Ethel Shanas, eds., *Handbook of Aging and the Social Sciences*. New York: Van Nostrand, 1976, p. 255.

20. U.S. Bureau of the Census, "A Statistical Portrait of Women in the U.S.," *Current Population Reports*, P-23, no. 58 (1976): 10.

21. Barsby and Cox, *op. cit.*, p. 137.

22. Stephen J. Tordella, *Reference Tables, Net Migration of Persons Aged 0 to 64 and 65 and over for United States Counties, 1970 to 1975*. Madison, WI: Applied Population Laboratory, University of Wisconsin, 1980, p. 7.

23. For an account of the rural-urban migration, see T. Lynn Smith and Paul E. Zopf, Jr., *Demography: Principles and Methods*. 2nd ed. Port Washington, NY: Alfred, 1976, pp. 498-513. Cf. John Reid, "Black America in the 1980s," *Population Bulletin* 37 (1982): 18-20.

24. Reid, *ibid.*, p. 20.

25. Long, *op. cit.*, p. 139.

26. U.S. Bureau of the Census, "Geographic Mobility...," *op. cit.*, p. 3.

27. Barsby and Cox, *op. cit.*, p. 17.

28. Shaw, *op. cit.*, pp. 22-24.

29. Barsby and Cox, *op. cit.*, pp. 16-17.

30. For a discussion of the reversal, see Calvin L. Beale, *The Revival of Population Growth in Nonmetropolitan America.* Washington, DC: Economic Research Service, U.S. Department of Agriculture, 1975. See also David Brown and Calvin L. Beale, "Diversity in Post-1970 Population Trends," in Amos H. Hawley and Sara Mazie, eds., *Nonmetropolitan America in Transition.* Chapel Hill, NC: University of North Carolina Press, 1981, pp. 27-71.

31. U.S. Bureau of the Census, *1980 Census of Population, Supplementary Reports,* PC80-S1-5, *Standard Metropolitan Statistical Areas and Standard Consolidated Statistical Areas: 1980* (1981), p. 1.

32. Calvin L. Beale, "Internal Migration," in van der Tak, *op. cit.*, p. 42.

33. Glenn V. Fuguitt and Stephen J. Tordella, "Elderly Net Migration," in Longino and Jackson, *op. cit.*, pp. 199-200.

34. John M. Stahura and Sidney M. Stahl, "Suburban Characteristics and Aged Net Migration," *Research on Aging* 2 (1989): 3-4.

35. *Ibid.*, p. 19.

36. Tim B. Heaton, William B. Clifford and Glenn V. Fuguitt, "Changing Patterns of Retirement Migration," *Research on Aging* 2 (1980): 101.

37. Flynn, *op. cit.*, p. 166.

38. Rives, *op. cit.*, p. 156.

39. Jeanne C. Biggar, "Reassessing Elderly Sunbelt Migration," in Longino and Jackson, *op. cit.*, pp. 183-185.

40. Soldo, *op. cit.*, p. 15. See also Jeanne C. Biggar, Charles F. Longino, Jr. and Cynthia B. Flynn, "Elderly Interstate Migration: The Impact on Sending and Receiving States, 1965 to 1970," in Longino and Jackson, *op. cit.*, pp. 217-232.

41. Biggar, Longino and Flynn, *op. cit.*, p. 229.

42. Sullivan and Stevens, *op. cit.*, pp. 159-177.

43. Cribier, *op. cit.*, p. 257.

44. Barsby and Cox, *op. cit.*, p. 10.

45. Everett S. Lee, "Migration of the Aged," in Longino and Jackson, *op. cit.*, p. 132.

46. Robert F. Wiseman, "Why Older People Move: Theoretical Issues," in Longino and Jackson, *op. cit.*, p. 151.

47. Parts of these five components are adapted from Wiseman, *ibid.*, p. 145. See also Ralph R. Sell and Gordon F. De Jong, "Toward a Motivational Theory of Migration Decision Making," *Journal of Population,* 1 (1978): 313-335.

48. Anne S. Lee, "Return Migration in the United States," in Daniel Kubat, Anthony H. Richmond and Jerzy Zubrzycki, eds., *Policy and Research on Migration: Canadian and World Perspectives,* special issue of *International Migration Review* 8 (1974): 286-291. Cf. William J. Serow, "Return Migration of the Elderly in the U.S.A.: 1955-60 and 1965-70," *Journal of Gerontology* 33 (1978): 288-295.

274

49. Wiseman, *op. cit.*, pp. 150-151.

50. Carp, *op. cit.*, pp. 244; 255.

51. Kenneth F. Ferraro, "Relocation Desires and Outcomes Among the Elderly," *Research on Aging* 3 (1981): 167-169.

52. Barsby and Cox, *op. cit.*, p. 3.

Chapter 11

Some Implications of America's Aging Population

The preceding chapters have examined America's elderly population largely on the basis of data collected by federal agencies and essentially as a group, though with many subdivisions. The analysis should not imply that the elderly population is homogeneous, however, or ignore its tremendous variety. Yet the elderly do have things in common besides occupying the same age-category: The majority are women and many problems of the elderly are the problems of women;[1] older people share the consequences of the aging process itself, such as slower reaction times, a growing awareness of death, and changes in the circle of kin and friends. They also share various societal consequences of growing old in a youth-oriented society, though it is no more useful to deny the real effects of aging than it is to turn them into discriminatory stereotypes. Most elderly also want to remain as active as they can for as long as they can, and while that means a job or volunteer work for many, "active" has much more diverse meanings.

Therefore, despite certain broad similarities and shared concerns, the traits that are thought of as typically old, even by many elderly, differ widely from person to person. As in their younger years, the elderly are optimistic or pessimistic, well adjusted or poorly adjusted, gregarious or withdrawn, or anywhere between those extremes. There is no "typical" older person or experience with aging,[2] and policies for the elderly need to account much more than they do for individual differences. In that context we conclude the book with a look at the prospects of faster increases in the older population than are now expected, and at the impact of aging on the elderly and on American society.

Intervening in the Aging Process

Revolutionary Technologies

New technology promises to intervene in mortality and the aging process to the degree that significant increases could occur in life expectancy
and even the life span itself. As large as we now expect the elderly
population to be in the next century, projections of numbers and proportions could be dwarfed by the demographic results of such innovation; the
social, economic, and political consequences of an elderly population that
greatly exceeds present expectations would be tremendous. The possibility hinges on three types of biomedical research: (1) efforts to prevent,
diagnose, and treat more effectively the three major causes of death —
heart disease, cancer, and stroke; (2) research into the aging process itself
and the prospect to slow it down significantly; and (3) work designed to
uncover and manipulate the social conditions that affect aging and
death.[3] In turn, these efforts produce two categories of technology, both
of which will increase the numbers and percentages of the elderly.

Curve-squaring technologies. Successful efforts that would increase the
number of middle-aged people who live longer would add to the population in all of the older years, but especially the 80s and 90s, and would do
so in a relatively short time. The top half of Figure 11-1 shows how such
improvements would change the number of survivors among each 100,000
Americans in specific age groups and the nation's age distribution in
general. The solid line represents the current survival ratios and the
dotted line represents those that would result after full implementation of
the new life-saving technologies, which tend to square the curve before it
falls off sharply. The curve-squaring technologies are mostly efforts to
control the degenerative diseases and to increase the life expectancy of
older people, contrasted with earlier efforts to control infectious and
parasitic diseases and to allow a larger percentage of infants to survive to
the older ages. As a result, in 2025 life expectancy at birth may be as high
as 85 years and the number of elderly people will be larger than now
projected; so will their percentage if no new baby-boom occurs.[4]

These life-saving technologies include prevention, diagnosis, and treatment of the three major causes of death; the use of artificial organ
substitutes; and improvements in the environment, such as stress
management, dietary modifications, and reductions in the proportion of
smokers. Many specific aspects of these technologies are already well
advanced and will probably improve significantly by 2000;[5] the three
major causes of death may even be substantially overcome within 50
years. Indeed, as we saw in Chapter 9, the death rate from heart disease

has fallen steadily since 1960, while new research into the genetic ante-
cedents of cancer promises to uncover a common element among the
hundreds of types of that disease and possibly to bring it under control,
perhaps with a vaccine.[6]

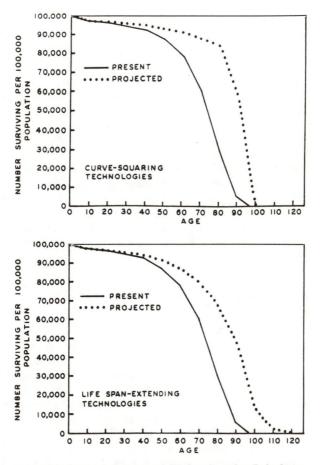

Figure 11-1. Effects of Curve-Squaring and Life Span-Extending Technologies
Source: Subcommittee on Human Services of the House Select Committee on Aging, *Future
Directions for Aging Policy: A Human Services Model,* Pub. no. 96-226. Washington, DC:
U.S.Government Printing Office, 1980, p. 110.

Life span-extending technologies. Another group of advances, which overlaps partly with the curve-squaring technologies, involves intervention in the process of aging itself and includes efforts to alter the ways that cells, organs, and whole bodily systems age, and to regenerate tissue. The lower half of Figure 11-1 shows how the number of survivors per 100,000 would increase at various ages as a result of these advances. The life span-extending technologies are more difficult to achieve than those directed primarily at disease control and prosthesis, and their principal demographic effects lie farther in the future.

Moreover, if such efforts are to extend the life *span* (as contrasted to life *expectancy*), they will have to be applied relatively early in life and not just when people have reached middle age. This is because they deal with the long-term effects of diet and temperature, the progressive breakdown of the immune system, the loss of tissue elasticity, the number of times cells can replicate, the gradual accumulation of cell substances that speed aging, the tendency for membranes to incur permanent damage, the process of abnormal oxidation, and other occurrences that influence human aging from the first day of life.[7]

It is not possible to conquer aging completely and make the human life span infinite, but much of the practical technology necessary to extend it significantly now exists or soon will. Therefore, the assumption that the life span is fixed at 100 years or so is outdated, and the advances that will probably come in the next century will lower the death rate even more and increase the numbers of elderly people, and most likely their percentages as well.

Effects of Increased Longevity

These technological breakthroughs are helping to age the nation's population and will speed that process even more in the future. At the same time, the financial resources necessary to meet the needs of the burgeoning elderly population are not keeping pace, as evidenced by problems with Medicare and the Social Security retirement fund crisis, which finally became serious enough to produce the compromise ameliorative legislation of 1983. The increases in life expectancy and the life span, on the one hand, and the unwillingness or inability to meet the needs of the elderly, on the other, represent a major dilemma for the United States and other developed countries now, and eventually they will do so for the entire world.

Demographically, the consequences will be profound. Projections made by the U.S. Bureau of the Census in 1977 anticipated that by 2025 elderly people would number about 51 million and be 17 per cent of the total population, but revisions in 1982 anticipated 59 million elderly by 2025 and that they would be almost 20 per cent of the total.[8] Those revisions account for the effects of curve-squaring technologies already operable, but if the technologies fulfill their potential, people aged 65 and older may well number 74 million and be 23 per cent of the total by 2025.[9] Recall, too, that by 2025 the large baby-boom generation will be aged 65 and over and that significant increases in their life expectancy will swell the ranks of the elderly very rapidly. In turn, the demographic changes may force us to raise retirement ages significantly, partly because many elderly will need to work, but basically because the employed population may be unable or unwilling to support a huge dependent group whose average retirement age is 62 or 65 or even 70, but who still have many years of life expectancy ahead.

As the elderly population grows and other changes occur, the nuclear family — already altered by divorce, migration, and other dynamics — may decline further in importance. But the significance of the modified extended family may increase and even be supplemented by quasi-families that provide intimate social bonds for the elderly outside the traditional family structure. The four-generation family may even become more commonplace, though the communication gap between the age extremes may prove unbridgeable, with middle-aged and young-old adults attempting to mediate between youth and the old-old. Two- and three-generation gaps may become common. Families will also experience higher health costs, because health needs increase with age and there will be more elderly, and because health care is a growth industry. Those costs may be offset some, however, if the needs are concentrated among the oldest people and the curve-squaring technologies make the young-old relatively healthy as a group.[10]

Some Basic Problem Areas

Some of the consequences of an aging population are not merely challenges for the nation, but are problems for older people themselves; they find many results real and immediate, not just the probable changes to be confronted in the next century. Many of the problems stem from prejudice, while others show that the nation was simply unprepared for the rapid increase in its elderly population. In our preoccupation with youth, we long studied and attempted to deal with the needs of the young, while until recently those of the elderly were neglected; in a throwaway society young people are perceived as a useful and envied commodity, whereas the elderly are thought to be used up and worn out. Because we also value change and deplore obsolescence, the past and the carriers of its culture seem irrelevant to the present and the future, so we isolate many elderly — a process that begins well before age 65. As a result of these realities, made more urgent by increases in the elderly population, some needs of older people are met less well than are those of younger ones. Consequently, while it is inaccurate to view old age *as* a social problem, it is a time *beset* by particular problems, many of which arise more from the social system than from the aging process itself.[*11*]

Income Maintenance

A decent level of living is probably the most urgent concern of the elderly, with health a close second, but the need for adequate income is poorly met for at least the quarter of all older people, who live below the poverty line or not far above it. The problem is especially acute for women and minorities, but on the average all elderly people suffer income reductions of at least a third when they retire, while many of their living costs do not fall. For many people, the resources available are far short of the 70 per cent or so of prior income that is necessary for most elderly to maintain a life style reasonably close to that of their preretirement years.

Moreover, Social Security, on which a large share of elderly persons depend heavily, still fails to prevent poverty or near-poverty for about a third of those who have little or no other income, while private pension plans cover only a minority of all elderly and provide low average benefits. Even the SSI program provides minimal amounts that barely enable survival, though it is really part of a more comprehensive package of provisions contained in the Older Americans Act of 1965 and its subsequent amendments. That Act created Medicare in 1965 to help with hospital expenses for Social Security recipients aged 65 and over and to provide a voluntary program, financed partly by participants' premiums, to help with doctors' fees and related costs; it also established Medicaid for those elderly who are too poor to pay Medicare premiums and deductibles.

SSI, financed from general revenues, also grew out of the Act in 1974 as a way to guarantee at least some income to people who are elderly, blind, or disabled, and federally provided amounts may be supplemented by the states. The Social Security Act has been amended to include disability payments, to raise the ceiling on the income one could earn and still receive full benefits, to lower to 62 the age at which one could begin to draw reduced benefits, to pay benefits to everyone aged 72 and older no matter what their income or former job status, to provide an income-floor for all elderly, and to guarantee periodic cost-of-living increases in benefits.[*12*] The federal government also makes grants to the states for public assistance, though not only for the elderly.

But the greatly expanded scope and cost of the programs, their failure still to provide enough income for the poorest people, and their tendency to oversubsidize the affluent are problems that coalesced into the Social Security financial crisis. The system simply ended up paying out far more than it took in, and the increased taxation of workers to "solve" that problem may soon prove to be prohibitively high.

The obsolete actuarial assumptions on which permissible retirement age is based are also part of the problem, and the system is even subject to considerable "leakage": Illegal aliens, for example, sometimes hold jobs covered by Social Security and may be able to receive benefits, while perhaps $100 million has been paid to dead people! Moreover, these difficulties may well become worse than was anticipated in the 1983 reforms, because the projected numbers of elderly people must certainly be revised upward. Life expectancy will surely rise, while the ratio of workers to retirees will continue to fall, especially if the trend toward early retirement resumes. It may not, however, because additional increases in the cost of living, even at a lower rate, will force some elderly people to continue working, provided they can get the jobs, and the Social Security crisis of the early 1980s will be seen as a mere prelude to the escalating costs of the various programs, especially retirement and Medicare. Private pension plans are unlikely to expand sufficiently, because even those already in force are paying out large sums that could go for wages; they are also used to prevent employee movement from company to company and are so plagued by paper work that small companies shun them.[13]

In short, the demographic trends, rising costs, and early retirement trend of the last several years may all conspire to reduce the average relative income of the elderly below present levels and further erode their economic well-being. Even the ameliorative efforts underway seem inadequate to prevent poverty for a significant share of the larger elderly population that will be with us in the first quarter of the next century.[14] This is one of the great challenges to the ingenuity of America's financial managers, and any policy to keep the elderly fully integrated in the society will be hampered if significant proportions lack adequate incomes.

The continuing reform of income-maintenance needs to address several questions: (1) How do incomes and expenditures actually change when one retires? (2) On what basis should retirement incomes be determined and how should they differ according to prior earnings, marital status, and other characteristics? (3) What level of living is reasonable and attainable for the elderly, assuming they are to have the same relative advantages as younger people? (4) Can and should income inequities be smoothed out, or should they continue to reflect the income disparities of people's earlier years? (5) How should other assets, such as paid-up home mortgages and help from family members, be weighed in assessing income adequacy for older people? (6) How can the taxation situation be improved for the elderly, especially real estate taxes and sales taxes on food and other necessities?[15]

These and other questions are not new and they have been addressed repeatedly. But none of them has been answered definitively, partly because policies for the elderly lack coordination and still permit many to become financial casualties. Significant numbers still fall close to or below the poverty line when they retire, and SSI and cost-of-living increases in Social Security benefits are not enough to prevent continuing financial erosion for many. Even the Older Americans Act has been amended to shift more responsibility to state and local governments, and finally back onto the elderly and their families. Thus, the basic causes of the financial problems of many elderly lie not in the lack of national resources, but in attitudes that still place the needs of older people too low on the list of national priorities, in forced retirement and limited work opportunities, and in a general view of the elderly as charity cases rather than as full participants in the socioeconomic system. Unless those attitudes change, income maintenance will continue to be a problem as the older population grows rapidly.[16]

Despite the deficiencies in income maintenance, in 1980 about $155 billion were allocated to Social Security, Medicare, and other federal programs primarily for the elderly. Therefore, the economic impact of the growing elderly population is tremendous, consisting largely of their withdrawals from rather than contributions to national funds. Figure 11-2 shows how federal expenditures were allocated in 1980, and emphasizes the overwhelming significance of retirement and health costs in the total picture; those expenditures now draw so heavily on public funds disbursed through Social Security taxes and general revenues, that they have become a serious problem of public finance and a huge burden for the working population.[17]

Health Care

The elderly are already the largest users of health resources, which they will continue to be as their numbers and proportions grow and higher percentages move into the old-old category, even if life expectancy is extended appreciably and most young-old remain healthy. Moreover, the elderly are increasingly likely to seek medical care, largely because they are better educated about health and more can afford the personal costs of help than could their parents. At present, they are half again as likely as middle-aged people to visit doctors and they appear disproportionately in the hospital population, account for 95 per cent of all nursing home residents, and have average medical costs that are about four times those of younger people. Moreover, the situation is complicated by the two contradictory goals of American health care policy — high quality care and cost containment — reflected in the periodic furor over "socialized medi-cine" and the mistrust of all care except that provided by highly trained physicians and registered nurses.

As a result, while Medicare and Medicaid are a boon to the elderly, Medicare especially is heavily biased toward institutions and provides poor coverage for people looked after at home. It thereby forces many elderly into nursing homes to receive benefits during convalescence, but even those benefits are relatively short term. And because the nation's whole health system is oriented to acute illness and dramatic intervention, it tends to treat elderly people with chronic illnesses by subsidizing institutionalization rather than home care. In turn, that raises the cost of care, from $6.5 billion for Medicare and Medicaid in 1967, the first full year those programs operated, to about $75 billion in 1983, or 9.5 per cent of all federal expenditures. The amount may be twice as high in 1988, despite rising deductibles and fewer hospital days that can be compen-sated. The emphasis on institutionalization in Medicare also deprives many elderly of the nurturing and support they would receive from family members or other caregivers at home. Proposed reforms are under con-sideration, including those that would make patients and the providers of care, such as hospitals, pay a larger share to head off serious Medicare

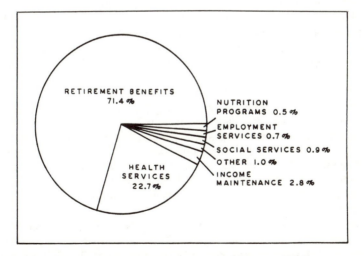

Figure 11-2. Allocation of the Federal Dollar Spent on Benefits for the Elderly
Source: Subcommittee on Human Services of the House Select Committee on Aging, *Future Directions for Aging Policy: A Human Services Model,* Pub. no. 96-226. Washington, DC: U.S.Government Printing Office, 1980, p. 31.

deficits. But if anything like the present practices continue, the cost of medical care for the growing elderly population will become even more formidable, or many will be forced to use up their own financial resources because of illness; some will be neglected entirely. Here again is the dilemma between care and costs.[18]

The degenerative diseases of old age often produce long, expensive periods of disability, especially for people aged 75 and older, and as in the case of income, poor health and the ability to pay for care are distributed unevenly throughout the elderly population. Those with the lowest social status are most affected by the degenerative illnesses, least likely to seek help, and least able to pay for it, though the Medicaid program for the elderly poor does help. But even with that program and Medicare, older people still bear relatively heavy personal health care expenses. Moreover, since only about 14 per cent of the noninstitutionalized elderly are completely free of chronic illnesses, such as arthritis, heart disease, hypertension, diabetes, arteriosclerosis, and Alzheimer's Disease,[19] the cost to them and the society is already large; it will grow much larger.

These realities argue for more physician's assistants, practical nurses, and others who can provide lower cost care for many illnesses and who can help with the activities of daily living; for careful monitoring of doctors, hospitals, and nursing homes to reduce overcharging; and for improved coverage of cost-effective hospice and home care. Home care also needs to be more innovative, however, because the proportion of women under age 65 who work is now so high that many elderly people cannot receive attention during the day from a member of the family. Better health education and information also are necessary for the elderly, so that more problems can be avoided or improved through diet, accident prevention, and reduced smoking, alcohol abuse, and misuse of medication. Proper nutrition is an especially acute problem for those who need financial assistance to buy better food and help to prepare it.[20]

In addition, we need more attention to mental health, especially malfunctions that strike because of organic bran damage from other problems, but also depression and other effects of widowhood, solitude, and the feeling of having been discarded. Such efforts are especially important for the dying, and in late 1983 Medicare regulations were broadened to provide new hospice benefits for them, 90 per cent of whom have cancer, though even those payments were below the levels proposed earlier.

Finally, because the elderly often require a special clinical approach, more physicians need to be trained in geriatric specialties. At present, less than half the medical schools offer elective courses in this field and few require them, partly because there is little federal assistance for geriatric programs,[21] but also because many doctors prefer to work with younger patients whose illnesses are more likely to be successfully treated.

Housing

About 70 per cent of the elderly own homes, but many of the houses are old and in need of repairs that some older people with reduced incomes cannot make. Therefore, more housing assistance is indicated, not just to repair dwellings but also to get many elderly out of high-crime areas and facilities that are inappropriate for those with physical disabilities. Moreover, many elderly people live alone in houses that are too large for their needs and carry high property taxes. As a result, a significant proportion of older people would probably live somewhere else if they had a choice, and many would rent if they could find decent, low-cost, relatively small apartments in safe neighborhoods.

If the trend for older people to migrate to nonmetropolitan places continues, more and better housing will be necessary in those villages and towns. In addition, widowhood and living alone call for more satisfactory group quarters, which should not always be nursing homes or retirement high-rises, but ought to include additional relatively small units in which quasi-families can develop. Older homes can be rehabilitated to house six or eight persons functioning as a social group. To provide the best atmosphere they probably should include people of both sexes, but given the low sex ratio in the older years, that probably would mean one or two men and several women. Such arrangements, which some elderly are already using, need to overcome prejudices, counterproductive moralizing, zoning restrictions, and other obstacles, because they are one way to solve several housing problems of the elderly. Those difficulties include the prohibitive costs of maintaining one-person households, the frailty that prevents many elderly from operating a home by themselves, and the need for care that many disabled persons have.

Quasi-family residences would keep many elderly in the community and out of institutions, and would even prevent their having to reside with adult children who cannot accommodate an aged parent. Congregate housing often does require outside social and health services, but those are more easily delivered to a group than to scattered individuals living alone, and the group arrangement is a better guarantee of proper nutrition, physical care, protection, and emotional support by others who share the experience of being elderly.[22] These needs are especially acute for elderly minority groups, women, and rural residents, who occupy a disproportionate share of the dilapidated housing.

There is already an extensive network of governmental programs designed to provide housing for the elderly, but many needs remain unmet. The 1974 Housing and Community Development Act, for example, is supposed to encourage builders to provide better rental units, including residential facilities for the elderly and the handicapped.[23] But only a small percentage of the elderly actually benefit from governmental housing programs, and almost a third live in "substandard, deteriorating or dilapidated housing."[24] Moreover, housing costs often take a disproportionately large share of the older person's total income, especially that of the elderly woman who lives alone and rents. Therefore, even the programs that do exist are insufficient to meet the housing needs of many elderly.

Work, Retirement, and Leisure

Despite the trend toward early retirement, more elderly would like to work, especially part time, than can find jobs. That is particularly true during times of substantial inflation, when one's planned retirement income proves inadequate and the level of living falls. But even when inflation rates are low, a truly full-employment economy would provide jobs for all who wished to work and who had or could acquire the necessary skills, and would ensure an adequate income, whether from work or other sources. In an economy with less than full employment, several questions arise that affect the elderly directly or indirectly: (1) Who is to get the scarce jobs and on what basis? (2) Should the elderly with modest retirement incomes be allowed jobs at all, presumably at the expense of younger people without nonwork income? (3) If the elderly who wish to work are not allowed to do so, at what level and for how long should the working population support them? (4) What is the most practical balance between a group of working elderly who take jobs that younger workers could hold, and a group of dependent elderly who take no jobs but who must be supported by the younger working population? Concomitantly, does the growing elderly population have to impose an increasing burden on younger people no matter which way the balance tips? (5) What obligations does society have to support its elderly and to supply housing, income, medical care, and other needs? What is the nature of the obligation, if one exists at all? (6) In a less than full-employment economy are the elderly expendable? By what criteria can their existence be justified if they don't produce?[25]

These and other questions are significant now but will become more so as the large baby-boom group reaches age 65 and must be supported by relatively small younger cohorts. Moreover, any significant increases in life expectancy and life span will make these questions some of the nation's most burning issues in the first quarter of the next century, when they will call for a major reappraisal of the work and retirement roles of the elderly. We are in a time when more nonworking elderly are living longer in retirement. In response the society can choose to shoulder a growing burden for their support; it can let more elderly people work longer at their present jobs, but thereby restrict the ascension of middle-aged workers to the positions held by some older ones; or it can force the elderly to take jobs no one else wants.

Each of these alternatives has obvious shortcomings for one group or another, but they represent the problems an aging population faces. They also underscore the situation in which the elderly are caught, the intergenerational clash that may intensify in the future, and the need for new work alternatives, such as more part-time jobs, flextime, and job sharing. Perhaps even old alternatives will be refurbished, such as one spouse limiting his/her labors to the home while the other works for wages, although the inflation that increased the number of two-earner couples in the first place would need to be eliminated for such an option to be realistic. If inflation were fully contained, however, the retirement incomes of more elderly people would suffice; fewer would compete for available jobs and the costs of Social Security would not escalate quite as fast as they do now. In any case, if we are to improve or merely maintain the economic situation of a rapidly growing elderly population and still not damage that of younger people, then work and other economic relations call for fundamental reorganization. Most urgently, the elderly need to know their incomes won't be ravaged by inflation or insolvency in the Social Security system, and that there will be more jobs for those who must work.[26]

The Question of Disengagement

The morale of the elderly is affected by the extent to which they remain full social participants, although participation is influenced far more by how a person spent his/her earlier life than by aging per se and is, therefore, highly individualized.[27] Consequently, the frequent notion that the elderly progressively withdraw — disengage — from society needs to be treated very cautiously, for it is sometimes a way to rationalize measures that exclude the elderly from social participation. Disengagement theory may also reinforce certain stereotypes about the elderly and help justify the view of them as a social problem.[28] That view keeps us from dealing constructively with the growing political involvement and power of the elderly, and with the probable intergenerational clash that lies ahead, for it falsely assumes older people will inevitably withdraw quietly into senescence. Instead, more elderly persons are rejecting the role of grateful beneficiary of policies allegedly created on their behalf by others, and are becoming directly involved in the development of those policies.[29] At that level, at least, they are more socially aware than ever.

But older people live their retirement years in a great variety of ways, and while some are social activists and others have essentially withdrawn into themselves, the majority range between these extremes.[30] Some disengage physically when activity becomes more difficult and energy wanes; others disengage psychologically by shifting their concern from the outer to the inner world of personal feelings and thoughts; still others disengage socially by withdrawing progressively from the social systems in which they participated. Furthermore, disengagement theory assumes that *most* elderly people go through these three processes; some of its proponents argue that disengagement enables the elderly to accept the inevitability of decline and death and of having their functions taken over by the young.[31]

In fact, older people do tend to withdraw gradually from *some* activities as they age, especially the work force, and their range of activities often grows smaller, though there are many individual exceptions. Many disengage from sex because of widowhood, declining health, boredom, and the fear of failure, though a significant number maintain or even increase their sexual activity. Moreover, other kinds of involvement do not decline, such as club memberships and church attendance, and the older person who becomes completely isolated is quite uncommon. Consequently, a certain degree of disengagement seems true for most elderly, but it is rarely total; significant minorities, such as the Gray Panthers, are anything but disengaged from the social and political systems and are even trying to change those systems. Moreover, since the elderly relate more to their own age cohort than to others, there is some tendency for an aged subculture to emerge, complete with group consciousness born of certain common experiences.[32] It is easy to carry that idea too far, however, and to see the elderly as a homogeneous mass. *Tendencies* among a majority of older persons do not demonstrate *universal characteristics;* nor should they deny the wide range of individuality and the plethora of minority contingents that pervade the total elderly population.

Victimization

Elderly people are not much more likely statistically to be the victims of crime than are other age groups, but this obscures the fact that many urban elderly are virtual prisoners in their homes because they fear street crime. In fact, a Harris survey commissioned by the National Council on the Aging found that nearly a quarter of all elderly people rate the fear of crime as a very serious problem that often caused their self-imposed isolation.[33] In that sense, abnormally large percentages of older people are victimized by the fear of assault, robbery, and other crimes, even though reported crimes against them may not seem disproportionately numerous. Moreover, we don't know how many older victims fail to report crimes and harassment because of threats of retaliation. Clearly, the fears and realities call for greater protection of the elderly, more efforts to compensate actual victims, and community action, such as watch programs and crime-prevention education. Some of the efforts should also be directed toward adolescents, who are the major perpetrators of crimes against vulnerable older people.[34] Some elderly also live in public or other housing where general crime rates are high, and they are easy prey to those who know their movements and when their pension checks arrive.

Elderly people are particularly susceptible to confidence games and frauds, because many living on fixed incomes are eager to increase their funds if possible, while some are too inexperienced or lonely to resist the overtures of friendly strangers. Many are simply too naive and trusting, while others desperately want cures for arthritis, other chronic illnesses, and even the cosmetic consequences of aging, and are victims of fad foods, elixirs, and gadgets. Moreover, those who are terminally ill are tempted to buy anything that promises life;[35] cancer-curing gimmicks are especially appealing. In short, many elderly, especially the poor and the less educated, are easy victims of hoodlums, confidence artists, and unscrupulous salespeople, and are unable to get protection or help after a crime occurs.

Political Consequences of an Aging Population

The difficulties encountered in reforming Social Security so as not to favor the well-to-do showed that certain large groups of elderly persons have considerable political power. Moreover, their strength has grown as the numbers and proportions of older people have increased, and as they have developed a more coordinated vested interest in preserving present privileges and obtaining new ones. Thus, while the elderly may be conservative on some issues, the politically active ones often espouse liberal positions on major issues. The mandatory retirement age was raised to 70, for example, because of the political power of certain elderly groups and their spokespeople, and even that limit may be swept away in another surge of "gray power." That power also kept the 1983 Social Security changes from significantly penalizing the present elderly and shifted the major impact onto relatively young working people, not onto those who are already old and beneficiaries of the system. In fact, the presumed conservatism of older people may actually reflect their defense of views and positions which were liberal or radical when the elderly were young, but which have become conservative only because new ideas and stances have come along.[36]

Politicians, always sensitive to where power and influence lie, can be expected to promote more favorable legislation for the elderly as the population ages, and may even fail to enact the most appropriate long-term Social Security reforms in their fear of gray power. They are virtually certain to divert funds from other programs as their constituencies become older and more vocal, and many politicians who assume that people grow more conservative as they age can be expected to sound more conservative themselves. But on many "bread-and-butter" issues the young and the elderly may disagree sharply, thus catching politicians in the middle. For example, the elderly are concerned to derive maximum benefits from the Social Security system, often without much heed to the burden they may place on people who are still working; the latter are concerned to contain the cost of supporting the elderly, though many also sympathize with the need for adequate programs, partly to protect their own parents and partly to prepare the way for their own retirement. Nonetheless, there is an incipient political conflict inherent in the variable vested interests of the two age groups, and it may become heated and overt if younger workers feel they are forced to carry an unfair burden. That burden can only become heavier if the growing elderly population has to be dependent because of mandatory retirement, restrictive hiring decisions, and other discrimination,[37] or if they choose to be so because of early and prolonged retirement.

It is unlikely that the elderly voting population will ever be a majority able to promote only their own interests, but they have enough potential power to influence many issues if their views are consolidated into bloc voting, especially if younger groups remain fragmented. In some cases, their votes could constitute a plurality. But whether they consolidate fully or not, the elderly have already grown more powerful and vocal politically and are fighting for more of their interests. Some concessions to them are long overdue and represent the gradual decline of discrimination. But the elderly also have the potential power to demand measures that younger people will oppose, especially on such national issues as pensions and in such retirement areas as Florida. Whether the clash of interests precipitates new discrimination will depend heavily on whether American society continues policies that keep most elderly dependent, or promotes new ones that foster greater independence without jeopardizing the positions of younger people. The directions of change will be quite different according to which approach dominates.

The impending choices also imply that it is pointless and even destructive to treat all elderly persons alike, which we tend to do, and that more attention should be paid to need as a criterion in providing benefits and less to age per se. Age, after all, is not a universally applicable index of health, productivity, adjustment, or financial well-being, and it has become an expensive decision-making criterion that American society probably can't afford in such a blanket fashion much longer.[38] At the very least, we need to distinguish between the needs of the affluent and the poor and the young-old and the old-old, though each of these groups is also far from homogeneous. Ultimately, the fundamental question in any set of changes and policies is: "What form should society take so that, in old age, a human being can still be a human being?"[39]

Public and Private Responsibilities

The growth of the elderly population in American society has generated growth in public programs on their behalf, and the Older Americans Act represents the role of the federal government in their well-being. Under the OAA the elderly are assumed to have the right to the following:

1. An adequate income.
2. The best possible physical and mental health.
3. Suitable housing.
4. Full restorative services.
5. Opportunity for employment with no age discrimination.
6. Retirement in health, honor, and dignity.
7. Pursuit of meaningful activity.
8. Efficient community services.
9. Immediate benefit from proven research knowledge.
10. Freedom, independence, and the free exercise of individual initiative.[40]

But we have seen that a significant share of the elderly population lacks some or even most of these things, and for them the ideals seem unattainable. In addition, the federal effort to realize the goals has grown so costly that its support network cannot possibly help all those elderly persons who are in slums, below the poverty level, or chronically ill. The Social Security payroll tax has already grown astronomically, from 5.2 per cent on maximum taxable earnings of $7,800 in 1971, to 6.7 per cent on a maximum of

$32,700 in 1982, to an already legislated 7.65 percent on a maximum of $66,900 in 1990, and wage earners face even greater increases after that in order to support the aging baby-boom population. The tax rate could rise to 15 per cent by the middle of the next century, and even that may not be enough to meet the need. The high costs of Medicare and other programs also add greatly to the burden, especially for people whose final days or months require expensive life-support systems and other costly heroic measures to prolong life or ease its ebb.

Furthermore, given the necessarily impersonal nature of governmental programs, they can do little to reduce loneliness, facilitate communication between the generations, or provide loving environments. Those functions, along with much financial responsibility for housing, health care, and other needs, lie with families, friends, churches, neighborhoods, and other small "natural" social groups that add meaning to the lives of older people. In fact, this informal network provides virtually all of the home care for the disabled elderly, solace during bereavement and loneliness, guidance in seeking formal assistance, and the feeling of continued significance even in old age.

Consequently, the future of America's growing elderly population will be shaped by a partnership of formal and informal support networks, each doing essentially different things, but all reasonably coordinated and mutually reinforcing. Even so, how many elderly people will we allow to fall between the cracks of this complex structure? The dozens of federal efforts already miss many of the elderly people, partly because the latter cannot deal with the maze of programs, regulations, and bureaucrats. Therefore, the delivery of services is not well coordinated and the things that are available are not always well used. Even the informal networks exclude many elderly persons, especially solitary women.

Some solutions to these problems lie in a more rational and comprehensive way to structure formal programs and deliver their services. The Comprehensive Older Americans Act Amendments of 1978 attempted some such reforms, though the major problems persist. The 1981 White House Conference on Aging also tried to bring more focus into the various programs, oriented around six major issues, and its efforts may produce significant improvements.

But the basic solution resides in changed attitudes about the elderly, so that they are seen as a valuable resource for the society rather than as its discards and charity cases. Negative stereotypes and attitudes about older people are still common and as emotionally nurtured as those about other groups forced into minority status. Therefore, we need more basic research to deal with a core problem: The source and nature of anti-elderly prejudice and discrimination.[41] Until basic attitudes change, we will patch at the problems of the elderly but won't solve them, and will continue to view the elderly themselves as a problem. The change calls for exactly the kind of consideration the rest of us want for ourselves, both in our younger years and when we reach the older ages.

Summary

The aging of America's population has powerful implications for the elderly, the younger population, and the nation and society as a whole. Moreover, because recent projections of the size of the elderly population seem certain to prove too low as curve-squaring and life span-extending technologies unfold, the impact of that aging will be greater than anticipated. Those technologies, which include efforts to control the major causes of death and to intervene in the aging process itself, will increase life expectancy by allowing more people to reach age 65 and by extending the average lifetime for persons already in that age group. The segment aged 75 and older will increase especially rapidly as we lengthen the average life span.

For the elderly themselves, the principal concerns of aging are income maintenance, health care, housing, and the relationship between work and leisure. In addition, the ability to live a meaningful existence, fully engaged in such social pursuits as they wish, is also fundamental. So is the fear of victimization, especially among poorer older people who live in high-crime-rate areas. The ways in which we now meet these concerns reflect a mixture of discrimination, benevolence, and hesitation, especially about the costs and the job prospects of younger people and their own aging.

One of the most pressing long-term problems is the huge and growing cost of the complex Social Security system, which now provides escalating retirement benefits to a rapidly growing older population; survivors' benefits to widows, widowers, and dependent children; disability benefits to various age groups; and Medicare and Medicaid benefits to those who are ill or disabled. There is urgent need for ongoing reforms to supplement the 1983 changes in the retirement system, but the proposals are influenced in certain ways by the dependent elderly, and in others by the working population and employers who must help finance the system. This generational clash of interests and the opposing political power it represents result in large part from other policies that have converted most of the elderly population into a nonworking one.

Thus, age discrimination and even the benevolence that accompanies it have had very expensive consequences, though even the reasons for the discrimination are complex. In a society which seems unable to sustain a full-employment economy, for example, there is certain justification to pension older workers so that young ones can enter the labor force and middle-aged ones can move up. Nonetheless, those practices also show that we have not fulfilled our innovative potential to provide jobs for people of all ages who want and need them.

The aging of America's population, therefore, produces an intricate network of social, economic, and political consequences, many of which are serious social problems because the system is still poorly prepared to deal with such a large influx of older citizens and to balance humane concerns against practical realities.

NOTES

1. Mary Barberis, "America's Elderly: Policy Implications," *Population Bulletin* 35 (1981): 5.

2. Judith Murphy and Carol Florio, "Older Americans: Facts and Potential," in Ronald Gross, Beatrice Gross and Sylvia Seidman, eds., *The New Old: Struggling for Decent Aging.* Garden City, NY: Doubleday, 1978, p. 54.

3. Theodore J. Gordon, "Prospects for Aging in America," in Matilda White Riley, ed., *Aging from Birth to Death.* Boulder, CO: Westview Press, 1979, p. 183.

4. Subcommittee on Human Services of the House Select Committee on Aging, *Future Directions for Aging Policy: A Human Services Model,* Pub. no. 96-226. Washington DC: U.S. Government Printing Office, 1980, pp. 109-110.

5. *Ibid.,* pp. 111-112.

6. See Sharon McAuliffe and Kathleen McAuliffe, "Closing In on Cancer," *Reader's Digest* (March, 1983): 59-64.

7. Gordon, *op. cit.,* p. 186.

8. For the data, see U.S. Bureau of the Census, "Projections of the Population of the United States: 1977 to 2050," *Current Population Reports,* P-25, no. 704 (1977), table 11; "Projections of the Population of the United States: 1982 to 2050," (advance report), *Current Population Reports,* P-25, no. 922 (1982), table 2.

9. Gordon, *op. cit.,* p. 189.

10. These potential impacts are from *ibid.,* pp. 191-195.

11. Paul B. Horton and Gerald R. Leslie, *The Sociology of Social Problems.* 7th ed. Englewood Cliffs, NJ: Prentice-Hall, 1981, pp. 178-179.

12. Organisation for Economic Co-operation and Development, *Socio-economic Policies for the Elderly.* Paris: OECD, 1979, pp. 141-142.

13. J. John Palen, *Social Problems.* New York: McGraw-Hill, 1979, p. 398.

14. Subcommittee on Human Services.., *Future Directions..., op. cit.,* pp. 99-101.

15. Several of these questions are adapted from OECD, *Socio-economic Policies..., op. cit.,* pp. 157-158.

16. Carroll L. Estes, "Social Policy Alternatives: A Redefinition of Problems, Goals, and Strategies," in Harold Cox, ed., *Aging.* 3rd ed. Guilford, CT: Dushkin, 1983, p. 211.

17. Jacob S. Siegel, "Prospective Trends in the Size and Structure of the Elderly Population, Impact of Mortality Trends, and Some Implications," in U.S. Bureau of the Census, *Current Population Reports,* P-23, no. 78 (1979): 20.

18. Beth J. Soldo, "America's Elderly in the 1980s," *Population Bulletin,* 35 (1980): 40-41.

19. Barberis, *op. cit.,* pp. 7-8.

20. National Council on the Aging, *Perspective on Aging* 9 (1980): 37-38.

21. Subcommittee on Human Services, *op. cit.,* p. 106.

22. Several of the points in this section are from *ibid.,* pp. 91-94.

23. OECD, *Socio-economic Policies...,* *op. cit.,* pp. 145-146.

24. Barberis, *op. cit.,* p. 7.

25. Subcommittee on Human Services, *op. cit.,* pp. 94-95.

26. Joseph J. Spengler, *Population and America's Future.* San Francisco: Freeman, 1975, p. 108.

27. Kurt W. Back and Kenneth J. Gergen, "Cognitive and Motivational Factors in Aging and Disengagement," in Ida Harper Simpson and John C. McKinney, eds., *Social Aspects of Aging.* Durham, NC: Duke University Press, 1966, p. 303.

28. Estes, *op. cit.,* p. 212.

29. Palen, *op. cit.,* p. 412.

30. OECD, *op. cit.,* p. 158.

31. Erdman Palmore, *Social Patterns in Normal Aging: Findings from the Duke Longitudinal Study.* Durham, NC: Duke University Press, 1981, pp. 3-4.

32. For an analysis of this matter, see Charles F. Longino, Jr., Kent A. McClelland and Warren A. Peterson, "The Aged Subculture Hypothesis: Social Integration, Gerontophilia and Self-Confidence," *Journal of Gerontology* 35 (1980): 758-767.

33. Louis Harris & Associates, *The Myth and Reality of Aging in America.* Washington, DC: National Council on the Aging, 1975, pp. 29; 30.

34. National Council on the Aging, *Perspective on Aging, op. cit.,* p. 27.

35. Herman J. Loether, *Problems of Aging.* 2nd ed. Belmont, CA: Dickenson, 1975, pp. 112-113.

36. Ralph Thomlinson, *Population Dynamics: Causes and Consequences of World Demographic Change.* 2nd ed. New York: Random House, 1976, pp. 350-351.

37. Spengler, *op. cit.,* pp. 99-100.

38. On this question, see Bernice L. Neugarten, ed., *Age or Need? Public Policies for Older People.* Beverly Hills, CA: Sage, 1982.

39. OECD, *op. cit.,* p. 165.

40. Soldo, *op. cit.,* pp. 28-29.

41. Erdman Palmore, "Attitudes Toward the Aged: What We Know and Need to Know," *Research on Aging* 4 (1982): 333.

Bibliography

American Cancer Society, *Cancer Facts and Figures,* New York: American Cancer Society, 1983.

Anderson, Trudy B., "The Dependent Elderly Population: A Function of Retirement," *Research on Aging* 3 (1981): 311-324.

Angel, Ronald and Marta Tienda, "Determinants of Extended Household Structure: Cultural Patterns or Economic Need?" *American Journal of Sociology* 87 (1982): 1360-1383.

Apt, Patricia Harper and Roger Heimstra, "A Model for Learning Resource Networks for Senior Adults," *Educational Gerontology* 5 (1980): 163-173.

Atchley, Robert C., "The Process of Retirement: Comparing Women and Men," in Maximiliane Szinovacz, ed., *Women's Retirement,* Beverly Hills, CA: Sage, 1982, chapter 10.

Atchley, Robert C., "Retirement: Leaving the World of Work," *Annals of American Academy of Political and Social Science* 464 (1982): 120-131.

Atchley, Robert C., *The Sociology of Retirement,* Cambridge, MA: Schenkman, 1976.

Atchley, Robert C. and Judith L. Robinson, "Attitudes Toward Retirement and Distance from the Event," *Research on Aging,* 4 (1982): 299-313.

Back, Kurt W. and Kenneth J. Gergen, "Cognitive and Motivational Factors in Aging and Disengagement," in Ida Harper Simpson and John C. McKinney, eds., *Social Aspects of Aging,* Durham, NC: Duke University Press, 1966, chapter 18.

Back, Kurt W. and Carleton S. Guptill, "Retirement and Self-Ratings," in Ida Harper Simpson and John C. McKinney, eds., *Social Aspects of Aging,* Durham, NC: Duke Univerity Press, 1966, chapter 7.

Barberis, Mary, "America's Elderly: Policy Implications," *Population Bulletin,* 35 (1981).

Barsby, Steve L. and Dennis R. Cox, *Interstate Migration of the Elderly,* Lexington, MA: Heath, 1975.

Beale, Calvin L., "Internal Migration," in Jean van der Tak, "U.S. Population: Where We Are; Where We're Going," *Population Bulletin,* 37 (1982): 42.

Beale, Calvin L., *The Revival of Population Growth in Nonmetropolitan America,* Washington, DC: Economic Research Service, U.S. Department of Agriculture, 1975.

Beauvoir, Simon de, *Coming of Age,* New York: Putnam's Sons, 1972.

Belbin, R. Meredith, "Retirement Strategy in an Evolving Society," in Frances M. Carp, ed., *Retirement,* New York: Behavioral Publications, 172, chapter 6.

Berman, Phyllis W. and Estelle R. Ramey, eds., *Women: A Developmental Perspective,* Washington, DC: National Institutes of Health, 182.

Bernard, Jessie, *Remarriage,* New York: Dryden Press, 1956.

Biggar, Jeanne C., "Reassessing Elderly Sunbelt Migration," in Charles F. Longino, Jr. and David J. Jackson, *Migration and the Aged,* special issue of *Research on Aging,* 2 (1980): 177-190.

Biggar, Jeanne C., Charles F. Longino, Jr. and Cynthia B. Flynn, "Elderly Interstate Migration: The Impact on Sending and Receiving States, 1965 to 1970," in Charles F. Longino, Jr. and David J. Jackson, eds., *Migration and the Aged,* special issue of *Research on Aging,* 2 (1980): 217-232.

Binstock, Robert H. and Ethel Shanas, eds., *Handbook of Aging and the Social Sciences,* New York: Van Nostrand, 1976.

Bouvier, Leon F., "America's Baby Boom Generation: The Fateful Bulge," *Population Bulletin* 35 (1980).

Brickfield, Cyril F., "Rags to Riches — or Reality? Economic Prospects for the Elderly in the 1980s," in Kurt Finsterbusch, ed., *Social Problems 82/83,* Guilford, CT: Dushkin, 1982: 132-133.

Brockway, James M., Tanya K. Brockway and Marcia B. Steinhauer, *Kentucky Demographics: Migration Patterns of Kentucky's Older Population,* Louisville, KY: Urban Studies Center, University of Louisville, 1980.

Brody, Elaine M., "The Aging of the Family," *Annals of American Academy of Political and Social Science,* 438 (1978): 13-27.

Brody, Elaine M., statement in House Select Committee on Aging, "Families: Aging and Changing," June 4, 1980: 52-61.

Brown, David and Calvin L. Beale, "Diversity in Post-1970 Population Trends," in Amos H. Hawley and Sara Mazie, eds., *Nonmetropolitan America in Transition,* Chapel Hill, NC: University of North Carolina Press, 1981: 27-71.

Brubaker, Timothy H., ed., *Family Relationships in Later Life,* Beverly Hills, CA: Sage, 1983.

Butler, Robert N., "Ageism," in Kurt Finsterbusch, ed., *Social Problems 82/83,* Guilford, CT: Dushkin, 1982, pp. 125-131.

Calderone, Mary S., "Sex and the Aging," in Ronald Gross, Beatrice Gross and Sylvia Seidman, eds., *The New Old: Struggling for Decent Aging,* Garden City, NY: Doubleday, 1978: 205-208.

Califano, Jr., Joseph A., "The Aging of America: Questions for the Four-Generation Society," *Annals of American Academy of Political and Social Science* 438 (1978): 96-107.

Carp, Frances M., "Housing and Living Environments of Older People," in Robert H. Binstock and Ethel Shanas, eds., *Handbook of Aging and the Social Sciences,* New York: Van Nostrand, 1976, chapter 10.

Carp, Frances M., ed., *Retirement,* New York: Behavioral Publications, 1972.

Carp, Frances M. and Abraham Carp, "It May Not Be the Answer, It May Be the Question," *Research on Aging* 3 (1981): 85-100.

Clark, Robert L., Juanita Kreps and Joseph J. Spengler, "Aging Population: United States," in John A. Ross, ed., *International Encyclopedia of Population,* v. 1, New York: Free Press, 1982: 31-40.

Coale, Ansley J., "The Effects of Changes in Mortality and Fertility on Age Composition," *Milbank Memorial Fund Quarterly* 34 (1956): 79-114.

Coale, Ansley J., "How a Population Ages or Grows Younger," in Ronald Freedman, ed., *Population: The Vital Revolution,* Garden City, NY: Doubleday, 1964, chapter 3.

Collins, Glenn, "The Good News about 1984," *Psychology Today* 12 (1979): 34-48.

Congressional Budget Office, *Work and Retirement: Options for Continued Employment for Older Workers*, Washington, DC: U.S. Government Printing Office, 1982.

Cottrell, Fred, *Aging and the Aged*, Dubuque, IA: Wm. C. Brown, 1974.

Council on Environmental Quality and U.S. Department of State, *The Global 2000 Report to the President*, v. 2, *The Technical Report*, Washington, DC: U.S. Government Printing Office, 1980.

Cowgill, Donald O., "Residential Segregation by Age in American Metropolitan Areas," *Journal of Gerontology* 33 (1978): 446-453.

Cox, Harold, ed., *Aging*, 3rd ed., Guilford, CT: Dushkin, 1983.

Cribier, Francoise, "A European Assessment of Aged Migration," in Charles F. Longino, Jr. and David J. Jackson, eds., *Migration and the Aged*, special issue of *Research on Aging*, 2 (1980): 255-270.

Cumming, Elaine and William E. Henry, *Growing Old: The Process of Disengagement*, New York: Basic Books, 1961.

Datan, Nancy and Nancy Lohman, eds., *Transitions of Aging*, New York: Academic Press, 1980.

David Henry P., "Eastern Europe: Pronatalist Policies and Private Behavior," *Population Bulletin* 36 (1982).

Davis, Kingsley, "Population and Welfare in Industrialized Societies," *Population Review* 6 (1962): 17-29.

Davis, Kingsley and Pietronella van den Oever, "Age Relations and Public Policy in Advanced Industrial Societies," *Population and Development Review* 7 (1981): 1-18.

Dixon, J.C., ed., *Continuing Education in the Later Years*, Gainesville, FL: University of Florida Press, 1963.

Dono, John E., Cecilia M. Falbe, Barbara L. Kail, Eugene Litwak, Roger H. Sherman and David Siegal, "Primary Groups in Old Age," *Research on Aging* 1 (1979): 403-433.

Drake, Joseph, *The Aged in American Society*, New York: Ronald Press, 1958.

Duberman, Lucile, *Marriage and Its Alternatives*, New York: Praeger, 1974.

Easterlin, Richard A., "What Will 1984 Be Like? Socioeconomic Implications of Recent Twists in Age Structure," *Demography* 15 (1978): 397-421.

Eklund, Lowell, "Aging and the Field of Education," in Matilda White Riley, John W. Riley, Jr. and Marilyn E. Johnson, eds., *Aging and Society*, v. 2, *Aging and the Professions*, New York: Russell Sage Foundation, 1969, chapter 11.

Estes, Carroll L., "Social Policy Alternatives: A Redefinition of Problems, Goals, and Strategies," in Harold Cox, ed., *Aging*, 3rd ed., Guilford, CT: Dushkin, 1983: 210-220.

Fengler, Alfred P. and Nicholas Danigelis, "Residence, the Elderly Widow, and Life Satisfaction," *Research on Aging* 4 (1982): 113-135.

Ferrara, Peter J., *Social Security: Averting the Crisis*, Washington, DC: Cato Institute, 1982.

Ferrara, Peter J., *Social Security: The Inherent Contradiction,* Washington, DC: Cato Institute, 1980.

Ferraro, Kenneth F., "Relocation Desires and Outcomes among the Elderly," *Research on Aging* 3 (1981): 166-181.

Fingerhut, Lois A., "Changes in Mortality among the Elderly: United States, 1940-78," *Vital and Health Statistics* Analytical Studies, series 3, no. 22 (1982).

Fingerhut, Lois A., "Chartbook," in National Center for Health Statistics, *Health, United States, 1982,* PHS Pub. no. 83-1232 (1982): 6-37.

Fingerhut, Lois A. and Harry M. Rosenberg, "Mortality among the Elderly," in National Center for Health Statistics, *Health, United States, 1981,* PHS Pub. no. 82-1232 (1981): 15-24.

Finsterbusch, Kurt, ed., *Social Problems 82/83,* Guilford, CT: Dushkin, 1982.

Flynn, Cynthia B., "General versus Aged Interstate Migration, 1965-1970," in Charles F. Longino, Jr. and David J. Jackson, eds., *Migration and the Aged,* special issue of *Research on Aging,* 2 (1980): 165-176.

Folger, John K. and Charles B. Nam, *Education of the American Population,* Washington, DC: U.S. Government Printing Office, 1967.

Foner, Anne and Karen Schwab, *Aging and Retirement,* Monterey, CA: Brooks/Cole, 1981.

Freedman, Ronald, ed., *Population: The Vital Revolution,* Garden City, NY: Doubleday, 1964.

Fuguitt, Glenn V. and Stephen J. Tordella, "Elderly Net Migration," in Charles F. Longino, Jr. and David J. Jackson, eds., *Migration and the Aged,* special issue of *Research on Aging,* 2 (1980): 191-204.

Fullerton, Howard N., "The 1995 Labor Force: A First Look," in U.S. Bureau of Labor Statistics, *Economic Projections to 1990,* Bulletin 2121, Washington, DC: U.S. Government Printing Office, 1982: 48-58.

Gibson, Rose C., "Blacks at Middle and Late Life: Resources and Coping," *Annals of American Academy of Political and Social Science,* 464 (1982): 79-90.

Giesen, Carol Boellhoff and Nancy Datan, "The Competent Older Woman," in Nancy Datan and Nancy Lohman, eds., *Transitions of Aging,* New York: Academic Press, 1980, chapter 4.

Givens, Jr., Harrison, "An Evaluation of Mandatory Retirement," *Annals of American Academy of Political and Social Science* 438 (1978): 50-58.

Glick, Paul C., "Differential Mortality," in U.S. Bureau of Census, "Population of the United States, Trends and Prospects: 1950-1990," *Current Population Reports,* P-23, no. 49 (1974): 41-50.

Glick, Paul C., "The Future of the American Family," in U.S. Bureau of Census, *Current Population Reports,* P-23, no. 78 (1979): 1-6.

Golant, Stephen M., "Future Directions for Elderly Migration Research," in Charles F. Longino, Jr. and David J. Jackson, eds, *Migration and the Aged,* special issue of *Research on Aging,* 2 (1980): 271-278.

Golant, Stephen M., ed., *Location and Environment of the Elderly Population,* New York: Wiley, 1979.

Goldscheider, Calvin, "Differential Residential Mobility of the Older Population," *Journal of Gerontology* 21 (1981): 103-108.

Gordon, Theodore J., "Prospects for Aging in America," in Matilda White Riley, ed., *Aging from Birth to Death,* Boulder, CO: Westview Press, 1979, chapter 10.

Goudy, Willis J., "Antecedent Factors Related to Changing Work Expectations," *Research on Aging* 4 (1982): 139-157.

Graves, Edmund and Robert Pokras, "Expected Principal Source of Payment for Hospital Discharges: United States, 1979," in National Center for Health Statistics, *Advance Data from Vital and Health Statistics,* no. 75 (1982): 1-10.

Greenough, William C. and Francis P. King, *Pension Plans and Public Policy,* New York: Columbia University Press, 1976.

Gross, Ronald, "I Am Still Learning," in Ronald Gross, Beatrice Gross and Sylvia Seidman, eds., *The New Old: Struggling for Decent Aging,* Garden City, NY: Doubleday, 1978, pp.364-369.

Gross, Ronald, Beatrice Gross and Sylvia Seidman, eds., *The New Old: Struggling for Decent Aging,* Garden City, NY: Doubleday, 1978.

Grove, Robert D. and Alice M. Hetzel, *Vital Statistics Rates in the United States, 1940-1960,* Washington, DC: National Center for Health Statistics, 1968.

Hardy, Melissa A., "Social Policy and Determinants of Retirement: A Longitudinal Analysis of Older White Males," *Social Forces* 60 (1982): 1103-1122.

Harris, Charles S., *Fact Book on Aging: A Profile of America's Older Population,* Washington, DC: National Council on the Aging, 1978.

Harris, Louis & Associates, *The Myth and Reality of Aging in America,* Washington, DC: National Council on the Aging, 1975.

Harris, Louis & Associates, "Myths about Life for Older Americans," in Ronald Gross, Beatrice Gross and Sylvia Seidman, eds., *The New Old: Struggling for Decent Aging,* Garden City, NY: Doubleday, 1978, pp. 90-119.

Hauser, Philip M., "Aging and World-Wide Population Change," in Robert H. Binstock and Ethel Shanas, eds., *Handbook of Aging and the Social Sciences,* New York: Van Nostrand, 1976, chapter 3.

Heaton, Tim B., William B. Clifford and Glenn V. Fuguitt, "Changing Patterns of Retirement Migration," *Research on Aging* 2 (1980): 93-104.

Hicks, Nancy, "Life after 65," in *Social Problems 81/82,* Guilford, CT: Dushkin, 1981: 159-161.

Horton, Paul B. and Gerald R. Leslie, *The Sociology of Social Problems,* 7th ed., Englewood Cliffs, NJ: Prentice-Hall, 1981.

House Select Committee on Aging, "Families: Aging and Changing," Washington, DC: U.S. Government Printing Office, June 4, 1980.

International Labour Office, *Year Book of Labour Statistics, 1979,* Geneva: International Labour Office, 1979.

Jackson, Jacquelyne Johnson, "Death Rate Trends of Black Females, United States, 1964-1978," in Phyllis W. Berman and Estelle R. Ramey, eds., *Women: A Developmental Perspective,* Washington, DC: National Institutes of Health, 1982: 23-35.

Jackson, Jacquelyne Johnson, *Minorities and Aging,* Belmont, CA: Wadsworth, 1980.

Janson, Philip and Karen Frisbie Mueller, "Age, Ethnicity, and Well-Being," *Research on Aging* 5 (1983): 353-367.

Kalish, Richard A., "Death and Dying in Social Context," in Robert H. Binstock and Ethel Shanas, eds., *Handbook of Aging and the Social Sciences,* New York: Van Nostrand, 1976, chapter 19.

Kalish, Richard A., "Death and Survivorship: The Final Transition," *Annals of American Academy of Political and Social Science,* 464 (1982): 163-173.

Kalish, Richard A., *Late Adulthood: Perspectives on Human Development,* Monterey, CA: Brooks/Cole, 1975.

Kamerschen, David R., "On an Operational Index of 'Overpopulation'," *Economic Development and Cultural Change* 13 (1965): 169-187.

Keating, Norah and Judith Marshall, "The Process of Retirement: The Rural Self-Employed," *The Gerontologist* 20 (1980): 437-443.

Keyfitz, Nathan, "Age Distribution as a Challenge to Development," *American Journal of Sociology* 70 (1965): 659-668.

Keyfitz, Nathan and Antonio Golini, "Mortality Comparisons: The Male-Female Ratio," *Genus* 31 (1975): 1-33.

Kinsey, Alfred, Wardell Pomeroy and Paul Gebhard, *Sexual Behavior in the Human Female,* Philadelphia: Saunders, 1953.

Kinsey, Alfred, Wardell Pomeroy and Clyde Martin, *Sexual Behavior in the Human Male,* Philadelphia: Saunders, 1948.

Kleiman, Ephraim, "A Standardized Dependency Ratio," *Demography* 4 (1967): 876-893.

Kobrin, Frances E., "The Fall in Household Size and the Rise of the Primary Individual in the United States," *Demography* 13 (1976): 127-138.

Kreps, Juanita M., "The Economy and the Aged," in Robert H. Binstock and Ethel Shanas, eds., *Handbook of Aging and the Social Sciences,* New York: Van Nostrand, 1976, chapter 11.

Kubat, Daniel, Anthony H. Richmond and Jerzy Zubrzycki, eds., *Policy and Research on Migration: Canadian and World Perspectives,* special issue of *International Migration Review,* 8 (1974).

Lee, Anne S., "Return Migration in the United States," in Daniel Kubat, Anthony H. Richmond and Jerry Zubrzycki, eds., *Policy and Research on Migration: Canadian and World Perspectives,* special issue of *International Migration Review,* 8 (1974): 283-300.

Lee, Everett S., "Migration of the Aged," in Charles F. Longino, Jr. and David J. Jackson, eds., *Migration and the Aged,* special issue of *Research on Aging,* 2 (1980): 131-135.

Lee, Ronald D., "Demographic Forecasting and the Easterlin Hypothesis," *Population and Development Review* 2 (1976): 459-468.

Lerner, I.M., *Heredity, Evolution and Society,* San Francisco: Freeman, 1968.

Loether, Herman J., *Problems of Aging,* 2nd ed., Belmont, CA: Dickenson, 1975.

Lohman, Nancy, "Life Satisfaction Research in Aging: Implications for Policy Development," in Nancy Datan and Nancy Lohman, eds., *Transitions of Aging,* New York: Academic Press, chapter 2.

Long, Larry H., "Migration Differentials," in U.S. Bureau of Census, "Population of the United States, Trends and Prospects: 1950-1990," *Current Population Reports,* P-23, no. 49 (1974): 129-140.

Long, Larry H., "Migration Differentials by Education and Occupation: Trends and Variations," *Demography* 10 (1973): 243-258.

Longino, Jr., Charles F. and David L. Jackson, eds., *Migration and the Aged,* special issue of *Research on Aging,* 2 (1980): 131-280.

Longino, Jr., Charles F., Kent A. McClelland and Warren A. Peterson, "The Aged Subculture Hypothesis: Social Integration, Gerontophilia and Self-Conception," *Journal of Gerontology* 35 (1980): 758-767.

Lopata, Helena Znaniecki, "Loneliness: Forms and Components," *Social Problems* 17 (1969): 248-262.

Lopata, Helena Znaniecki, "The Widowed Family Member," in Nancy Datan and Nancy Lohman, eds., *Transitions of Aging,* New York: Academic Press, 1980, chapter 6.

Madigan, Francis C., "Are Sex Mortality Differentials Biologically Caused?" *Milbank Memorial Fund Quarterly* 35 (1957): 203-223.

Manley, Charles R., "The Migration of Older People," *American Journal of Sociology* 59 (1954): 324-331.

Manton, Kenneth G. and Eric Stallard, "Temporal Trends in U.S. Multiple Cause of Death Mortality Data: 1968 to 1977," *Demography* 19 (1982): 527-547.

Markle, Gerald E., "Sex Ratios at Birth: Values, Variance, and Some Determinants," *Demography* 11 (1974): 131-142.

Matras, Judah, *Introduction to Population,* Englewood Cliffs, NJ: Prentice-Hall, 1977.

McAuliffe, Sharon and Kathleen McAuliffe, "Closing in on Cancer," *Reader's Digest,* March, 1983: 59-64.

McCluskey, Neil G. and Edgar F. Borgatta, eds., *Aging and Retirement: Prospects, Planning, and Policy,* Beverly Hills, CA: Sage, 1981.

McNamara, Regina, "Migration Measurement," in John A. Ross, ed., *International Encyclopedia of Population,* v. 2. New York: Free Press, 1982, pp. 448-450.

McNamara, Regina, "Mortality Trends," in John A. Ross, ed., *International Encyclopedia of Population,* v. 2. New York: Free Press, 1982, pp. 459-461.

Metropolitan Life Foundation, *Statistical Bulletin* 63 (1982).

Michael, Robert T., Victor R. Fuchs and Sharon R. Scott, "Changes in the Propensity to Live Alone: 1950-1976," *Demography* 17 (1980): 39-56.

Morgenstern, Oskar, *National Income Statistics: A Critique of Macroeconomic Aggregation,* Washington, DC: Cato Institute, 1979.

Murphy, Judith and Carol Florio, "Older Americans: Facts and Potential," in Ronald Gross, Beatrice Gross and Sylvia Seidman, eds., *The New Old: Struggling for Decent Aging,* Garden City, NY: Doubleday, 1978, pp. 50-57.

Nam, Charles B. and Susan O. Gustavus, *Population: The Dynamics of Demographic Change,* Boston: Houghton Mifflin, 1976.

Nam, Charles B., Norman L. Weatherby and Kathleen A. Ockay, "Causes of Death which Contribute to the Mortality Crossover Effect," *Social Biology* 25 (1978): 306-314.

National Caucus on the Black Aged, "A Generation of Black People," in Ronald Gross, Beatrice Gross and Sylvia Seidman, eds., *The New Old: Struggling for Decent Aging,* Garden City, NY: Doubleday, 1978, pp. 281-283.

National Center for Health Statistics, "Advance Report of Final Mortality Statistics, 1979," *Monthly Vital Statistics Report* 31 (1982).

National Center for Health Statistics, "Advance Report of Final Mortality Statistics, 1980," *Monthly Vital Statistics Report* 32 (1983).

National Center for Health Statistics, "Advance Report of Final Natality Statistics, 1980," *Monthly Vital Statistics Report* 31 (1982).

National Center for Health Statistics, "Annual Summary of Births, Deaths, Marriages, and Divorces: United States, 1981," *Monthly Vital Statistics Report* 30 (1982).

National Center for Health Statistics, "Final Mortality Statistics, 1978," *Monthly Vital Statistics Report* 29 (1980).

National Center for Health Statistics, *Health, United States, 1981,* PHS Pub. no. 82-1232 (1981).

National Center for Health Statistics, *Health, United States, 1982,* PHS Pub. no. 83-1232 (1982).

National Center for Health Statistics, *Vital Statistics of the United States, 1978,* v. 2, sec. 5, *Life Tables* (1980).

National Center for Health Statistics, *Vital Statistics of the United States, 1977,* v. 3, *Marriage and Divorce* (1981).

National Center for Health Statistics, *Vital Statistics of the United States, 1970,* v. 2, *Mortality,* part A (1974).

National Center for Health Statistics, *Vital Statistics of the United States, 1977,* v. 2, *Mortality,* part A (1981).

National Council on the Aging, *The Myth and Reality of Aging in America,* Washington, DC: NCOA, 1975.

National Council on the Aging, "NCOA Public Policy Agenda," *Perspective on Aging* 9 (1980): 12-39.

National Council on the Aging, *Perspective on Aging,* 9 (1980).

National Council on the Aging, "Special Concerns II," *Perspective on Aging* 9 (1980): 20-27.

Neugarten, Bernice L., "The Rise of the Young-Old," in Ronald Gross, Beatrice Gross and Sylvia, eds., *The New Old: Struggling for Decent Aging,* Garden City, NY: Doubleday, 1978, pp. 47-49.

Neugarten, Bernice L., ed., *Age or Need? Public Policies for Older People,* Beverly Hills, CA: Sage, 1982.

Norland, Joseph A., "Measuring Change in Sex Composition," *Demography,* 12 (1975): 81-88.

O'Gorman, Hubert, "False Consciousness of Kind: Pluralistic Ignorance among the Aged," *Research on Aging* 2 (1980): 105-128.

Omran, Abdel R., "The Epidemiologic Transition: A Theory of the Epidemiology of Population Change," *Milbank Memorial Fund Quarterly* 49 (1971): 509-538.

Organisation for Economic Co-operation and Development, *Socio-economic Policies for the Elderly,* Paris: OECD, 1979.

Palen, J. John, *Social Problems,* New York: McGraw-Hill, 1979.

Palmore, Erdman, "Attitudes toward the Aged: What We Know and Need to Know," *Research on Aging* 4 (1982): 333-348.

Palmore, Erdman, *Social Patterns in Normal Aging: Findings from the Duke Longitudinal Study,* Durham, NC: Duke University Press, 1981.

Pampel, Fred C., "Changes in the Propensity to Live Alone: Evidence from

Consecutive Cross-Sectional Surveys," *Demography* 20 (1983): 433-447.

Pampel, Fred C., *Social Change and the Aged,* Lexington, MA: Heath, 1981.

Patterson, George F., "Income," in U.S. Bureau of Census, "Population of the United States, Trends and Prospects: 1950-1990," *Current Population Reports,* P-23, no. 49 (1974): 163-172.

Petersen, William, *Population,* 3rd ed., New York: Macmillan, 1975.

Priebe, John A., "Occupation," in U.S. Bureau of Census, "Population of the United States, Trends and Prospects: 1950-1990," *Current Population Reports,* P-23, no. 49 (1974): 151-157.

Ramey, Estelle R., "The Natural Capacity for Health in Women," in Phyllis W. Berman and Estelle R. Ramey, eds., *Women: A Developmental Perspective,* Washington, DC: National Institutes of Health, 1982, pp. 3-12.

Reid, John, "Black America in the 1980s," *Population Bulletin,* 37 (1982).

Riley, Matilda White, ed., *Aging from Birth to Death,* Boulder, CO: Westview Press, 1979.

Riley, Matilda White, "Introduction: Life Course Perspectives," in Matilda White Riley, ed., *Aging from Birth to Death,* Boulder, CO: Westview Press, 1979, pp. 3-13.

Riley, Matilda White and Anne Foner, *Aging and Society,* v. 1, *An Inventory of Research Findings,* New York: Russell Sage Foundation, 1968.

Riley, Matilda White, Marilyn E. Johnson and Anne Foner, eds., *Aging and Society,* v. 3, *A Sociology of Age Stratification,* New York: Russell Sage Foundation, 1972.

Riley, Matilda White, John W. Riley, Jr. and Marilyn E. Johnson, eds., *Aging and Society,* v. 2, *Aging and the Professions,* New York: Russell Sage Foundation, 1969.

Rives, Jr., Norfleet W., "Researching the Migration of the Elderly," in Charles F. Longino, Jr. and David J. Jackson, eds., *Migration and the Aged,* special issue of *Research on Aging,* 2 (1980): 155-163.

Ross, John A., ed., *International Encyclopedia of Population,* 2 vols., New York: Free Press, 1982.

Schneider, Paula J. and Thomas J. Palumbo, "Social and Demographic Characteristics of the Labor Force," in U.S. Bureau of Census, "Population of the United States, Trends and Prospects: 1950-1990," *Current Population Reports,* P-23, no. 49 (1974): 142-151.

Schulz, James C., "Income Distribution and the Aging," in Robert H. Binstock and Ethel Shanas, eds., *Handbook of Aging and the Social Sciences,* New York: Van Nostrand, 1976, chapter 22.

Sell, Ralph R. and Gordon F. De Jong, "Toward a Motivational Theory of Migration Decision Making," *Journal of Population* 1 (1978): 313-335.

Serow, William J., "Return Migration of the Elderly in the U.S.A.: 1955-60 and 1965-70," *Journal of Gerontology* 33 (1978): 288-295.

Shanas, Ethel and Gordon F. Streib, eds., *Social Structure and the Family: Generational Relations,* Englewood Cliffs, NJ: Prentice-Hall, 1965.

Shanas, Ethel and Marvin B. Sussman, eds., *Family, Bureaucracy, and the Elderly,* Durham, NC: Duke University Press, 1977.

Shaw, R. Paul, *Migration Theory and Fact: A Review and Bibliography of Current Literature,* Philadelphia: Regional Science Research Institute, 1975.

Sheldon, Henry D., *The Older Population of the United States,* New York: Wiley, 1958.

Sheppard, Harold L., "Aging and Manpower Development," in Matilda White Riley, John W. Riley, Jr. and Marilyn E. Johnson, eds., *Aging and Society,* v. 2, *Aging and the Professions,* New York: Russell Sage Foundation, 1969, chapter 6.

Sheppard, Harold L., "The Issue of Mandatory Retirement," *Annals of American Academy of Political and Social Science,* 438 (1978): 40-49.

Sheppard, Harold L., "Work and Retirement," in Robert H. Binstock and Ethel Shanas, eds., *Handbook of Aging and the Social Sciences,* New York: Van Nostrand, 1976, chapter 12.

Shryock, Henry S., *Population Mobility within the United States,* Chicago: Community & Family Study Center, University of Chicago, 1964.

Shryock, Henry S. and Jacob S. Siegel, *The Methods and Materials of Demography,* 2 vols., Washington, DC: U.S. Government Printing Office, 1973.

Siegel, Jacob S., "On the Demography of Aging," *Demography* 17 (1980): 345-364.

Siegel, Jacob S., "Prospective Trends in the Size and Structure of the Elderly Population, Impact of Mortality Trends and Some Implications," in U.S. Bureau of the Census, *Current Population Reports,* P-23, no. 78 (1979): 7-22.

Simpson, Ida Harper and John C. McKinney, eds., *Social Aspects of Aging,* Durham, NC: Duke University Press, 1966.

Simpson, Ida Harper, Kurt W. Back and John C. McKinney, "Work and Retirement," in Ida Harper Simpson and John C.McKinney, eds., *Social Aspects of Aging,* Durham, NC: Duke University Press, 1966, chapter 2.

Simpson, Ida Harper, Richard L. Simpson, Mark Evers and Sharon Sandomirsky Poss, "Occupational Recruitment, Retention, and Labor Force Cohort Representation," *American Journal of Sociology* 87 (1982): 1287-1313.

Sirrocco, Al, "An Overview of the 1980 National Master Facility Inventory Survey of Nursing and Related Care Homes," in National Center for Health Statistics, *Advance Data from Vital and Health Statistics,* no. 91 (1983):1-5.

Smith, T. Lynn and Paul E. Zopf, Jr., *Demography: Principles and Methods,* 2nd ed., Port Washington, NY: Alfred, 1976.

Soldo, Beth J., "America's Elderly in the 1980s," *Population Bulletin* 35 (1980).

Spengler, Joseph J., *Population and America's Future,* San Francisco: Freeman, 1975.

Spengler, Joseph J., "Some Economic and Related Determinants Affecting the Older Worker's Occupational Role," in Ida Harper Simpson and John C. McKinney, eds., *Social Aspects of Aging,* Durham, NC: Duke University Press, 1966, chapter 1.

Stahura, John M. and Sidney M. Stahl, "Suburban Characteristics and Aged Net Migration," *Research on Aging* 2 (1980): 3-22.

Stimson, Ardyth, Jane F. Wise and John Stimson, "Sexuality and Self-Esteem among the Aged," *Research on Aging* 3 (1981): 228-239.

Streib, Gordon F., "Social Stratification and Aging," in Robert H. Binstock and Ethel Shanas, eds., *Handbook of Aging and the Social Sciences,* New York: Van Nostrand, 1976, chapter 7.

Streib, Gordon F. and Clement J. Schneider, *Retirement and American Society,* Ithaca, NY: Cornell University Press, 1971.

Subcommittee on Human Services of the House Select Committee on Aging, *Future*

Directions for Aging Policy: A Human Services Model, Pub. no. 96-226, Washington, DC: U.S. Government Printing Office, 1980.

Sullivan, Deborah and Sylvia A. Stevens, "Snowbirds: Seasonal Migrants to the Sunbelt," *Research on Aging* 4 (1982): 159-177.

Sussman, Marvin B., "An Analytical Model for the Sociological Study of Retirement," in Frances M. Carp, *Retirement,* New York: Behavioral Publications, 1972, chapter 2.

Thomlinson, Ralph, *Population Dynamics: Causes and Consequences of World Demographic Change,* 2nd ed., New York: Random House, 1976.

Tordella, Stephen J., *Reference Tables, Net Migration of Persons Aged 0 to 64 and 65 and Over for United States Counties, 1970 to 1975,* Madison, WI: Applied Population Laboratory, University of Wisconsin, 1980.

Treas, Judith and Vern L. Bengston, "The Demography of Mid- and Late-Life Transitions," *Annals of American Academy of Political and Social Science* 464 (1982): 11-21.

Uhlenberg, Peter, "Demographic Change and Problems of the Aged," in Matilda White Riley, ed., *Aging from Birth to Death,* Boulder, CO: Westview Press, 1979, chapter 8.

United Nations, *Demographic Yearbook, 1979,* New York: United Nations, 1979.

United Nations, *Demographic Yearbook, 1980,* New York: United Nations, 1980.

United Nations, *Demographic Yearbook, 1981,* New York: United Nations, 1981.

U.S. Bureau of the Census, "America in Transition: An Aging Society," *Current Population Reports,* P-23, no. 128 (1983).

U.S. Bureau of the Census, *1980 Census of Population, General Population Characteristics,* reports for states, 1981.

U.S. Bureau of the Census, *1980 Census of Population, Supplementary Reports,* PC80-S1-1, *Age, Sex, Race, and Spanish Origin of the Population by Regions, Divisions, and States: 1980,* 1981.

U.S. Bureau of the Census, *1980 Census of Population, Supplementary Reports,* PC80-S1-5, *Standard Metropolitan Statistical Areas and Standard Consolidated Statistical Areas: 1980,* 1981.

U.S. Bureau of the Census, *1980 Census of Population, Supplementary Reports,* PHC80-S1-1, *Provisional Estimates of Social, Economic, and Housing Characteristics,* 1982.

U.S. Bureau of the Census, "Characteristics of the Population below the Poverty Level: 1980," *Current Population Reports,* P-60, no. 133 (1982).

U.S. Bureau of the Census, "Demographic Aspects of Aging and the Older Population in the United States," *Current Population Reports,* P-23, no. 59 (1978).

U.S. Bureau of the Census, "Educational Attainment in the United States: March 1979 and 1978," *Current Population Reports,* P-20, no. 35 (1980).

U.S. Bureau of the Census, "Estimating After-Tax Money Income Distributions Using Data from the March Current Population Survey," *Current Population Reports,* P-23, no. 126 (1983).

U.S. Bureau of the Census, "Farm Population of the United States: 1980," *Current Population Reports,* P-27, no. 54 (1981).

U.S. Bureau of the Census, "Geographic Mobility: March 1975 to March 1980," *Current Population Reports,* P-20, no. 368 (1981).

U.S. Bureau of the Census, "Illiteracy in the United States: November 1969," *Current Population Reports*, P-20, no. 217, (1971).

U.S. Bureau of the Census, "Marital Status and Living Arrangements: March 1980," *Current Population Reports*, P-20, no. 365 (1981).

U.S. Bureau of the Census, "Mobility of the Population of the United States: March 1970 to March 1975," *Current Population Reports*, P-20, no. 285 (1975).

U.S. Bureau of the Census, "Money Income of Households, Families, and Persons in the United States: 1980," *Current Population Reports*, P-60, no. 132 (1982).

U.S. Bureau of the Census, *Negroes in the United States, 1920-32*, Washington, DC: U.S. Government Printing Office, 1935.

U.S. Bureau of the Census, "Persons of Spanish Origin in the United States: March 1980," (advance report) *Current Population Reports*, P-20, no. 361 (1981).

U.S. Bureau of the Census, "Population of the United States, Trends and Prospects: 1950-1990," *Current Population Reports*, P-23, no. 49 (1974).

U.S. Bureau of the Census, "Projections of the Population of the United States: 1977 to 2050," *Current Population Reports*, P-25, no. 704 (1977).

U.S. Bureau of the Census, "Projections of the Population of the United States: 1982 to 2050," *Current Population Reports*, P-25, no. 922 (1982).

U.S. Bureau of the Census, *Sixteenth Census of the United States: 1940, Characteristics of the Population, U.S. Summary*, 1943.

U.S. Bureau of the Census, *Sixteenth Census of the United States: 1940. The Labor Force, U.S. Summary*, 1943.

U.S. Bureau of the Census, "The Social and Economic Status of the Black Population in the United States: An Historical View, 1790-1978," *Current Population Reports*, P-23, no. 80 (1979).

U.S. Bureau of the Census, "Some Demographic Aspects of Aging in the United States," *Current Population Reports*, P-23, no. 43 (1973).

U.S. Bureau of the Census, *State and Metropolitan Area Data Book, 1982*, Washington, DC: U.S. Government Printing Office, 1982.

U.S. Bureau of the Census, *Statistical Abstract of the United States: 1960*, Washington, DC: U.S. Government Printing Office, 1960.

U.S. Bureau of the Census, *Statistical Abstract of the United States: 1979*, Washington, DC: U.S. Government Printing Office, 1979.

U.S. Bureau of the Census, *Statistical Abstract of the United States: 1981*, Washington, DC: U.S. Government Printing Office, 1981.

U.S. Bureau of the Census, *Statistical Abstract of the United States: 1982-83*, Washington, DC: U.S. Government Printing Office, 1982.

U.S. Bureau of the Census, "1976 Survey of Institutionalized Persons: A Study of Persons Receiving Long-Term Care," *Current Population Reports*, P-23, no. 69 (1978).

U.S. Bureau of the Census, *U.S. Census of Population: 1950, Detailed Characteristics, U.S. Summary*, 1953.

U.S. Bureau of the Census, *U.S. Census of Population: 1960, Characteristics of the Population, U.S. Summary*, 1964.

U.S. Bureau of the Census, *U.S. Census of Population: 1960, Detailed Characteristics, U.S. Summary*, 1964.

U.S. Bureau of the Census, *U.S. Census of Population: 1960, Subject Reports, Mobility for States and State Economic Areas*, 1963.

U.S. Bureau of the Census, *U.S. Census of Population: 1970, Detailed Characteristics, U.S. Summary,* 1973.

U.S. Bureau of the Census, *U.S. Census of Population: 1970, General Population Characteristics, U.S. Summary,* 1972.

U.S. Bureau of the Census, *U.S. Census of Population: 1970, General Population Characteristics,* reports for states, 1971.

U.S. Bureau of the Census, *U.S. Census of Population: 1970, Subject Reports, Mobility for States and the Nation,* 1973.

U.S. Bureau of Labor Statistics, *Economic Projections to 1990,* Bulletin 2121, Washington, DC: U.S. Government Printing Office, 1982.

U.S. Bureau of Labor Statistics, *Handbook of Labor Statistics, 1980,* Washington, DC: U.S. Government Printing Office, 1980.

U.S. Bureau of Labor Statistics, *Labor Force Statistics Derived from the Current Population Survey: A Databook,* 2 vols., Washington, DC: U.S. Government Printing Office, 1982.

U.S. Census Office, *Ninth Census of the United States, Vital Statistics of the United States,* 1872.

van der Tak, Jean, "U.S. Population: Where We Are; Where We're Going," *Population Bulletin,* 37 (1982).

Voss, Paul R., "The Increasing Ranks of Elderly Veterans: Where They Will Be in 1990," paper presented to the Southern Regional Demographic Group, Greensboro, NC, October 6-8, 1982.

Webber, Irving L., "The Educable Aged," in J.C. Dixon, ed., *Continuing Education in Later Years,* Gainesville, FL: University of Florida Press, 1963, pp. 14-25.

Weeks, John R., *Population: An Introduction to Concepts and Issues,* 2nd ed., Belmont, CA: Wadsworth, 1981.

Wiseman, Robert F., "Why Older People Move: Theoretical Issues," in Charles F. Longino, Jr. and David J. Jackson, eds., *Migration of the Aged,* special issue of *Research on Aging,* 2 (1980): 141-154.

World Health Organization, *Manual of the International Statistical Classification of Diseases, Injuries, and Causes of Death, Ninth Revision,* Geneva: WHO, 1977.

Zopf, Jr., Paul E., *Population: An Introduction to Social Demography,* Palo Alto, CA: Mayfield, 1984.

Zopf, Jr., Paul E., *Sociocultural Systems,* Washington, DC: University Press of America, 1978.

Zopf, Jr., Paul E., "Variations in Support Burdens as Measured by the Dependency Ratio," *Greek Review of Social Research,* no. 19-20 (1974): 29-43.

Indexes

Author and Source Index

Subject Index

317

318

occupations of, 150-52
poverty status of, 195, 200, 203, 204-5, 206-7, 208
sex composition among, 57, 61-63, 66-67, 69-70, 74
survivorship of, 32-34

Cancer, 230-31, 233, 234, 235, 237. *See also* Cause of death
increase in death rate for, 233, 236, 237
Cause of death, 230-38
age-specific rates for, 213, 230-32
race differences in, 233-35
sex differences in, 218, 233
trends in, 231, 235-38
Competent older women, 76-77
Comprehensive Older Americans Act Amendments, 292
Crime, 289
"Crossover" by race in death rates, 219-20, 226, 234
Curve-squaring technologies, 276-77

Death rate. *See* Mortality
Decision-making process in migration, 265-66
Demographic processes, 4-5. *See also* Fertility; Internal migration; Mortality
Dependency ratio, 39-48
formula for, 39
international comparisons of, 40-43
projections of, 46-48
race differences in, 43-44
retired population and, 179
trends in, 44-46
Developed nations: aging in, 11
dependency ratios in, 40-42
labor force in, 141-43
marital status in, 85
mortality in, 216, 217
retirement in, 178
Developing nations: dependency ratios in, 41-43
labor force in, 141-43
marital status in, 85
retirement in, 178
Disengagement, 128, 287-88
from labor force, 139-40, 177-78
Distribution of elderly, 18-24

changes in, 24-26
by race and sex, 24
by residence, 21-24
by states, 19-21
Divorced people, 84, 105-6. *See also* Labor Force

Economically active population, 142. *See also* Labor Force
Educational needs, 127-31
reasons for, 127-28
responses to, 129-31
Educational status, 111-32. *See also* Educational needs; Illiteracy
improvement in, 129-31
indexes of, 112-16
internal migration and, 255-57
labor force participation and, 146
marital status differences in, 119-20
mortality differences by, 220-21
occupations and, 150
poverty status and, 206-7
projections of, 125-26
race differences in, 117, 122-23
retirement and, 173
rewards of, 130-31
sex differences in, 117, 122-23
trends in, 121-25
Elderly poor. *See* Poverty status
Elderly population:
age composition of, 29-53
age-specific death rates of, 214-26
cause of death in, 230-38
common features of, 275
dependency ratio and, 39-48
as dependent group, 180-81
disengagement of, 128, 139-40, 177-78, 287-88
educational needs of, 127-31
educational status of, 111-32
geographic distribution of, 18-24
growth of, 9-13, 17-18
health care for, 282-85
housing for, 285-86
implications of, 275-86
income of, 186-201, 280-82
increasing life span of, 278
institutionalization of, 99-103
internal migration of, 243-71
leisure among, 286-87
life expectancy of, 34-35, 226-30, 276-77

LIBRARY
OF
MOUNT ST. MARY'S
COLLEGE
EMMITSBURG, MARYLAND